JOHANNES FEICHTINGER, HERBERT MATIS,
STEFAN SIENELL, HEIDEMARIE UHL (EDS.)

THE ACADEMY OF SCIENCES IN VIENNA 1938 TO 1945

AUSTRIAN ACADEMY OF SCIENCES

Austrian Academy
of Sciences Press

Vienna 2014

JOHANNES FEICHTINGER, HERBERT MATIS,
STEFAN SIENELL, HEIDEMARIE UHL (EDS.)

The Academy of Sciences in Vienna 1938 to 1945

together with Silke Fengler

Translation from German:
Nick Somers, Cynthia Peck-Kubaczek

Austrian Academy
of Sciences Press

ÖAW

Vienna 2014

Translation of the exhibition catalog
Johannes Feichtinger, Herbert Matis, Stefan Sienell, Heidemarie Uhl (eds.)
Die Akademie der Wissenschaften in Wien 1938 bis 1945. Katalog zur Ausstellung (Vienna 2013).
ISBN 978-3-7001-7367-0

Illustrations on the cover:
Background: ÖNB, Bildarchiv, Sign. L32608C
Seal: AÖAW, Siegelsammlung

British Library Cataloguing in Publication data
A Catalogue record of this book is available from the British Library

Printed on chlorine-free bleached cellulose, acid free, non-ageing paper

ISBN 978-3-7001-7537-7

Gesamtherstellung / produced by: Ferdinand Berger & Söhne Ges.m.b.H., A-3580 Horn

http://hw.oeaw.ac.at/7537-7
http://verlag.oeaw.ac.at

Printed and bound in the EU

Table of Contents

Preface to the English edition

Some preliminary remarks are necessary to ensure the correct use and better understanding of the English translation of the German edition published in March 2013. The use of quotation marks (“ ”) denotes a quote taken from a published source or a citation from a scholarly work, for which a footnote indicating that source will always be given. Quotation marks will also be used for specific National Socialist expressions and jargon. In as far as these terms are already widely understood in (American) English, they will be printed in normal script, otherwise in italics. Furthermore, all quotes from unpublished primary sources will be italicized.

All quotations, be they from scholarly works or from unpublished texts, have been translated into English, even though the original texts were, as a rule, in German!

The term “Academy of Sciences” as the translation for “Akademie der Wissenschaften” appears frequently in the text. The editors are aware of the fact that the English term “sciences” is generally used to denote the natural sciences only, whereas the German term “Wissenschaften“ also includes the “Humanities and Social Sciences.” However, since the (albeit inadequate) English designation “Austrian Academy of Sciences“ is well established for the “Österreichische Akademie der Wissenschaften,” this has been adopted in the present volume.

The translation “full member” for “wirkliches Mitglied” and “ordinary member” for “ordentliches Mitglied” is ambivalent insofar as both the two German terms and the two English terms can be used synonymously. Their difference lies only in that with the so-called “Vorläufige Satzung” (Provisional Statutes) of July 1938, the term “ordinary member,” then in force in the German Reich, was adopted in favor the Austrian term “full member“ used until that point. With the reinstitution of the Academy Statutes of 1922/1925, the term “full member” was once again used in Vienna from 1945 on.

For the translation of specific National Socialist terminology, Robert A. Michael and Karin Doerr's *Nazi-Deutsch. An English lexicon of the language of the Third Reich = Nazi German* (Westport/Conn., 2002) was consulted.

The editors would like to thank Nick Somers and Cynthia Peck-Kubaczek for the translation as well as Joanna White for copy-editing.

The Editors

Preface

The "Anschluss" of Austria with the National Socialist German Reich in March 1938 signified a profound break for the Academy of Sciences in Vienna. On 18 March 1938 the longtime Academy President Oswald Redlich resigned; on recommendation of the remaining members of the Presiding Committee, the Academy General Assembly of 25 March requested corresponding Academy member Fritz Knoll to safeguard "*the interests of the regional administration of the Nazi party in Austria with regard to the Academy of Sciences until the final regulation of the Academy Statutes.*" The botanist Knoll was an illegal Nazi and, on 15 March, had become the commissarial rector of the University of Vienna. "Meritorious" Nazis were immediately appointed as directors of the Academy institutes. Under the newly elected President Heinrich Srbik, the Academy of Sciences was "enthusiastically and dutifully at the exclusive service of the Greater German *Volksstaat* [people's State]," as Srbik declared in his inaugural speech in November 1938. The scholarly activities should stand – as stated programmatically in the new Statutes – in "the service of the German people."

With the Nazis' seizure of power, Academy members and staff members were forced to leave the Academy for political and "racial" reasons. They were persecuted and expelled; they died in Nazi concentration camps. Not only were human tragedies connected to this, but also irretrievable losses for Austrian scholarship. Academy Organizations like the Institute for Radium Research, the Institute for Experimental Biology (Vivarium), and the Phonogram Archive lost their key research personnel; worldwide pioneering research programs and international research collaborations were broken off.

With the restoration of democracy and the rule of law in 1945, freedom of research became the maxim of the Academy of Sciences. Regaining the status of a scientific institution of international standing and emphasizing the Austrian focus of research were priorities, the latter also reflected in the name being changed to "Austrian Academy of Sciences" (in 1947).

The year 1945 was not a "zero hour." In addition to breaks, there were also continuities in the research institutes as well as the association of scholars. In dealing with Nazism, the Academy took an ambivalent stance, albeit on a legal basis: In the early postwar period, the membership of former Nazis was provisionally *ruhendgestellt,* or held in abeyance. A few years later – pursuant to the Amnesty Law of 1948 – practically all former Nazi party members, even high-ranking officials, were re-admitted as members.

It took decades before the Academy dealt more intensively with its history during the Nazi era. In 1997, on the occasion of the 150th anniversary of the Academy's founding, the publication of the essay by Herbert Matis entitled *Zwischen Anpassung und Widerstand. Die Akademie der Wissenschaften in den Jahren 1938–1945* [Between

Accommodation and Resistance. The Academy of Sciences in the years 1938–1945] provided a first critical historiographical account.

In 2013, the Academy is using the 75th anniversary of the "Anschluss" in March 1938 as an occasion to present an exhibition and publish a catalog investigating the reactions of the Academy to the Nazi power takeover, the Academy's involvement in the Nazi domination apparatus, and the impact this had on the postwar period. Special attention has been devoted to the members and staff of the Academy who were victims of Nazi persecution. A plaque dedicated to them was unveiled on 11 March 2013 in the main building of the Academy. Their names and biographies will be made available in a virtual memorial book on the Academy website.

In dealing critically with the history of its own institution, the Academy is consonant with the other Academies of Science in the German-speaking world. And it is in the very bringing together of recent and ongoing research upon which the exhibition and catalog are based, as well as in collaborating in research projects at Academies of Science in Germany, that it becomes clear that a comprehensive scholarly analysis of the history of the Austrian Academy of Sciences during the twentieth century remains a desideratum.

Helmut Denk,
President of
the Austrian Academy of Sciences

I. THE "ANSCHLUSS" AND NAZI RULE

The "Anschluss" and Nazi Rule. Austria 1938–1945

When on the afternoon of 12 March 1938 Adolf Hitler set off from his home town of Braunau am Inn and, following the troops of the German army, began his triumphal journey through Linz and on to Vienna, hundreds of thousands of Upper Austrians, Lower Austrians, and Viennese cheered him along the main roads. "Flowers marked the path of the clanking tanks and armored vehicles," reported the *Times* correspondent. On 15 March 1938, at Vienna's Heldenplatz, the "leader and chancellor of the German nation and empire" bombastically announced "the entry" of his homeland into the German Reich. Again on his "journey through the Ostmark" from 3 to 9 April, Hitler was greeted by hundreds of thousands in Graz, Klagenfurt, Innsbruck, Salzburg and Linz – by around 400,000 Styrians in Graz alone. Photos and films of these events were seen around the world.[1]

Fig. 1: Hitler's speech on Vienna's Heldenplatz on 15 March 1938

[1] See Hanisch (1994), *Schatten*, pp. 337–45; see also Botz (2008), *Nationalsozialismus*; Schmidl (1987), *März*, and Williams (2005), *Gau*.

The "Anschluss" had already been preceded by five years of Nazi rule in the German Reich. Hitler, as a propaganda speaker for nationalist combat units in Bavaria, had been bashing the Treaty of Versailles since 1919, as well as drumming up support for a solidly united *"Volksgemeinschaft"* ["people's community"], for the "removal of the Jews from German society," and for "national revival." The electoral successes of the Nazi Party in 1930, fed primarily by the devastating consequences of the world economic crisis and mass unemployment, had started Hitler's triumphal march, and it continued with the Nazi Party winning a relative majority in the Reichstag for the first time in the elections on 31 July 1932. How was it possible, Hans-Ulrich Thamer rightly asks, "for a nation that was highly developed politically, culturally, and technically to apparently voluntarily submit itself to a one-party rule that had repeatedly and openly expressed its goals of persecution, extermination, and conquest?" And: "How could a social and political nobody achieve such an effect?"[2]

Even if Ian Kershaw, Hans-Ulrich Wehler, and Hans-Ulrich Thamer convincingly clarify this with Max Weber's concept of charismatic authority, for those born later it is difficult to understand how a political outsider – talking and gesticulating strangely, using repeated violent expressions, a power amateur – could become the focal point of collective fears, desires of salvation, dreams of omnipotence, and hysteria in one of the world's leading industrial nations. While on one hand Hitler was a political fanatic and racist, he was also a calculating realist who could produce the appearance of rationality and trustworthiness. There is no doubt that he impressed supporters and opponents with his Manichean views and threatening outbursts of energy. But at the same time, Hitler's criminal designs and extermination fantasies, his ideas of racial purity and world domination were, basically, very far removed from the moral attitudes of most Germans (and Austrians). Nonetheless – as shown by the assassination of Austrian Chancellor Engelbert Dollfuss by Austrian Nazis on 25 July 1934 – the gap between the Nazi elite and the simple morality of the people could be masked by extensive measures of deception, suppression, and intimidation.[3]

The appointment of Hitler as Chancellor was not a "seizure of power," but a legal transfer of power from the elderly Reich President Paul von Hindenburg and his Berlin power cartel. The establishment of a totalitarian Nazi regime only began after the Reichstag fire in late February and the *Ermächtigungsgesetz* [Enabling Act] of 22 March 1933, but by August 1934 it had led to the Nazis exercising comprehensive control over the state and society. The first anti-Semitic employment bans and boycotts began in April 1933. They were followed at the beginning of May 1933 by the public burning of "un-German literature," at which time the "racial" and political "cleansing" of the universities and academies was also introduced. The experts in

[2] Thamer (1986), *Verfügung*, p. 19. See also Steiner (2011), *Triumph*, p. 10, and Wildt/Krumeich (2012), *Nationalsozialismus*.

[3] See Kershaw (1998), *Hitler*; Kershaw (2000), *Hitler*; Wehler (2008), *Gesellschaftsgeschichte*; Thamer/Erpel (2010), *Hitler*, pp. 18–9, and Frevert (2008), *Gefühle*, p. 31.

constitutional law Hans Kelsen and Hermann Heller, the economists Emil Lederer and Moritz Julius Bonn, the sociologist Karl Mannheim, the philosopher Max Horkheimer, the historian Ernst Kantorowicz, and the Protestant theologian Paul Tillich were dismissed from their posts; Thomas Mann, Alfred Döblin, and Ricarda Huch resigned from the Prussian Academy of Arts, and Franz Werfel, Fritz von Unruh, and Jakob Wassermann were expelled. But more than a few professors, writers and artists sided with National Socialism: Martin Heidegger and Carl Schmitt, Gerhart Hauptmann and Heinrich George, Wilhelm Furtwängler and Richard Strauss, Gustaf Gründgens, Emil Jannings, and Werner Kraus.[4]

Since not only the Nazi Party and the SS were "working towards the Führer," but also the armed forces, the Foreign Ministry, relevant economic sectors, and last but not least, many workers in the defense industry and highway construction projects, by the time of the Summer Olympics in 1936 Hitler had already reached a level of fame that no German chancellor had enjoyed since Bismarck. Of course the terrorist side of the Nazi regime, which was building concentration camps all over the country and persecuting, torturing, and murdering people, must not be overlooked. Nevertheless, the Austrian chancellor Kurt Schuschnigg, who actually held legitimist views but who, under intense political pressure both domestically and internationally and ruling monocratically, saw himself forced by the 1936 July Agreement to tolerate the Austrian Nazis and affirm Austria as a culturally "German state." Many contemporaries saw this as a first step towards the "Anschluss."[5]

Although the idea of an "Anschluss" that had been formed in 1918/19 was still alive in many German and Austrian professors, teachers, officers, officials, diplomats, lawyers, doctors, economists, engineers, journalists, and writers, no one foresaw Hitler announcing on 5 November 1937 to his foreign policy makers and the head of the *Wehrmacht* [armed forces] that he was striving to annex Austria and Czechoslovakia, possibly already in 1938. Hitler argued that this was necessary to expand the German *"Lebensraum"* [living space], increase the security of Germany's borders, and to establish twelve new divisions of the army. At the Berghof near Berchtesgaden he accused Schuschnigg of "treason" against the German people, and demanded amnesty for arrested Nazis, the appointment of the Viennese lawyer Arthur Seyss-Inquart as Minister of the Interior, and the integration of the Austrian economic system into the German. Schuschnigg still wanted to hold a referendum on Austria's independence on 13 March, but gave way in the face of SS and SA activities in Vienna and under the pressure of Berlin's ultimatum. On the evening of 11 March he announced that Austria would retreat from violence. To avoid bloodshed, the country's armed forces would offer no resistance.[6]

---

[4] See Thamer (1986), *Verführung*, pp. 299–304, and Wehler (2008), *Gesellschaftsgeschichte*, pp. 600–7.

[5] See Jedlicka (1977), *Juliabkommen*.

[6] See Schuschnigg (1946), *Requiem*, pp. 39–42; Kershaw (2000), *Hitler*, pp. 119–25, and Williams (2005), *Gau*, pp. 88–93.

Parallel to the takeovers by Austrian Nazis beginning in a number of cities and provinces, the entry into the country of the *Wehrmacht* on the morning of 12 March was cheered on by hundreds of thousands of Austrians. Encouraged by his enthusiastic reception in Linz, on the evening of 13 March Hitler signed the "Law on the Reunification of Austria with the German Reich." Practically overnight, Austria became a German province.

Many people had to hide in the first days of the "Anschluss", especially in Vienna. Together with the entry of the *Wehrmacht, Reichsführer-SS* Heinrich Himmler and his henchmen arrived at the airfield in Aspern and immediately began to arrest not only followers of the Schuschnigg regime, but also socialists, communists, and Jews. Many Jews were abused and tortured by the Nazi mob and large numbers of Jewish shops were looted. Stefan Zweig, who had already emigrated to London, received terrible news from Vienna: "University professors had to scrub the streets with their bare hands, religious white-bearded Jews were dragged into the synagogue by jeering boys and forced to do knee-bends and shout in chorus, 'Heil Hitler'."[7]

The Archbishop of Vienna, Cardinal Theodor Innitzer, assured Hitler of the loyalty of Austrian Catholics, while Karl Renner, the Social Democratic chancellor in the years 1918–1920, endorsed the "Anschluss" in the *Neues Wiener Tagblatt*. The head of the Austrian peace delegation in 1919 found the "Anschluss" a "true compensation for the humiliation of 1918 and 1919, for Saint-Germain and Versailles." In fact, on 10 April 1938 more than 99 percent of Austrians voted for the "list of our leader Adolf Hitler" and the "Anschluss".[8] There has been discussion in Austria since that day about how many Austrians would actually have voted for the "Anschluss" had a secret referendum been conducted with electoral observers from the League of Nations. One would certainly have seen quite heterogeneous groups among those voting against: Jews, who were unquestionably the most threatened, devout Catholics and officials of the *Vaterländische Front* [Fatherland's Front], monarchists, the core of the social democratic industrial workers and their representatives, as well as the communists. Together these numbered perhaps a million out of four million eligible voters. Nonetheless, this would still have resulted in a clear majority of about 75 percent for "Anschluss" with Hitler's Germany. Thus, we can assume that in March/April 1938, the thinking of a clear majority of Austrians was in line with that of Cardinal Innitzer and the former chancellor Renner.[9]

The U.S. international law expert Charles G. Fenwick gave a profound assessment of the significance of the "Anschluss" for international law and politics: "[...] Today we witness not a customs treaty between two independent states, not even a confederation of Austria and Germany leaving the national integrity of Austria unpaired, but the complete assimilation of Austria into Germany. Austria is henceforth to be a

[7] Zweig (1970), *Welt*, p. 458. See also Welzig (2010), *"Anschluss"*.

[8] See *Neues Wiener Tagblatt*, 3 April 1938. See also Rauscher (1995), *Renner*, pp. 297–301.

[9] See Hanisch (1994), *Schatten*, pp. 345–7.

mere province of Germany, the name of the country, whose origins go back to the tenth century or earlier, is now erased from the annals of international law."[10]

The "assimilation" of Austria was particularly beneficial for the Nazi armaments industry: The Austrian economy delivered iron, lead and zinc ore, magnesite, petroleum, timber, milk, butter and cheese; Austria had productive commodity and manufacturing industries with a large number of skilled laborers; and the Austrian National Bank had currency holdings of 460 million Austrian schillings, gold bullion worth 296 million schillings, clearing assets of 150 million schillings, and gold deposits in the Bank of England worth 80 million schillings. And indeed, Austrian banks and industries were immediately seized by the Reichsbank, Deutsche Bank, and Dresdner Bank, as well as by the Reichswerke Hermann Göring, an industrial conglomerate.[11]

The "Anschluss" not only involved "assimilation," but it also meant rejection and expulsion, especially the expulsion of the intelligentsia. Some of Austria's intellect only survived in exile: Sigmund Freud's psychoanalysis, Joseph Schumpeter's "Theory of Economic Development," Friedrich Hayek's neo-liberalism, Hans Kelsen's "Pure Theory of Law", Ludwig Wittgenstein's philosophy of language, Otto Neurath's isotype system, Kurt Gödel's mathematical theories, the physics theories of Erwin Schrödinger and Wolfgang Pauli, Karl Popper's philosophy of science, and Ernst Gombrich's history of art.[12] Between 1938 and 1945, twenty-one full and corresponding members had to leave the Academy of Sciences in Vienna: Emil Abel (physical chemistry), Franz Boas (anthropology), Walther Brecht (German philology), Ernst Theodor Brücke (physiology), Karl Bühler (philosophy), Victor Moritz Goldschmidt (mineralogy), Berthold Hatschek (zoology), Hermann Franz Mark (physical chemistry), Victor Franz Hess (experimental physics), Alfred Hettner (geography), August Loehr (numismatics), Hans Horst Meyer (pharmacology), Stefan Meyer (physics), Eduard Norden (classical philology), Wolfgang Pauli (biological and physical chemistry), Ernst Peter Pick (pharmacology), Alfred Francis Přibram (history), Erwin Schrödinger (theoretical physics), Franz Eduard Suess (geology), Josef Weninger (anthropology), and Richard Willstätter (chemistry).[13]

From 1 September 1939, the *Wehrmacht*, now incorporating large numbers of Austrian troops – mountain, infantry, and soon also armored divisions – marched under Hitler's command: first against Poland, then in the spring of 1940 against Denmark, Norway, the Netherlands, Belgium, Luxembourg, and France, in the spring of 1941 against Yugoslavia and Greece, and from 22 June 1941 against the Soviet Union. In the course of the war, over 1.3 million men and boys from Austria served in the *Wehrmacht* and *Waffen-SS*, about 220 reached the rank of general, and 247,000 found a violent death in theaters of war across Europe. The names of the

[10] See Fenwick (1938), *Comment*, p. 312.
[11] See Schausberger (1981), *Anschluss*, pp. 244–70.
[12] See Johnston (2006), *Geistesgeschichte*, pp. xii–xvii.
[13] See Matis (1997), *Anpassung*, pp. 27–35.

dead can be read on thousands of Austrian war memorials. But despite heavy losses at Stalingrad and on other fronts, and despite the Allies' Moscow Declaration on the restoration of Austria, most Austrian soldiers fought until the capitulation, hoping to return to their native Austria. Austrian officers and soldiers were also involved in war crimes – especially in Yugoslavia and the Soviet Union.[14]

As a result of population policy measures, from April 1938 there was a disproportionate increase in marriages in Austria, as well as a significant increase in births. This continued until 1943. Furthermore, National Socialism weakened traditional ties to family, religion, and social class. From January to November 1938, the Nazi programs for creating jobs – especially accelerated arms policies – were able to increase the number of employed persons from about 1.5 to 2.1 million, while in the same period the number of unemployed fell from 500,000 to less than 150,000. By establishing and expanding arms factories in Linz, Steyr, St. Valentin, Simmering, Wiener Neustadt, Graz, and Ranshofen, and building hydropower plants in Ybbs-Persenbeug, Kaprun, Schwabegg, and Lavamünd, the industrial base of the *"Ostmark"* was greatly expanded. During the war, the Nazi authorities protected the food industry by introducing mechanized farming and through the *Reichserbhofgesetz* [Reich Farm-Inheritance Law] of 1933 and a debt-relief program. The social policies introduced by the Nazis included the German social security law, increased wages, and regulated maternity leave, but also the requirement that everyone work, which in the end became *"totaler Arbeitseinsatz"* [total work deployment], which increasingly affected women as well. In addition, during the course of the war, up to 350,000 people – prisoners of war and concentration camp inmates – were used as forced laborers in industries and agriculture.[15]

The Nazi terror system consisted above all of the SS and the police forces (Gestapo, criminal police, security services), who also built concentration camps in which a total of 16,493 Austrian resistance fighters were killed. About 100,000 people perished in Mauthausen concentration camp, built in 1938, above all Poles, Hungarians, Yugoslavs, Italians, Spaniards, and citizens of the Soviet Union and France. Between 1940 and 1944 about 20,000 people were victims of Nazi euthanasia in Schloss Hartheim in Upper Austria, and another 10,000 sick prisoners from Dachau and Mauthausen concentrations camps were murdered there. At least 2,700 Austrian resistance fighters were sentenced to death by the *"Volksgerichtshof"* ["people's court"] and the Vienna Court of Appeals, as were more than 500 Austrian soldiers and officers by military courts and other military tribunals.[16]

The first deportations of Austrian Jews to the recently formed *Generalgouvernement* [General Government – occupied Polish territories] took place in the autumn of

---

[14] See Germann (2006), *"Österreicher,"* and Grischany (2007), *Austrians*.

[15] See Tálos (1988), *NS-Herrschaft*, pp. 28–9, 53, 55–7, 83, 104, 109–10, 131, and Bukey (2000), *Hitler's Austria*, pp. 91–2, 129–30.

[16] See Neugebauer (1988), *NS-Terrorsystem*, pp. 163–83.

1939 and continued on a massive scale – not only to Theresienstadt, but also to Auschwitz and other extermination camps – from the fall of 1941. The premeditated implementation as well as its pan-European dimension of the Shoah, for which the Hitler regime was exclusively responsible, is still unparalleled in world history. Hitler had already threatened the extermination of the Jews at the Reichstag in January 1939; on 12 December 1941, a day after declaring war on the United States, he repeated his threat to senior party leaders, as noted by Joseph Goebbels in his diary: "Regarding the Jewish question, the Führer is determined to make a clean sweep. He foretold the Jews that if they caused another world war [sic!], they would experience their annihilation. This was not just a turn of phrase. The world war is here; the annihilation of the Jews must be the necessary consequence."[17]

In fact, about 5.6 million European Jews were killed in the Shoah. About 65,000 of the approximately 190,000 Jews in Austria were victims of the Nazi extermination policy. Under strictest secrecy, thousands of SS officers, members of the security services, the security police, the Gestapo and the criminal police, concentration camp guards, policemen, gendarmes, and field policemen were involved in the *"Endlösung"* [final solution], as were members of the *Wehrmacht*, railroad employees, and workers in the defense industry.[18]

Hitler and the Nazi regime were a symbol of an "absolute" political claim to power; of the principle of dictatorial leadership, including a leader's cult; of an increasingly militarized *"Volksgemeinschaft"* ["people's community"]; of the continued economic and social corruption of its own people; of hitherto unforeseen and increasingly radical state repression and use of violence; of an unprecedented manipulation of the media to control and mobilize the masses; of the exclusion, denunciation, and persecution of alleged or actual enemies; of the tremendously destructive power of the biologistic ideology of "racial superiority," including its two core elements of "eliminating the Jews" and acquiring *"Lebensraum"* [living space] in the east; of incredible cynicism in exploiting tensions in international relations; of a brutal war with no respect for international martial law; and of the ruthless enslavement and extermination of entire peoples.[19]

In the end, Hitler's only legacy was destruction: "No architectural testimony, no works of art, no political structures or economic models, least of all a moral state – in short, nothing was left for future generations."[20]

Arnold Suppan

---

[17] Quoted in Evans (2010), *Reich*, p. 331.

[18] See Hilberg (1990), *Vernichtung*, pp. 1299–300; Kundrus (2010), *Holocaust*, pp. 130–5, and Benz (1996), *Dimension*.

[19] See Frei (2007), *Broszat*, and Kershaw (2011), *Ende*.

[20] Kershaw (2000), *Hitler*, p. 9. The technical innovations in power plants, motorized vehicles, tanks, aircraft and rockets developed by German and Austrian scientists and engineers would have also been accomplished without the Nazi regime.

The initial reactions to the "Anschluss" in the Academy of Sciences

On 12 March 1938 German *Wehrmacht* [armed forces] and SS and police units had marched into Austria and, just one day later, a law was passed "on the Reunification of Austria with the German Reich", thus fixing the "Anschluss". On 15 March, the Führer and Reich Chancellor Adolf Hitler gave a highly feted speech on Heldenplatz in Vienna.

Fig. 2: Oswald Redlich, 1940

At the Academy, President Oswald Redlich declared his resignation on 18 March 1938 at the first General Assembly after the "Anschluss".[1] He read his declaration, dated 16 March and addressed to the Presiding Committee, aloud: *At this moment when the preparations for the next Academy elections are commencing I see myself compelled to make a decision I have contemplated for some time and to declare that I hereby*

[1] See AÖAW, Minutes of the General Assembly of 18 March 1938 (A 932). On the following, see Graf-Stuhlhofer (1995), *Akademie*, pp. 134–5, as well as Matis (1997), *Anpassung*, pp. 10–6.

step down from my role as President of the Academy. As I lay down the position of President, I would like to thank the honorable gentlemen of the Presiding Committee and all the honorable members of the Academy for having given me so many years of their trust. It is the pride of my life that I was allowed to stand at the head of our Academy's most excellent body of members. I sincerely wish our Academy of Sciences a happy future; may it flourish and prosper in the newly unified Greater German Reich.[2] The nearly 80-year-old historian had presided over the Academy through almost the entire interwar period, after having succeeded the physicist Victor Lang. At this time the Presiding Committee was headed by zoologist Karl Grobben, who had temporarily taken over the office after the death of Vice-President Hans Molisch on 8 December 1937.[3] Grobben addressed a few words of thanks to Redlich, before he too announced his resignation. A new deputy Vice-President was decided by acclamation. The anatomist Ferdinand Hochstetter accepted his election and immediately took over the session's chair, *since the outgoing President had left the meeting.*[4] Hochstetter addressed the attending members of the Academy with the following words: *The Academy of Sciences is subject to the overwhelming impact of a huge event, the transformation of the independent state of Austria into a province of the German Reich. The longing of millions of Germans, both within and beyond our small homeland, for the Greater German Reich has been fulfilled. We are all awed by the enormity of the historical fact, and, with burning hearts, desire a happy future for the shared large homeland, of which our native land is henceforth a part. But full of deep piety we are also all thinking about the glorious history of Austria. Our treasured academy has served our country for ninety years; at the same time, it has always been a precious possession of the entire German people and an enricher of German culture. We are all filled with the conviction that this German task is a great duty with which our Academy has been charged, also for the future; we want to meet this obligation by expending our best efforts for the benefit of the people and the Reich.*[5]

Hochstetter then submitted a draft of a telegram to Adolf Hitler, which had been composed by the Secretary Heinrich Srbik.[6] It read as follows:

[2] AÖAW, Minutes of the General Assembly of 18 March 1938 (A 932), Annex I (copy), reproduced in Matis (1997), *Anpassung*, p. 11. Redlich's handwritten text is found in AÖAW, Allgemeine Akten, No. 142/1938.

[3] Grobben had only been elected as deputy Vice-President at the General Assembly of 28 January 1938 (A 930), with 41 of 42 votes cast.

[4] AÖAW, Minutes of the General Assembly of 18 March 1938 (A 932).

[5] AÖAW, Minutes of the General Assembly of 18 March 1938 (A 932), Annex III, reproduced in Matis (1997), *Anpassung*, pp. 12–3.

[6] See AÖAW, Allgemeine Akten, No. 143/1938. The telegram was dispatched the same day.

To the Führer and Reich Chancellor Adolf Hitler in Berlin!
The Academy of Sciences in Vienna, at the moment the head of the Union of German Academies, has at its General Assembly of 18 March decided to present its respectful compliments to the leader of the united German people and to pledge him ~~unswerving~~ loyalty ~~and unconditional obedience~~. It promises to serve the greater German People's Reich, to which Austria has returned home, with all its intellectual and moral force, and ~~not to waver~~ never to waver in the work of preserving and improving German culture, to which it has always been dedicated.

~~The Presiding Committee of Ak. Grobben, Schweidler, von Srbik.~~
The Academy of Sciences in Vienna

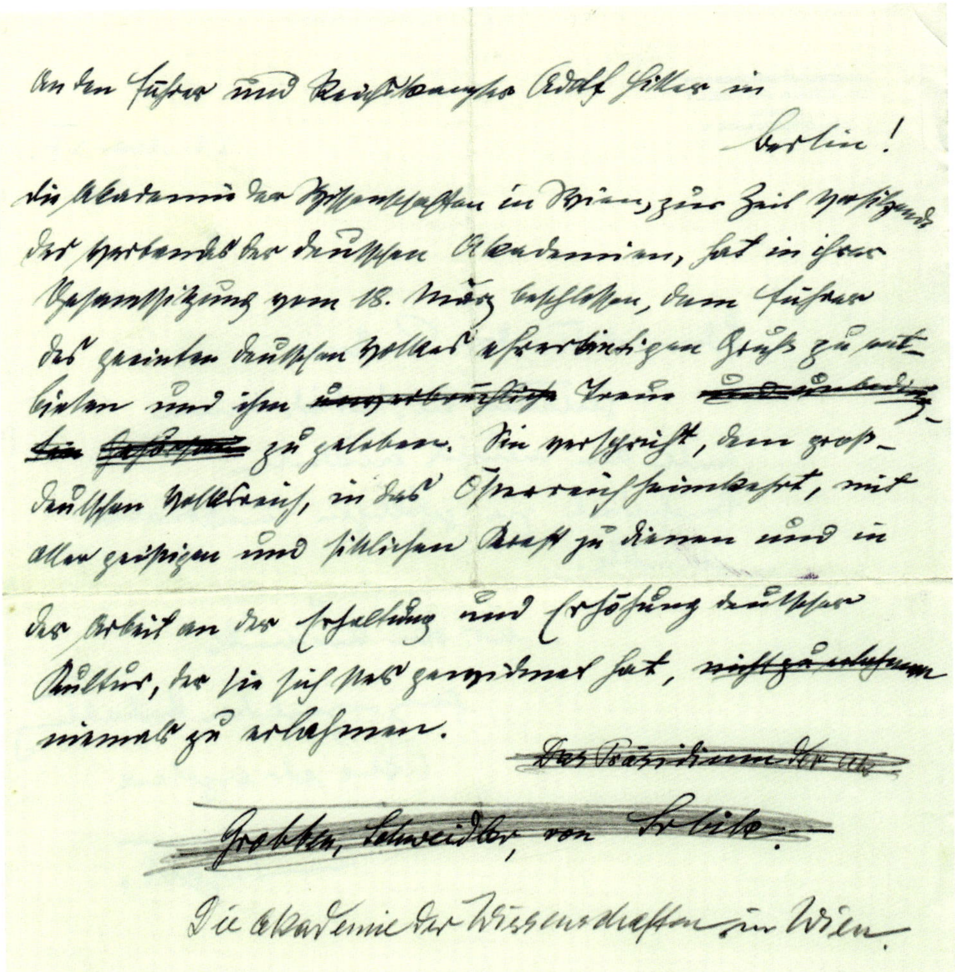

Fig. 3: Draft of the telegram from the Academy to Hitler

It is unclear when the changes were made to the text;[7] in any event the Assembly minutes only mention that the draft was *unanimously approved.* The General Assembly ended with the decision to direct copies of this telegram to Education Minister Oswald Menghin, who was responsible for the Academy, and to the "Official News Agency" (the name at that time of today's Austria Press Agency). Furthermore, telegrams with greetings were to be sent *to all German Academies* (Berlin, Göttingen, Heidelberg, Leipzig, and Munich). The Bavarian Academy of Sciences responded that it *gratefully recalls, in this momentous historical hour, the faithful intellectual defense that the Vienna Academy had without hesitation afforded its German Reich sisters in the difficult years after 1918* [and] *wishes for it and all of us, in the closest union, doubly fruitful work for the intellectual life of our great German people.*[8]

At the next General Assembly, which took place on 25 March, it was decided among other things to request Fritz Knoll *to safeguard the interests of the Nazi leadership in Austria at the Academy of Sciences until the final regulation of the Academy Statutes.*[9] It was also decided to postpone the elections and the Ceremonial Session to the fall, and to set up a committee for the revision of the Statutes.[10]

The question of the Presidency was now on the agenda. Paragraph 5 of the 1922 By-Laws, which were applicable at that time, simply stated: "Elections shall be effected by absolute majority." The Statutes, also dating from 1922, augmented this in paragraph 8, subparagraph 4 by merely stating that the election of the Presiding Committee members required the confirmation of the Federal President.[11] But there was no longer a Federal President. Certainly, the subsequent course of events corresponded to the requirements of the By-Laws only to a limited degree. The legal historian Moriz Wlassak suggested proposing the current Secretary Heinrich Srbik to the Federal Ministry of Education in Vienna as the future President. The proposal was adopted with 43 of 44 votes cast.[12] This was preceded by a letter from the senior member of the Section for Humanities and the Social Sciences, the legal historian Hans Voltelini, to all the ordinary members of his Section: *The Reichsstatthalter* [Reich Governor Arthur Seyss-Inquart] *and the Minister of Education* [Oswald Menghin] *have expressed the intention of appointing the Secretary of the Section for Humanities and the Social Sciences, Professor Heinrich von Srbik, as President of the Academy of Sciences. Prof. Srbik has, however, stated that he would accept this appointment only on the condition that a*

[7] The deletions in the text (*unswerving* and *and unconditional obedience*) and the change (*never to waver* rather than *not to waver*) were added in ink, the change in the signature in pencil, which could be an indication that the former were made before the text was presented to the General Assembly and the latter on the basis of its presentation.

[8] AÖAW, Allgemeine Akten, No. 143/1938.

[9] AÖAW, Minutes of the General Assembly of 25 March 1938 (A 933). See the essay in this volume by Klaus Taschwer, "Expelled, burnt, sold, forgotten, and suppressed," p. 47.

[10] See the essay in this volume by Herbert Matis, "The revision of the Statutes," p. 87.

[11] See Meister (1947), *Geschichte*, p. 157. The Statutes and By-Laws of 1922 are printed in the *Almanach* for 1923, 73 (1924), pp. 14–21, and pp. 22–46.

[12] See AÖAW, Minutes of the extraordinary General Assembly of 1 April 1938 (A 934).

nomination in his favor has come from the side of the Academy. Thus the election of the President of the Academy must be concluded at the Academy General Assembly on 1 April of this year.[13] Wlassak, *as longest elected f*[ull] *member of the Academy* took up this suggestion and proposed Srbik, explaining in an open letter dated 31 March: *The named person has dedicated much of his excellent scholarly work to the study of earlier and later threads that indissolubly linked the German Ostmark with the German Reich. To me he currently seems to be the right man to serve at the head of the Academy. An age-old dream has become a reality. No one can welcome these events with a more joyful heart than a*

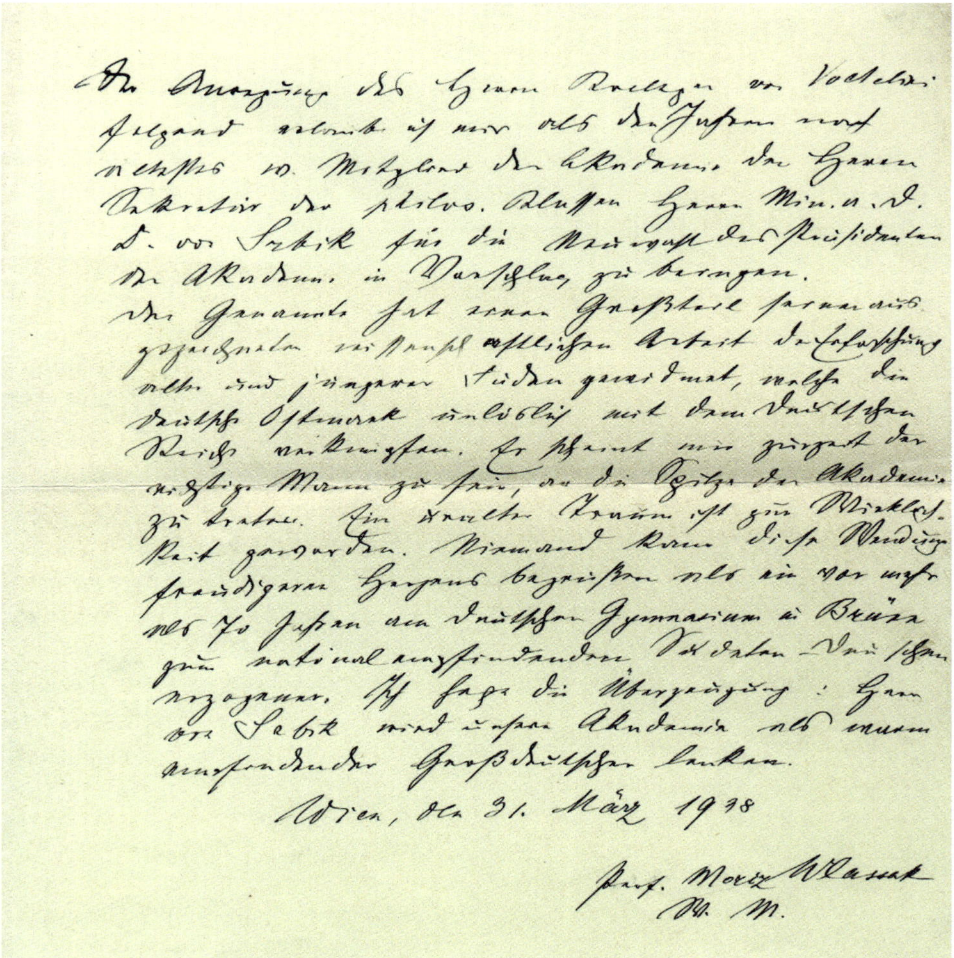
Der Anregung des Herrn Kollegen von Voltelini folgend erlaube ich mir als der Jahren nach ältestes w. Mitglied der Akademie den Herrn Sekretär der philos. Klasse Herrn Min. a. D. Dr. von Srbik für die Neuwahl des Präsidenten der Akademie in Vorschlag zu bringen.
Der Genannte hat einen Großteil seiner ausgezeichneten wissenschaftlichen Arbeit der Erforschung alter und jüngerer Fäden gewidmet, welche die deutsche Ostmark unlöslich mit dem Deutschen Reiche verknüpften. Er scheint mir zurzeit der richtige Mann zu sein, an der Spitze der Akademie zu stehen. Ein uralter Traum ist zur Wirklichkeit geworden. Niemand kann diese Wendung freudigeren Herzens begrüßen als ein vor mehr als 70 Jahren am deutschen Gymnasium in Brünn zum national empfindenden Volksdeutschen erzogener. Ich hege die Überzeugung: Herr von Srbik wird unsere Akademie als ein warm empfindender Großdeutscher lenken.

Wien, den 31. März 1938

Prof. Moriz Wlassak
w. M.

Fig. 4: Wlassak's proposal of Srbik for election as President of the Academy (31 March 1938)

[13] AÖAW, Wahlen, Box 4, Folder "1938," Voltelini to all full members of the Section for Humanities and the Social Sciences on 29 March 1938, sent through the Academy Chancellery on 30 March.

Sudeten German who was raised with national sentiments more than 70 years ago at the German grammar school in Brno. I cherish the conviction: Mr. von Srbik will guide our Academy as a warmly sensitive Greater German.[14]

In the absence of a Federal President, on 2 April the Presiding Committee of the Academy turned to the Minister of Education Menghin, who had not participated in the special session – which he, in his capacity as a full member would have been entitled to do – and reported that the Academy had decided to propose Srbik *for nomination as President.*[15] Through this wording, the letter had a slightly different emphasis than the Statutes would have required: According to the Statutes, the result of a presidential election could be confirmed only by the Federal President; here however, a candidate was being proposed. For the Academy, of greater concern than the formulation was fact that *in established practice, according to which the post of Academy President alternates between the two Academy Sections, in this case an exception in favor of the Section for Humanities and the Social Sciences would be taking place, but in later cases, if practicable, consideration should again be taken of the established practice.*[16]

The confirmation from the government was slow in coming, because the Ministry also did not know who was responsible for appointing Srbik as President. After urging from the side of the Academy, it was declared that the file had come back from Berlin with the remark that although the confirmation was a matter for the *Reichsstatthalter*, that the Reich Minister of the Interior agreed with the vote. Seyss-Inquart wanted to hand over the certificate of appointment, dated 28 June, in person.[17] This only occurred on 26 September in the rooms of the *Reichsstatthalterei* [situated in the former parliament]. After congratulations from Seyss-Inquart, Srbik stated among other things: *It was one of the happiest moments of my life when I was able to tell myself, in the decisive days of March of this year, that I have done my bit for the intellectual preparation of the Greater German Reich. This Reich was the passionate longing of my youth and the silent and strong hope and work of many years of my manhood. The Greater German Reich has become reality, thanks to the genius of our Führer and the will of the German people. Let me promise that I will work for the people and the Reich as long my strength allows it!*[18]

Stefan Sienell

[14] AÖAW, Wahlen, Box 4, Folder "1938."

[15] Ibid. Aktenzahl 157/1938, Presiding Committee to Menghin on 2 April 1938.

[16] AÖAW, Wahlen, Box 4, Folder "1938."

[17] See AÖAW, Wahlen, Box 4, Folder "1938," Junk to Srbik on 29 July 1938. Two days earlier, Srbik had written to Hans Hirsch, who in the meantime had been elected as Srbik's successor as a Secretary of the Academy and was also not yet confirmed: "I don't know whether my appointment is still being delayed because of political decisions. If it does not go through by 1 September, I will resign." Kämmerer (1988), *Srbik*, p. 490, Letter No. 313. Apparently Srbik was calmed by Junk's letter.

[18] *Wiener Zeitung*, 27 September 1938, pp. 6–7, where the exact words exchanged between Seyss-Inquart and Srbik are printed. The appointment document presented to Srbik is held at the AÖAW, Urkundensammlung, No. 10. Illustration on p. 39.

I. 1. The Protagonists

The Presiding Committee of the Academy during the Nazi Era

Since the founding of the Academy, the composition of the Presiding Committee has been based on the principle of balance between the two Sections. It consists of a President, Vice-President, and two Secretaries, one for each of the Academy's two Sections, namely the Section for Humanities and the Social Sciences and the Section for Mathematics and the Natural Sciences. The President and Vice-President are from different Sections and, until the Statutes were modified in 2010, they were both Presidents of their Sections. The Secretary of the Section that did not provide the President acted as Secretary General.

On 16 March 1938, Academy President Oswald Redlich and Karl Grobben, elected interim Vice-President after the death of Hans Molisch in 1937, both resigned. According to the Statutes, Grobben should have assumed the Presidency following Redlich's resignation, but as he had also resigned, the Academy was faced with a hitherto unknown situation of having neither a President nor a Vice-President. The Presiding Committee consisted merely of the two Secretaries, who continued to exercise their functions.

According to the 1922 Statutes (with the amendment of 1925), in the event of the death of a member of the Presiding Committee a temporary substitute was to be chosen until the next election without the need for confirmation by the Federal President, which was normally required. This procedure was applied here: an interim Vice-President, the 77-year-old anatomist Ferdinand Hochstetter, was chosen by acclamation, and pursuant to the Statutes he was also to assume the role of the President on a temporary basis. The meetings of the Section for Humanities and the Social Sciences were chaired as per the Statutes by the most senior member, the 76-year-old jurist and legal historian Hans Voltelini, while the two Secretaries, Egon Schweidler and Heinrich Srbik, retained their former functions. In this uncertain situation the Academy seems to have relied on the principle of seniority.

In contrast to generally accepted democratic principles, the Nazis espoused the "Führer principle." This meant that the authorities in power usually gave important positions to Party members. As part of the Nazi *"Gleichschaltung"* [alignment/consolidation] in business, science, and associations, commissarial directors were appointed immediately after the *"Anschluss"*. Already at the Academy General Assembly on 25 March 1938, in which the elections and Ceremonial Session were also postponed until the fall, corresponding member inland Fritz Knoll, who had recently been appointed commissarial rector of the University, was asked by the remaining members of the Presiding Committee, namely Hochstetter, Schweidler, and Srbik, *to safeguard the interests of the regional administration of the Nazi party in Austria at the Academy of Sciences until the final regulation of the Academy Statutes.*[1] Moreover, in implementing the "Führer principle," on 29 March *Reichsstatthalter* [Reich Governor] Arthur Seyss-Inquart and Minister of Education Oswald Menghin announced their intention to appoint Heinrich Srbik, former Secretary of the Section for Humanities and the Social Sciences, as the new President.[2] Srbik insisted, however, that he would accept the appointment only on the basis of a prior election by the members of the Academy.[3] The status and tasks of the new Nazi representative in the Academy were unclear. It was primarily a gesture of acceptance of the new power relationships, but it was apparent that Knoll's position would expire once the new Statutes had been drawn up and a new Academy Presiding Committee had been established. About a year later, the newly elected President Srbik stated that he would henceforth exercise the functions of the Nazi representative himself. The *Gauleitung*

Fig. 5: Heinrich Srbik

Fig. 6: Egon Schweidler

[1] AÖAW, Minutes of General Assembly of 25 March 1938 (A 933). The Presiding Committee had agreed this three days earlier at its own meeting. See AÖAW, Minutes of the meeting of the Presiding Committee of 22 March 1938.

[2] See the essay in this volume by Stefan Sienell, "The initial reactions to the 'Anschluss' in the Academy of Sciences," pp. 24–6.

[3] See AÖAW, Wahlen, Box 4, Folder "1938," No. 157/1938.

Fig. 7: Ernst Späth

Fig. 8: Hans Hirsch

[supreme regional Nazi Party authority] noted this on 9 March 1939, and for its part the Academy expressed its thanks on 16 March 1939 to Knoll, who had been made an ordinary member in November 1938.

The election of the new Presiding Committee should in fact have taken place on the basis of new Statutes and the Academy had established a special commission for that purpose.[4] However, as the new Statutes were not approved by the Reich Ministry for Science, Education, and Culture in Berlin until 22 July 1938, the President was elected at an extraordinary General Assembly on 1 April 1938 on the basis of the Provisional Statutes. This meant, however, that action had been taken on an uncertain legal basis; there was no longer a Federal President, for example, to confirm the elected members of the Presiding Committee as provided for in the Academy Law and Statutes. This legal uncertainty found expression not least in the letter from the Academy to Federal Minister of Education in Vienna Menghin, which stated merely that it had resolved *to put Srbik forward for appointment as President.*[5] Menghin did not attend the extraordinary General Assembly, although as a full member he was entitled to do so.

[4] See AÖAW, Minutes of the General Assembly of 25 March 1938 (A 933).
[5] AÖAW, Wahlen, Box 4, Folder "1938," No. 157/1938, of 2 April 1938.

A. 934

AKADEMIE DER WISSENSCHAFTEN IN WIEN

PROTOKOLL

der ausserordentlichen Gesamtsitzung
am 1. April 1938.

Anwesend: Der stellvertretende Vizepräsident Hochstetter
Der Generalsekretär Schweidler
Der Sekretär der phil.-histor. Klasse Srbik

Die wirklichen Mitglieder:

Adametz
Benndorf
Bittner
Dopsch
Durig
Eder
Egger, Rudolf
Graff
Grobben
Hartmann
Hauler
Hillebrand
Himmelbauer
Hirsch
Hochstetter
Kralik
Kretschmer
Kruppa
Mache
Mark
Meister
Mewaldt
Nadler
Oberhummer
Patsch
Pintner
Praschniker
Prey
Radermacher
Redlich
Reininger
Schaffer
Schaffernak
Schlosser
Skrabal
Späth
Suess
Tschermak
Voltelini
Wenger
Wilhelm
Wirtinger
Wlassak

Der Generalsekretär legt das Protokoll der ausserordentlichen Gesamtsitzung vom 25.März vor.

Zur Kenntnis.

143 Die Bayerische Akademie in München dankt für den telegraphischen Gruss anlässlich der Einverleibung Oesterreichs ins Grossdeutsche Reich.

Zur Kenntnis.

157 Das w.M.Wlassak schlägt vor, den bisherigen Sekretär w.M.von Srbik beim Unterrichtsministerium als künftigen Präsidenten der Akademie in Vorschlag zu bringen.

Bei der Abstimmung entfallen 43 Stimmen von 44 Stimmen mit Ja auf w.M.von Srbik.

Es wird demnach w.M. von Srbik dem Ministerium vorgeschlagen werden.

151 Der Generalsekretär erstattet namens der Statuten-Kommission kurzen Bericht über die in der gestrigen Sitzung der Kommission durchberatenen neuformulierten Paragraphe der Satzung der Akademie.

Zur Kenntnis.

158 Der Generalsekretär stellt namens des Präsidiums den Antrag, die Wahlsitzungen sowie die Feierliche Sitzung auf unbestimmte Zeit zu verschieben.

Angenommen.

Fig. 9: Minutes of the extraordinary General Assembly of 1 April 1938

In doing so, the Academy was following a motion put forward by legal historian Moriz Wlassak, former Secretary of the Section for Humanities and the Social Sciences, that the 59-year-old historian Srbik be proposed to the Minister of Education as future President.[6] Srbik was elected thereupon by 43 of the 44 votes cast. At the General Assembly of 20 May 1938, the remaining members of the Presiding Committee were also elected. The former Secretary General Egon Schweidler became the new Vice-President. The new Secretary General was the chemist Ernst Späth, and the Secretary of the Section for Humanities and the Social Sciences was another historian, Hans Hirsch, who died, however, in 1940, to be replaced by the specialist in German language and literature, Dietrich Kralik-Meyrswalden.[7]

Fig. 10: Dietrich Kralik-Meyrswalden

Because of the uncertain legal situation after the "Anschluss", confirmation of the elections by the state authorities did not come until later. After Minister of Education Menghin had announced that he was not the competent authority, the appointment proposal was sent to Berlin, from where the file was returned with a note that confirmation of the proposed President was a matter for *Reichsstatthalter* Seyss-Inquart in Vienna. Seyss-Inquart formally confirmed Srbik's election on 28 June 1938. Since the

[6] See AÖAW, Minutes of the extraordinary General Assembly of 1 April 1938 (A 934).

[7] After Hirsch's death he was elected deputy Secretary at the Section meeting of 16 October 1940 (C 2623) and formerly confirmed on 13 June 1941.

Reichsstatthalter wanted to hand over the appointment decree in person but Srbik was indisposed at the time due to illness, the decree was not presented until 26 September, when a small ceremony was held at the *Reichsstatthalterei* [the former parliament]. Seyss-Inquart spoke of the *Central European role of the German Ostmark* as a bulwark of the German people in the south-east, while the new President Srbik, who had joined the Nazi Party in May 1938 and who had been nominated by the *Reichsstatthalter* as a candidate for the Reichstag in Berlin, defined the role of the Academy in this connection as follows: *When speaking of a German cultural mission by this German tribe and country, the Vienna Academy may claim to have played a most honorable role in the achievements of many generations and can also say with pride that its activities have always been designed to further the glory and wellbeing of the pan-German people.*[8]

According to the provisions applicable to German academies, with which the Vienna Academy had been associated since 1893 in a so-called "Cartel," members, including those of the Presiding Committee, were to be appointed by the Reich Minister of Science, Education, and Culture. There were therefore no independent elections within the Academy but only the possibility of proposing "suitable members,"[9] who were then appointed by the Reich minister. It seems that in Vienna, the new situation had not been fully appreciated. The Nazis did not want elections whose results were then confirmed by the state authorities, but wished to appoint the officials in accordance with the Nazi "Führer principle." If the *Reichsstatthalter* approved the election of the new Academy President, it was in some way as the arrogated legal successor of the Austrian Federal President.

Srbik took up office on 1 October 1938. After approval of the new Statues on 22 July 1938, the other members of the Presiding Committee were definitively appointed not by the *Reichsstatthalter* but by the Reich Minister of Science, Education, and Culture, effective as of 14 November 1938. At the General Assembly of 16 December 1938, President Srbik announced that the Presiding Committee members had now been appointed by the Reich Minister of Science, Education, and Culture.[10] Thus the Presiding Committee was not complete until late fall 1938.

On 1 February 1940, the Vienna Academy of Sciences was formally assigned to the Reich Ministry of Science, Education, and Culture in Berlin.[11] *Gauleiter* [regional Nazi Party leader] Josef Bürckel, Reich Commissioner for the reunification of Austria with the German Reich, and the (formerly Austrian) Ministry of Interior and Cultural Affairs were instructed to hand over to the Ministry of Science, Education, and Culture in Berlin all files in their possession concerning the Academy.[12]

Herbert Matis

[8] *Wiener Zeitung*, 27 September 1938, p. 6.
[9] Provisional Statutes, § 8, in: *Almanach* for 1938, 88 (1939), p. 12.
[10] See AÖAW, Minutes of the General Assembly of 16 December 1938 (A 941).
[11] See AÖAW, Minutes of the General Assembly of 9 February 1940 (A 950).
[12] See AÖAW, Allgemeine Personalakten, Box 2, Folder 9, No. 30/1940 of 31 January 1940.

Fig. 11: The Presiding Committee at the Ceremonial Session on 23 November 1938 (Späth, Srbik, Schweidler, Hirsch)

Heinrich (von) Srbik (1878–1951) and the Academy of Sciences

Srbik[1] is sometimes described as the "greatest," "most important," and "most eminent" Austrian historian of the twentieth century.[2] These superlatives are due, above all, his monumental 1925 biography *Metternich*.[3] This first major portrait, written with empathy and even sympathy, of the *bête noire* of previous bourgeois historiography not only gave hitherto unknown popularity[4] to this *Vormärz* statesman but also gave the author himself – just three years after his appointment to the University of Vienna in 1922 – the status of a mandarin among German-speaking historians, with great popular appeal and political relevance. Srbik had in fact received his first professorship (Graz 1912) on the basis of monographs, written mainly on the economic history of the Austrian hereditary lands and in the tradition of the Institute for Austrian Historical Research (IFÖG), an establishment that shunned any reference to the present day. It was not until 1919 that his first publication with contemporary relevance appeared, which suggested an affinity to Social Democracy.[5] His sympathy for Metternich now made him appear more as a conservative, and Srbik indeed described himself in the book as a moderate conservative.[6] This is the source of his later assessment of himself as such, an attitude that, before 1945, was shared both by many

[1] For details of Srbik's life, see Pesditschek (2012), *Srbik*, with extensive bibliography. For reasons of space, this article will reference the relevant pages in the work, which, in turn, will also encounter additions here. I would like to thank Martin Peters in particular for the critical reading of the manuscript and Stefan Sienell for the outstanding support within the AÖAW.

[2] See Pesditschek (2012), *Srbik*, p. 263.

[3] Srbik (1925), *Metternich*. It was not before his death that a third volume appeared, published by his most loyal student, Taras Borodajkewycz, from his papers: Srbik (1954), *Metternich*. Mention should also be made of the choice of publishing company, F. Bruckmann in Munich, which also published Houston Stewart Chamberlain's anti-Semitic second-rate work *Die Grundlagen des neunzehnten Jahrhunderts* (Munich, 1899). For the publishers' relationship to Hitler, see most recently Bohnenkamp (2010), *Egeria*, pp. 34–7.

[4] See Hübner (1991), *Geschichte*, sheets 102–16 (particularly 102), and Traska/Lind (2012), *Leopoldi*, p. 165.

[5] Srbik (1919), *Revolution*. For comments on this essay, see Pesditschek (2012), *Srbik*, pp. 274–6.

[6] Srbik (1925), *Metternich*, vol. 1, p. 49: The author "makes no secret of his moderate, historically based conservative conviction."

Nazis and also by Carl Friedrich Goerdeler,[7] one of the 20 July 1944 conspirators,[8] and which continued after 1945.[9]

Fig. 12: Heinrich Srbik

But if conservatism, as Michael Oakeshott defines it, means "to prefer the familiar to the unknown, the tried to the untried, fact to mystery,"[10] then it cannot apply to Srbik, who after 1945 set his hopes on the utopia of an "undogmatic, non-Marxist orthodox socialism."[11] In the fall of 1898, Srbik joined 'Gothia', an association of German students that idolized Georg Schönerer. The basic acceptance of his proto-Nazi, anti-Semitic, and anti-Slav doctrine must have produced a strong feeling of inferiority in Srbik, knowing that his paternal grandfather had started out as a "Czech farm hand."[12] Throughout his life he thus sought to avoid any sign of being pro-Slav, as his name might have suggested. Until his death he remained steadfastly convinced

---

7 Srbik apparently gave differing versions of the year in which Goerdeler visited him in Vienna, as was his wont in other respects as well. He told the conservative historian, resistance fighter, and Goerdeler biographer Gerhard Ritter (see Pesditschek (2012), *Srbik*, p. 314, n. 263) that it was in 1944, whereas to his historian colleague Wilhelm Bauer he cited the year 1938. See Bauer (1951), *Srbik*, p. 358.

8 See Pesditschek (2012), *Srbik*, pp. 312–4.

9 See Pesditschek (2012), *Srbik*, p. 265.

10 Oakeshott (1991), *Rationalism*, p. 408.

11 Pesditschek (2012), *Srbik*, p. 317. In this context mention should be made of his supervision of a doctoral thesis in 1940 written by the future left-wing socialist Minister of Justice Christian Broda, who was notable for his "strict rejection of liberalism and the demand for the (total) politicization of man." See Wirth (2011), *Broda*, pp. 90–1.

12 Pesditschek (2012), *Srbik*, pp. 268–9.

that the Germans should "lead" the Slav peoples of Central Europe or *Zwischeneuropa*,[13] and this brings us to the core of his life's work, a "pan-German view of history," as he himself called it. In principle this was an ideological project and it is clear that with the help of this ideology, Srbik hoped not only to write another extensive historical work,[14] but to write history itself. He was not merely in favor of a political union of the German Reich and "German Austria." Rather a Greater Germany should, according to Srbik, incorporate all the German diaspora settlement areas, in other words no less than the whole of Central Europe and *Zwischeneuropa*, in order to ensure, in this way, the aforementioned German "leadership" of the Slav and other non-Germanic peoples living there. There was a further important element in Srbik's ideology, the "rehabilitation" of the Habsburg monarchy. In this context Srbik emphasized in particular that the Dual Monarchy perpetuated the "universalistic" idea of the Holy Roman Empire of German nation. From this Srbik inferred the timeless right of Germans to "lead" Europe, if not the whole world. He consciously accepted[15] that the realization of the aims of the "pan-German view of history" would inevitably demand new "hecatombs of blood sacrifices."[16]

For Austria, realization of the pan-German concept after January 1933 meant union with the Nazi German Reich. Srbik now stepped up his pan-German propaganda. The first two volumes of *Deutsche Einheit*, which appeared in 1935, were unquestionably intended as a plea for rapid annexation and were understood in Austria as such. Between 1933 and 1938 Srbik sought, as far as was possible, to promote the interests of the Nazis in other ways as well. As such, he was evidently perceived in this period by many Nazis and also by opponents of Nazism as a staunch National Socialist.[17]

For Srbik personally, the spring and summer of 1938 must have been euphoric months. During this time he published a series of exultant articles in various newspapers and magazines, starting with the *Völkischer Beobachter*, and even ended his own private correspondence (until mid-August 1938) with "Heil Hitler!"[18]

---

[13] Which "is defined as the line from Danzig to Trieste and from Riga to Odessa and is characterized for us by islands of Germaness [*Streudeutschtum*]." Srbik (1937 and 1938), *Mitteleuropa*, p. 5.

[14] Srbik (1935–42), *Einheit*.

[15] Srbik's own formulation for an event that he himself evidently regarded as positive. Pesditschek (2012), *Srbik*, p. 302.

[16] Pesditschek (2012), *Srbik*, pp. 284–90, 300–2.

[17] Pesditschek (2012), *Srbik*, pp. 291–7; Ebneth (1976), *Wochenschrift*, pp. 39, 178–9, 187, 239, and Oberkofler (1999), *Huter*, pp. 54–5.

[18] See Pesditschek (2012), *Srbik*, p. 297.

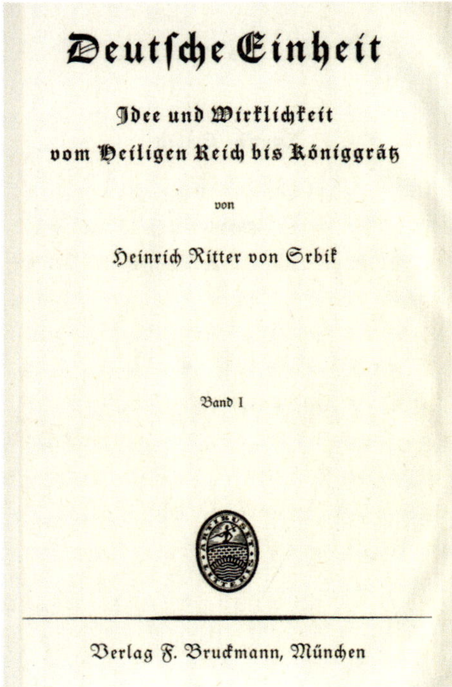

Deutsche Einheit

Idee und Wirklichkeit
vom Heiligen Reich bis Königgrätz

von

Heinrich Ritter von Srbik

Band I

Verlag F. Bruckmann, München

Fig. 13: *Deutsche Einheit*, front page

It was at this time as well that he accepted the "election"[19] as President of the Academy of Sciences in Vienna and the "appointment as member of the Greater German Reichstag by the Führer and Reich Chancellor" (both in April 1938),[20] which was followed by membership of the Nazi Party on 1 May 1938.[21]

[19] Matis (1997), *Anpassung*, p. 16. Seyss-Inquart and Menghin had originally planned to apply the "Führer principle" directly to the Academy and to appoint Srbik as President without a prior election. Srbik, however, insisted on an "election" even though the outcome was naturally not in question. See the essay in this volume by Stefan Sienell, "The initial reactions to the 'Anschluss' in the Academy of Sciences," pp. 24–6.

[20] In his "letter of justification" of 3 September 1945, Srbik writes that "I had been placed on the election list without my knowledge or will and had only learned of it on the radio. [...] I was persuaded to become a member of the Reichstag not least in the interests of the Academy of Sciences, whose welfare I had been entrusted with." There was an alternative version (also attributable to Srbik himself) in circulation saying that he had learned of his appointment from the newspaper. Pesditschek (2012), *Srbik*, p. 298.

[21] "In recognition of his services to German unity, he was given the low membership number 6.104.788." Pesditschek (2012), *Srbik*, p. 298. See also the quote in Oberkofler (1999), *Huter*, p. 126 ("the conscientiously worn Nazi Party badge").

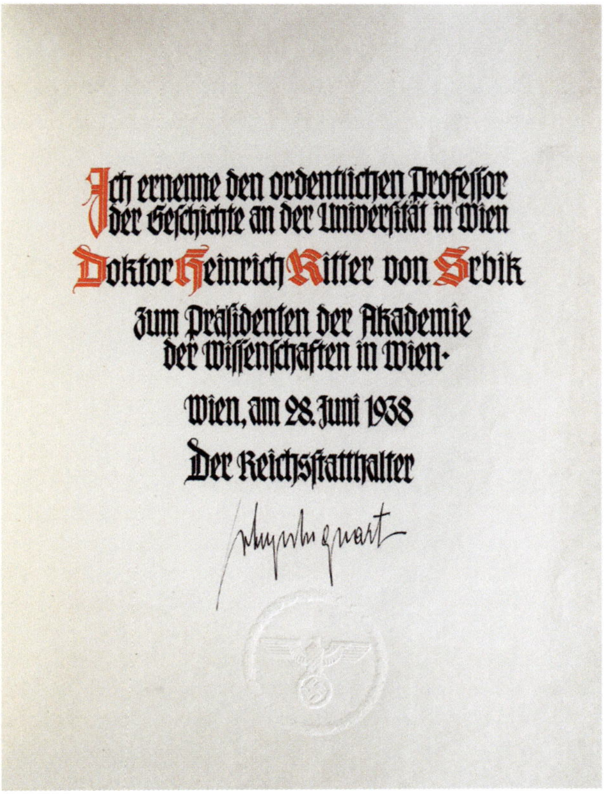

Ich ernenne den ordentlichen Professor
der Geschichte an der Universität in Wien
Doktor Heinrich Ritter von Srbik
zum Präsidenten der Akademie
der Wissenschaften in Wien.
Wien, am 28. Juni 1938
Der Reichsstatthalter

Fig. 14: Document appointing Srbik as Academy President

As President of the Academy, Srbik generally towed the government line. In his inaugural address at the Ceremonial Session of the Academy in 1942, for example, he quoted approvingly from a letter apparently written from the front by a student that a "purely vegetative, hormic" way of life prevailed in the Soviet Union, and a year later at the same ceremony he called the Russian campaign a "battle of the soul against the machine, of love against hate."[22] Occasionally, however, he also tried to outsmart the Berlin headquarters, albeit in an inconsequential manner. He did so with the approval of the other *"Ostmark"* Nazi Academy members who, like him, became embittered soon after the "Anschluss" at Berlin's condescension towards Vienna.[23] In spite of the great contribution – in his view – that he had made to the "Anschluss", Srbik had to

[22] Pesditschek (2012), *Srbik*, p. 309, n. 244. See also Oberkofler (2012), *Spiegel und Pleyer*, pp. 167–9.

[23] See the essay in this volume by Felicitas Seebacher, "'Increasing the achievements of German science by all available means,'" pp. 141–8.

settle for a token position without any real political influence.[24] Because he was not yet a Party member at this time, he could not exercise the function of Nazi Party representative of the Academy but had to delegate it[25] to the botanist Fritz Knoll.[26] Reference is made in this regard to paragraph 10 of Srbik's "letter of justification" of 3 September 1945, his subjective review of his achievements as President of the Academy.[27]

The letter fails to mention an alleged incident, cited in the memoirs[28] of a generally uncritical admirer of Srbik as a further example of his "courage" as President of the Academy, in which "in the first meeting of the Academy after the Anschluss […] the Secretary General of the Academy read out an annual report" paying homage to

[24] For further details, see Pesditschek (2012), *Srbik*, pp. 306–8, 311.

[25] See most recently Seliger (2010), *Scheinparlamentarismus*, pp. 565–7, 569–71, and Oberkofler (2012), *Bemerkungen*, p. 3. According to Leitner (2010), *Christian*, passim, Fritz Knoll must have been a more amenable Nazi than his namesake Kurt Knoll, rector of the Institute of Economics and Business Administration and *Gaudozentenbundführer* [*Gau* head of the Nazi Association for University Teachers] in Vienna. See also the essay in this volume by Klaus Taschwer, "The two careers of Fritz Knoll," pp. 45–52.

[26] Massiczek (1978), *Situation*, p. 225. A short time later, however, Srbik enjoyed "such trust by the Nazis that he was able to take over from Knoll as the Academy's Nazi Party representative." Oberkofler (1983), *Stellungnahmen*, p. 120. See also Matis (1997), *Anpassung*, pp. 19–20, and Oberkofler (2012), *Bemerkungen*, p. 3.

[27] Pesditschek (2012), *Srbik*, pp. 310–1. He writes in his "letter of justification": "To mention but a few examples, I supported the award of the Grillparzer Prize to the poet Max Mell against the objections of Reich Minister Göbbels [sic], parried the attack by the Reich Propaganda Office against the further publication of the 'Archive for Austrian History' by the Academy, and, as chairman of the 'Commission for Modern History of Austria' […] prevented its name from being changed to 'Commission for the Modern History of the Ostmark.'" As a further example of "at least modest successes," he cites "the publication of the work of Abraham a S[ancta] Clara, saying that in doing so the Academy had honored the great Augustinian hermit and *Altösterreich's* [Habsburg Austria's] heroic era." Finally, he refers to "an episode lasting six months until January 1945: the accusation made against me in Vienna to Reich Minister Rust because I had given a congratulatory letter on behalf of the Academy to the old Archduke Eugen, last curator and long-term honorary member of the Academy, in honor of his eightieth birthday. After a hard struggle, I managed to extract from Minister Rust and Reichsleiter Schirach the written satisfaction due to myself and the Academy." As concerns Mell, he had also called for "Anschluss" with Nazi Germany in his writings. He was still applying for Party membership when he was awarded the Grillparzer Prize. Even after 1945 he was regarded by most members of the Austrian P.E.N. Club as a "Nazi writer" unworthy of being a member of this literary association; this at least is the tenor of a text published twice from the papers of the Jewish author Hermann Hakel, who for his part had appreciated Mell: Hakel (1991), *Äste*, pp. 68–9 / Hakel (2011), *Von denen ich weiss*, p. 205. More compromising from a recent point of view was the election on 27 May 1941 of the staunch Nazi writer Erwin Guido Kolbenheyer as an honorary member of the Academy, which had been advocated by Srbik in the hope, directly after the Mell affair, of *creating a strong counterweight that would surpass the significance of the award of the prize to Mell* (AÖAW, Grillparzer Prize 1941).

[28] See Spitzmüller (1955), *Ursach*.

three recently deceased Jewish Academy members.[29] Srbik did not, however, oppose the expulsion of "non-Aryan" members.[30] In spite of his friendly relations with his fellow-historians of Jewish descent, Hans Rothfels and Friedrich Engel-Janosi, Srbik had basically held strong anti-Semitic views since his student days, which he also expressed between 1938 and 1945 in his (more or less) scholarly publications.[31]

Also missing from Srbik's list of achievements as Academy President is his intervention on behalf of Johan Huizinga, described by a number of writers as successful.[32] The famous, generally conservative Dutch (cultural) historian had been a *persona ingratissima* for the Nazis since the 'Von-Leers-incident' in early 1933[33] and had been arrested on 7 August 1942 by the Nazi occupying authorities under the former *Reichsstatthalter* [Reich Governor] Seyss-Inquart, who had been Reich Commissioner for the occupied Netherlands since 29 May 1940, and transported as a hostage to Sint-Michielsgestel concentration camp. At the instigation of Huizinga's friend Willem Jan Mari van Eysinga,[34] Srbik wrote two letters to his former compatriot and comrade-in-arms calling for Huizinga's release,[35] but in his reply on 2 September 1942, Seyss-Inquart emphatically denied his request[36]

---

29 "When I asked Srbik after the meeting how he had managed to do this, he told me that the *Gauleiter* [regional Nazi Party leader] had indeed asked him to remove the homage to the three Jewish scholars, but he had replied that in that case he would not be able to hold the meeting because a refusal to mention these names would cause international embarrassment for the Academy." Ibid., p. 404, quoted in Pesditschek (2012), *Srbik*, p. 311.

30 Except in one case, that of the geologist Franz Eduard Suess. See Matis (1997), *Anpassung*, p. 30. See also the essay in this volume by Herbert Matis "Exclusion of members," pp. 53–9.

31 For details, see Pesditschek (2012), *Srbik*, pp. 302–6; Oberkofler (2012), *Spiegel und Pleyer*, p. 213; Reiter (1999), *Zerstört*, p. 610, and Rupnow (2010), *Brüche*, pp. 82–4.

32 See Matis (1997), *Anpassung*, p. 56.

33 For details, see most recently Krumm (2011), *Huizinga*, pp. 201–3.

34 See Huizinga (1991), *Briefwisseling III*, p. 350 (letter of 16 August to his wife), and van der Lem (1993), *Huizinga*, p. 269.

35 See Huizinga (1991), *Briefwisseling III*, p. 346, nn. 3 and 4. Srbik's first letter presumably received no reply.

36 See AÖAW, Minutes of the General Assembly of 27 November 1942 (A 974), and AÖAW, PA Johan Huizinga, Seyss-Inquart to Srbik of 2 September 1942 (part of the letter published in Dutch translation in van der Lem (1993), *Huizinga*, p. 271), reproduction given above. Two days later, on 4 September, Huizinga was declared *unfit for the camp* (AÖAW, PA Johan Huizinga, Van Eysinga to Srbik on 13 September 1942) and transferred to the hospital in Den Bosch. After transfer back to the camp he was released on 25 October (nominally) for health reasons. See van der Lem (1993), *Huizinga*, pp. 272–3, 290, and also Krumm (2011), *Huizinga*, pp. 237–8. This fortunate turn of events is interpreted by a friend of Huizinga as having been due to Srbik's intervention; see Jan der Hoeve, chairman of the Dutch Academy of Sciences and former rector of the University of Leiden, to Srbik on 5 November 1942 (AÖAW, PA Johan Huizinga): "As our common friend Prof. Dr. J. Huizinga has been released, I should like to thank you sincerely for your contribution to his liberation." In view of Seyss-Inquart's reply and the chronology, however, I believe it highly unlikely that Srbik's intervention in fact contributed to Huizinga's release – which was, *nota bene*, a banishment from Leiden. See also Strupp (2000), *Huizinga*, p. 42, n. 100, who ascribes to him "only a subordinate role," and Krumm (2011), *Huizinga*, p. 238 ("The reason for Huizinga's release [...] cannot be determined with certainty.").

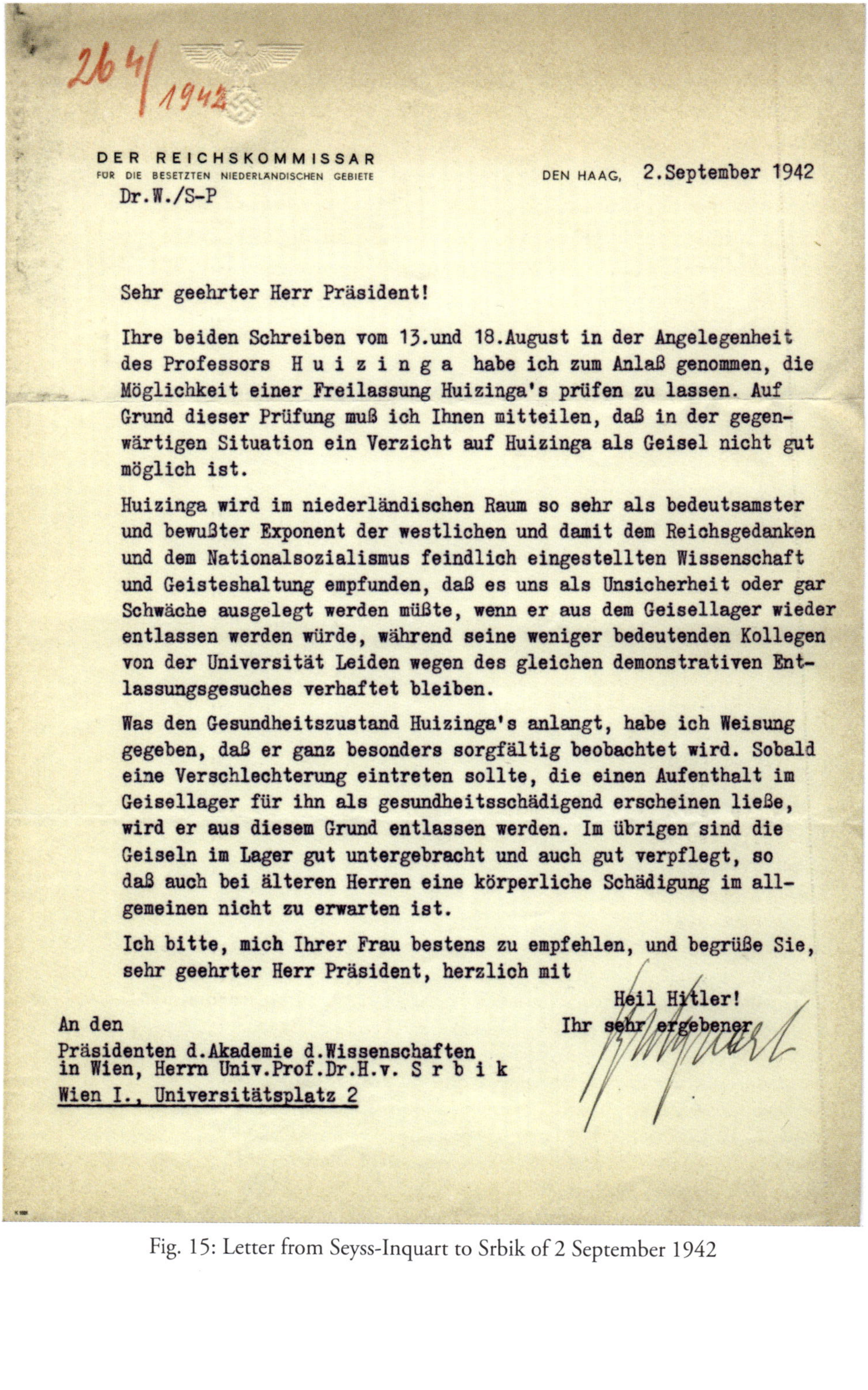

264/1942

DER REICHSKOMMISSAR
FÜR DIE BESETZTEN NIEDERLÄNDISCHEN GEBIETE
Dr.W./S-P

DEN HAAG, 2.September 1942

Sehr geehrter Herr Präsident!

Ihre beiden Schreiben vom 13.und 18.August in der Angelegenheit des Professors H u i z i n g a habe ich zum Anlaß genommen, die Möglichkeit einer Freilassung Huizinga's prüfen zu lassen. Auf Grund dieser Prüfung muß ich Ihnen mitteilen, daß in der gegenwärtigen Situation ein Verzicht auf Huizinga als Geisel nicht gut möglich ist.

Huizinga wird im niederländischen Raum so sehr als bedeutsamster und bewußter Exponent der westlichen und damit dem Reichsgedanken und dem Nationalsozialismus feindlich eingestellten Wissenschaft und Geisteshaltung empfunden, daß es uns als Unsicherheit oder gar Schwäche ausgelegt werden müßte, wenn er aus dem Geisellager wieder entlassen werden würde, während seine weniger bedeutenden Kollegen von der Universität Leiden wegen des gleichen demonstrativen Entlassungsgesuches verhaftet bleiben.

Was den Gesundheitszustand Huizinga's anlangt, habe ich Weisung gegeben, daß er ganz besonders sorgfältig beobachtet wird. Sobald eine Verschlechterung eintreten sollte, die einen Aufenthalt im Geisellager für ihn als gesundheitsschädigend erscheinen ließe, wird er aus diesem Grund entlassen werden. Im übrigen sind die Geiseln im Lager gut untergebracht und auch gut verpflegt, so daß auch bei älteren Herren eine körperliche Schädigung im allgemeinen nicht zu erwarten ist.

Ich bitte, mich Ihrer Frau bestens zu empfehlen, und begrüße Sie, sehr geehrter Herr Präsident, herzlich mit

Heil Hitler!
Ihr sehr ergebener

An den
Präsidenten d.Akademie d.Wissenschaften
in Wien, Herrn Univ.Prof.Dr.H.v. S r b i k
Wien I., Universitätsplatz 2

Fig. 15: Letter from Seyss-Inquart to Srbik of 2 September 1942

In early March 1945 Srbik moved to his second residence in Ehrwald, Tyrol, transferring "responsibility for the Academy" in his absence to Eduard Pernkopf,[37] rector of the University of Vienna.[38] From there he was not to return again to Vienna for fear of the Red Army "machine." Although not literally an "illegal" (albeit only in a formal sense), he was dismissed as an academic teacher and his membership of the Academy held in abeyance.[39] In spring 1948 he was awarded a pension thanks to the protection offered by the socialist Federal Minister of the Interior Oskar Helmer,[40] and at the end of 1948 his membership of the Academy was reactivated.[41] Officially, however, Srbik remained *persona non grata*. At his burial in Ehrwald after a highly productive – although only in terms of volume – final period of creativity, in which he expressed no regret whatsoever for his earlier actions, but reproduced his old views (even if partially concealed),[42] "neither the Academy of Sciences nor the University of Vienna nor the government were directly represented."[43] By way of reparation, however, there were no less than three obituaries from within the Academy: one written by his historian colleague Wilhelm Bauer, also a staunch anti-Semite, in the Academy *Almanach*, fully in line with the unwritten laws of this genre,[44] and also personal appreciations by two former students, Günther Hamann and Adam Wandruszka,[45] in volume 115 of the *Anzeiger der phil.-hist. Klasse* of 1979. Here (particularly in Hamann's portrait) shines a leading light who shares little more with the dark figure of the genuine supporter of Nazism that can be reconstructed from the other evidence[46] – typifying Albert Müller's definition of an "Austro-Nazi" at best[47] – than a name and basic biographical details.

Martina Pesditschek

[37] See most recently Seliger (2010), *Scheinparlamentarismus*, pp. 567–71.

[38] Pesditschek (2012), *Srbik*, p. 315.

[39] He remained a "sought-after consultant in the Academy agenda." Oberkofler (2012), *Bemerkungen*, p. 3.

[40] See Höbelt (1999), *VdU*, pp. 17, 56.

[41] See Pesditschek (2012), *Srbik*, p. 315.

[42] For details, see Pesditschek (2012), *Srbik*, pp. 315–22. For Srbik's later activities in support of his old German national milieu, see Höbelt (1999), *VdU*, p. 144; Oberkofler (1999), *Huter*, pp. 82–3, 87–8, and Oberkofler (2008), *Grass*, pp. 92–6, 98–9.

[43] Spitzmüller (1955), *Ursach*, p. 405.

[44] See Bauer (1951), *Srbik*; see on this Oberkofler (2012), *Bemerkungen*, p. 3.

[45] Hamann (1979), *Nachkriegserinnerungen*; Wandruszka (1979), *Srbik*. On Wandruszka, see Oberkofler (2012), *Bemerkungen*, S. 7.

[46] See Pesditschek (2012), *Srbik*, pp. 309–10, n. 246.

[47] See most recently Leitner (2010), *Christian*, p. 68; Müller (1997), *Adaptierung*, pp. 609–10.

The two careers of Fritz Knoll

How a botanist furthered the Nazi Party's interests after 1938 – and successfully lived it down after 1945

A long life as an academic often ends with late recognition. Such was the case with the botanist Fritz Knoll, who died in February 1981 at the age of 97 after having been a member of the Academy of Sciences for 45 years. In 1965 he was awarded the "Austrian Cross of Merit for Science and Art 1st Class", and four years earlier he had already received the "Rector Memorial Award" from the Academic Senate of the University of Vienna *in recognition* [of the] *honorable and courageous discharge of duties in difficult times.*[1] This was not the only award that Fritz Knoll received for his rectorship from 1938 to 1943, which was indeed remarkable in many ways. Already in March 1943, the tenured staff of the University of Vienna had allowed themselves *to express to your Magnificence our deeply felt devotion and gratitude on the occasion of the completion of your term of office as rector of the National Socialist University of Vienna.* [...] *Heil Hitler!*[2]

Fig. 16: Fritz Knoll (1943)

[1] AÖAW, Papers of Fritz Knoll, Box 5, Folder 8, document commemorating his term as rector of the University of Vienna, 1938–43.

[2] AÖAW, Papers of Fritz Knoll, Box 5, Folder 6, letter from the authorities of the University of Vienna at the end of Knoll's rectorship, 1943.

In the long history of the University of Vienna, which was founded in 1365, Knoll's five-year term of office was something exceptional. The botanist was the only rector to be appointed by the political authorities in contravention of the university's right to self-government. This also applies to his function as the authorized Nazi Party representative for the Academy of Sciences, although he held this position for a shorter period of just under a year. But how did Fritz Knoll become the *Magnifizenz* [rector] of one of the largest and oldest universities in Europe? What did he achieve as Nazi Party representative of the Academy and university rector? And how did he manage, after 1945, to start a new career at the Academy of Sciences and to receive such recognition in later life?

While Knoll's academic career is well documented,[3] little study has been made to date of his political career. He appears to have been an early supporter of German nationalism. He was a member of the Gothia singing fraternity and member of the board of the Deutscher Klub,[4] founded in 1908 as a forum for German national academics. On 1 July 1933 he joined the *NS-Lehrerbund* [Nazi Teachers' Union] and after 1934 he was one of the few university professors to evade mandatory membership of the *Vaterländische Front* [Fatherland's Front].[5] There is further concrete evidence of Knoll's Nazi leanings from this time. A report by the secret police to the regional leadership of the *Vaterländische Front* of 7 July 1937 stated that in his department there was *an insufferably provocative Nazi majority of teachers, students, and staff.* He applied for membership of the Nazi Party in November 1937 and was given the membership number 6.235.774. Another report from the Nazi era, quoted several times by Party representatives, states that long before 1938 he came to lectures in boots and black riding breeches as a way of demonstrating his support for National Socialism to the students.[6]

After the "Anschluss" Knoll came into his own. On 15 March the regional Nazi authorities commissioned him with immediate effect *to safeguard the interests of the provincial administration of the Nazi party in Austria at the University of Vienna.*[7] It is not easy to establish why the Nazi Party chose Fritz Knoll of all people. The main reason could well be that more suitable candidates had been dismissed by the Austro-Fascists in 1934 – which does not mean that Knoll was not a fervent Nazi. One of his first tasks was to rid the university "quickly and thoroughly of all professors and lecturers who were not suitable to teach at a National Socialist university," as it said

---

[3] For a scholarly biography of Knoll, see Ehrendorfer (1983), *Knoll*, and Ehrendorfer (1984), *Knoll.*

[4] Knoll mentions both memberships in his application for membership of the Nazi Party, in ÖStA-AdR, Gauakt Fritz Knoll, BMI/GA 38749.

[5] All details taken from Gauakt Fritz Knoll, ÖStA-AdR, BMI/GA 38749.

[6] Ibid. The original report was written by *Dozentenbundführer* [head of the Nazi Association for University Teachers] Arthur Marchet.

[7] The letter is contained in AÖAW, Papers of Fritz Knoll, Box 1, Folder 1, and in his Gauakt in ÖStA-AdR.

in a contemporary report.[8] He completed this task to perfection. On 23 April 1938 some 252 teachers were removed from the University of Vienna on "racial" or political grounds. "After the cleansing of the teaching and research establishment of racially and ethnically impure academics it has now become possible for the first time for the German teacher and academic to act as a model in every respect for German youth," reported Knoll three years later. "For that reason the Jew has also disappeared from our academic circles now and for all times."[9]

At the same time Knoll was also making his way in the Academy of Sciences. As a corresponding member inland since 1934, he was asked at the General Assembly of 25 March *until the final regulation of the Academy Statutes, to safeguard the interests of the regional administration of the Nazi party in Austria at the Academy of Sciences.*[10] Confirmation from the regional Nazi Party authorities came on 29 March 1938.[11] Knoll's work involved, amongst other things, the dismissal of Jewish staff from institutes run by the Academy as the principal research body. In the case of the Institute for Radium Research and the Institute for Experimental Biology (BVA), this meant severe losses, since Jewish researchers in physics and biology had had little chance of a university career since the early 1920s and were therefore particularly heavily represented in these two research establishments.[12]

Knoll's brief Academy intermezzo came to an end on 16 March 1939, when President Heinrich Srbik took over the interests of the Nazi Party. In his reply, Knoll stated that it was *quite convenient that I am now released again from one of my many obligations.*[13] Knoll was also elected shortly afterwards as an ordinary member of the Academy, a move that was not only political. At a meeting of the Election Committee on 24 February 1938, the Academy had already decided to elect an ordinary member for botany at the next elections. The candidates on 22 November 1938 were Fritz Knoll and Friedrich Weber; Knoll prevailed.[14]

Knoll remained rector of the University of Vienna until March 1943, during which time he had plenty of opportunity to promote Nazism in the academic world. One of his most prominent speeches was given in 1941 in Bucharest, when he discussed the question of Jews in academia. He said, amongst other things: "It cannot be said that the Jew is incapable of research. A correctly established scientific fact remains one even if it is established by a Jew. This is not what Nazism opposes [...]. Jewish research does not differ in general from Jewish journalism. Both are designed to

---

[8] Bereichsstudentenführung Süd-Ost (1938), yearbook, p. 60.

[9] Knoll (1942), *Wissenschaft*, p. 23.

[10] AÖAW, Minutes of the extraordinary General Assembly of 25 March 1938 (A 933).

[11] See AÖAW, Papers of Fritz Knoll, Box 1, Folder 1.

[12] See Taschwer (2013), *Geheimsache*. For details of the perfidious "cleansing" of the Vivarium, see the essay in this volume by Klaus Taschwer, "Expelled, burnt, sold, forgotten, and suppressed," pp. 101–11.

[13] AÖAW, Papers of Fritz Knoll, Box 1, Folder 1, Knoll to Srbik of 23 March 1939.

[14] See AÖAW, Wahlen, Box 4, Folder "1938."

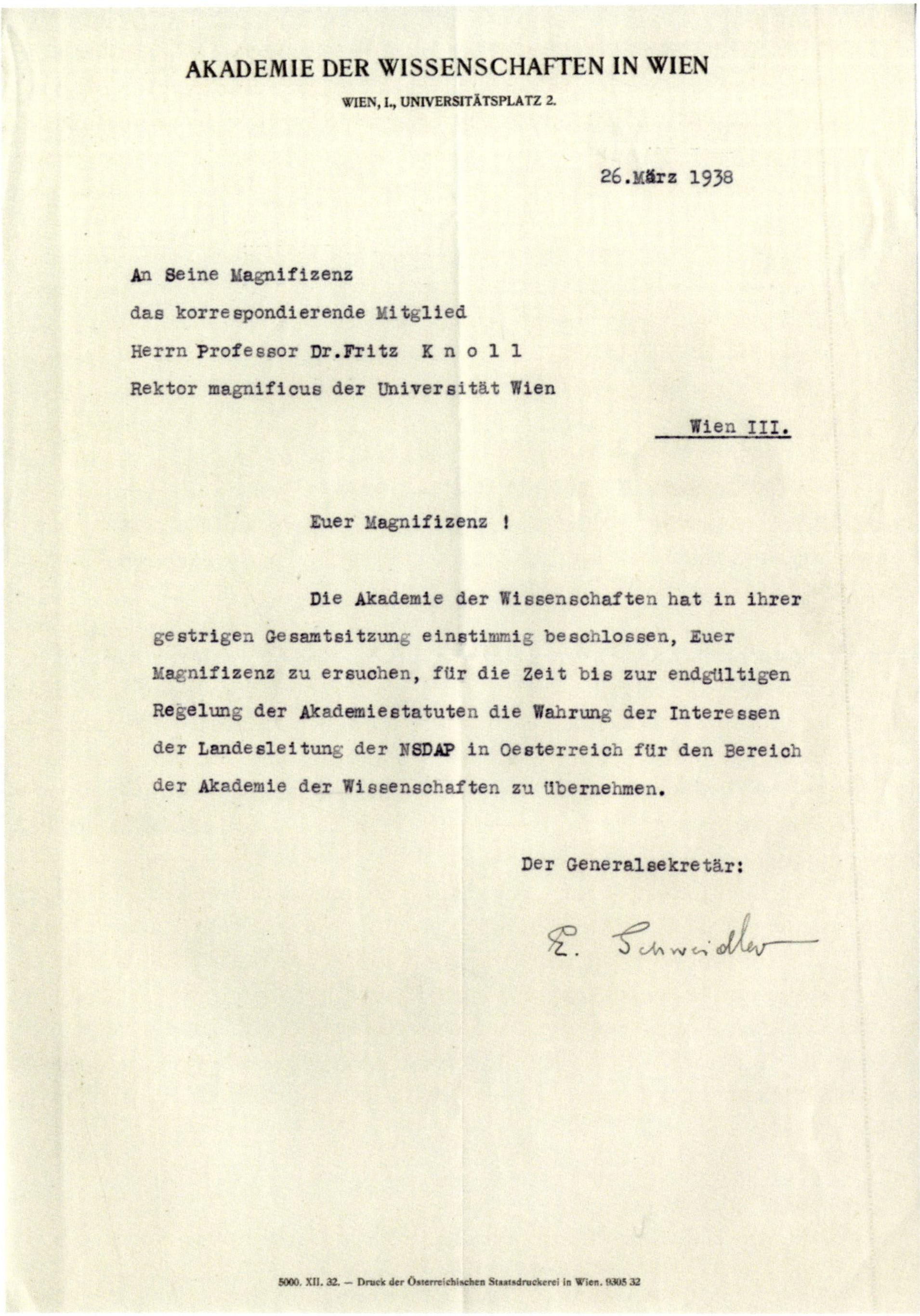

AKADEMIE DER WISSENSCHAFTEN IN WIEN

WIEN, I., UNIVERSITÄTSPLATZ 2.

26. März 1938

An Seine Magnifizenz
das korrespondierende Mitglied
Herrn Professor Dr. Fritz K n o l l
Rektor magnificus der Universität Wien

Wien III.

Euer Magnifizenz !

Die Akademie der Wissenschaften hat in ihrer gestrigen Gesamtsitzung einstimmig beschlossen, Euer Magnifizenz zu ersuchen, für die Zeit bis zur endgültigen Regelung der Akademiestatuten die Wahrung der Interessen der Landesleitung der NSDAP in Oesterreich für den Bereich der Akademie der Wissenschaften zu übernehmen.

Der Generalsekretär:

E. Schweidler

5000. XII. 32. – Druck der Österreichischen Staatsdruckerei in Wien. 9305 32

Fig. 17: Schweidler's letter to Knoll of 26 March 1938

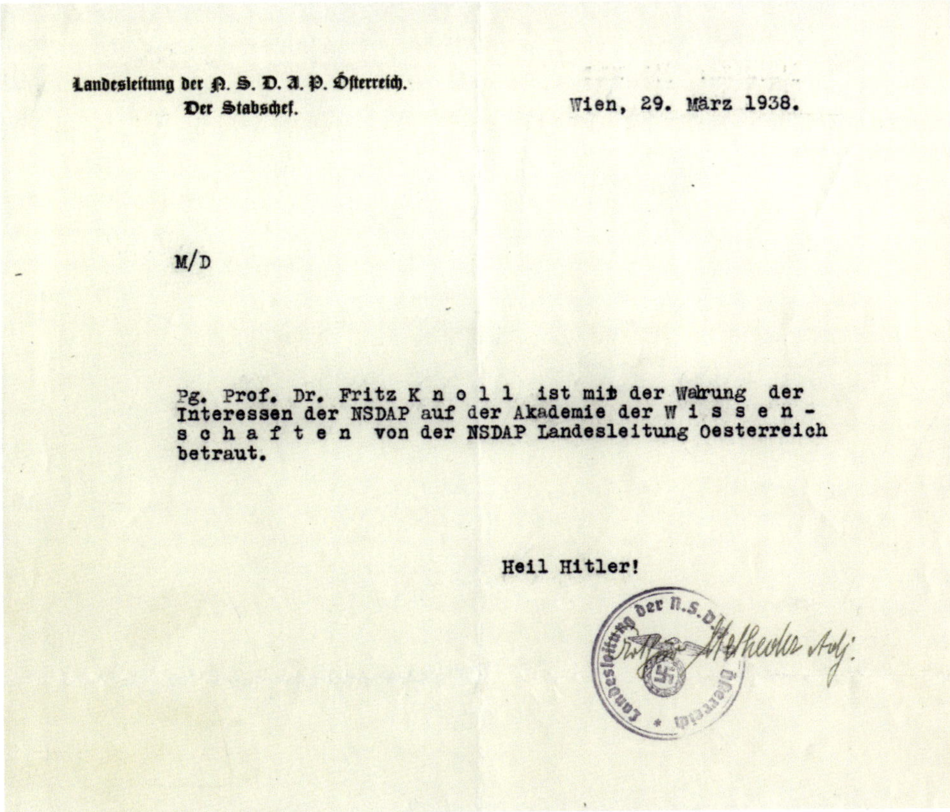

Landesleitung der N. S. D. A. P. Österreich.
Der Stabschef.

Wien, 29. März 1938.

M/D

Pg. Prof. Dr. Fritz K n o l l ist mit der Wahrung der Interessen der NSDAP auf der Akademie der W i s s e n - s c h a f t e n von der NSDAP Landesleitung Oesterreich betraut.

Heil Hitler!

Fig. 18: Letter of the Nazi Party to Knoll of 29 March 1938

further the Jewish desire for international standing and world domination. Jewish researchers prefer certain areas of work and in some cases have even created them so as to promote their racially linked capabilities […] for 'the world' and hence against the German people."[15]

In March 1943 Knoll resigned the rectorship of the University of Vienna in favor of the anatomist Eduard Pernkopf. This was prompted in part by a decision of the Reich Ministry of Science, Education, and Culture of November 1941 that even in times of war, the rectorship should change at least every three years and at the latest after five years.[16] There had also been objections from the students and the SS to Knoll. On 10 August 1938, for example, the south-east section of the Reichsstudentenführung [Reich Student Leadership] suggested that Knoll's mandate should not be renewed, claiming that Knoll did not have *the leadership qualities required by an*

[15] Knoll (1942), *Wissenschaft*, p. 23.

[16] See ÖStA-AdR, Gauakt Heinrich Srbik, BMI/GA 49317, Sheet 26–7, report on the rectorship question at the University of Vienna.

establishment like the University of Vienna, which had lost its way and become stuck in the liberalist era.[17] This did not endanger Knoll's rectorship at the time, however, but there was also an ex post critical evaluation of Knoll. A letter written by an *SS-Hauptsturmführer* on 19 April 1943 stated that he was the wrong person to have been commissarial rector: *Above all he was unimposing and in many respects too weak.* [...] *Many of his decisions often showed a lack of instinct, so much so that in some cases they raised doubts about his political disposition. Knoll is extremely ponderous, ideologically unsound, and above all reluctant to take clear steps and accept consequences.*[18]

Fig. 19: Fritz Knoll

This harsh criticism of Knoll's personality was to prove fortunate. He was dismissed from public office in June 1945 by decree of the *Staatsamt für Volksaufklärung, für Unterricht und Erziehung und für Kultusangelegenheiten* [State Office for Public

[17] ÖStA-AdR, Gauakt Fritz Knoll, BMI/GA 38749, letter to Pg. Dr. Capra, personal assistant of *Gauleiter* [regional Nazi Party leader] Globocnik.

[18] ÖStA-AdR, Gauakt Fritz Knoll, BMI/GA 38749, signature of the *SS-Hauptsturmführer* illegible.

Enlightenment, Education, and Cultural Affairs] on account of his membership of the Nazi Party, and the Academy also held his membership in abeyance [*stellte ruhend*]. In 1947, however, Knoll's case was reviewed by the authorities. The humiliating assessment by the SS probably now played into Knoll's hands. He also claimed in his own defense that in his speech in Bucharest he had played down Nazi ideology. He may still have represented the *official Nazi point of view, but by this time he was already becoming a "heretic."*[19]

Whatever the reason, in December 1947 Knoll received notification that under paragraph 17, subparagraph (3), of the *Verbotsgesetz* [law banning re-engagement in National Socialist activities] he was classified as "less incriminated." For that reason his dismissal from the university was transformed into retirement. And when the Amnesty Law came into force, Knoll's full membership of the Academy could be reactivated.[20] From this time he worked primarily at the Academy of Sciences since he was still banned from entering the university.[21] In his later years Knoll thus became an amateur historical researcher. Academy President Heinrich Ficker commissioned Knoll to edit the volume *Österreichische Naturforscher und Techniker* (1951), which was designed to demonstrate "the contribution of Austrians to achievements in natural research and engineering and hence the general progress of mankind," as Ficker wrote in the introduction.[22] Knoll had a free hand; the only criteria for inclusion in the book were that the researchers and engineers should be sufficiently important and also no longer living. A further book edited by Knoll, *Österreichische Naturforscher, Ärzte und Techniker*, was published in 1957.

The amateur historian's choice of co-authors appears somewhat puzzling today. Some former Nazis including Knoll himself, the paleontologist Kurt Ehrenberg, and the anatomist Eduard Pernkopf wrote several of the articles. Even more remarkable are the omissions in the 450-page large-format publication. To mention just three examples: Stefan Meyer (1872–1949), physicist and long-serving head of the Institute for Radium Research at the Academy of Sciences, Hans Przibram (1874–1944), zoologist and founder and long-standing head of the Institute for Experimental Biology (BVA), who was murdered in the Theresienstadt concentration camp, or Eugen Steinach (1861–1944), physiologist, world-famous pioneer of hormone research and BVA department head. All three were Jewish researchers who in part "created their own areas of work," as Knoll put it in 1941/42.[23] All three were first dismissed from the Academy and the University of Vienna in 1938 under Knoll's direction – and

---

[19] Dr. Franz Speta private archive, Linz, letter from Knoll or his legal representative, undated.

[20] AÖAW, Papers of Fritz Knoll, Box 1, Folder 1, notification by President Heinrich Ficker of 16 June 1948.

[21] See AÖAW, Papers of Fritz Knoll, Box 2, Folder 10, correspondence with Lothar Geitler regarding the Botanical Institute of the University of Vienna, particularly Geitler's letter of 7 January 1949.

[22] Österreichische Akademie der Wissenschaften (1951), *Naturforscher*, p. 7.

[23] Knoll (1942), *Wissenschaft*, p. 23.

barely twenty years later he consistently eliminated them from the official history of science in Austria published by the Academy. Again, as Knoll said in 1941/42: "Thus the Jew has disappeared from our academic circles now and for all times."[24]

In the year the second volume appeared, the 74-year old botanist became Secretary of the Section for Mathematics and the Natural Sciences and, the following year, Secretary General of the Academy, a position he held until 1964. In 1967 the now 84-year-old received one final honor: the General Assembly passed a resolution awarding him the silver "Bene Merito" medal for particular services to the Austrian Academy of Sciences.[25]

Klaus Taschwer

---

[24] Knoll (1942), *Wissenschaft*, p. 23.
[25] See *Almanach* for 1966, 117 (1967), p. 145.

I. 2. Consequences of the "Anschluss"

Exclusion of members

The first victim of any dictatorship is justice. After the Nazis came to power in the German Reich in 1933, they also followed the practice of changing the laws to give their actions, which violated all human rights, the semblance of legality. Injustice was given a façade of legitimacy in this way, so that the perpetrators could say that they had only "done their duty." Within a few weeks of the "Anschluss," the universities and higher education institutes experienced "cleansing," dismissals, and "racial" discrimination on the basis of the Law for the Reconstitution of the Civil Service that had been in force in the German Reich since 1933. According to this law, officials who "for racial or political reasons could not swear the oath of allegiance to the Führer were to refrain indefinitely from carrying out any duties." As a result Jews and officials regarded as "politically unreliable," i.e. declared opponents of the regime and persons known publicly as "supporters of the former system," were dismissed from their posts in public service,[1] something which also applied to the universities.

After the "Anschluss", the *"Gleichschaltung"* [alignment/consolidation] of the Academy of Sciences took place somewhat later than at the universities. This was due to the fact that the state's capacity to intervene was more limited, and also because the new regime clearly thought that intervention in the universities, where there was direct contact with young students, was more important. Some of the lecturers and professors dismissed from the universities were still able to attend meetings of the Academy for almost nine more months and also took part in the election of the new Presiding Committee.

This changed abruptly in the late fall of 1938. The Nuremberg Laws denied citizenship to "non-Aryans," and the Statutes approved in October 1938, which made citizenship a precondition for ordinary membership, already indirectly excluded such persons. It is interesting to note that the Academy itself was not proactive, but merely reacted to an initiative by the authorities. It received a note on 22 November 1938 from the Federal Ministry of Education *regarding the suspension of non-Aryan members.*[2] A General Assembly was convened on that day. The minutes do not mention any discussion of the exclusion of Jewish members but after the meeting, the Presiding Committee sent a memorandum to all members inland in which reference was

[1] Weinert (1983), *Massnahmen*, pp. 127–34.
[2] AÖAW, Protokollbuch 1938, No. 425.

made to this note. At the General Assembly of 16 December 1938, a decree from Bernhard Rust, Reich Minister for Science, Education, and Culture, was announced demanding the suspension of *non-Aryan* members. It was decided *to suggest personally to the Jewish members that they resign voluntarily.*[3]

Fig. 20: Stefan Meyer

Fig. 21: Hans Horst Meyer

At this time the ordinary members Stefan Meyer (physics) and Hans Horst Meyer (pharmacology) had already resigned of their own accord, on 24 November and 13 December 1938 respectively.[4] The minutes of the meeting go on to say: *Regarding the anticipated decree on the departure of the* [added by hand '*Mischlinge*' *and*] *members of Jewish descent, it is decided to wait for receipt of the decree and then after more exact interpretation of the expression* [added by hand '*Mischling*' and] '*of Jewish descent*' *to arrange for the exit of those concerned in a similar fashion.*[5] Thereupon, ordinary member Berthold Hatschek (zoology), corresponding members Alfred Francis Přibram (history), Ernst Peter Pick (pharmacology), and Emil Abel (physical chemistry), and corresponding member abroad Eduard Norden (classical philology, Berlin) also announced their departure at the end of the year.

[3] AÖAW, Minutes of the General Assembly of 16 December 1938 (A 941).

[4] As head of the Institute for Radium Research, full member Stefan Meyer had already been retired on the basis of a note from the Ministry of Education of 28 May 1938, No. 9492/II/6. He survived the Nazi era in Bad Ischl and died in 1949. See Reiter (2000), *Meyer*.

[5] AÖAW, Minutes of the General Assembly of 16 December 1938 (A 941).

At the General Assembly of 27 January 1939,[6] reference was made to the December 1938 decree of the Ministry of Interior and Cultural Affairs, section IV, *by which Jews were to be excluded from German universities and scientific institutions.*[7] Then President Heinrich Srbik announced the departure of ordinary members Stefan Meyer,

Fig. 22: Berthold Hatschek

Fig. 23: Emil Abel

Hans Horst Meyer, and Berthold Hatschek, and corresponding members Abel, Pick, Norden, and Přibram. The former corresponding members abroad Richard Willstätter and Wolfgang Pauli were notified that as a result of the decrees of the Reich Ministry of Science, Education, and Culture and the Ministry of Interior and Cultural Affairs, section IV, their membership had been terminated. At the same time they were thanked for their academic work until then. The Ministry was then informed that *all members who are Jews or deemed to be so according to the Nuremberg Laws had left the Academy either through their voluntary departure or through their deletion from the Academy's lists.*[8] In February 1939 the decree from the Reich Minister for Science, Education, and Culture was finally promulgated ordering the exclusion of "Mischlinge" and "persons, married or related to Jews [*jüdisch versippt*]" as they were described in the contemptuous diction of the Nazi regime. At the General Assembly of the Academy of 24 February 1939, President Srbik reported on the decree and announced

[6] See AÖAW, Minutes of the General Assembly of 27 January 1939 (A 942).
[7] AÖAW, Minutes of the General Assembly of 27 January 1939 (A 942).
[8] AÖAW, Minutes of the General Assembly of 27 January 1939 (A 942).

the termination of membership of corresponding member abroad Wolfgang Pauli.[9] The corresponding members Ernst Theodor Brücke (physiology), Josef Weninger (anthropology), and August Loehr (numismatics)[10] also "resigned" in early 1939.[11]

Fig. 24: Wolfgang Pauli

Fig. 25: Franz Eduard Suess

In one individual case, that of ordinary member Franz Eduard Suess (geology), who had been a full member since 1915, documented efforts were made to prevent his exclusion. On 18 April 1939 the Academy addressed an application to Reich Minister of Education Rust to allow Suess to remain in the Academy.[12] Rust rejected the application in a note dated 2 December 1939 and issued a decree in this matter on 9 January 1940, which was announced without further comment at the General Assembly of 9 February 1940. President Srbik stated *that* [...] *the former ordinary*

[9] See AÖAW, Minutes of the General Assembly of 24 February 1939 (A 943).

[10] August Loehr resigned at the meeting of the Section for Humanities and the Social Sciences of 19 April 1939, while the *Almanach* gives the date as 29 March 1939. See AÖAW, Minutes of the meeting of the Section for Humanities and the Social Sciences of 19 April 1939 (C 2600), *Almanach* for 1939, 89 (1940), p. 79.

[11] The *Almanach* for 1939, 89 (1940), p. 79, states incorrectly that Ernst Theodor Brücke left the Academy on 20 February 1939, although an inquiry "regarding Aryan descent" was not sent to him until 23 February 1939, and he was informed of the termination of his membership on 4 May 1939.

[12] See AÖAW, Protokollbuch 1939, No. 191.

member of the Academy Franz Eduard Suess is no longer a member of the Academy. Replacements were immediately elected to fill the vacant positions in two commissions.[13]

Fig. 26: Victor Franz Hess

Fig. 27 Erwin Schrödinger

A further note was received on 25 August 1939 and shortly afterwards, a decree from the Reich Minister *regarding corresponding members abroad who are Jews or 'jüdisch versippt' persons*[14] and *regarding the termination of membership of Jews, Mischlinge, and 'jüdisch versippt' persons* which President Srbik announced at the General Assembly of 9 February 1940.[15] The next stage in the exclusions was reached with a further decree by the Reich Minister of 3 October 1940, terminating the membership of seven members of the Academy,[16] namely ordinary members Walther Brecht (German studies) and Hermann Franz Mark (physical chemistry), corresponding members Karl Bühler (philosophy and psychology), Victor Franz Hess (experimental physics, Nobel Prize 1936), and Erwin Schrödinger (physics, Nobel Prize 1933), and corresponding members abroad Franz Boas (anthropology) and Alfred Hettner

[13] Although the *Almanach* for 1939, 89 (1940), p. 79, gives the termination of Suess's membership as 2 December 1939, he continued to take part regularly in meetings until 15 December 1939. See AÖAW, General Assembly of 9 February 1940 (A 950).

[14] AÖAW, Protokollbuch 1939, No. 388.

[15] AÖAW, Minutes of the General Assembly of 9 February 1940 (A 950).

[16] See AÖAW, Minutes of the General Assembly of 25 October 1940 (A 957).

(geography). It is interesting to note that there were three Nobel Prize winners amongst the excluded members. A further decree by Minister Rust referred again to *the exclusion of non-Aryan corresponding members abroad*, which resulted in the deletion of Viktor Moritz Goldschmidt (mineralogy, Oslo) from the list of members.[17] The state authorities did not only demand the exclusion of *non-Aryans and 'jüdisch versippt' persons*, however. The Reich Ministry of Science, Education, and Culture decree also called for the termination of membership of former Polish university professors from all German scientific associations.[18]

Ausgetreten sind die ordentlichen Mitglieder:

Endlicher, Stephan, am 11. März 1848.
Desseffy, Emil Graf, am 9. März 1849.
Meyer, Stefan, am 24. November 1938.
Meyer, Hans Horst, am 13. Dezember 1938.
Hatschek, Bertold, am 31. Dezember 1938.
Sueß, Franz Eduard, am 2. Dezember 1939.
Brecht, Walter, am 3. Oktober 1940.
Mark, Hermann, am 3. Oktober 1940.

Ferner die korrespondierenden Mitglieder:

Pribram, Alfred Francis, im Dezember 1938.
Norden, Eduard, am 20. Dezember 1938.
Pick, Ernst P., am 1. Jänner 1939.
Abel, Emil, am 4. Jänner 1939.
Pauli, Wolfgang, am 28. Jänner 1939.
Willstätter, Richard, am 28. Jänner 1939.
Brücke, Ernst, am 20. Februar 1939.
Loehr, August, am 29. März 1939.
Weninger, Josef, am 3. Mai 1939.
Boas, Franz, am 3. Oktober 1940.
Bühler, Karl, am 3. Oktober 1940.
Hettner, Alfred, am 3. Oktober 1940.
Hess, Victor, am 3. Oktober 1940.
Schrödinger, Erwin, am 3. Oktober 1940.
Goldschmidt, Viktor M., am 12. Februar 1941.

Fig. 28: List of resigned members (Almanach for 1943)

[17] AÖAW, Minutes of the General Assembly of 16 May 1941 (A 962).
[18] AÖAW, Minutes of the General Assembly of 4 July 1941 (A 964).

A total of six ordinary members, nine corresponding members inland, and six corresponding members abroad were excluded in this way. To judge from the list of the "departed members," as they were euphemistically called in the *Almanachs* for 1938 to 1943, and the dates of their exclusion, the Nazi *"Gleichschaltung"* had no effect on the membership of the Academy for nearly nine months. The Academy itself was inactive during this time and later on was also in no hurry to exclude members who were disapproved of by the regime on "racial" or political grounds. The procedure thereafter was also painstakingly bureaucratic, which in this case was to the benefit of those concerned. It would be an exaggeration to describe this as an act of internal resistance; it is nevertheless interesting given the large number of fervent supporters of Nazism in the Academy at the time. The exclusion of Jewish Academy members was also the main agenda item at the Congress of German Academies in Berlin in 1937, which members of the Vienna Academy also attended, but it was not discussed further in Vienna.[19] It was only when a definite official order came from the authorities that the Vienna Academy reacted to the various notes and decrees from the ministries – and this was also an indication of the confusion regarding competences that existed at the time. While the official orders were sometimes noted without comment and carried out, attempts were also made in other cases to find a "more elegant" method of exclusion by advising the members concerned to resign "voluntarily." The memorandum to members suggested that those affected by the Nuremberg Laws should take appropriate measures of their own accord. The systematic implementation of the Reich-Citizen Law of 1938, which deprived Jews of citizenship, removed any remaining prospects of protecting Jewish members or staff from the Nazi state. Where pressure from the regime was less severe, for example in regard to (the few but no less prominent) "supporters" of the authoritarian *Ständestaat* [Corporate State], now judged political opponents, they retained their membership of the Academy.[20]

The authorities acted much more swiftly with regards to the staff of the Academy, who, unlike the members, were not respected scholars in the public eye. Attempts were made to anticipate the official exclusion of members of the Academy by suggesting that they give up their membership voluntarily, whereas staff members were simply dismissed without notice.[21]

Herbert Matis

---

[19] See Grau (1995), *Wissenschaftsakademien*, p. 48. It is also interesting to note that the Presiding Committee refused to acquire a bust of Hitler: *Offer for a bust of the Führer costing RM 480 is rejected for lack of funds.* AÖAW, Minutes of the Presiding Committee meeting of 1 July 1938, item 8.

[20] Whereas, for example, corresponding member inland Othmar Spann, whose supposedly comprehensive social philosophy played a prominent role in the authoritarian *Ständestaat*, lost his chair at the University of Vienna, he continued to be listed as a member of the Academy under the heading "Reich citizens." The ethnologist and member of a Catholic missionary order Father Wilhelm Schmidt SVD, also classified in the Nazi diction as a "system supporter" of the Dollfuss-Schuschnigg era, left for Fribourg, Switzerland, after he had been forced to give up his position at the University of Vienna, and became a corresponding member abroad.

[21] Grau (1995), *Wissenschaftsakademien*, p. 46.

Filling of vacant positions following the exclusion of ordinary members

There were six full or ordinary members among the 21 members of the Academy who were excluded or resigned between 1938 and 1941. They deserve particular attention because ordinary members have much more influence than corresponding members inland or abroad. Paragraph 10 of the Statutes of 1938 states: "Ordinary members shall be entitled to attend all meetings of their Section and the Academy as a whole and to vote on resolutions. [...] All ordinary members must be convened specially to Election Meetings and General Assemblies in which resolutions on changes to the Statutes or By-Laws are to be adopted. Unless specified otherwise in the Statutes, elections and resolutions shall be adopted by the absolute majority of the ordinary members present."[1] The meetings make decisions not only on the composition of the Academy through elections, but also on the establishment or closure of research institutes. Corresponding members inland or abroad have more of an advisory function; they have no direct impact on Academy policy.

Through the exclusion or "*departure*" of six ordinary members on political or "racial" grounds, their positions became vacant and could be filled again. There was now the question of how this was to be done. The Election Commission (Schweidler, Späth, Mache, Prey, Suess, Himmelbauer, Durig, Hochstetter, and Hartmann) noted at its meeting of 16 February 1939[2] that six positions for ordinary members had become vacant – one on account of the death of the astronomer Karl Hillebrand, one through the failure to fill a vacancy at the elections of the previous year, one through the classification of the engineer Karl Terzaghi as an *ordinary member not counted towards the maximum number*,[3] and finally three vacancies *through the departures of Messrs Bert*[h]*old Hatschek, Hans Horst Meyer, and Stefan Meyer*.[4] The Election Commission suggested that only four of the six vacant positions should be filled, with one position being attached to the technical sciences.[5] Of the other three, at least one

---

[1] Copy of the Statutes in Meister (1947), *Geschichte*, pp. 240–2, here p. 241.

[2] AÖAW, Wahlen, Box 4, Folder "1939," No. 93/1939.

[3] This formulation refers to paragraph 6 of the Statutes of the time, decreed on 22 July 1938 by the Reich Minister for Science, Education, and Culture, which stated: "Should an ordinary member move from Austria, his membership shall remain in force but shall not be counted towards the maximum number." This maximum number was 33 per Section, of whom 22 were required to live in or near Vienna. Copy of the Statutes in Meister (1947), *Geschichte*, pp. 240–2, here p. 240. For Terzaghi's domicile, see the obituary in the *Almanach* for 1962, 112 (1963), pp. 549–50.

[4] AÖAW, Wahlen, Box 4, Folder "1939," No. 150/1939.

[5] The technical sciences were already well represented by three ordinary members (Hartmann, Schaffernak, and Terzaghi), while medicine had no representation. See the hectographed list of the scientific disciplines represented in the Section for Mathematics and the Natural Sciences 1939 in AÖAW, Wahlen, Box 4, Folder "1939."

should be filled by a physicist and one by a geologist. The Section followed the recommendations of the Election Commission at its meeting of 23 February 1939.[6]

Fig. 29: Rudolf Saliger

By the meeting of the Section for Mathematics and the Natural Sciences on 5 June 1939,[7] two proposals had been received for the position designated for a representative of the technical sciences, both put forward by Friedrich Schaffernak, namely the corresponding members Karl Federhofer (mechanics, Graz) and Rudolf Saliger (reinforced concrete construction and statics, Vienna). Both were placed on the list for election by the Academy as a whole on the following day. Federhofer received 24 votes and Saliger 17. The Section for Mathematics and the Natural Sciences had four candidates for the three other ordinary member positions. Apart from Federhofer and Saliger, mentioned above, there were corresponding member inland Fritz Kohlrausch (physics, Graz, proposed by Hans Benndorf) and corresponding member inland Otto Ampferer (geology, Vienna, proposed by Franz Eduard Suess). As Federhofer had already been elected for the position designated for technical sciences, there were just three candidates remaining for the three vacant positions, all of whom easily

[6] See AÖAW, Minutes of the meeting of the Section for Mathematics and the Natural Sciences of 23 February 1939 (B 2602).

[7] See AÖAW, Minutes of the meeting of the Section for Mathematics and the Natural Sciences of 5 June 1939 (B 2608).

exceeded the 22-vote majority required for election. Ampferer obtained 40 votes, Kohlrausch 39, and Saliger 34.[8] As the Election Commission had proposed, a physicist and a geologist were thus elected. Since the exclusion of Hans Horst Meyer, pharmacology was no longer represented in the Academy;[9] zoology was represented by Leopold Adametz, Karl Grobben, and Theodor Pintner, while Stefan Meyer's position was effectively taken over by Fritz Kohlrausch.

Franz Eduard Suess, who had proposed Otto Ampferer, was deleted from the list of members on "racial" grounds by decree of Reich Minister of Education Bernhard Rust of 9 January 1940.[10] The Election Commission of the Section for Mathematics and the Natural Sciences, consisting of Schweidler, Späth, Hochstetter, and Kruppa, met on 7 March 1940.[11] They noted that there were six vacant positions for election to ordinary member: two on account of the deaths of Josef Schaffer (histology) and Friedrich Emich (chemistry), one through the *departure*[12] *of Franz Eduard Suess (geology), and one through the transfer of Mr. Hermann Mark* [chemistry] *to the list of those ordinary members who did not count towards the maximum number*;[13] and two others, whose positions had not been filled the previous year. The Election Commission suggested that one position be tied to the medical group. In addition it gave one recommendation each for geology and geography and suggested that a position in chemistry be left vacant.[14] These recommendations were implemented at the Section meeting held the same day.[15]

---

[8] Rudolf Saliger was thus one of only 57 persons to this day to have been elected a full member without having previously been a corresponding member.

[9] It was not until 1959 that a pharmacologist, Franz Theodor Brücke, was again elected as a full member. Richard Rössler and Adolf Jarisch, both corresponding members inland, had represented the discipline until then. Brücke was elected a corresponding member inland in 1957.

[10] See Matis (1997), *Anpassung*, p. 30.

[11] See AÖAW, Wahlen, Box 4, Folder "1940," No. 63/1940.

[12] Hectographed letter by Srbik on the positions to be voted on in AÖAW, Wahlen, Box 4, Folder "1940," No. 104/1940.

[13] Ibid. See also facsimile of the letter from Mark from London of 18 September 1938 overleaf. Apparently Mark's position had not yet been filled in the 1939 elections in view of his short visit to the United States. After it transpired that Mark was remaining permanently in the United States, his position was declared vacant for the 1940 elections.

[14] See AÖAW, Wahlen, Box 4, Folder "1940," No. 63/1940.

[15] See AÖAW, Minutes of the meeting of the Section for Mathematics and the Natural Sciences of 7 March 1940 (B 2620).

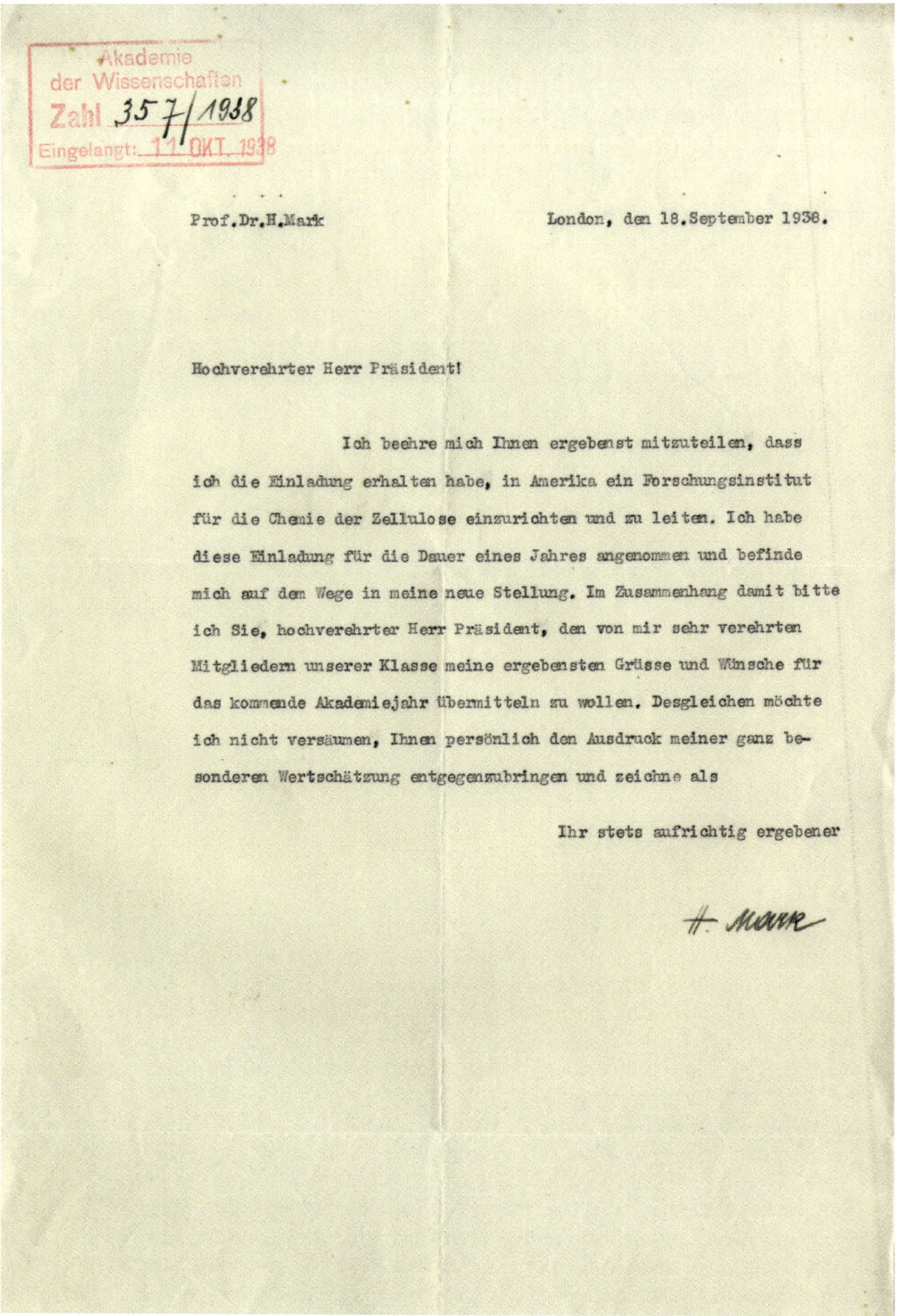

Akademie der Wissenschaften
Zahl 357/1938
Eingelangt: 11 OKT. 1938

Prof.Dr.H.Mark London, den 18.September 1938.

Hochverehrter Herr Präsident!

Ich beehre mich Ihnen ergebenst mitzuteilen, dass ich die Einladung erhalten habe, in Amerika ein Forschungsinstitut für die Chemie der Zellulose einzurichten und zu leiten. Ich habe diese Einladung für die Dauer eines Jahres angenommen und befinde mich auf dem Wege in meine neue Stellung. Im Zusammenhang damit bitte ich Sie, hochverehrter Herr Präsident, den von mir sehr verehrten Mitgliedern unserer Klasse meine ergebensten Grüsse und Wünsche für das kommende Akademiejahr übermitteln zu wollen. Desgleichen möchte ich nicht versäumen, Ihnen persönlich den Ausdruck meiner ganz besonderen Wertschätzung entgegenzubringen und zeichne als

Ihr stets aufrichtig ergebener

H. Mark

Fig. 30: Letter from Mark to Srbik of 18 September 1938

Fig. 31: Eduard Pernkopf

Hochstetter suggested two corresponding members inland for the position of a representative of medicine, namely the anatomist Eduard Pernkopf and the hygienist Roland Grassberger. At the Section meeting of 29 May 1940,[16] Pernkopf obtained 12 of the 21 votes cast, Grassberger just 9.[17] No candidates were proposed for the disciplines geography and geology, and only Ludwig Flamm (physics, proposed by Heinrich Mache) and Hermann Weber (zoology, proposed by Theodor Pintner) were to be voted on. Both received 20 of the 21 possible votes and were placed on the electoral list. The necessary majority was achieved in all three cases at the General Assembly of 30 May 1940, and so Pernkopf (33 of 46 votes), Flamm (44 of 46), and Weber (38 of 46) were elected as ordinary members, with Weber becoming the successor for Berthold Hatschek's discipline. The Reich Minister for Science, Education, and Culture confirmed the elections in a letter of 7 August 1940.[18]

[16] See AÖAW, Minutes of the meeting of the Section for Mathematics and the Natural Sciences of 29 May 1940 (B 2623).

[17] The minutes are incorrect here in stating, *Thus both names were entered on the electoral list*. Both names appeared on the voting slip for the electoral meeting of the General Assembly. The mistake was noticed there and only Pernkopf stood for election.

[18] See AÖAW, Wahlen, Box 4, Folder "1940," No. 179/1940, reported at the General Assembly of 25 October 1940 (A 957).

There was thus no successor for Franz Eduard Suess's discipline at this time. Geology was represented among the ordinary members only by Otto Ampferer, whom Suess himself had proposed the year before.

At the General Assembly on 25 October 1940, in which confirmation of the elections of 30 May 1940 was given, the decree ordering a further seven members *to be excluded from the Academy* was announced. They included two ordinary members, the physical chemist Hermann Franz Mark and the Germanist Walther Brecht. The latter was the first and only ordinary member of the Section for Humanities and the Social Sciences who had to leave the Academy for political reasons. It had little influence on the 1941 elections. The Actuary Junk wrote regarding the four vacant positions for ordinary members (three through the deaths of Hans Hirsch, Albert Ehrhard, and Max Layer, and one *as a result of the exclusion of Mr. Brecht* on 1 February 1941): *It is to be noted in this regard that of these four positions, only two are to be filled, since the positions of Messrs Ehrhard and Brecht do not count towards the maximum number of ordinary members.*[19] In the minutes of the meeting of the Election Commission of the Section for Humanities and the Social Sciences of 19 February 1941, no mention was therefore made of the consequences of Brecht's exclusion.[20] Regarding ordinary members, it was suggested positions be designated for political science and law, and a recommendation in favor of history of art was made. German philology still had four representatives among the ordinary members, namely Dietrich Kralik-Meyrswalden, Josef Nadler, Josef Schatz, and Konrad Zwierzina. At the General Assembly of 27 May 1941, the economist Hans Mayer was elected as an ordinary member with 30 of 47 votes (proposed by Leopold Wenger). The second candidate, Rudolf Köstler, received only 17 of 47 votes and therefore failed to get a majority. The position of ordinary member without discipline (with the recommendation for history of art) was filled by Hans Sedlmayr with 38 of 47 possible votes.[21]

The Section for Mathematics and the Natural Sciences made no reference to the exclusion of Hermann Franz Mark. The normal lists, which show how many positions are vacant and why, mentioned only two positions made vacant by the deaths of Philipp Furtwängler (mathematics) and Leopold Adametz (zoology), and three others, as only three of the six vacant positions had been filled the previous year. Only the minutes of the Election Commission of the Section for Mathematics and the Natural Sciences appear to take account of Mark, with the acceptance of the application by Späth *to reserve 1 ordinary member position for chemistry.*[22] After Mark's departure, chemistry was still well represented among the ordinary members by Josef

[19] AÖAW, Wahlen, Box 4, Folder "1941," without number. The comment refers to the fact that because of his move to Munich, Brecht had been classified in 1926 as a corresponding member abroad, but had become an ordinary member again in 1938. See obituary in the *Almanach* for 1950, 100 (1951), p. 382. Therefore he was not counted towards the maximum number.

[20] See AÖAW, Wahlen, Box 4, Folder "1941," No. 44/1941.

[21] All details according to AÖAW, Minutes of the General Assembly of 27 May 1941 (A 963).

[22] AÖAW, Wahlen, Box 4, Folder "1941," No. 45/1941.

Fig. 32: Hans Sedlmayr

Maria Eder, Anton Skrabal, and Ernst Späth, together with the ordinary member Wilhelm Schlenk, who had worked in Berlin since 1921 and in Tübingen since 1936.[23] On 27 May 1941 the General Assembly elected the histologist Siegmund Schumacher-Marienfrid, the mathematician Karl Mayrhofer, the geologist Franz Heritsch, and the zoologist Leopold Karl Böhm as ordinary members of the Section for Mathematics and the Natural Sciences.

Vacant positions were dealt with quite pragmatically in subsequent elections. They were filled without reference to the discipline, a method that had been the case in the past and is still practiced today. When it was thought expedient to prefer a particular discipline for the purpose of parity, the Election Commission designated the relevant discipline, which was generally confirmed by the Section. This method ensured that a particular discipline continued to be represented in the future. This concept of foresight can be seen in the case of geology. In the elections of June 1939 this discipline was designated, and Otto Ampferer was elected at the suggestion of Franz Eduard Suess.[24] After Suess' exclusion in January 1940, no further geologist was elected at the following election in May, but in 1941 Franz Heritsch was elected.

---

[23] See obituary of Schlenk in the *Almanach* for 1943, 93 (1943), p. 212.

[24] The exclusion of Suess had been under consideration since February 1939. See Graf-Stuhlhofer (1995), *Akademie*, p. 137; Matis (1997), *Anpassung*, p. 30, and the essay in this volume by Herbert Matis, "Exclusion of members," pp. 53–9.

Regarding the political affiliations of the proponents, which cannot discussed in detail here, the statements by Graf-Stuhlhofer[25] and Matis[26] that “Nazi sympathies did not have a significant influence on the chances of being elected”[27] seem to be borne out. As for the disciplines, there appears to be no difference in preference before 1938 or after 1945.

Stefan Sienell

[25] See Graf-Stuhlhofer (1995), *Akademie*, pp. 144–6.
[26] See Matis (1997), *Anpassung*, pp. 35–8.
[27] Matis (1997), *Anpassung*, p. 37.

Consequences for the academic staff. The case of Leo Hajek

Staff at the Academy have always stood in the shadow of the usually more well-known members, and the history of the institution is often written with the focus on its members. This essay takes a look at the staff and their experiences. The year 1938 brought incisive changes for the Academy. Until then it had been an institution that was, to a large degree, independent of the state.[1] In contrast to the situation with regard to members, however, state authorities had direct access to staff and public officers. In particular, the Law for the Reconstitution of the Civil Service[2] gave the new authorities the possibility of dismissing those politically opposed to Nazism and those defined by it as Jewish.[3] In summer 1938 the situation became even more critical with the application of the Nuremberg Laws in Austria.[4]

The role of the Academy of Sciences as a research institute was not as pronounced in the 1930s and 1940s as it is today. Only a few institutes and commissions had full-time staff. Many commissions were managed by academics employed by the university who continued their research in the Academy's facilities.[5] The departments of the Academy with the largest number of staff members were the Institute for Experimental Biology in the Prater, the Institute for Radium Research, the Commission for Editing the Corpus of critically amended texts of the Latin Church Fathers, the Commission for Archeological Research in Asia Minor, the Phonogram Archive Commission, and the Commission for Editing an Austrian-Bavarian Dictionary.

Directly after the "Anschluss", the staff members of the Academy were sent questionnaires investigating earlier membership of parties, associations, lodges, etc. Military status and any military service during World War I was also queried. A separate point concerned membership of the Nazi Party or an affiliated association. Several inquiries reached the Academy after the "Anschluss" from the Federal Ministry of Education, the Ministry of Interior and Cultural Affairs, section IV (both in Vienna), and the Administrative Offices of Institutions of Higher Education in Vienna that were directly or indirectly concerned with the *Verordnung zur Neuordunung des österreichischen Berufsbeamtentums* [Regulation for the Reorganization of the Austrian Civil Service].[6] Pursuant to a decree by Reich Chancellor Adolf Hitler of 15 March 1938, all "public officials of Austria [...]" had to "swear an oath of service on entering

[1] For the legal status of the Academy of Sciences since its founding, see Kopetz (2006), *Akademie.*

[2] Gesetzblatt für das Land Österreich, No. 160/1938.

[3] See Matis (1997), *Anpassung*, pp. 27, 34.

[4] Gesetzblatt für das Land Österreich, No. 298/1938.

[5] See Matis (1997), *Anpassung*, p. 28.

[6] See Reichsgesetzblatt 1938, Part I, No. 87.

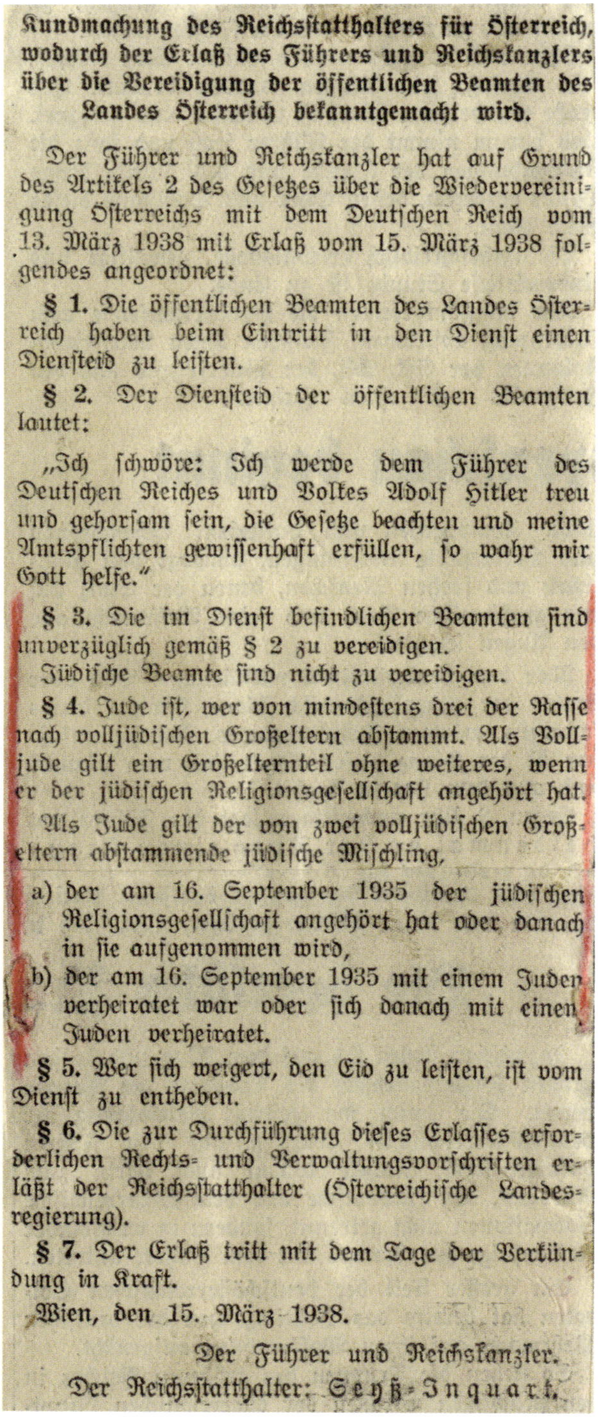

Kundmachung des Reichsstatthalters für Österreich, wodurch der Erlaß des Führers und Reichskanzlers über die Vereidigung der öffentlichen Beamten des Landes Österreich bekanntgemacht wird.

Der Führer und Reichskanzler hat auf Grund des Artikels 2 des Gesetzes über die Wiedervereinigung Österreichs mit dem Deutschen Reich vom 13. März 1938 mit Erlaß vom 15. März 1938 folgendes angeordnet:

§ 1. Die öffentlichen Beamten des Landes Österreich haben beim Eintritt in den Dienst einen Diensteid zu leisten.

§ 2. Der Diensteid der öffentlichen Beamten lautet:

„Ich schwöre: Ich werde dem Führer des Deutschen Reiches und Volkes Adolf Hitler treu und gehorsam sein, die Gesetze beachten und meine Amtspflichten gewissenhaft erfüllen, so wahr mir Gott helfe."

§ 3. Die im Dienst befindlichen Beamten sind unverzüglich gemäß § 2 zu vereidigen.

Jüdische Beamte sind nicht zu vereidigen.

§ 4. Jude ist, wer von mindestens drei der Rasse nach volljüdischen Großeltern abstammt. Als Volljude gilt ein Großelternteil ohne weiteres, wenn er der jüdischen Religionsgesellschaft angehört hat.

Als Jude gilt der von zwei volljüdischen Großeltern abstammende jüdische Mischling,

a) der am 16. September 1935 der jüdischen Religionsgesellschaft angehört hat oder danach in sie aufgenommen wird,

b) der am 16. September 1935 mit einem Juden verheiratet war oder sich danach mit einem Juden verheiratet.

§ 5. Wer sich weigert, den Eid zu leisten, ist vom Dienst zu entheben.

§ 6. Die zur Durchführung dieses Erlasses erforderlichen Rechts- und Verwaltungsvorschriften erläßt der Reichsstatthalter (Österreichische Landesregierung).

§ 7. Der Erlaß tritt mit dem Tage der Verkündung in Kraft.

Wien, den 15. März 1938.

Der Führer und Reichskanzler.

Der Reichsstatthalter: Seyß-Inquart.

Fig. 33: Announcement of 15 March 1938

the service" (paragraph 1). Moreover, "officials already in service [...] are to take the oath. Jewish officials shall not take the oath" (paragraph 3). The following oath was sworn at the Academy of Sciences in Vienna: *I swear | I will be loyal and obedient | to the Führer | of the German Reich and people | Adolf Hitler, | observing the laws | and fulfilling my duties | conscientiously | so help me God.*[7] Under paragraph 5, anyone who refused to take the oath was to be dismissed immediately.

The Academy was repeatedly called upon by the official authorities listed above to provide a list of employees who had been retired or dismissed after 13 March 1938. The Academy's replies normally consisted of the one succinct sentence: [...]*notice is given that within operational field of the Academy of Science there were no public officers in employ whose political behavior or professional suitability have, according to official criteria, given occasion for concern.*[8] It was not until early 1940 that Academy President Heinrich Srbik sent an additional notification in connection with these inquiries to the Reich Ministry of Science, Education, and Culture in Berlin[9] stating that *the Academy* [...], *in accordance with the decree of the Reich Minister for Science, Education, and Culture of 31 January 1940, W E 308/40,* [has] *only included personnel employed directly in its secretariat in the required overview. Since the inquiry by the Reich Minister for Science, Education, and Culture now indicates that personnel in institutes belonging to the Academy are not listed elsewhere and that a list of the staff of all institutes belonging to the Academy (with the exception of the Institute for Radium Research) is required from the Academy, this list is hereby supplied.*[10] However, this new list drawn up in early 1940 does not provide adequate answers regarding dismissed or forcibly retired personnel. It must be assumed that several staff members had been obliged to leave the Academy before 1940. These persons no longer appear in the 1940 list, however. It is only by counting the vacant positions in some commissions that it can be inferred that persons formerly employed there had already lost their positions. It is not, however, possible to make claims with certainty.

One employee whose dismissal in 1938 has been documented is Leo Hajek, head of the Phonogram Archive from 1928 until he was forced to emigrate. After years as a regular assistant and repeated efforts by the Academy Presiding Committee – through President Oswald Redlich, Secretary General Egon Schweidler – and chairman of the Phonogram Archive Commission Karl Luick to have him classified as a *Beamter der allgemeinen Verwaltung* [general administrative civil servant], the request was finally granted in 1937 by the Federal Ministry of Education, and he was

---

[7] See AÖAW, Allgemeine Personalakte, Box 2, Folder 9, No. 145/1938, Oath.

[8] AÖAW, Allgemeine Personalakte, Box 2, Folder 9 of 4 July 1938.

[9] At this time the Reich Ministry of Science, Education, and Culture in Berlin was responsible and had taken over all agendas relating to the Academy of Sciences in Vienna; on the Reich Ministry see Nagel (2012), *Bildungsreformer*.

[10] AÖAW, Allgemeine Personalakte, Box 2, Folder 9, ad No. 30/1940. For the dismissals at the Institute for Radium Research, see Reiter (1988), *Wissenschaftsemigration*.

AKADEMIE DER WISSENSCHAFTEN IN WIEN

WIEN, I., UNIVERSITÄTSPLATZ 2.

Ansprache des Generalsekretärs bei der Vereidigung der Akademieangestellten am 23.März 1938.

Deutsche Volksgenossen !

Als Angestellte der Akademie der Wissenschaften in Wien, einer Körperschaft, die durch ein staatliches Gesetz begründet ist und vom Staat erhalten wird, haben Sie sich hier versammelt, um den gesetzlichen Bestimmungen entsprechend, dem Oberhaupt unseres Staates, dem Führer und Reichskanzler ADOLF HITLER den Eid der Treue zu leisten.

Wer in den letzten 12 Tagen Augen- und Ohrenzeuge der Vorgänge gewesen ist, welche die Vereinigung Oesterreichs mit dem Deutschen Reiche begleitet haben, braucht nicht erst belehrt zu werden, dass dieses Ereignis ebensosehr von weltgeschichtlicher Bedeutung ist wie es auch die Berufspflichten und Lebensbedingungen des Einzelnen in einschneidender Weise beeinflusst.

Sie haben bisher einer Institution gedient, deren Aufgabe schon in unserem alten Vaterlande Oesterreich die Förderung der Wissenschaft und damit der deutschen Kultur war. An dieser Aufgabe hat sich nichts geändert und ich bin überzeugt, dass Sie im neuen Staate, dem grossen Deutschen Reich,

5000. XII. 32. – Druck der Österreichischen Staatsdruckerei in Wien. 9305 32

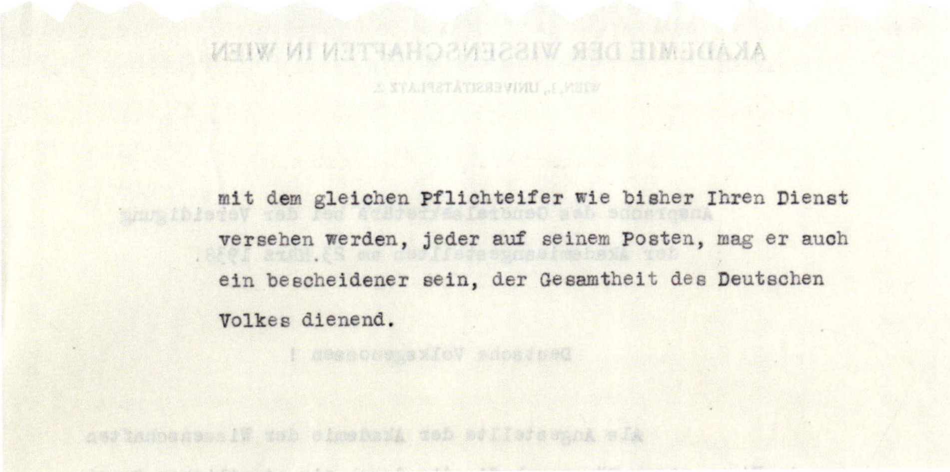

mit dem gleichen Pflichteifer wie bisher Ihren Dienst versehen werden, jeder auf seinem Posten, mag er auch ein bescheidener sein, der Gesamtheit des Deutschen Volkes dienend.

Fig. 34: Speech by Schweidler of 23 March 1938

appointed "Kustos 1st Class."[11] As late as January 1938, the question was raised at a Presiding Committee meeting as to whether an award should be given to Hajek or a statement of thanks and recognition issued by the Presiding Committee for his 25 years of service. Schweidler wrote by hand on this application that it was *approved in principle* and that an *acknowledgement by the Academy was to be noted for October 1938.*[12] Although Hajek was apparently a respected researcher, the "Anschluss" in March 1938 put an end to his career. According to Secretary General Ernst Späth, he performed no further official duties in the Phonogram Archive after 18 June 1938.[13] Thanks to his teaching at the University of Vienna and his international reputation, he was given a position at Ohio State University in Columbus, Ohio. This made it possible for him to emigrate to the United States. According to the record of the police headquarters at Berggasse in Vienna's 9th district dated 18 July 1939, Hajek was listed as having deregistered from residency in Vienna for New York on 3 June 1939. His address in the United States was given as the Voice, Speech, and Sound Science Research Laboratory of the Ohio State University in Columbus, Ohio. From there Hajek applied to be retired. This application was forwarded from the Academy to the Ministry of Interior and Cultural Affairs, section IV, in Vienna, on 5 June 1939.[14] On 5 February 1940, a letter was sent by the Reich Commissioner for the unification of Austria with the German Reich to the *Kustos der Akademie der Wissenschaften in Wien Dr. Leo Israel Hajek* informing him that his employment with the

[11] See AÖAW, Personalakte Leo Hajek.

[12] AÖAW, Phonogrammarchiv, Box 1, Folder 4, No. 118/1938, entry by Actuary Viktor Junk of 7 January, dealt with at the Presiding Committee meeting of 28 January 1938.

[13] See AÖAW, Phonogrammarchiv, Box 1, Folder 4, supplement to the report of the Academy to the Ministry of Interior and Cultural Affairs of 30 May 1939.

[14] See AÖAW, Phonogrammarchiv, Box 1, Folder 4, No. 275/1939.

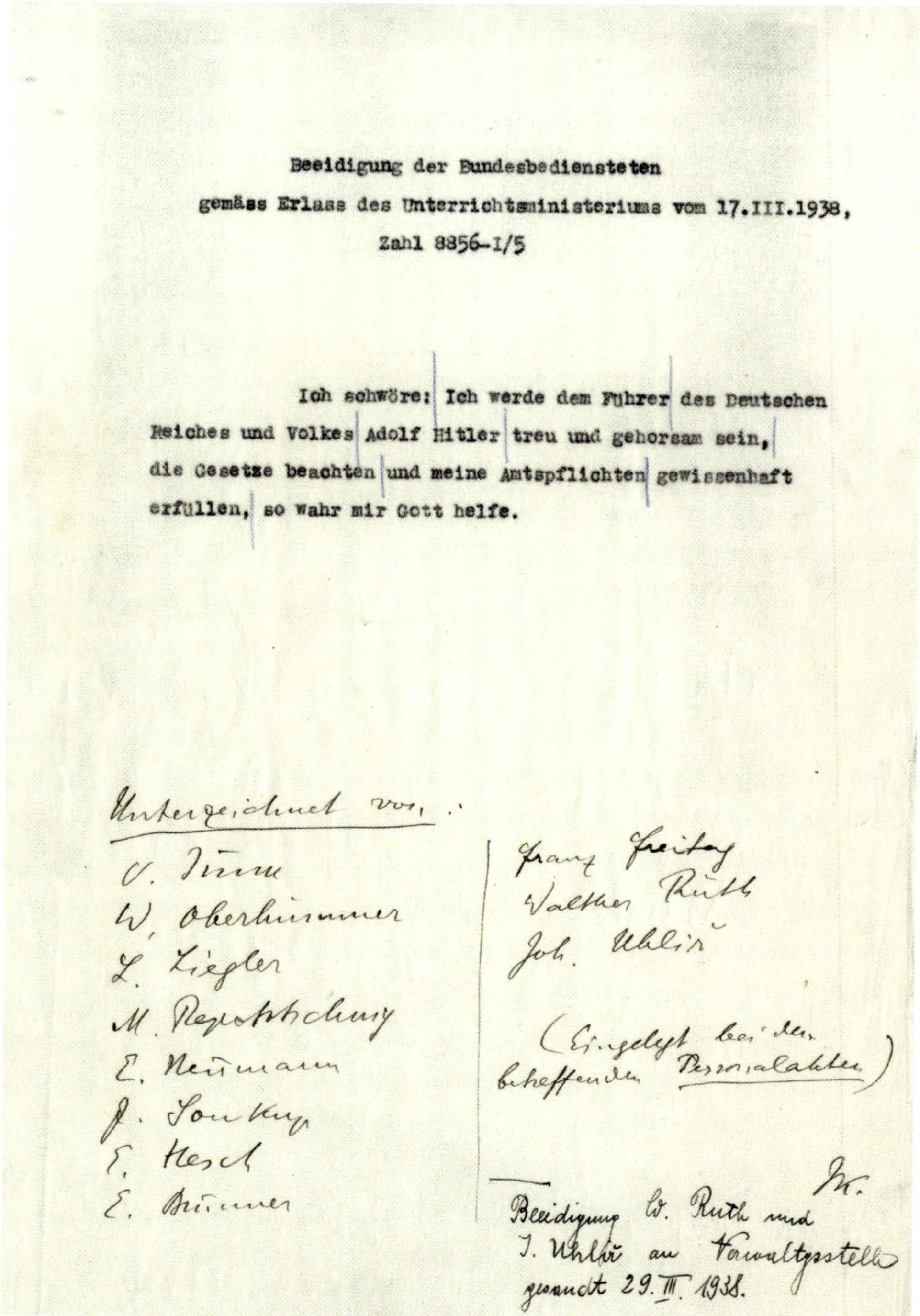

Beeidigung der Bundesbediensteten
gemäss Erlass des Unterrichtsministeriums vom 17.III.1938,
Zahl 8856-I/5

Ich schwöre: Ich werde dem Führer des Deutschen Reiches und Volkes Adolf Hitler treu und gehorsam sein, die Gesetze beachten und meine Amtspflichten gewissenhaft erfüllen, so wahr mir Gott helfe.

Unterzeichnet von:

W. Oberhummer
L. Ziegler
E. Neumann
E. Brunner

Franz Freitag
Walther Ruth
Joh. Uhlíř

(Eingelegt bei den betreffenden Personalakten)

Beeidigung W. Ruth und J. Uhlíř an Verwaltungsstelle gesandt 29. III. 1938.

Fig. 35: Swearing in of state employees

Fig. 36: Leo Hajek in front of the gramophone horn (c. 1928)

civil service had been terminated as he had deregistered with the police on 3 May 1939 from Vienna to New York without obtaining prior permission from the highest service authority. The date of termination was put at 30 June 1939.[15] This decision was forwarded to Hajek by the Academy on 20 February 1940.

Walter Ruth had already been nominated as Hajek's provisional successor on 4 May 1938,[16] and he was officially appointed head of the Phonogram Archive in 1942. On 3 May 1939 Academy President Heinrich Srbik reported to the Reich Ministry of Science, Education, and Culture that *the current commissarial head, Dr. Walter RUTH, was fully qualified both academically and ideologically*. Moreover, he had *also been recommended by the Party as an Illegal* [member of the Nazi Party before 12 March 1938] and thus deserved *every promotion on account of his services during the period of prohibition*.[17] The way in which Walter Ruth came to occupy this leading position is by no means unique in the Austrian academic landscape. The *"Gleichschal-*

[15] See AÖAW, Phonogrammarchiv, Box 1, Folder 4, No. 951/1940.

[16] See AÖAW, Phonogrammarchiv, Box 1, Folder 4, minutes of the Phonogram Archive Commission of 4 May 1938. See essay in this volume by Johannes Feichtinger, "Science 'in the service of the German people,'" pp. 123–32.

[17] AÖAW, Phonogrammarchiv, Box 1, Folder 4, No. 92/1939. In the files of the Dictionary Commission, Ruth is mentioned in the minutes of the meeting of 4 November 1947 to discuss the affairs of the Commission for the Austrian-Bavarian Dictionary. Ruth's incrimination as an Illegal was dealt with but this was ultimately deemed to be irrelevant. Following his dismissal in 1945, Ruth was then re-employed by the Academy. See AÖAW, FE-Akten, Wörterbuch-Kommission, Box 1, No. 1518/1947.

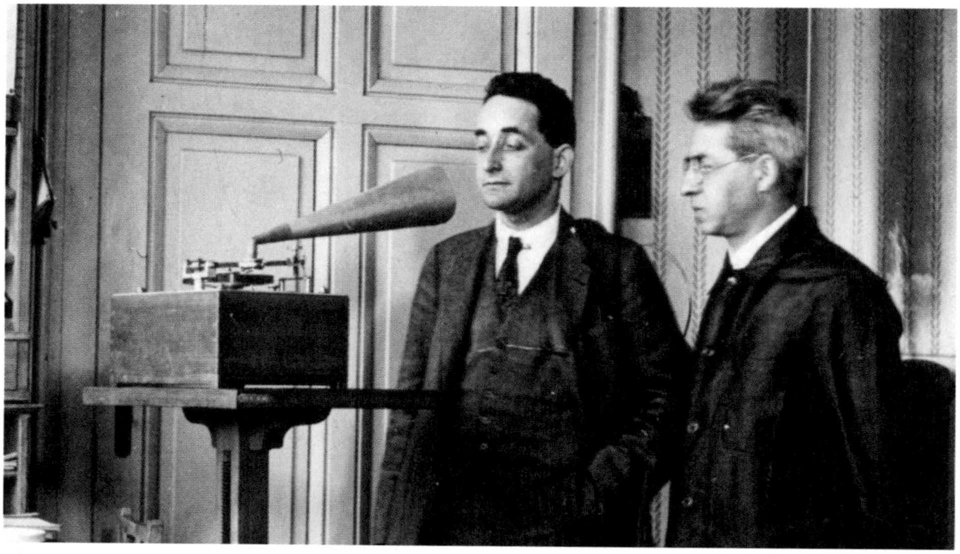

Fig. 37: Leo Hajek with archive phonograph type IV (c. 1928)

tung" [alignment/consolidation] – in this case unforced – of academic institutions is typical of the first phase after the assumption of power by the Nazis in March 1938. The aim was to create institutions that were loyal to the Nazis. For this purpose, persons of Jewish descent and political opponents in leading positions were removed and replaced by persons trusted by the Nazi Party. A typical example of this procedure is the University of Vienna. Fritz Knoll, the newly appointed rector of the university, was able to report to the Reich Ministry of Science, Education, and Culture ten days after his appointment that "the basic structure of the internal organization of the University is complete. […] Everything is functioning in an orderly manner."[18]

The "Anschluss" brought significant personnel changes for the Academy of Sciences. The example of Leo Hajek also shows that the expulsion of Jewish intelligentsia after the "Anschluss" was carried out in an extensively uniform fashion in all public institutions. As part of the *"Gleichschaltung"* of public institutions, leading positions were filled by politically reliable persons. At the same time, politically or "racially" unacceptable persons were dismissed. At the University of Vienna, for example, almost half of the teachers were dismissed.[19] The absence of a complete list of employees immediately after the "Anschluss" makes it difficult to determine the changes that took place in the Academy's staff. There is also no conclusive information about persons working independently in the Academy's institutions. Since all personnel files were transferred to the Archive of the Academy of Sciences in 2011, it is now possible to investigate personnel changes within the administrative staff.

Marlene Wahlmüller

[18] Quoted in Lichtenberger-Fenz (2000), *Geordnete Bahnen*.

[19] See Mühlberger (1993), *Vertriebene Intelligenz 1938*, p. 7.

Administrative staff

Actuaries

Since the founding of the Academy in 1846/47, there had always been one actuary responsible for the affairs of the Section for Mathematics and the Natural Sciences and one for the Section for Humanities and the Social Sciences, one of whom was also responsible for the affairs of the Academy as a whole.[1] Following the death of Emil Kohl in June 1924, the position of First Actuary was taken over by the then Second Actuary Viktor Junk.[2] Junk, who had joined the Academy on 1 March 1900 as a *Konzeptsbeamter* [paralegal secretary] with the title of *Erster Kanzlist* [First Chancellery Clerk], retired on 1 February 1945 after almost 45 years of services and after having been on sick leave since the summer of 1944. He joined the Nazi Party in April 1933 (membership number 1.616.309) and was thus an *"Alter Kämpfer"* [Old Comrade] as well as the holder of a "Führer Medal to Commemorate 13 March 1938."[3] He was succeeded as First Actuary by the former Second Actuary Wilfried Oberhummer.

Oberhummer, who had a doctorate in chemistry, joined the Academy as an actuary on 1 June 1937. His duties were described in 1937 as *planning work, keeping the minutes and administration of the files of the Section for Mathematics and the Natural Sciences, supervision of the printing of papers of the Section for Mathematics and the Natural Sciences, librarian of the Academy library.*[4] He succeeded Haas as Second Actuary until 31 January 1945. For most of World War II he was classified as "indispensable;" his only military service was from 26 March to 29 July 1941 in Intelligence Reserve Battery No. 44 in Wels. Between June 1938 and 1942 he was an applicant for membership of the Nazi Party and subsequently became a member.[5]

In a highly documented case, Senate II of Special Commission at First Instance of the University of Vienna concerning the assessment of Oberhummer under paragraph 21 of the *Verbotsgesetz* [law banning re-engagement in National Socialist activities], found at its session of 10 July 1946 that *he would unreservedly and at all times*

---

[1] These two functions were originally called First Actuary and First Chancellery Clerk and then from 1903 First and Second Actuary.

[2] On Junk: ÖBL 3 (1965), pp. 152–3. See also Ranzmaier (2010), *Germanistik*, passim, esp. p. 438. Unless otherwise indicated, the biographical details and quotations in this essay are based on the respective AÖAW personnel files.

[3] See AÖAW, PA Viktor Junk, list of candidates for Loyalty Medal (July 1941) and letter by Srbik to the Registrar of academic institutions of higher education of 24 June 1941 (No. 170/1941).

[4] Detailed description in AÖAW, PA Wilfried Oberhummer, No. 123/1937, Academy to Federal Ministry of Education of 12 March 1937.

[5] See AÖAW, PA Wilfried Oberhummer, red file No. 75 (1946).

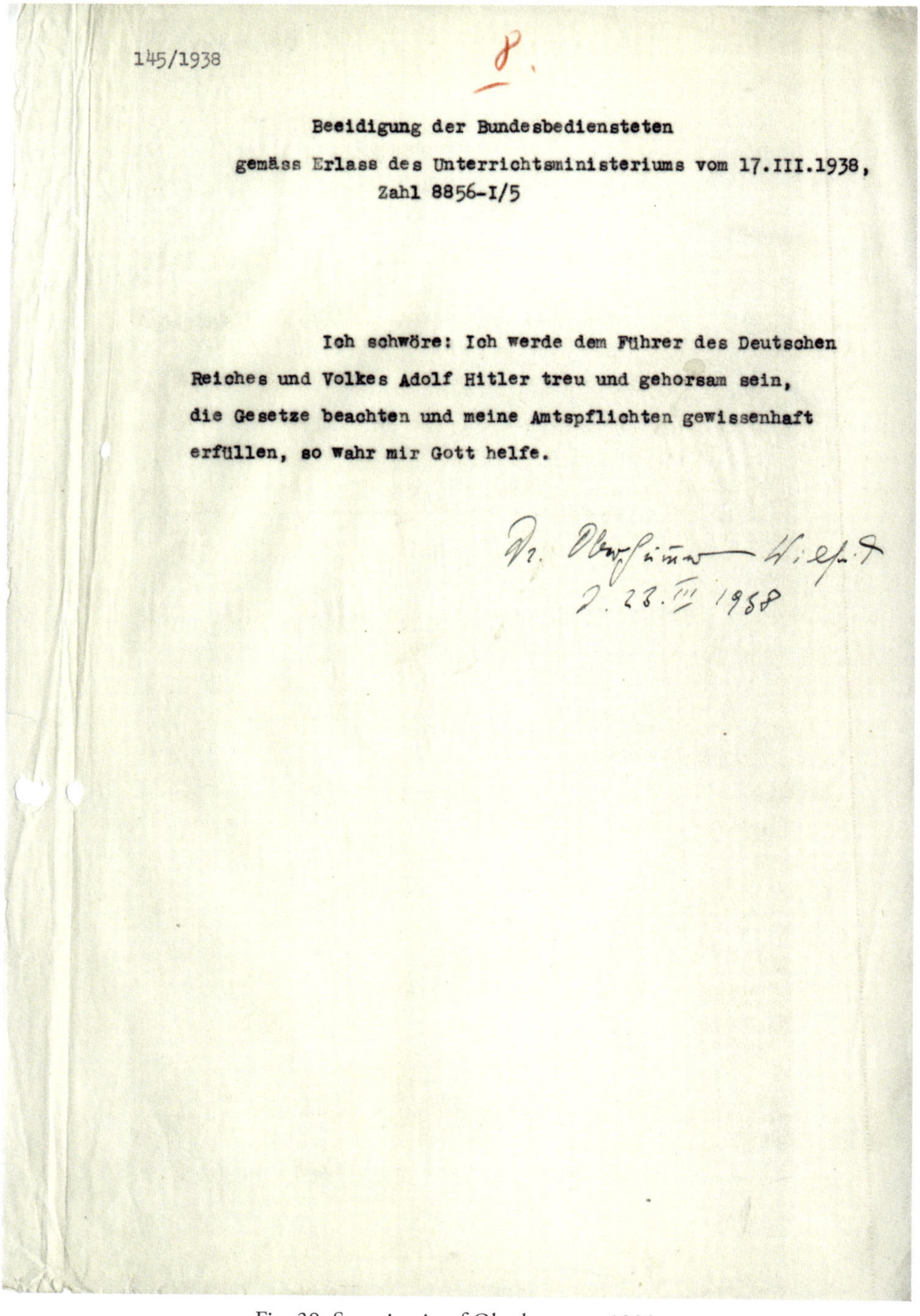

145/1938

8.

Beeidigung der Bundesbediensteten

gemäss Erlass des Unterrichtsministeriums vom 17.III.1938, Zahl 8856-I/5

Ich schwöre: Ich werde dem Führer des Deutschen Reiches und Volkes Adolf Hitler treu und gehorsam sein, die Gesetze beachten und meine Amtspflichten gewissenhaft erfüllen, so wahr mir Gott helfe.

Fig. 38: Swearing in of Oberhummer 1938

support an independent Republic of Austria. Reasons for the decision: Based on the statements by the defendant and witnesses and the documents presented, the Senate was of the opinion that Dr. Oberhummer was swayed, on the basis of his support of a Greater Germany, by the Nazi ideology and required no particular persuasion to join the Betriebs-SA [Academy's internal SA organization for employees] *and the Party. He soon became disillusioned, however, and distanced himself from the Party without leaving it, as he did not believe this was possible. According to the credible testimony of Major-General Slavik, his activities as deputy propaganda officer in the Reichskriegerbund* [Reich Warrior League] *had nothing to do with the Party. Oberhummer's later attitude (no Hitler greeting, no uniform, no Party badges, communication with political miscreants and their promotion) indicates that he had distanced himself from the Nazi Party and its ideology.*[6]

Oberhummer's duties during the war and thereafter were considerable: "He was in charge of the Secretariat, represented the Academy on international committees, was responsible for various official inquiries, and supervised the exchange of the Academy's publications with some 810 scientific institutions. The establishment of new Academy institutes that began in 1963 brought a vast amount of difficult work." Although he officially retired in 1965, he did not actually withdraw until 31 December 1974 as there was no suitable successor. In 1971 he was given the title *Hofrat* [Court Councilor] and in 1972 the "Bene Merito" medal from the Academy.[7]

Fig. 39: Award of the "Bene Merito" medal to Oberhummer (1972)

[6] Transcriptions in AÖAW, PA Wilfried Oberhummer. See also his *Anlage zum Personalblatt* of 6 June 1945 in AÖAW, Politischer Fragebogen der Mitarbeiter, from which some of the formulations have been more or less borrowed.

[7] See *Almanach* for 1971, 122 (1972), pp. 32–3.

Fig. 40: Oberhummer at his desk (c. 1973)

The Chancellery staff

The Chancellery employee Emma Neumann, daughter of the former actuary Emil Kohl, was subordinate to the actuaries. She joined the Academy *as a clerk subject to notice of dismissal at any time* on 14 May 1924 after graduation from commercial college. Starting in January 1928, as a full-time employee of the Chancellery Neumann was responsible for keeping records of incoming documents including indexing, for all filing as well as for sending corrected proofs to authors. The Academy applied for her to become tenured in public office, but by 1951 at least this had still not been achieved. After 1 October 1938 she was taken on as a salaried employee. She gave notice on personal grounds on 1 August 1945[8] after having already taken two months unpaid leave. From 15 November 1946 onwards she was employed by the Department of Mechanical Technology at the Vienna College of Technology.

Apart from Neumann, Josef Soukup was also employed in the Academy administration. He entered service on 1 May 1903 as an *Unterbeamter* [lower civil servant] and was employed as janitor and porter. His duties as janitor were taken over by Emerich Hesch in 1922, enabling Soukup to concentrate more on the library and publication archive. From around 1924 to 1933 he was a member of the Social Democratic Party and *Bund der öffentlichen Angestellten* [Association of Public Servants]. An inquiry in 1937 by the *Vaterländische Front* [Fatherland's Front] – to which Soukup belonged from 1934 to 1938 – requesting that the 71-year-old he be allowed to retire was rejected on account of his indispensability. He finally retired on 1 April

[8] See AÖAW, Ministerium, No. 5/1946.

1941 and died the following year. In June 1941 he stated that he was not a member of the Nazi Party or an affiliated group.

Soukup was replaced by Rudolf Thiel. A qualified bookbinder, he had worked in various companies since 1922 as an office clerk or assistant with periods of unemployment in between, in some cases quite lengthy (e.g. from 1932 to 1938). He was employed by the Academy from 1 June 1940 to replace Ferdinand Weiss, who had been drafted into the armed forces. Thiel too had been called up for *service of several weeks' duration,* with a start date as soon as 8 October 1940. The Academy attempted to prevent this in the fall of 1940, stating that Thiel was *currently the only attendant available to the Academy for the most urgent business. He is responsible for heating all rooms (seven large rooms and halls), keeping order in the Academy library (20,000 volumes), for the daily mail, and in particular for the monthly dispatch of the Academy's scientific publications abroad, a function that needs to be maintained for propaganda reasons, that involves the packing, franking, and shipment of several hundred packages.* The Academy's intensive efforts to retain Thiel were successful only until 20 May 1942. After he had been drafted, Thiel was held in custody in Munich for a period in 1943 for allegedly listening to a Swiss radio station in the summer of 1943. After the war, from which Thiel and Weiss both returned, Thiel took over the now retired Soukup's functions. He was responsible for the library and publication archive and retired on 31 December 1967.[9]

The shoemaker Ferdinand Weiss, mentioned above, entered into employment at the Academy on 10 February 1939. On 9 February 1940 the Academy reported to the Ministry that *Weiss, who had been referred to it from the Office of Employment,* [...] *has a correct and positive political attitude. The Academy would also like to point out that Ferdinand Weiss is used only for menial work such as carrying coal, heating the stoves, cleaning rooms, taking messages, and the like. The statement in the letter written by the district headquarters of the Nazi Party [Kreisleitung] that Ferdinand Weiss is sympathetic to Jews is no doubt attributable to the fact that before the change Weiss had worked as a clerk in a Jewish company for 10 years.*

Weiss was drafted into the armed forces on 1 June 1940 and served in the Soviet Union, Hungary, and Slovakia. He was given civil servant status on 13 January 1942 after Soukup's retirement made a position vacant. From May until 27 August 1945 he was in a U.S. prisoner of war camp before taking up his employment at the Academy again. On 28 October 1947 his position was described as follows: *work in the publication archive, acceptance of incoming printed matter, care of same, dispatch to the publishers and preparation for exchange of publications, registering book locations.* Weiss was named an *Oberaufseher* [senior supervisor] on 1 March 1960; he retired on 31 July 1969.

[9] See AÖAW, Minutes of the General Assembly of 15 December 1967 (A 1181).

Fig. 41: Official stamp of the Academy

Fig. 42: Official seal of the Academy

The accountants

Leopold Liegler was recruited on 19 June 1913 *on probation as an assistant to the accountant with a monthly salary of K 140.00* and employed on 1 January 1914 as *Rechnungsassistent* [accounts assistant]. His application to replace Kohl as First Actuary in 1924 was unsuccessful. After the departure of the accountant Streicher, Liegler took over his position in 1925 and managed the Academy's double-entry bookkeeping thereafter. He was a member of the Social Democratic Party from around 1924 until 1933 and of the *Vaterländische Front* from 1934 to 1937. He was a good friend of Karl Kraus and was himself a literary scholar and critic. At his request, the Academy applied in June 1945 for Liegler's retirement, as he had not been able to carry out his functions as head of accounts since August 1942 on account of a serious heart complaint.[10] Liegler retired at the end of February 1946.

On 13 October 1949, the *Österreichische Zeitung* wrote about Liegler, who had died shortly beforehand: *Those who had the opportunity of meeting the late Leopold Liegler in late 1944 and early 1945 would not have thought it possible that this deathly ill man with his weakened, crippled body would continue to live for several months. But in this organism dwelt a tough, strong spirit, kept alive by the passionate wish to experience the end of the hated Nazi rule, and this stubborn will not only rescued Liegler but, after the liberation of Vienna, seemed to transform him from a terminally ill man into a healthy, flourishing, and rejuvenated person. With fiery enthusiasm he set about the work pressing from all sides of building up a new state.*

Liegler was assisted by Marie Repototschnig, née Calabek. She worked in the Academy from 1 November 1911 to 31 December 1915 as a Chancellery assistant and thereafter – after her employment had been confirmed – as *Kanzleioffiziantin* [chancellery officiant] and, from 1 March 1925, as bookkeeping assistant. In a letter

[10] See AÖAW, PA Leopold Svajda, Academy to District Military Command of 24 August 1942.

to the Presiding Committee of 25 November 1938 she wrote that she *had sympathized with the Party in every respect, as could be seen from the enclosed confirmation from the N.S.D.A.P.*[11] *This must have come to the attention of the authorities in power at the time because in the crisis of 1934, I received a warning from the Vaterländische Front, City Center, via the Presiding Committee of the Academy regarding my political behavior.* [...] *Only through the benevolent and protective intervention of the Presiding Committee was I saved from disaster.*[12] She retired on 1 April 1941 because of health reasons.

Her successor was the jurist Leopold Svajda, who had worked previously in the Ministry of Finance, which was dissolved at the end of fiscal year 1940/41. From 2 December 1940 he completed a *fully satisfactory four-month probationary period*[13] and thereafter took over Repototschnig's position in the Academy. Officially, *with effect from 1 April 1941, Svajda is appointed Steuersekretär* [tax commissioner] *with secondment to the Registrar of academic institutions of higher education in Vienna (which should read Academy of Sciences) and transferred to Section P of the Oberfinanzpräsidium* [higher tax office].[14] In August 1942 he was classified as "indispensable" *until further notice* and hence exempted from military service; after May 1942 he was solely responsible for the Academy accounts because of Liegler's ill-health.[15] From 22 February to 1 March 1945 he completed officer training in the "*Volkssturm*" [German home guard made up of old men and boys during the last months of World War II]. He belonged neither to the Nazi Party nor to any affiliated group.

After Liegler retired at the end of February 1946, Svajda officially became Academy accountant. The Academy wrote to the Federal Ministry of Education in 1950 in connection with an application to promote Svajda to the grade *Dienstpostengruppe IV*: *It is not least thanks to his vigilance, willingness, and conscientiousness that the library stacks, whose contents are worth millions, survived the most difficult war and post-war period without any losses.*[16] Svajda was appointed *Amtssekretär* [department secretary]

[11] AÖAW, PA Marie Repototschnig, letter from the Vienna Nazi Party Gau leadership of 24 November 1938: *It is hereby confirmed that the husband of Mrs. Marie Repototschnig, Pg. Ludwig Repototschnig, has been a member of the N.S.D.A.P. since 1934 and was an enthusiastic member during the illegal period and with his wife's knowledge generously provided the illegal formations with food. Pg. Repototschnig was also imprisoned for some time for Nazi activities. He and his wife are in every way reliable and politically unblemished.* A letter from *district headquarter VII* (Kreisleitung VII) of the Vienna Gau of the Nazi Party of 7 July 1939 confirmed her as an *Old Comrade of the Ostmark* [...] *because she demonstrated exceptional service to the Party before 11 March 1938.* Ibid.

[12] AÖAW, PA Marie Repototschnig.

[13] AÖAW, PA Leopold Svajda, Academy to Registrar of academic institutions of higher education of 18 March 1941.

[14] AÖAW, PA Leopold Svajda, explanation of the Registrar of academic institutions of higher education in Vienna to the Academy of 26 August 1941.

[15] See AÖAW, PA Leopold Svajda, Academy to District Military Command of 24 August 1942.

[16] AÖAW, PA Leopold Svajda, letter of 4 July 1950.

on 1 January 1945 and *wirklicher Amtsrat* [full department head] on 1 July 1955. He retired at the end of 1961.

On 20 October 1942 Lucia Freiberg began work at the Academy as a wartime assistant and was employed as a middle grade civil servant in the accounts department. Her recruitment had been necessary on account of Liegler's ill-health. She was promoted in 1947 to the *Gehobener Fachdienst* [upper grade civil servant]. On 1 January 1962 she succeeded Svajda as head of accounts and retired with the rank of *Amtsdirektorin* [department director] at the end of May 1983.

The janitor

Fig. 43: Marie Hesch

Marie Hesch succeeded her husband, Emerich Hesch, as janitor of the Academy after his death in April 1939. It is thanks to her great personal commitment that the Academy building and its contents were protected from plundering after the liberation of Vienna in 1945. When she reached the age of 65 her employment as a cleaning lady was terminated by the Ministry with effect from 31 December 1953, but she continued to work as janitor.[17] She left at her own request on 15 November 1956 on health grounds. After requesting *the further payment of a small monthly allowance,*[18]

[17] AÖAW, Minutes of the General Assembly of 23 October 1953 (A 1060).
[18] AÖAW, Minutes of the General Assembly of 9 November 1956 (A 1084).

she received the proceeds of a collection among the Academy members, which were handed to her at a small farewell celebration.

Stefan Sienell

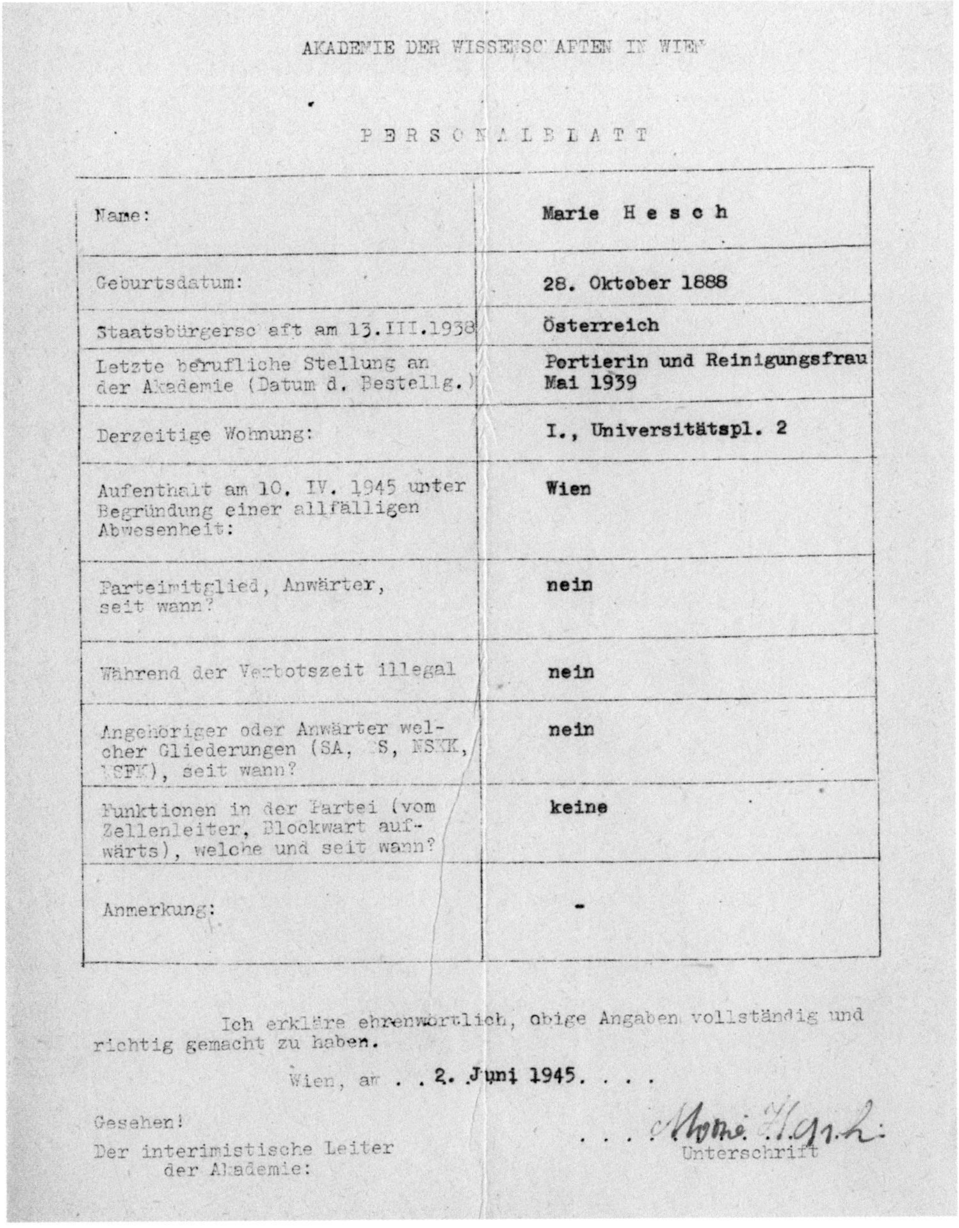

AKADEMIE DER WISSENSCHAFTEN IN WIEN

P E R S O N A L B L A T T

Name:	**Marie H e s c h**
Geburtsdatum:	**28. Oktober 1888**
Staatsbürgerschaft am 13.III.1938	**Österreich**
Letzte berufliche Stellung an der Akademie (Datum d. Bestellg.)	**Portierin und Reinigungsfrau Mai 1939**
Derzeitige Wohnung:	**I., Universitätspl. 2**
Aufenthalt am 10. IV. 1945 unter Begründung einer allfälligen Abwesenheit:	**Wien**
Parteimitglied, Anwärter, seit wann?	**nein**
Während der Verbotszeit illegal	**nein**
Angehöriger oder Anwärter welcher Gliederungen (SA, SS, NSKK, NSFK), seit wann?	**nein**
Funktionen in der Partei (vom Zellenleiter, Blockwart aufwärts), welche und seit wann?	**keine**
Anmerkung:	**-**

Ich erkläre ehrenwörtlich, obige Angaben vollständig und richtig gemacht zu haben.

Wien, am . . **2. Juni 1945**. . . .

Gesehen!
Der interimistische Leiter
der Akademie:

. . . Marie Hesch
Unterschrift

Fig. 44: Questionnaire Marie Hesch 1945

The revision of the Statutes

In the *Bundesgesetzblatt für die Republik Österreich* [Federal Law Gazette of the Republic of Austria] of 14 October 1921 (BGBL. No. 569), paragraph 3 states: "The Academy of Sciences in Vienna shall function on the basis of Statutes whose validity must be confirmed by the Federal President." The Statutes (*Satzung*), confirmed in 1922 and augmented with an Amendment in 1925, were replaced in 1938 by Provisional Statutes.[1]

Already at the extraordinary General Assembly of 25 March 1938, a Statutes Commission was set up consisting of the ordinary members Hochstetter, Schweidler, Srbik, Durig, Hartmann, Himmelbauer, Mache, Späth, Redlich, Wenger, Hirsch, Meister, Radermacher, and Dopsch, as well as the corresponding member inland Ficker.[2] In order to meet the changed circumstances, the Commission was charged with drafting new Statutes that conformed with the legal situation of the German academies. The Advisory Commission was also charged with formulating the new By-Laws necessitated by the new Statutes.[3]

At the General Assembly of 8 April 1938, Secretary General Egon Schweidler gave a first report on the work of the Advisory Commission and presented a draft of the new Statutes. The draft was discussed paragraph by paragraph and finally adopted with minor changes. The final stylistic editing was reserved for the Presiding Committee, whereupon the new Statutes were to be forwarded for approval to Berlin.[4] The correspondence was not undertaken directly with Berlin, however, but with the Department of Interior and Cultural Affairs, section IV, in Vienna. This section also conveyed to the Academy the new Statutes (albeit still titled Provisional) as approved by the Reich Ministry of Science, Education, and Culture as per the decree of 22 July 1938. President Heinrich Srbik reported to the General Assembly of 21 October 1938 on the establishment of the new Statutes and the changes, emphasizing his gratitude for the support of *Oberregierungsrat* [senior councilor] Hans Huber, who headed the Austria Office in the Reich Ministry of Science, Education, and Culture in Berlin. In this function Huber also played a significant role in the "cleansing" of Austrian universities in 1938.[5]

The changes to some points in the Statutes resulted simply out of the need to adapt to the provisions of the German academies. Thus, in accordance with the German usage full members were called ordinary members and the separation of corresponding members between those in Austria and those abroad was abolished. While

[1] See Kopetz (2006), *Akademie*, pp. 139–42.

[2] See AÖAW, Minutes of General Assembly of 25 March 1938 (A 933).

[3] See AÖAW, Minutes of General Assembly of 25 March 1938 (A 933), and AÖAW, Minutes of General Assembly of 21 October 1938 (A 939).

[4] See AÖAW, Minutes of General Assembly of 8 April 1938 (A 935).

[5] See AÖAW, Minutes of General Assembly of 21 October 1938 (A 939).

Fig. 45: Academy building (1935)

the task of the Academy had been to promote science "in every way," whereby "when carrying out its duties, it has the right to support and assistance from the Federal Government,"[6] the Academy's tasks were now defined as the advancement of science "in the service of the German people"; "[the Academy] is under the special protection of the Reich."[7] At the General Assembly of 8 March 1940, President Srbik was to notify the members that some smaller changes in the Statutes had become necessary.[8]

In 1941, Minister Rust then attempted to adapt the Statutes of the Vienna Academy to those of the other German academies. President Srbik informed the General Assembly on 17 October 1941 about this; the minutes state, however: *The President reported on the draft of the Academy Statutes received from the Reich Minister during the academic holidays and requested the belated approval of the objections and suggestions he had made. The Academy as a whole granted the belated approval.*[9]

At the General Assembly of 2 July 1943, he pointed out that the Minister of Science, Education, and Culture had envisaged earmarking a net Reich subsidy for the Academy, while maintaining its legal autonomy.[10]

The original number of 66 full (now: ordinary) members, 33 in each Section, was retained, although now instead of 17, at least 22 members of each Section were to reside in or near Vienna. If a member transferred his residence outside the "Land of Austria" while maintaining Reich citizenship, ordinary membership was to be retained but it was not to be included in the maximum number of members. If a current ordinary member became a citizen of a foreign country, his membership was automatically re-designated as corresponding member abroad. The total number of corresponding members was to remain at 160, of which each Section was to have 80. While up to this point the number of nationals in each Section had been limited to 35 and that of foreigners to 45, it was now determined that of the 80 corresponding members in each Section, at least 55 were to have Reich citizenship. Of these, at least 25 nationals had to have their domicile in the "Land of Austria." Of the foreign corresponding members, however, "German ethnicity is to be represented accordingly." The number of honorary members was limited to a maximum of eight for the Academy, elected by both Sections, and to a maximum of ten per Section.[11]

Probably the most significant change in the Statutes had to do with the election and confirmation of elected members, because here is where the deepest intervention in the Academy's autonomy occurred: Paragraph 7 of the Statutes formerly read, as it did again after 1945 and still does today: "Through the completed election, the

---

[6] BGBl. of 14 October 1921, No. 569, §2.

[7] The Provisional Statutes are printed in the *Almanach* for 1938, 88 (1939), pp. 9–16, but also in Meister (1947), *Geschichte*, pp. 240–2, here: §2.

[8] See AÖAW, Minutes of General Assembly of 8 March 1940 (A 951).

[9] AÖAW, Minutes of General Assembly of 17 October 1941 (A 965).

[10] AÖAW, Minutes of General Assembly of 2 July 1943 (A 980).

[11] *Almanach* for 1938, 88 (1939), p. 11. See also Meister (1947), *Geschichte*, p. 181.

§ 7.

Die Akademie wählt ihre Mitglieder nach der in der Geschäftsordnung bestimmten Wahlordnung. Durch die vollzogene Wahl erwerben die Gewählten ohneweiters die Rechte der Mitgliedschaft.

§ 8.

Das Präsidium der Akademie setzt sich zusammen aus einem Präsidenten, einem Vizepräsidenten und zwei Sekretären. Der Präsident und der Vizepräsident, ebenso die zwei Sekretäre müssen verschiedenen Klassen angehören. Einer der Sekretäre leitet neben den Geschäften der Klasse, der er angehört, auch die Geschäfte der Gesamtakademie und führt den Titel Generalsekretär.

Die Amtsdauer des Präsidenten und des Vizepräsidenten beträgt drei Jahre, die der beiden Sekretäre vier Jahre.

Der Präsident, der Vizepräsident, der Generalsekretär und der zweite Sekretär werden in Gesamtsitzungen der Akademie aus den wirklichen Mitgliedern gewählt und sind nach Ablauf ihrer Amtsdauer wieder wählbar, der Präsident und Vizepräsident jedoch nur mit drei Vierteln der abgegebenen Stimmen bei Anwesenheit von zwei Dritteln der wirklichen Mitglieder.

Die Wahlen der Mitglieder des Präsidiums bedürfen der Bestätigung durch den Bundespräsidenten.

Fig. 46: Statute of 1922, §§ 7 and 8

elected persons shall automatically acquire the rights of membership."[12] It now read: "The completed election must be confirmed by the Minister of Science, Education, and Culture. The confirmation may be withdrawn."[13] And while until then paragraph 8 stated that the election of the members of the Presiding Committee had to be confirmed by the Federal President, the new Statutes limited the rights of the Academy in that it could merely propose persons coming from the ranks of the ordinary members for nomination to the Minister for Science, Education, and Culture. The appointment was a matter for the Reich Minister. And whereas in the old Statutes the principle of collegiality was emphasized: "The Presiding Committee is made up of a President, a Vice-President and two Secretaries,"[14] it now read: "At the head of the

[12] Statutes of 1922, and Amendment of 26 February 1925 in the *Almanach* for 1937, 87 (1937), p. 13.

[13] Provisional Statutes in the *Almanach* for 1938, 88 (1939), p. 12.

[14] Statutes of 1922, and Amendment of 26 February 1925 in the *Almanach* for 1937, 87 (1937), p. 13.

§ 7.

Die Akademie wählt ihre Mitglieder nach der in der Geschäftsordnung bestimmten Wahlordnung.

Die vollzogene Wahl bedarf der Bestätigung durch den Reichsminister für Wissenschaft, Erziehung und Volksbildung. Die Bestätigung ist widerruflich.

§ 8.

An der Spitze der Akademie steht der Präsident der Akademie. Er wird vertreten und unterstützt durch einen Vizepräsidenten und zwei Sekretäre. Der Präsident und der Vizepräsident, ebenso die zwei Sekretäre müssen verschiedenen Klassen angehören. Einer der Sekretäre leitet neben den Geschäften der Klasse, der er angehört, auch die Geschäfte der Gesamtakademie und führt den Titel Generalsekretär.

Die Amtsdauer des Präsidenten und des Vizepräsidenten beträgt drei Jahre, der beiden Sekretäre vier Jahre.

Der Präsident, der Vizepräsident, der Generalsekretär und der zweite Sekretär werden aus der Zahl der ordentlichen Mitglieder vom Reichsminister für Wissenschaft, Erziehung und Volksbildung ernannt. Die Akademie kann geeignete Mitglieder vorschlagen.

Fig. 47: Statute of 1938, §§ 7 and 8

Academy is the President of the Academy. He is represented and supported by a Vice-President and two Secretaries."[15]

Reich Minister Rust was able to impose a change of Statutes on the Berlin Academy in which the "Führer principle," the strict application of the Reich-Citizen Law, as well as a relaxing of the geographical restrictions for ordinary members were explicitly defined. In contrast, the Statutes of the Vienna Academy were subject to relatively small changes, and thus offered few opportunities for enforcing the "Führer principle" at the Vienna Academy.

The contents of paragraphs 9 to 11, in which the tasks of the Presiding Committee and members' rights were set out, were not changed. In paragraph 12, which had previously also explicitly regulated postage and fee waivers as well as tax exemptions, and had also guaranteed the Academy the right to "utilize the active support of federal and regional authorities for projects of its own or which it had arranged," the relevant provisions were replaced by the phrase "the scholarly activities of the Academy shall

[15] Provisional Statutes in the *Almanach* for 1938, 88 (1939), p. 12.

be promoted by the Reich and state agencies." While paragraph 15 had previously stated that the statements of accounts were to be examined by the independent *Rechnungshof* [Court of Auditors], this control was now exercised by the responsible Ministry itself. In contrast, the other parts of the old Statutes were adopted virtually unchanged, with any changes only concerning language conformity. New, however, was an additional paragraph 20, in which it was stated: "The By-Laws and Amendments to the Statutes and By-Laws are subject to the approval of the Minister for Science, Education, and Culture."[16]

It has frequently been pointed out that these Statutes were also remarkable in that the "Land of Austria" is mentioned more than once (and indeed until 1945). In the spring of 1938 this definitely still corresponded to official usage. Thus announcement of the federal law of 13 March 1938 in connection with the "Anschluss" also spoke of the "reunification of Austria with the German Reich." It was only on 24 May 1938 that the "Land of Austria" was divided into seven *Gaue* [highest regional organizational units of the Nazi Party]. This meant that in the course of 1938, Austria was also linguistically extinguished and replaced by the term *"Ostmark."* A Führer decree of 1942 introduced the official designation Danube and Alpenreich *Gaue*. The continued existence, year after year and thus at a time when it had already officially long been suppressed, of the expression "Land of Austria"[17] in Provisional Statutes as printed in the *Almanach* at least reflects a certain stubbornness on the part of the Academy as an institution.[18]

The Provisional Statutes shared the fate of so many provisional matters: they remained in force throughout the Nazi era and were replaced in 1945 by the original Statutes of 1922, including their Amendment of the year 1925.

Herbert Matis

---

[16] Provisional Statutes in the *Almanach* for 1938, 88 (1939), p. 16.

[17] This is also pointed out by Graf-Stuhlhofer (1995), *Akademie*, pp. 135 and 159.

[18] But even departments in the so-called Altreich still used this designation in the 1940s, and some firms retained the term "Austria" in their company names throughout the Nazi era.

I. 3. New programmatic and structural orientation

Speeches by Academy President Heinrich (von) Srbik at the Ceremonial Sessions

The highpoint of the Ceremonial Session, which according to the By-Laws was to take place every year on or near the date of the foundation of the Academy on 30 May, was the speech by the Academy President, in which he went into the Academy's current problems or gave programmatic statements on its academic policy.

The official speech given by President Oswald Redlich in 1937 in celebration of the ninetieth anniversary of the Academy's founding was still in this tradition, as it pointed out the function of scholarship and research in society: "The urge for knowledge is a divine spark in the human breast. Science serves this urge, it investigates nature and all works of mankind. It is an achievement of the nineteenth century, which is now so often vilified for having devised and defined the demand for strict scientific research and method for this sacred urge, in other words the spirit of free but critically controlled, truthful, and impartial striving for knowledge. It is the exalted task and duty of science and thus of academies of science to consciously adhere to, uphold, and defend this achievement."[1]

In the first Ceremonial Session after the "Anschluss", held exceptionally not in the spring but on 23 November 1938, the new President Heinrich Srbik gave an unusually long address on the theme: "German scholarship and the Vienna Academy in the Greater German Reich." Among other points, Srbik emphasized "the community of blood, soil, spirits, and hearts, and the epochal changes in the body of the people and the Reich." He did not fail to mention the "incomparable creativity and will of the Führer," which had brought about this "national drive of immense depth and potency in the people."[2] The prevailing zeitgeist – and probably a personal verbal gesture on the part of the speaker – was reflected in an overblown pathos that is alien to us today. The use at every possible opportunity in the speeches by Academy Presidents documented in the *Almanachs* for the years 1938 to 1943 of phrases such as *"deutsche Volksgemeinschaft"* ["German people's community"], "service to the German people," "decision-making power of the spiritual and moral element," "spiritual overarching of peoples," "spiritual homeland front," "fertility of the German spirit," or "idea of the eternal Reich" also have a disturbing effect.

---

[1] *Almanach* for 1937, 87 (1937), p. 183.

[2] *Almanach* for 1938, 88 (1939), pp. 163–4.

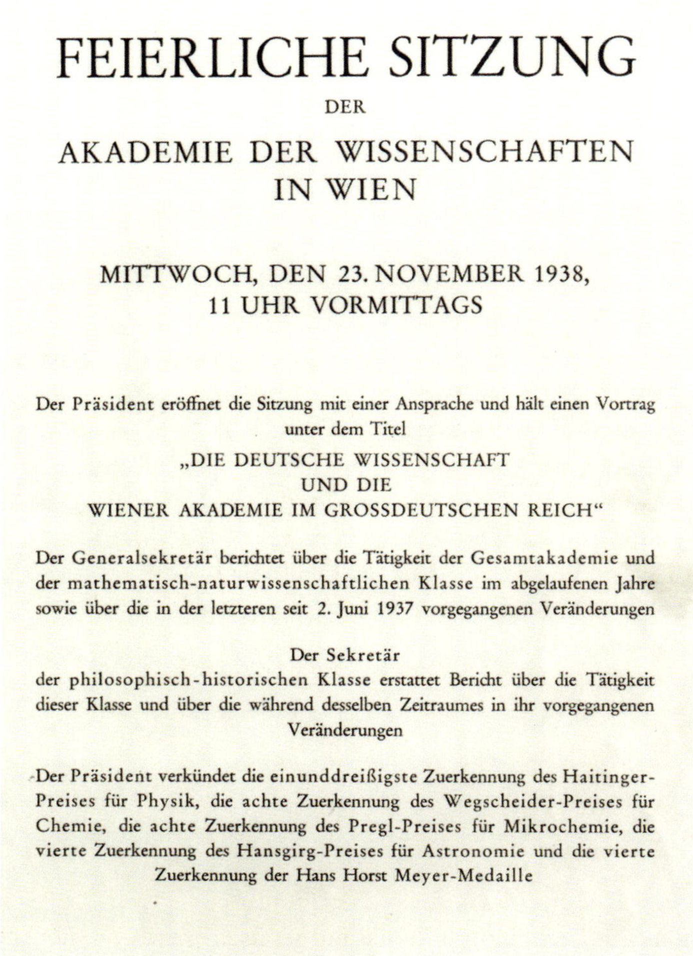

FEIERLICHE SITZUNG
DER
AKADEMIE DER WISSENSCHAFTEN
IN WIEN

MITTWOCH, DEN 23. NOVEMBER 1938,
11 UHR VORMITTAGS

Der Präsident eröffnet die Sitzung mit einer Ansprache und hält einen Vortrag unter dem Titel
„DIE DEUTSCHE WISSENSCHAFT
UND DIE
WIENER AKADEMIE IM GROSSDEUTSCHEN REICH“

Der Generalsekretär berichtet über die Tätigkeit der Gesamtakademie und der mathematisch-naturwissenschaftlichen Klasse im abgelaufenen Jahre sowie über die in der letzteren seit 2. Juni 1937 vorgegangenen Veränderungen

Der Sekretär
der philosophisch-historischen Klasse erstattet Bericht über die Tätigkeit dieser Klasse und über die während desselben Zeitraumes in ihr vorgegangenen Veränderungen

Der Präsident verkündet die einunddreißigste Zuerkennung des Haitinger-Preises für Physik, die achte Zuerkennung des Wegscheider-Preises für Chemie, die achte Zuerkennung des Pregl-Preises für Mikrochemie, die vierte Zuerkennung des Hansgirg-Preises für Astronomie und die vierte Zuerkennung der Hans Horst Meyer-Medaille

Fig. 48: Program of the Ceremonial Session 1938

"How could the Academy of Sciences in Vienna, now that Austria had entered the Greater German Reich and the age-old yearning for a greater German community of states has been fulfilled, how could the supreme academic community on the soil of the old Ostmark stand apart when Austria has again become the Ostmark of the united German People's state and the Reich has been enlarged and enriched by millions of Germans?"[3] […] "Our Academy links up organically with its German past by placing itself with fervor and a sense of duty in the service of the greater German People's state."[4]

[3] *Almanach* for 1938, 88 (1939), p. 164.
[4] *Almanach* for 1938, 88 (1939), p. 169.

Fig. 49: Srbik bust with quotes from his speeches

Srbik then spoke of "the question of the entitlement to exist of the old major research communities, the German academies of sciences"[5] and emphasized in this regard: "Scholarship of a creative nature is in its most profound sense not an end in itself, but in the service of something higher. It must experience the here and now of its own people and of peoples and influence its design. [...] If it does not want to waste its best energies, scholarship should not set itself apart from life and people or lose itself in impossible ideas of complete objectivity, which can never be attained."[6]

Compared with Redlich's speeches, Srbik[7] makes disproportionate use of the words "German," "Germany," and "German-ness," which occur in practically every second sentence. This is in keeping with the start of his speech in 1938, in which he confirms the "continuity of the national idea in the Vienna Academy." Word frequency

[5] *Almanach* for 1938, 88 (1939), p. 165.

[6] *Almanach* for 1938, 88 (1939), pp. 165, 169–70.

[7] The speeches by Redlich and Srbik lend themselves to comparison insofar as opening addresses by Presidents were given continuously after 1919. See *Festgabe* (1958). Redlich's nineteen speeches between 1919 and 1937 consisted of around 13,000 words, while Srbik's speeches between 1938 and 1943 amounted to just under 8,000; his 1944 speech was not published in 1945.

comparison also shows that apart from the inflationary use of "German," the words "people," "Reich," and "spirit" also appear frequently. For Redlich, by contrast, who in general had a wider vocabulary, we find frequent use of the words "Austria," "research," and "activity." A comparison on the basis of the keywords "national" and "international" also shows that Redlich repeatedly emphasized the international dimension of science and research, in particular the international association of academies in the world (1919, 1922, 1924, 1927, 1931), whereas Srbik mentions this dimension much less. He interprets the promotion of the international scientific collaboration of the Academy rather as a contribution to the "honor of the German name in the world" (1938).[8] A comparison on the basis of the words "serve" and "scholarship" reveals the fundamental difference in the two speakers' conception of scholarship. On several occasions, Redlich emphasizes on that scholarship primarily serves human knowledge, and (at the end of his 1937 speech) demands of it and of the Academy in particular that it should "uphold and defend the spirit of free but critically controlled, truthful, and impartial striving for knowledge."[9] In Srbik's speeches, by contrast, scholarship is seen almost exclusively in the service of the German people, being placed "in the service of a new awareness of the truth and of the people's honor, power, national unity, and freedom, and of the new idealism experienced by our people,"[10] so that the work of the Academy – referred to on several occasion as "service to the people" – should prove itself, for example, "in works that serve the German race, the German language, and questions of German national character, German soil, German law, and German art, German family and genealogy."[11] An analysis of the citations used also reveals a manifest break with tradition in 1938. Whereas Redlich is very keen to point to the Academy's continuity through his recurrent (eight) references to the the start its history in the revolutionary year of 1848 on the one hand, and through numerous mentions of earlier Presidents and tributes to various members and their research on the other, only two quotations in Srbik's 1938 speech (apart from the standard expression of thanks to Redlich) make reference to the Academy's tradition, and the two names – Leibniz and Grillparzer – are instrumentalized to highlight the connection between Austrian and German history.

[8] *Almanach* for 1938, 88 (1939), p. 167.
[9] *Almanach* for 1937, 87 (1937), p. 183.
[10] *Almanach* for 1938, 88 (1939), p. 176.
[11] *Almanach* for 1938, 88 (1939), p. 177.

Fig. 50: Auditorium at the Ceremonial Session 1939

The 1939 Ceremonial Session once again took place in spring, as was customary. The President's speech on this occasion was greatly affected by the incorporation of Sudetenland into the German Reich and the subsequent liquidation of Czechoslovakia, and the occupation of rump Czechoslovakia by the *Wehrmacht* [armed forces] and the creation of the Protectorate of Bohemia and Moravia. From Srbik's point of view, "the reorganization of the center of Europe through a grand idea has brought about great progress: [...] precious German ethnic soil has been returned to the Reich, and all the clouds that form, all the storms that could break out, will be unable to harm the solid structure of the German political body."[12]

The start of World War II, however, soon caused the initial euphoria about "the reorganization of the center of Europe" to fade away. In his relatively short speech of 1940, Srbik opined: "In the earth-shattering struggle of peoples and states that we are experiencing today, organizations for intellectual work such as our Academy of Sciences, do not, as a whole, have a widely audible voice." The commitment to the German people was, of course, present again, although on this occasion linked with the hope for peace in the near future: "The Academy as an intellectual community serves the German people and the Greater German Reich in immutable loyalty in time of war, as it will serve it when peace returns, and through the medium of its own people

[12] *Almanach* for 1939, 89 (1940), p. 166.

it also serves humanity. [...]. May a German peace illuminate our Ceremonial Session next year!"[13]

In his opening address in 1941, Srbik was forced to admit that an end to the war was not in sight: "The hope I spoke of a year ago has not yet been fulfilled: that a German peace would illuminate our Ceremonial Session. The immeasurable efforts in Germany's struggle for a new order in Europe and even in the world have not yet ended, the struggle on land and at sea continues to rage [...]. It is a millennial task with the most intense sense of responsibility that the German people has once again taken on today. German scholarship has no less duty in this people's task than the German sword and the German sense of beauty: German culture should radiate throughout the world, and the fertility of the German intellect should also fructify other peoples. Out of its loyalty to the people, the Reich, and the Führer, the Academy of Sciences in Vienna will also do its German duty. [...]. From such knowledge, strength and assurance of victory also flow to us, who can serve our people only with our intellect and not with weapons as well."[14]

On the day of the Ceremonial Session of the Academy in 1942, the President spoke of the need to take sides: "The side we take is that of the German people and Reich; the intellectual work must also incorporate and subordinate its own personality and creativity to it." Srbik also appealed for the "joyful fulfillment of duty to serve Germany" – which applied equally to the researcher in the hinterland as the "soldiers at the front."[15] Following the reports by the two Secretaries, the newly elected honorary member of the Academy, Nazi writer Erwin Guido Kolbenheyer, gave a speech on "the ethnic biological function of spiritual life and spiritual education."[16]

In the 1943 Ceremonial Session the President again spoke of the "commitment of loyalty to the people and the Reich" in the "difficult years of Germany's world struggle, and the global task of our German cultural work," of the "purest and most intense pan-German sentiments." He also announced his "conviction that the idea of the Reich and a new world order demands the sacrifice of one's own life for the nation's mission and generates new life." He even went as far as to say that one must "burn pure life itself in order to brighten the world as a sacrificial flame." Regarding the war of the German Reich against the Soviet Union he stated: "The realm of Goethe and Beethoven, the German judicial and economic system, European order and civilization, will extend to wherever the marching boots of the German musketeer will stop."[17]

This was the last of Srbik's speeches to be printed in the Academy *Almanach*. In the *Almanach* for 1944, which was not published until 1946, it says merely: "The President of the Academy of Sciences, Prof. Dr. Heinrich R. v. Srbik, opened the

[13] *Almanach* for 1940, 90 (1941), pp. 155–6.
[14] *Almanach* for 1941, 91 (1941), pp. 167–9.
[15] *Almanach* for 1942, 92 (1942), pp. 169–70.
[16] *Almanach* for 1942, 92 (1942), pp. 322–48.
[17] *Almanach* for 1943, 93 (1943), pp. 171–3.

Eröffnungsansprache

des Präsidenten der Akademie der Wissenschaften
Heinrich Ritter von Srbik.

Der Tag der feierlichen Sitzung der Akademie der Wissenschaften soll der Tag der Einkehr in uns selbst und der Rechenschaftslegung über unser Tun vor unserem Volk sein. Heute, da wir inmitten der gewaltigsten Umformung der ganzen Welt stehen und da dem deutschen Volk unabmeßbare Zukunftsaufgaben erwachsen, heute müssen wir uns vollends bewußt sein, daß die Wissenschaft nicht in einem gefreiten Bezirk, nicht auf einer stillen Insel inmitten eines brandenden Meeres lebt, sondern des Goethewortes eingedenk zu sein hat: „Wem um die Sache zu tun ist, der muß Partei zu nehmen wissen, sonst verdient er nirgends zu wirken.“ Die Partei, die wir ergreifen, ist die des deutschen Volks und Reichs; ihr hat auch der geistige Arbeiter seine Eigenpersönlichkeit und sein Schaffen einzugliedern und unterzuordnen. Wir glauben unerschütterlich, daß auch dieses Wirken der Vielheit der Wissenschaften, die in der Akademie zur idealen Einheit der Wissenschaft zusammengeschlossen sind, für unser Volk und für den Neuaufbau des Erdteils und der Welt unentbehrlich ist und sein wird. Wir sehen die Gesinnungsreinheit, das Streben nach Erkenntnis durch Forschung, die Strenge der Methode und den Verzicht auf alles Unechte für ein Daseinsgesetz der deutschen Wissenschaft an, und der Bekennermut, das als richtig Erkannte auch auszusprechen, darf und wird uns nicht entschwinden; aber wir wissen auch, wie lebensnötig die Wärme des männlichen Herzens und die freudige Erfüllung der deutschen Dienstpflicht ist — dem

Fig. 51: Srbik's speech at the 1942 Ceremonial Session, beginning

Ceremonial Session by welcoming the guests in a speech and handed the floor to the Secretary General for his report on the Academy as a whole and the Section for Mathematics and the Natural Sciences, and then to the Secretary for his report on the Section for Humanities and the Social Sciences."[18]

At the beginning of this *Almanach* it says: "Publication of the *Almanach* for 1944 is delayed on account of the destruction of the first composition by a bomb on the state printing works and the need to reconstruct the manuscript. The details regarding the Presiding Committee and members nevertheless reflect, in accordance with the purpose of the *Almanach* of gathering material for the history of the Academy, the situation in 1944 on the cutoff date of 31 December 1944, and the addresses of the members are also unchanged. By contrast, it appeared unnecessary to include the

[18] *Almanach* for 1944, 94 (1946), p. 101.

Statutes of the Academy and the Reich Association of German Academies of Sciences, which the changed circumstances have invalidated, or provisions regarding foundations, legacies, and gifts, which are in need of revision and review, or the list of institutes receiving the publications of the Academy of Sciences.

Vienna, February 1946.
For the Presiding Committee
of the Academy of Sciences:
J. Keil,
Secretary General."[19]

Herbert Matis

[19] *Almanach* for 1944, 94 (1946), p. 1.

Expelled, burnt, sold, forgotten, and suppressed

The permanent destruction of the Institute for Experimental Biology and its academic staff

Today only a street name recalls the existence of a research facility that wrote biological and medical history in the first decades of the twentieth century. In February 1957, *Vivariumsstrasse* in the Prater was named after the magnificent building built at the start of the Prater's *Hauptallee* for the Vienna World's Fair in 1873, functioning initially as an aquarium and known after 1888 as the Vivarium. After this and many other exhibition projects had come to nothing, three young and wealthy biologists from the Jewish bourgeoisie purchased the building in 1902: the zoologist Hans Przibram, just 28 years old, and the botanists Wilhelm Figdor (36) and Leopold Portheim (33). This triumvirate transformed the building into a private research institute, to which they gave the programmatic name the Institute for Experimental Biology (Biologische Versuchsanstalt, BVA). In subsequent years it developed into one of the leading research centers for experimental biology in the world.[1]

Equipped with what was, at that time, state-of-the-art laboratory infrastructure – including new types of temperature chambers – the researchers were attempting, as in chemistry and physics, to answer major biological questions by means of experiment. In so doing, they made the Institute for Experimental Biology into a sort of "breeding ground" of modern biology and a model for research institutes from New York to Moscow. Not only the infrastructure, but also the organization of the research was highly innovative: Scholars from different disciplines worked together, and laboratory facilities were made available to a constant stream of colleagues from Austria and other countries. Many doctoral theses by students at the University of Vienna – including that in 1910 of the later Nobel Prize winner Karl Frisch – were written at the Institute for Experimental Biology.

The research work most well known today to be conducted at the Institute for Experimental Biology were the spectacular breeding experiments by the eccentric zoologist Paul Kammerer, the first employee of the Institute for Experimental Biology who committed suicide following accusations of falsification that remain unresolved to this day. The researcher, who was very well reputed in his day, attempted to demonstrate the heritability of acquired characteristics in amphibians, but also carried out important work on the mutability of sex characteristics, and the significance of

---

[1] Some new articles have recently appeared about the Institute for Experimental Biology and its history; see Hofer (2001), *Goldscheid*, or Coen (2006), *Fin-de-Siècle Wien*. The best work remains Reiter (1999), *Zerstört*. The documentary novel by Lorenz (1952), *Sieg*, is still also worth reading, in particular pp. 127–234, 339–48.

Fig. 52: The Vivarium

cooperation in evolution.[2] The physiologist Eugen Steinach has also recently been rediscovered. From 1912 onwards he headed his own department in the Institute for Experimental Biology and was a pioneer in hormone research.[3] Steinach, who was nominated for the Nobel Prize five times, became world-famous for his anti-aging operation, which Sigmund Freud, among others, underwent. "To be steinached" was a common expression in the 1920s, and became so well known even in English that newspapers used it without further explanation. But many other researchers also contributed to the high regard in which the Institute for Experimental Biology was held and hence to the reputation of the Academy of Sciences, which became the owner of the institute in 1914.

In order to safeguard the existence of their private institute in the medium term, the three founders donated their unique facility to the Academy on 1 January 1914 after long-drawn-out negotiations. Moreover, Przibram, Portheim, and Figdor, together with Prizbram's brother Karl, supplied 300,000 krone to establish a foundation, an sum equivalent to over 2 million Euros today. After 1918 the institute suffered not only from the difficult economic conditions but also from the growing anti-Semitism of professors at the University of Vienna. Paul Kammerer, for example, was refused the title of extraordinary professor in 1918/19 for political and "racial"

[2] It is hard to obtain an overview of the literature on Kammerer; even without more recent publications. The three best works remain Koestler (1971), *Case*; Hirschmüller (1991), *Kammerer*, and Gliboff (2006), *Kammerer*.

[3] See, for example, Stoff (2004), *Jugend*, and Walch (2011), *Sexualhormone*.

reasons and thus abandoned his university career. Kammerer's main opponent was the paleontologist Othenio Abel who, in 1926, was motivated by anti-Semitism to prevent the habilitation of the zoologist Leonore Brecher and her colleague Paul Weiss, Hans Przibram's closest collaborators, who then left Austria for this reason.[4] In turn, Przibram himself had no chance of obtaining one of the two vacant zoology professorships in 1925 despite his impressive scientific achievements. In spite of the adverse circumstances and the lack of support from the Academy – Przibram was in a weak position within the university and was not a member of the Academy – he managed to keep the research going. Between 1914 and 1939, 284 papers, some of them of book length, came out of the institute's laboratories and were published by the Academy. Since 1903 over 250 researchers (around a quarter of them women) had worked there, either unpaid or funded almost exclusively from external sources.[5]

Fig. 53: Work station in the Vivarium (1931)

[4] See Taschwer (2013), *Geheimsache*, and Taschwer (2012), *Andenken*.

[5] According to unpublished research by Sabine Brauckmann. Gerd Müller has calculated that 175 BVA papers totaling 5,056 pages appeared in the *Archiv für Entwicklungsmechanik der Organismen*, the leading international journal in this field at the time. Quoted in Markl (2002), *Keimzelle*.

Fig. 54: Vivarium staff (1936)
Seated center: Leopold Portheim; standing 3rd from l.: Franz Köck

With the "Anschluss" came the onset of tragedy for the 35-year-old Institute for Experimental Biology. While the Academy's Presiding Committee carried out its exclusion of members for political and "racial" reasons after March 1938 in a bureaucratic and measured fashion, and in some cases *only on the explicit order of the Reichsstatthalterei* [office of the Reich Governor],[6] its attitude toward the Institute for Experimental Biology was quite the opposite. The first act of destruction was executed with military precision. The main parties responsible were Fritz Knoll, who had already been elected on 20 January 1938 to the Academy curatorium of the Institute for Experimental Biology,[7] and Franz Köck, who had succeeded Paul Weiss in 1927 as *Adjunkt* [administrative official] at the Institute for Experimental Biology, although he had been employed only as a specialist for the technical apparatus. Köck announced his National Socialist sympathies after 1938 and claimed a leading position for himself under the new political regime. On 17 March he ordered the *conditional closure* of the institute as well as preparations for its *reorganization*.[8] It is likely that the locks

[6] This was the text of the letter of 23 November 1942, in which the Nazi representative criticized Heinrich Srbik's 'wait and see' attitude. ÖStA-AdR, Gauakt Heinrich Srbik, BMI/GA 49317.

[7] From January 1938 the curatorium also included physicist and Academy Secretary Egon Schweidler, zoologist Karl Grobben, physiologist Arnold Durig, physical chemist Hermann Franz Mark, and geneticist and botanist Erich Tschermak-Seysenegg. Knoll was immediately appointed chairman.

[8] AÖAW, Papers of Fritz Knoll, Box 1, Folder 2.

AKADEMIE DER WISSENSCHAFTEN IN WIEN

WIEN I., UNIVERSITÄTSPLATZ 2.

A B S C H R I F T.

Wien, 4.April 1938.

Der Unterzeichnete,welcher im Kuratorium der Biologischen Versuchsanstalt mit der Wahrung der Interessen der Landesleitung der N S D A P in Österreich für den Bereich der Akademie der Wissenschaften betraut ist, beauftragt hiemit den Parteigenossen Universitätsprofessor Dr.Victor J U N K ,Aktuar der Akademie der Wissenschaften gemeinsam mit Frau Marie R E P O T O T S C H N I G ,Buchhaltungsassistentin der Akademie der Wissenschaften die Zeichnung für den Widmungsfond der Biologischen Versuchsanstalt erliegend bei der österr.Creditanstalt -Wiener Bankverein und für das Konto ordinario erliegend beim Postsparkassenamt in Wien zh übernehmen. Die bisherigen Zeichnungsberechtigten Univ.Prof.Dr.Hans P R Z I B R A M und Leopold v. P O R T H E I M werden hiemit von der Zeichnungsberechtigung enthoben .

Herr Ing.Franz K Ö C K ,Adjunkt der Biologischen Versuchsanstalt hat sich zur Fortführung der laufenden Agenden nunmehr mit beiden obgenannten neuen Zeichnungsberechtigten in Verbindung zu setzen.

f.d.Landesleitung der N S D A P :

gez. F.KNOLL

5000 III 29 — Druck der Österreichischen Staatsdruckerei in Wien. 3009 29

Fig. 55: Letter by Knoll of 4 April 1938

were changed already at this time and Jewish staff prevented from entering. On 4 April 1938 Fritz Knoll ordered *Party comrade University Professor Dr. Victor Junk, Actuary of the Academy of Sciences, together with Mrs. Marie Repototschnig, accounting assistant of the Academy of Sciences, to take over as signatories for the fund of the Institute for Experimental Biology* [...] *and the ordinary account* [...]. *The former signatories Univ.-Prof. Hans Przibram and Leopold von Portheim are hereby relieved of their signing authority.*[9]

The next day Köck was officially confirmed as sub-authorized agent for the Institute for Experimental Biology. And on 13 April 1938, a month and a day after the "Anschluss", the Academy direction issued the following order, which could not have been more cynical: *The Institute for Experimental Biology is to be closed from 6 p.m. this day for cleaning work that cannot be delayed and will remain closed until 25 April. At 8 a.m. on 26 April the Institute will be reopened to those members of staff who have applied for and been issued passes. The work places are to be left in proper condition by 6 p.m. today. Temporary passes, which may be revoked at any time, will be issued for work that cannot be postponed (care of animals, final work, etc.).*[10] The letter was signed by Knoll and the designated Academy President Heinrich Srbik.

From this time at the latest, Hans Przibram and Leopold Portheim, who had managed the institute for over 35 years and had donated it to the Academy, were no longer able to enter their institute. Przibram also had to abandon his private library. Eugen Steinach, physiology department head, was on a lecture tour abroad in March 1938 and never returned to Austria before his death in 1944. His villa at *Böcklinstrasse* 51 in the Pratercottage, a residential area between the Prater and the Danube Canal with large patrician houses, was "aryanized."

Of the other twenty-two male and eight female employees in March 1938, fifteen were of Jewish descent. They were all required to leave the Institute for Experimental Biology immediately; one other female and four other male researchers left 'voluntarily' in March 1938. This meant that the institute lost all of its department heads and two-thirds of its staff within a very short space of time. Egon Schweidler, Secretary General of the Academy, described the situation in his report for 1938 in somewhat less dramatic terms: "The Institute for Experimental Biology in the Prater is in the process of reorganization in terms both of the design of the building and improvements to the interior fittings, and the organization of its scientific activities."[11] Köck formulated it more explicitly on 4 May 1940 in a letter to the *Kurator der wissenschaftlichen Hochschulen* [Registrar of academic institutions of higher education]: *The Jews were removed after the changeover and where money from the Institute for Experimental Biology (private and state) was being used for the personal work of the Jews, Aryans*

[9] AÖAW, Papers of Fritz Knoll, Box 1, Folder 2; see facsimile overleaf

[10] AÖAW, Papers of Fritz Knoll, Box 1, Folder 2. See also AÖAW, Biologische Versuchsanstalt (Vivarium), Box 1, Folder 2.

[11] *Almanach* for 1938, 88 (1939), p. 188.

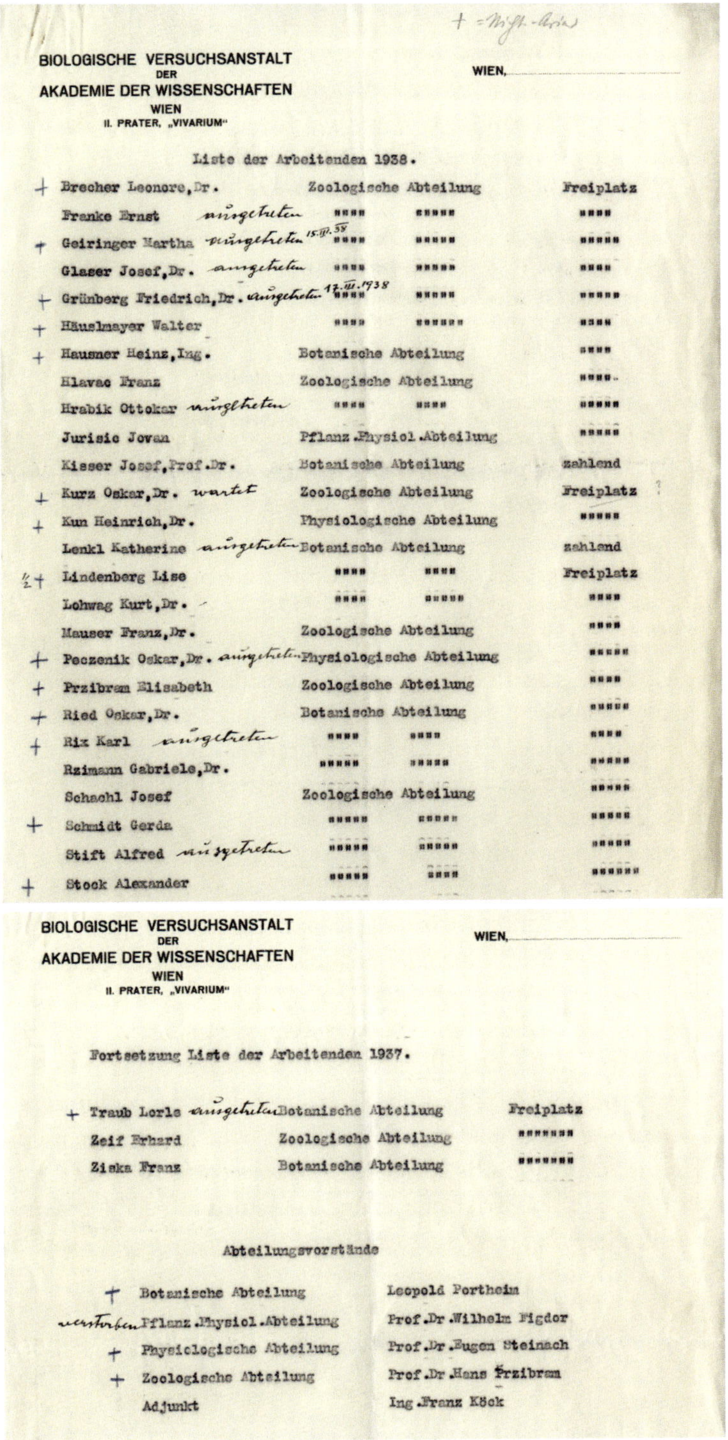

+ = Nicht-Arier

BIOLOGISCHE VERSUCHSANSTALT
DER
AKADEMIE DER WISSENSCHAFTEN
WIEN
II. PRATER, „VIVARIUM"

WIEN, ...

Liste der Arbeitenden 1938.

+	Brecher Leonore, Dr.	Zoologische Abteilung		Freiplatz
	Franke Ernst *ausgetreten*	""""	"""""	""""
+	Geiringer Martha *ausgetreten 15.III.38*	""""	"""""	"""""
	Glaser Josef, Dr. *ausgetreten*	""""	"""""	""""
+	Grünberg Friedrich, Dr. *ausgetreten 17.III.1938*	""""	"""""	"""""
+	Häuslmayer Walter	""""	""""""	""""
+	Hausmer Heinz, Ing.	Botanische Abteilung		""""
	Hlavac Franz	Zoologische Abteilung		"""".
	Hrabik Ottokar *ausgetreten*	""""	""""	"""""
	Jurisic Jovan	Pflanz.Physiol.Abteilung		"""""
	Kisser Josef, Prof. Dr.	Botanische Abteilung		zahlend
+	Kurz Oskar, Dr. *wartet*	Zoologische Abteilung		Freiplatz ?
+	Kun Heinrich, Dr.	Physiologische Abteilung		"""""
	Lenkl Katherine *ausgetreten*	Botanische Abteilung		zahlend
½ +	Lindenberg Lise	""""	""""	Freiplatz
	Lohwag Kurt, Dr.	""""	"""""	""""
	Mauser Franz, Dr.	Zoologische Abteilung		""""
+	Peczenik Oskar, Dr. *ausgetreten*	Physiologische Abteilung		"""""
+	Przibram Elisabeth	Zoologische Abteilung		""""
+	Ried Oskar, Dr.	Botanische Abteilung		"""""
+	Rix Karl *ausgetreten*	""""	""""	""""
	Rzimann Gabriele, Dr.	"""""	"""""	"""""
	Schachl Josef	Zoologische Abteilung		"""""
+	Schmidt Gerda	"""""	"""""	"""""
	Stift Alfred *ausgetreten*	"""""	"""""	"""""
+	Stock Alexander	"""""	""""	""""""

BIOLOGISCHE VERSUCHSANSTALT
DER
AKADEMIE DER WISSENSCHAFTEN
WIEN
II. PRATER, „VIVARIUM"

WIEN, ...

Fortsetzung Liste der Arbeitenden 1937.

+	Traub Lorle *ausgetreten*	Botanische Abteilung	Freiplatz
	Zeif Erhard	Zoologische Abteilung	"""""""
	Ziska Franz	Botanische Abteilung	"""""""

Abteilungsvorstände

+	Botanische Abteilung	Leopold Portheim
verstorben	Pflanz.Physiol.Abteilung	Prof. Dr. Wilhelm Figdor
+	Physiologische Abteilung	Prof. Dr. Eugen Steinach
+	Zoologische Abteilung	Prof. Dr. Hans Przibram
	Adjunkt	Ing. Franz Köck

Fig. 56: List of employees (1937–8)

were paid with this money; Aryans being paid with this money remained in the Institute for Experimental Biology. This was done so that the experience gained through years of scientific work would not be lost.[12] While the "Aryanization" of the funds was successful, the continuation of research work was a disaster. The only serious researcher to continue to work for a short time at the *Institute for Experimental Biology* after the "Anschluss" was the botanist Josef Kisser. After 1945 he became a professor at what is now the University of Natural Resources and Life Sciences, where he was rector three times. Köck's own research, which consisted mainly of mixing sawdust with bran and testing this for use as livestock feed, proved to be nonsense. The only thing that continued to function in any way was the public aquarium.

Following numerous complaints and accusations against Köck, Knoll was appointed as *"Gefolgschaftsführer"* of the Institute for Experimental Biology on 8 November 1939 and thus became responsible for it. Köck's dismissal took effect on 1 October 1940,[13] after he had brought about, amongst other things, *the destruction of ponds and terraria, the closure of parts of the scientific collection and several display cases, changes in the gardens*, in short *severe injury to the value of the institute.*[14] The Vivarium continued to exist until 1943 as an aquarium, as it had started out 70 years earlier. In June 1943 the Academy concluded an agreement with the Kaiser Wilhelm Society that allowed the Kaiser Wilhelm Institute for Cultivated Plant Research to use the institute's facilities, greenhouses, and gardens for its experimental research.

But what happened to the former employees of the institute? In her book *Biologen unter Hitler* [Biologists under Hitler], Ute Deichmann also discusses the zoology and botany professors at German and Austrian universities who were expelled and murdered by the Nazis. She starts with Hans Przibram, the only biology professor to die in a concentration camp.[15] The director of the Institute for Experimental Biology appears to have received an invitation from his former student Paul Weiss for the United States, but he underestimated the dangers posed by the Nazis. Before war broke out he was able to flee to the Netherlands, but they were occupied by German troops in the spring of 1940. On 3 March 1941, Przibram asked Fritz Knoll for a letter of support for his planned emigration to the United States. The letter was written by Knoll with the permission of the head of the Nazi Association for University Teachers Arthur Marchet, but the entire file was sent for a final decision to the Reich Ministry of Science, Education, and Culture in Berlin, effectively invalidating the letter from Vienna.[16] In April 1943 the Nazis deported Hans Przibram and his wife to Theresienstadt concentration camp, where Przibram's suffering ended on 20 May 1944. He died of nutritional edema; his wife Elisabeth, who was also listed as an

[12] AÖAW, Papers of Fritz Knoll, Box 1, Folder 2.

[13] See AÖAW, Papers of Fritz Knoll, Box 1, Folder 2, Knoll to Köck of 17 July 1940.

[14] AÖAW, Papers of Fritz Knoll, Box 1, Folder 2, unsigned letter of 3 June 1940, probably written by Knoll, page 2.

[15] See Deichmann (1995), *Biologen*, pp. 36–40.

[16] See UAW, Akademischer Senat, academic year 1939/40/41, ref. 1679.

employee of the Institute for Experimental Biology in March 1938, committed suicide the following day.[17]

These two were not the only Institute for Experimental Biology employees to meet their death through the Nazi terror. The zoologist Leonore Brecher was another victim.[18] Shortly after the "Anschluss" she went on an unpaid research trip to Cardiff but had to return and was deported on 14 September 1942 from Vienna to the Maly Trostinec extermination camp near Minsk, Belarus, and killed on 18 September, the day of arrival.[19] All that is known of her colleague Martha Geiringer, a doctoral student of Przibram, is that she was deported from Belgium to Auschwitz on 15 January 1943. The physiologist Heinrich Kun, Eugen Steinach's closest colleague, died in an unknown camp in Yugoslavia. Henriette Burchardt, also employed for several years with Steinach, was deported on 24 September 1942 from Vienna to Theresienstadt and from there to Auschwitz-Birkenau on 23 October 1944. Her precise date of death is also unknown. The Institute for Experimental Biology was thus, relative to its size, the research institute in Austria and the German Reich with the most victims of National Socialism.

During the last days of the war in Vienna, the physical destruction of the building itself took place, long after the staff had been forced to leave and the research activities abandoned. According to the eye-witness account of long-standing institute employee Albert Weiser, German combat units (SS and *Wehrmacht*) were quartered in the Institute for Experimental Biology with heavy armored fighting vehicles from 6 to 9 April 1945 and were responsible for the initial destruction. *On 11 April 1945 a fire broke out in several places at the same time in the Institute itself, probably as the result of an incendiary shell, which raged for two days. It was impossible to fight the fire because of the water shortage and, since the Institute was right in the combat area, the heavy shelling.*[20] What happened afterwards was described in 1947 in Richard Meister's *Geschichte der Akademie der Wissenschaften*: "The building of the Prater Institute for Experimental Biology, II., *Hauptallee* 1, was destroyed by fire in the last days of the war to such an extent that there was no possibility of restoring it with the Academy's resources."[21] Elsewhere he writes: "The available cash funds and proceeds from the sale of the burnt-out building will be [...] used, as the founders would have wished, to build the Biological Station in Lunz am See."[22] There is also a paragraph about the work of the

[17] On the fate of the Przibrams, see Przibram (1959), *Przibram*, p. 187; Koestler (1971), *Case*, pp. 121–2, and Reiter (1999), *Zerstört*, pp. 611–2.

[18] See Taschwer (2012), *Andenken*.

[19] This and the following data were researched at www.yadvashem.org.

[20] AÖAW, Biologische Versuchsanstalt (Vivarium), Box 4, Folder 2, commemorative record of events of April 1945.

[21] Meister (1947), *Geschichte*, p. 190.

[22] Meister (1947), *Geschichte*, p. 344. The question remains as to how those responsible in the Academy were able to fathom the wishes of the founders, all of whom, with the exception of Karl Przibram, were dead.

Fig. 57: The destroyed Vivarium

Institute for Experimental Biology – but not a word about the fact that no other Academy institute was harder hit by the events of 1938 to 1945. And, needless to say, nothing about the fate of Elisabeth and Hans Przibram, Wilhelm Figdor, Eugen Steinach, Leonore Brecher, Henriette Burchardt, Martha Geiringer, or Heinrich Kun. In the media, at least, there were protests at the abandonment of the burnt ruins. On 20 October 1948, *Neues Österreich* reported resignedly one last time about "the selling of biology" thus: "[…] at the heart of academia, in the traditional home of biology, material and even moral forces appear to have failed. Goodbye Vivarium! […] The Academy of Sciences has sold the building it received as a gift."

One person who cut out and kept this and other newspaper articles on the Institute for Experimental Biology, and who also collected further material on this research institute before 1938 and after 1945, was Fritz Knoll. It is possible that the botanist had a guilty conscience about the complete destruction of the research institute that had been entrusted to him. When he published two volumes on great Austrian natural scientists, engineers, and physicians in 1950 and 1957 on behalf of the Academy, he had two opportunities to recall the great history of the research institute and to pay tribute to its most important researchers. But the principle of repression was stronger: Knoll did not write a single word about any of them. And in essence, the eradication of the Institute for Experimental Biology from the collective memory of the history of science continues to have an effect to this day; even now there is no comprehensive portrayal of and tribute to this once world-famous institute of the Academy.

Klaus Taschwer

Transformations in research policy

In the history of the Academy of Sciences published in May 1947 as part of the centenary celebrations, the author, Vice-President Richard Meister, did not entirely cover up the Academy's activities during the Nazi era. On the contrary, he considered it to provide convincing evidence that "the majority of the members [...] resisted the subjugation of research to the primacy of politics."[1] "The work of the Academy – in terms of its business and the content and spirit of the work – was not significantly influenced by the political transformation [...], and in the work carried out and published during this time, [it] did not deviate from its position of research based on strict scientific objectivity."[2] That Meister's description distorts and even completely deforms the historical facts can be seen just from the fact that his contemporary, the ancient historian and long-serving Secretary General of the Academy (1945–59) Josef Keil, described it in the same year as *one of the most effective pieces of propaganda for intellectual Austria.*[3] Meister's claims are interesting for historians, however, because they indirectly point to the ambivalent relationship to politics that could be perceived among the Academy members after the "Anschluss" in 1938.

Scholarship and Politics – Alliances? Separate entities?

Within the Academy of Sciences some of the members adapted their research activities to National Socialist ideology; at the same time, others showed greater reserve in their reaction to the political demands of the new authorities. In spite of the "relatively small changes" in the Provisional Statutes (particularly regarding the admittance of new members),[4] many full members, who thanks to the Academy Law and Statutes had enjoyed a high degree of scientific autonomy during the First Republic, saw the demands made by the Nazi authorities as a comparatively major transformation. In practice, the interference by the Nazi regime far exceeded the extent of political intervention negotiated between the National Socialist authorities and the Academy and set out in the Provisional Statutes. It is not, therefore, surprising that some Academy members also soon began to assert themselves.[5] At the same time, many members sympathized with the Nazi Party and some were fervent National Socialists. The academic community reacted ambivalently to the new political situation: there was opportunistic adaptation by some members and individual attempts to resist demands by others. There are a number of examples to illustrate this ambivalence. Adaptation could be seen, for example, in the way in which, from 1938, the leading

---

[1] Meister (1947), *Geschichte*, pp. 181–2.

[2] Meister (1947), *Geschichte*, pp. 183, 186.

[3] AÖAW, Minutes of the General Assembly of 10 October 1947 (A 1013).

[4] Matis (1997), *Anpassung*, p. 25; see also the essay in this volume by Herbert Matis, "The revision of the Statutes," pp. 87–92.

[5] See Matis (1997), *Anpassung*, pp. 54–61.

figures in the Academy's institutions were replaced, as well as in the submissiveness with which Academy members accepted the transfer of institutes to the Kaiser Wilhelm Society. In the minutes of the meeting of 16 December 1938, it thus states: *The Ministry requested the Academy's opinion on the proposal that Privatdozent* [lecturer] *Dr. Gustav Ortner be nominated head of the Institute for Radium Research and as full professor at the Department of Physics II of the University.* Although the Statutes did not permit interference of this type, the Academy decided *to agree to the application by the Vice-President* [Egon Schweidler].[6] At the General Assembly of 27 October 1939, it was announced that Ortner had been appointed head of the Department by the Reich Minister of Science, Education, and Culture.[7] The transfer of institutes was also – as mentioned above – *acknowledged* without further resistance: *The Ministry of Interior and Cultural Affairs, section IV, gives notice of the decree of the Reich Minister for Science, Education, and Culture, that the further support of the two Kaiser Wilhelm Institutes, the Biological Station in Lunz and the Sonnblick Observatory, is no longer necessary.*[8]

However, there were discernable signs of self-assertion among the academy members. To prevent the political misuse of funds, the General Assembly decided on 8 March 1940 to add an additional paragraph to the Statutes for the Institute for Radium Research relating to the Kupelwieser Fund dedicated to it, as follows: *This Fund shall be used by the Institute for Radium Research by agreement with the Curatorium for PURELY SCIENTIFIC non-profit tasks* [author's emphasis] *carried out by the Radium Institute in accordance with the Statutes.*[9]

Some members and staff of the Academy used the new regime as a springboard for their careers. They did not stop at opportunistic adaptation, but took the initiative and became actively involved in research activities aimed at substantiating political beliefs. Active self-mobilization in both action and rhetoric attested to this. In the 72nd *Mitteilungen* [Bulletin] of the Phonogram Archive Commission, the new head of the Archive, Walter Ruth, stated: "In keeping with the most recent demands, the Phonogram Archive has set itself the task of promoting speech and singing education, thereby putting itself at the service of Nazi education. [...] Its proud task of acting as an outpost and preserver of German culture in the south-east should be an incentive and commitment for us in the future."[10] The contract concluded by ordinary member Viktor Christian between the in-house publishers of the Department of Oriental Studies of the University of Vienna and the *"Ahnenerbe"* [Ancestral Heritage] Foundation Publishing House gave control over the Academy's series the *Rudolf Pöchs Nachlass*

---

[6] AÖAW, Minutes of the General Assembly of 16 December 1938 (A 941).
[7] See AÖAW, Minutes of the General Assembly of 27 October 1939 (A 948).
[8] AÖAW, Minutes of the General Assembly of 6 June 1939 (A 946).
[9] AÖAW, Minutes of the General Assembly of 8 March 1940 (A 951). See also *Almanach* for 1940, 90 (1941), p. 138. The Assembly is erroneously dated 15 March 1940.
[10] Ruth (1941), *Phonogrammarchiv*, pp. 90–1.

Fig. 58: Institute for Radium Research

[Rudolf Pöch Papers] to the SS research institute.[11] Its aim was to provide scientific underpinning for the claim of supremacy of the Aryan race. The two volumes published by the Academy's Pöch Commission on the anthropology of Turkic peoples in Russia (1941) and the *Rassenkundliche Untersuchungen an Serben und Montenegrinern* (1943) were published by the *"Ahnenerbe"* [Ancestral Heritage] Foundation Publishing House in Berlin-Dahlem with, according to the title page "the support of the Academy of Sciences in Vienna."

This essay sheds some light on the self-assertion, opportunistic adaptation, self-mobilization and involvement of the Academy. On this central issue of research, first

[11] See BAB, NS 21/388 K., contract between the Department of Oriental Studies' in-house publishers and the *"Ahnenerbe"* Foundation Publishing House of 14 December 1938.

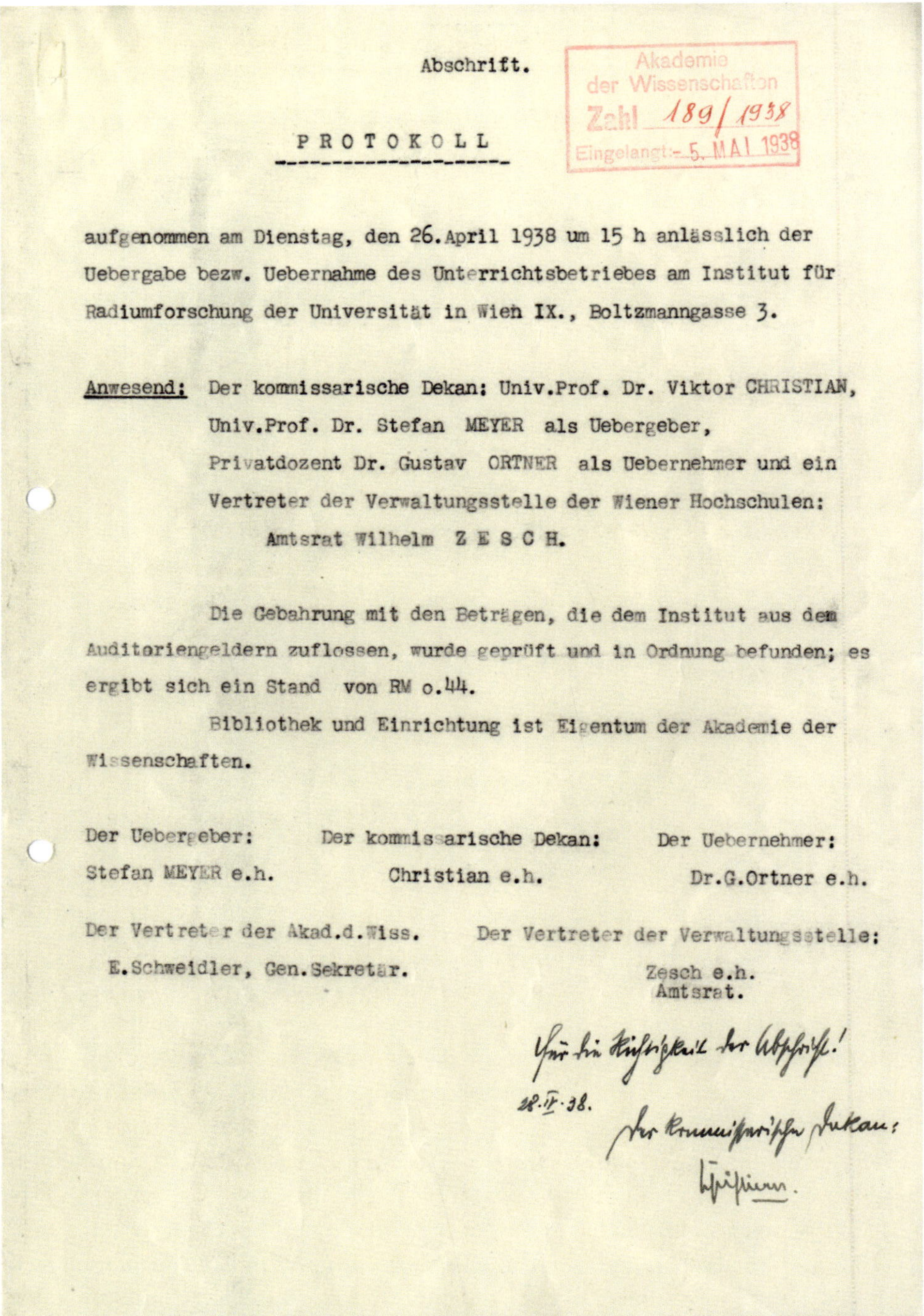

Abschrift.

Akademie der Wissenschaften
Zahl 189/1938
Eingelangt: 5. MAI 1938

PROTOKOLL

aufgenommen am Dienstag, den 26. April 1938 um 15 h anlässlich der Uebergabe bezw. Uebernahme des Unterrichtsbetriebes am Institut für Radiumforschung der Universität in Wien IX., Boltzmanngasse 3.

Anwesend: Der kommissarische Dekan: Univ.Prof. Dr. Viktor CHRISTIAN,
Univ.Prof. Dr. Stefan MEYER als Uebergeber,
Privatdozent Dr. Gustav ORTNER als Uebernehmer und ein
Vertreter der Verwaltungsstelle der Wiener Hochschulen:
Amtsrat Wilhelm ZESCH.

Die Gebahrung mit den Beträgen, die dem Institut aus dem Auditoriengeldern zuflossen, wurde geprüft und in Ordnung befunden; es ergibt sich ein Stand von RM o.44.

Bibliothek und Einrichtung ist Eigentum der Akademie der Wissenschaften.

Der Uebergeber: Stefan MEYER e.h.
Der kommissarische Dekan: Christian e.h.
Der Uebernehmer: Dr.G.Ortner e.h.

Der Vertreter der Akad.d.Wiss. E.Schweidler, Gen.Sekretär.
Der Vertreter der Verwaltungsstelle: Zesch e.h. Amtsrat.

Für die Richtigkeit der Abschrift!
28.IV.38.
Der kommissarische Dekan:
Christian.

Fig. 59: Transfer of the Institute for Radium Research of 26 April 1938

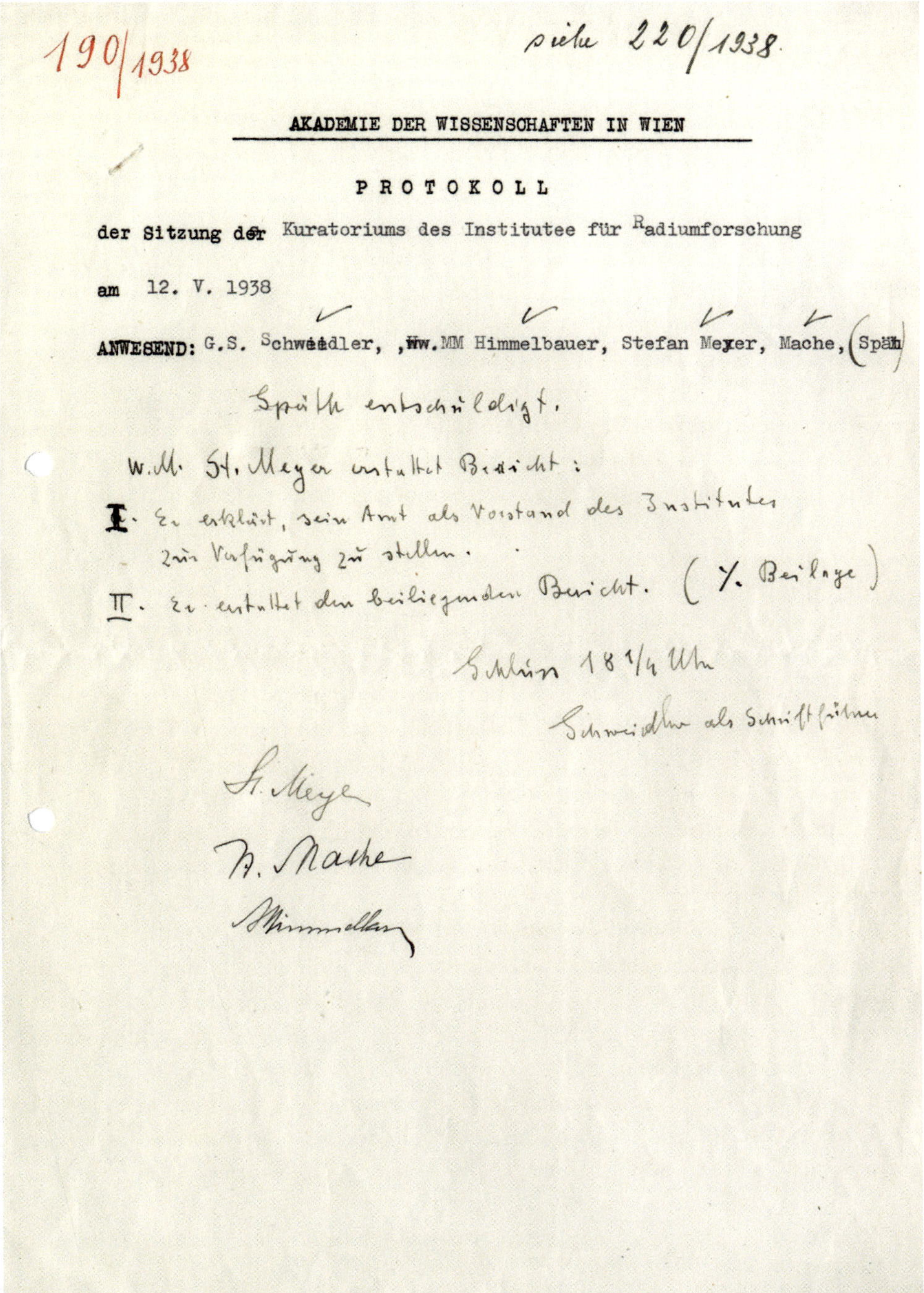

190/1938 siehe 220/1938

AKADEMIE DER WISSENSCHAFTEN IN WIEN

PROTOKOLL

der Sitzung der Kuratoriums des Institutee für Radiumforschung

am 12. V. 1938

ANWESEND: G.S. Schweidler, ,w.M. Himmelbauer, Stefan Meyer, Mache, (Späth)

Späth entschuldigt.

w.M. St. Meyer erstattet Bericht:

I. Er erklärt, sein Amt als Vorstand des Institutes zur Verfügung zu stellen.

II. Er erstattet den beiliegenden Bericht. (%. Beilage)

Schluss 18 1/4 Uhr

Schweidler als Schriftführer

St. Meyer

H. Mache

Himmelbauer

Fig. 60: Curatorium meeting of 12 May 1938

pioneering studies have been published by Mitchell G. Ash and Albert Müller who focus specifically on the German Reich and on the University of Vienna.[12] Regarding the Vienna Academy of Sciences and a comparative approach between research institutions, there is still a large gap that can be closed only by way of a major research project.

1938, or the so-called "new era"

In 1938, members of the Nazi Party were installed in leading positions in the scientific institutions that had employees, if these institutions were not already headed by illegal Nazis. The nomination processes revealed the opportunism of the Academy, which abandoned some of the relative autonomy it still had in doing so. The following tendency can be observed: In general, "racially" persecuted heads of the Academy's institutions were dismissed, as were some supporters of the authoritarian *Ständestaat* [Corporate State]; they were replaced by illegal Nazis. With this "upheaval" in personnel, internationally acclaimed scientific practices built up over years among the Academy institutions, as well as research programs and pioneering international research institutes were extinguished at a blow.[13] The following institutions were affected in this way.

At the Institute for Radium Research, the illegal Nazi Gustav Ortner replaced the full member Stefan Meyer, a pioneer of radium research who, together with his colleague Karl Przibram, had made the Institute world-famous. A quarter of the staff members, including Marietta Blau, Elisabeth Rona, Anni and Franz Urbach, Eduard Jahoda, Gustav Kürti, and Stefan Pelz, were also dismissed on "racial" grounds.[14] The institute continued to produce publications, but many fewer than before.

At the Institute for Experimental Biology (BVA) in the Prater, the board members and department heads Leopold Portheim, Eugen Steinach, and Hans Przibram were removed. The internationally renowned scientists working there and around two-thirds of the staff were dismissed after April 1938 on "racial" grounds.[15] The illegal Nazi Franz Köck became head of the Institute for Experimental Biology. On the basis of an "official party measure," he was appointed by the "trustee head of cultural associations and organizations" as the "authorized representative of the Academy's Institute for Experimental Biology" on 5 April 1938. This appropriation of the commissarial leadership was even questioned by the chairman of the Institute for Experimental Biology's Curatorium, rector of the University and ordinary member of the Academy of Sciences Fritz Knoll, in a letter to the *Kurator der wissenschaftlichen Hochschulen*

[12] See Ash (2010), *Wissenschaft*; Ash (2006), *Wissenschaftswandlungen*; Ash (2004), *Wissenschaftswandlungen*; Ash (2002), *Wissenschaft*, and Müller (1997), *Adaptierung*.

[13] See Reiter (1999), *Naturwissenschaften*, p. 184.

[14] See Reiter (2000), *Meyer*, p. 122; also Reiter (1988), *Wissenschaftsemigration*, pp. 709–29; Reiter (2006), *Naturwissenschaften*, p. 185, and Rosner/Strohmaier (2003), *Blau*, pp. 49–51.

[15] See the essay in this volume by Klaus Taschwer, "Expelled, burnt, sold, forgotten, and suppressed," p. 106.

[Registrar of academic institutions of higher education] in Vienna of 8 October 1940.[16] Research was discontinued in 1941 following the provisional closure of the institute.[17]

At the Phonogram Archive, the meritorious director Leo Hajek, for whose 25th anniversary celebrations plans were already being made before the "Anschluss", was replaced by his assistant Walter Ruth, who had already rendered services to the Nazi Party during its illegal period and who was made provisional director by a decision of the Phonogram Archive Commission of 4 May 1938.[18] Hajek was dismissed from the civil service on 30 June 1939 and had to emigrate the same year on account of "racial" persecution.[19] Thereafter the Phonogram Archive carried out research projects aimed at substantiating political beliefs.

With regards to the Biological Station in Lunz and the Gastein Research Institute, following the Nazi seizure of power in Austria, the association agreements with the Academy of Sciences in Vienna were dissolved. The original agency responsible for running the Biological Station in Lunz was an association founded in 1923 by the Kupelwieser Foundation, in which the Academy and the Kaiser Wilhelm Society were represented. In 1939 the association's assets were confiscated and it was dissolved by the *"Stillhaltekommissär"* ["Commissioner for Suspensions"] responsible for the *"Gleichschaltung"* ["alignment"] of associations, societies, and organizations. The Biological Station continued to operate under the Kaiser Wilhelm Society and the leadership of the illegal Nazi Party member Franz Ruttner with the same staff as before. The Academy continued to be represented at the Biological Station by the Vice-President of the Curatorium, the botanist Fritz Knoll. At the Gastein Research Institute, the supervisory function of the Academy Curatorium, whose members came from the Section for Mathematics and the Natural Sciences, was suspended in 1938. This institute was handed over to the municipalities of Badgastein and Bad Hofgastein. Ferdinand Scheminzky, a student of the Catholic conservative physiologist and ordinary member Arnold Durig, was replaced as head of the Institute by the illegal Nazi Party member Gerhard Kirsch.[20] After 1945, the Academy took over both institutes: Lunz in 1947 and Gastein in 1952.[21]

---

[16] See Reiter (1999), *Zerstört*, pp. 609–14.

[17] Meister (1947), *Geschichte*, p. 186. For details of the Institute for Experimental Biology, see also the essay in this volume by Klaus Taschwer, "Expelled, burnt, sold, forgotten, and suppressed," pp. 101–11.

[18] AÖAW, Phonogram Archive, Box 1, Folder 4, minutes of the meeting of the Phonogram Archive Commission of May 4, 1938.

[19] For details of Hajek see the essay in this volume by Marlene Wahlmüller, "Consequences for the academic staff. The case of Leo Hajek," pp. 69–76.

[20] Knierzinger (2012), *Forschungsinstitut*, pp. 121–2.

[21] A commission for the administration of the Biological Station in Lunz was set up in 1947 and a commission for the scientific management of the Gastein Research Institute in Bad Gastein in 1952. See *Almanach* for 1947, 97 (1948), p. 56, and *Almanach* for 1952, 102 (1953), p. 148.

Fig. 61: Sonnblick Observatory

The administration of the Sonnblick Observatory remained in the hands of the Sonnblick Association, with funding being provided by the Kaiser Wilhelm Society.[22] Ordinary member Heinrich Ficker was made chairman of the Sonnblick Association by order of the Reich Minister for Science, Education, and Culture on 23 January 1941.[23]

Of the dismissed institute directors, Stefan Meyer managed to survive the Nazi era in Bad Ischl. Ferdinand Scheminzky, a physiologist who had been highly appreciated in the authoritarian *Ständestaat*, was appointed extraordinary professor at the University of Innsbruck in 1942. Karl Przibram, Leopold von Portheim, Eugen Steinach, and Leo Hajek were persecuted and expelled on "racial" grounds. Hans Przibram died in the Nazi Theresienstadt concentration camp in 1944 after having initially escaped to the Netherlands.

The Academy, which was divided into commissions, saw the creation of a new *Kommission zur Herausgabe von Schriften zur Rassenkunde und menschlichen Erblehre* [Commission for the Publication of Documents on the Study of Race and Human Genetics] in 1942. It was hoped that this commission would produce findings that could be used politically. Other commissions were renamed. Fervent National Socialists were elected to some. Chairmen were sometimes replaced by other commission

[22] See *Almanach* for 1939, 89 (1940), p. 177.

[23] After 1939 the observatory on Hoher Sonnblick was of "increased military value" for the *Luftwaffe* [air force] and, as a result, the Association was able to continue to run it. See *Almanach* for 1941, 91 (1941), p. 190, and *Almanach* for 1942, 92 (1942), pp. 188–9.

members who belonged to the Nazi Party. The following examples bear witness to this development. In 1939 the Commission for the Promotion of Prehistoric Research and Excavations in Austria was renamed the Prehistoric Commission, and was run henceforth as an intersectional commission (made up of members of both the Section for Mathematics and the Natural Sciences, and the Section for Humanities and the Social Sciences), by the chairman Oswald Menghin, ordinary member of the Academy.[24] In 1940 the dean of the Faculty of Philosophy of the University of Vienna, *SS-Obersturmführer* and ordinary member Viktor Christian, was co-opted into this commission. In the intersectional Phonogram Archive Commission, ordinary member Arnold Durig was replaced the following year as chairman by another ordinary member, the Anglicist and Nazi Party member Friedrich Wild. In the intersectional Commission for the Pöch Estate, Viktor Christian replaced the ordinary member Ferdinand Hochstetter as chairman. Hochstetter remained in the Pöch Commission, and Durig in the Phonogram Archive Commission. In the Commission for the Publication of German Medieval Inscriptions, the Germanist Dietrich Kralik-Meyrswalden, an ordinary member of the Academy and a member of the Nazi Party, replaced the former director and long-standing President of the Academy, Oswald Redlich. In 1942, most Nazi Party members were active in the following commissions: Phonogram Archive Commission (eight Nazi Party members out of fourteen commission members), Commission for Public Lectures (eight out of thirteen), Commission for the Publication of German Medieval Inscriptions (seven out of ten), Balkan Commission (six out of seventeen), Commission for the Matthäus and Rudolf Much Foundation (six out of nine), Asia Minor Commission (five out of ten), Prehistoric Commission (five out of eight), Commission for the Publication of Writings on the Study of Race and Human Genetics (five out of eight), Egyptian Commission (four out of seven), Medieval Sources of Law (Weistümer) and Rent-roll Commission (three out of six), and the Historical Commission (three out of seven). Significantly, these commissions received the most state funding between 1938 and 1945.[25]

It should be pointed out that, in 1942, commission work was carried out predominantly by Academy members who did not belong to the Nazi Party, with the exception of Heinrich Srbik and Arnold Durig, who sat on nineteen and fourteen commissions, respectively. The most active Academy members were the physicist Egon Schweidler (member of 29 commissions and two delegations), the chemist Ernst Späth (member of 23 commissions), the classical philologist Ludwig Radermacher (18), the historian Oswald Redlich (17), the philologist Paul Kretschmer (13), and the historian Alfons Dopsch (12). It is notable and yet hardly surprising,

[24] For details on Menghin see Urban (2010), *Urgeschichte*.

[25] See the unpublished evaluation of the annual accounts of the Academy of Sciences for the period 1938–45 by the economist Johanna Aigner, MS., in the framework of the research project "Continuity and Transformation. The Austrian Academy of Sciences in the 20th Century," run by the Institute of Culture Studies and Theatre History and funded by the city of Vienna (MA 7).

therefore, that in many of the Academy's commissions there was "an extensive continuity in the research work."[26] The strikingly active collaboration of older ordinary members who were likely as not critical of the interventions by the new authorities would appear to indicate that many of those who were familiar with the Academy's high-level of autonomy before 1938 were, through their research, investing in the interests of the Academy's self-assertion. By contrast, other Academy members who had already belonged to the Nazi Party when it was still illegal, sympathized with National Socialism, and/or as members of the Nazi Party had been elected as members of the Academy after the "Anschluss", were key figures in the opportunistic adaptation, self-mobilization and self-motivated involvement of the Academy through projects that suited Nazi interests.

Summary

The transformation of research policy under National Socialism was the result of two developments: the abandonment of the extensive autonomy enjoyed by the Academy since 1921/22 and, in conjunction with this, the passive acceptance of extensive interference by the new authorities that had not been allowed for in the Statutes. It is to be assumed that some of the older Academy members spoke up for keeping research and politics separate. Nevertheless, at the same time most of them opportunistically accepted considerable non-statutory political interference. By order of the new state authorities, "racially" or politically unacceptable institute directors were replaced by relatively young illegal Nazi Party members. On its own initiative, the Academy reorientated commissions along National Socialist lines and also entered into political alliances. As the following essay shows, under the "special protection of the Reich" and in accordance with the Provisional Statutes, between 1938 and 1945 the Academy carried out "science in the service of the German people."[27]

Johannes Feichtinger

---

[26] Matis (1997), *Anpassung*, p. 42.
[27] *Almanach* for 1938, 88 (1939), p. 9.

Science "in the service of the German people"

According to the Provisional Statutes approved by the decree of the Reich Minister for Science, Education, and Culture of 22 July 1938, the task of the Academy of Sciences in Vienna was "to promote science in the service of the German people through independent research by its members and through stimulating and supporting external achievements."[1] The Academy dedicated itself to this task by carrying out research projects with civilian or military relevance and through approving grants for research whose role it was to substantiate political beliefs. The self-mobilization and self-motivated involvement of parts of the Academy was illustrated in the initiative of carrying out research projects within the core area of the Nazi ideology (racial and ethnicity research) and the Nazi state (nuclear research). This went hand in hand with a focus on research relevant to the state instead of on the basic scientific research that had prevailed hitherto. Self-mobilization was frequently linked with the aim of earning new financial and symbolic resources. The examples cited here bear witness to this trend.

Nuclear research

At the Institute for Radium Research, the new director Gustav Ortner attempted "to adapt the Institute, which had originally been devoted solely to radium research, as quickly as possible to the larger range of tasks of a modern nuclear physics institute."[2] Because of the secret work, vital to the war effort, on energy generation from nuclear processes, the Institute, which was merged with parts of the Department of Physics II of the University of Vienna in 1943 to become the Four-Year Plan Institute for Neutron Research headed by Nazi Party members Georg Stetter and Gustav Ortner, was granted generous special funding. As early as 1940 the Academy had supported the Institute with a subsidy of RM 12,000 from the remaining Reich grants from the years 1939 and 1940 for the *design of a high-voltage discharge tube (generation of high-speed canal rays)*.[3] New findings, however, were published "from 1939 in a much reduced quantity," as Meister commented critically in 1947.[4]

---

[1] *Almanach* for 1938, 88 (1939), p. 9.

[2] ÖStA-AdR, K 19/6147A, Georg Stetter, application for transformation of the extraordinary professorship for physics (radium research) into a full professorship, undated [January 1943], quoted in Fengler (2012), *Wüstentrockenheit*, p. 101.

[3] AÖAW, Minutes of the General Assembly of 25 October 1940 (A 957), Annex.

[4] Meister (1947), *Geschichte*, p. 186.

Racial research

From the early 1940s the Academy also supported projects associated with the study of race, partly through grant-funded research and partly on its own initiative. At the request of director Hans Kummerlöwe, who was commissioned to direct the so called *Wissenschaftliche Staatsmuseen* [state research museums] in Vienna, Academy President Srbik arranged grants for an extensive series of studies by the Anthropology Department of the Museum of Natural History in the Kaisersteinbruch prisoner of war camp (Stalag XVII A) in northern Burgenland, the first prisoner of war camp in Austria.[5] The examinations carried out by the department head and illegal Nazi Party member Josef Wastl were financed by the Academy committee for the administration of the Treitl legacy. Srbik drafted the approval of Kummerlöwe's application on 18 July 1940, even before the letters from the committee members had been received by the Academy Chancellery. The letter was sent after receipt of the expert opinions of 22 July 1940: The ordinary members Oswald Redlich, Egon Schweidler, Paul Kretschmer, Josef Maria Eder, and Ferdinand Hochstetter had more or less willingly but unanimously agreed to pay for ten assistants and a large amount of material (including 100 dozen photographic plates, 120 rolls of film, 60 rolls of Agfa Color film), together with a *subsidy* for the staff of the Museum of Natural History.[6] Srbik, who was also a member of the Treitl committee, had informed the other members that Ferdinand Hochstetter, who was responsible for anthropological work, and Viktor Christian were in accord on this matter.[7] Financing was also provided for the ethnologist Martin Gusinde as an additional researcher. Before approval, Srbik pointed out to Kummerlöwe that it would be *of unique value* if the *bodies of Africans who had died in Kaisersteinbruch* could be transferred *to the Anatomical Institute of the University of Vienna for scientific study*, because there were *only very few studies of the differences between races regarding the internal organs*.[8] The provisional results of the "studies of Belgian and French prisoners of war" carried out from 7 July to 7 November 1940 "by order of the Academy"[9] with a view to obtaining "insights into the racial composition of the peoples of western Europe"[10] were published in 1941 in the *Anzeiger der Akademie*: "3,517 individuals" were measured (including "north Africans," "negroes," and "Jews") and 20,000 photographs were taken. The main finding

---

[5] See AÖAW, Subventionen, Box 11, No. 264/1940, Kummerlöwe to Srbik of 5 July 1940.

[6] AÖAW, Subventionen, Box 11, No. 264/1940, members of the Treitl committee to Srbik (and Academy Chancellery) of 17 July 1940 (Redlich, Schweidler), 20 July 1940 (Kretschmer), 18 July 1940 (Eder), and 19 July 1940 (Hochstetter).

[7] AÖAW, Papers of Egon Schweidler, Box 1, Srbik to members of the Treitl committee of 16 July 1940.

[8] AÖAW, Subventionen, Box 11, No. 264/1940, Srbik to Kummerlöwe of 9 July 1940.

[9] This terminology was chosen in later publications on the activities of the Anthropology Department, see Teschler-Nikola/Berner (1998), *Abteilung*, p. 335.

[10] Another series of measurements in the Wolfsberg prisoner of war camp (Stalag XVIII) of members of the British Army was prevented by captured officers of the Royal Army with reference to the Hague Convention. See Berner (2011), *Gegenstände*, pp. 161–2.

was "that both Nordic and Mediterranean migrants had exerted a strong racial influence on the original Gallo-Celtic population in historical times."[11] On behalf of the Academy, Srbik also supported Kummerlöwe's application to the *Oberkommando* [Supreme Command] *der Wehrmacht* (OKW) for an "official military commission for anthropological and racial studies of prisoners of war." The application was rejected by the *Oberkommando* in spite of the *unusually favorable opportunity* and *the plethora of material* bearing witness to the *Soviet ethnological and racial mix.*[12]

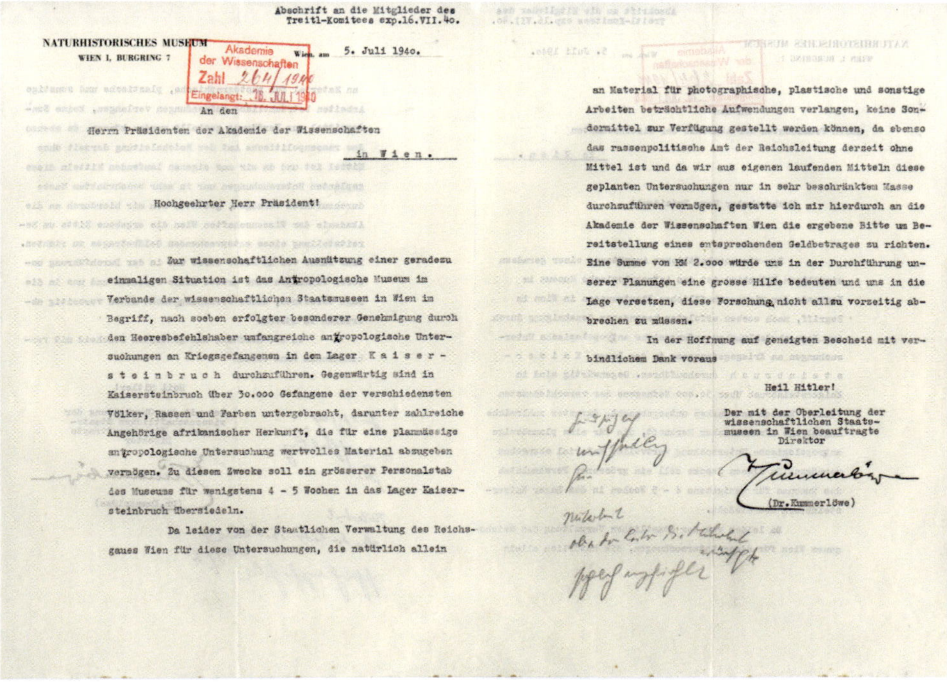

Abschrift an die Mitglieder des Treitl-Komitees exp.16.VII.4o.

NATURHISTORISCHES MUSEUM
WIEN I, BURGRING 7

Akademie der Wissenschaften
Zahl 264/1940
Eingelangt: 16. JULI 1940

Wien, am 5. Juli 194o.

An den
Herrn Präsidenten der Akademie der Wissenschaften
in Wien.

Hochgeehrter Herr Präsident!

Zur wissenschaftlichen Ausnützung einer geradezu einmaligen Situation ist das Antropologische Museum im Verbande der wissenschaftlichen Staatsmuseen in Wien im Begriff, nach soeben erfolgter besonderer Genehmigung durch den Heeresbefehlshaber umfangreiche antropologische Untersuchungen an Kriegsgefangenen in dem Lager Kaisersteinbruch durchzuführen. Gegenwärtig sind in Kaisersteinbruch über 3o.ooo Gefangene der verschiedensten Völker, Rassen und Farben untergebracht, darunter zahlreiche Angehörige afrikanischer Herkunft, die für eine planmässige antropologische Untersuchung wertvolles Material abzugeben vermögen. Zu diesem Zwecke soll ein grösserer Personalstab des Museums für wenigstens 4 - 5 Wochen in das Lager Kaisersteinbruch übersiedeln.

Da leider von der Staatlichen Verwaltung des Reichsgaues Wien für diese Untersuchungen, die natürlich allein an Material für photographische, plastische und sonstige Arbeiten beträchtliche Aufwendungen verlangen, keine Sondermittel zur Verfügung gestellt werden können, da ebenso das rassenpolitische Amt der Reichsleitung derzeit ohne Mittel ist und da wir aus eigenen laufenden Mitteln diese geplanten Untersuchungen nur in sehr beschränktem Masse durchzuführen vermögen, gestatte ich mir hierdurch an die Akademie der Wissenschaften Wien die ergebene Bitte um Bereitstellung eines entsprechenden Geldbetrages zu richten. Eine Summe von RM 2.ooo würde uns in der Durchführung unserer Planungen eine grosse Hilfe bedeuten und uns in die Lage versetzen, diese Forschung nicht allzu vorzeitig abbrechen zu müssen.

In der Hoffnung auf geneigten Bescheid mit verbindlichem Dank voraus

Heil Hitler!

Der mit der Oberleitung der wissenschaftlichen Staatsmuseen in Wien beauftragte Direktor

(Dr.Kummerlöwe)

Fig. 62: Application for subsidy by Hans Kummerlöwe of 5 July 1940

In 1942 the Academy started a special anthropological series on its own initiative at the *suggestion* of ordinary member Christian (now *SS-Hauptsturmführer*). For this purpose, a new Commission for the Publication of Writings on the Study of Race and Human Genetics was established consisting of ordinary members from both Sections, that is the Section for Mathematics and the Natural Sciences, and the Section for

[11] Wastl (1941), *Untersuchungen*. For the series of measurements, see Pawlowsky (2005), *Erweiterung*; Teschler-Nicola/Berner (1998), *Abteilung*, and Berner (2011), *Gegenstände*.

[12] AÖAW, Subventionen, Box 11, No. 264/1940, Kummerlöwe to Supreme Command of the *Wehrmacht* of 16 April 1941; ibid., Kummerlöwe to Srbik of 11 August 1941; Srbik to Supreme Command of the *Wehrmacht* of 21 August 1941, and Supreme Command of the *Wehrmacht* to Srbik of 10 September 1941.

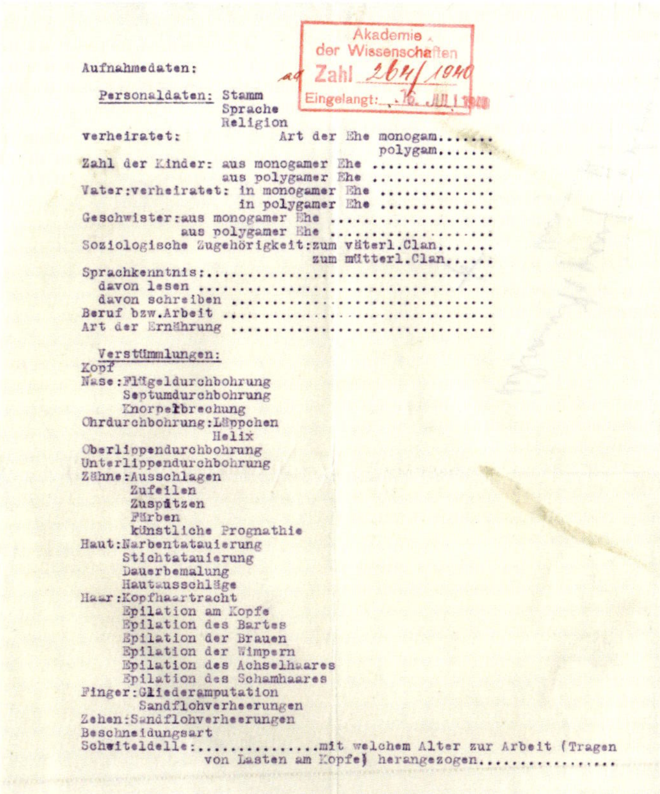

Akademie der Wissenschaften
ad Zahl 264/1940
Eingelangt: 16. JULI 1940

Aufnahmedaten:

Personaldaten: Stamm
Sprache
Religion

verheiratet: Art der Ehe monogam.......
polygam.......

Zahl der Kinder: aus monogamer Ehe ....
aus polygamer Ehe ....

Vater:verheiratet: in monogamer Ehe ....
in polygamer Ehe ....

Geschwister:aus monogamer Ehe ....
aus polygamer Ehe ....

Soziologische Zugehörigkeit:zum väterl.Clan.......
zum mütterl.Clan......

Sprachkenntnis:..................................
davon lesen ....
davon schreiben ....
Beruf bzw.Arbeit ....
Art der Ernährung ....

Verstümmlungen:
Kopf
Nase:Flügeldurchbohrung
Septumdurchbohrung
Knorpelbrechung
Ohrdurchbohrung:Läppchen
Helix
Oberlippendurchbohrung
Unterlippendurchbohrung
Zähne:Ausschlagen
Zufeilen
Zuspitzen
Färben
künstliche Prognathie
Haut:Narbentatauierung
Stichtatauierung
Dauerbemalung
Hautausschläge
Haar:Kopfhaartracht
Epilation am Kopfe
Epilation des Bartes
Epilation der Brauen
Epilation der Wimpern
Epilation des Achselhaares
Epilation des Schamhaares
Finger:Gliederamputation
Sandflohverheerungen
Zehen:Sandflohverheerungen
Beschneidungsart
Scheiteldelle:..............mit welchem Alter zur Arbeit (Tragen
von Lasten am Kopfe) herangezogen................

Fig. 63: "Registered data" form

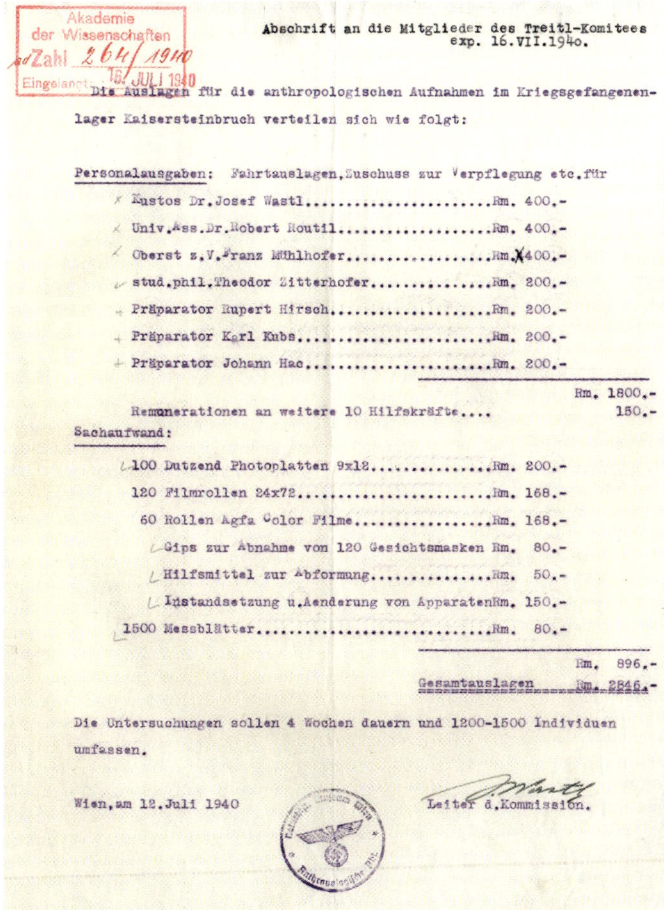

Akademie der Wissenschaften
ad Zahl 264/1940
Eingelangt: 16. JULI 1940

Abschrift an die Mitglieder des Treitl-Komitees
exp. 16.VII.1940.

Die Auslagen für die anthropologischen Aufnahmen im Kriegsgefangenenlager Kaisersteinbruch verteilen sich wie folgt:

Personalausgaben: Fahrtauslagen,Zuschuss zur Verpflegung etc.für

Kustos Dr.Josef Wastl........................	Rm. 400.-
Univ.Ass.Dr.Robert Routil....................	Rm. 400.-
Oberst z.V.Franz Mühlhofer...................	Rm. 400.-
stud.phil.Theodor Zitterhofer................	Rm. 200.-
Präparator Rupert Hirsch.....................	Rm. 200.-
Präparator Karl Kubs.........................	Rm. 200.-
Präparator Johann Hac........................	Rm. 200.-
	Rm. 1800.-
Remunerationen an weitere 10 Hilfskräfte....	150.-

Sachaufwand:

100 Dutzend Photoplatten 9x12................	Rm. 200.-
120 Filmrollen 24x72.........................	Rm. 168.-
60 Rollen Agfa Color Filme...................	Rm. 168.-
Gips zur Abnahme von 120 Gesichtsmasken	Rm. 80.-
Hilfsmittel zur Abformung....................	Rm. 50.-
Instandsetzung u.Aenderung von Apparaten	Rm. 150.-
1500 Messblätter.............................	Rm. 80.-
	Rm. 896.-
Gesamtauslagen	Rm. 2846.-

Die Untersuchungen sollen 4 Wochen dauern und 1200-1500 Individuen umfassen.

Wien,am 12.Juli 1940

Wastl
Leiter d.Kommission.

Fig. 64: Cost calculation

Humanities and the Social Sciences: physician Ferdinand Hochstetter, botanist Erich Tschermak-Seysenegg, biologist Fritz Knoll, physician Eduard Pernkopf, geographer Eugen Oberhummer, prehistorian Oswald Menghin, geographer Hugo Hassinger, and Viktor Christian. Christian and Hochstetter were made *responsible for publication.*[13] The commission worked "very scientifically," as Meister emphasized in 1947,[14] but not very productively, despite being well funded. In October 1940 the Section for Mathematics and the Natural Sciences had already approved a generous subsidy of RM 5,000 for the *publication of a special series on of studies on race from the German south-east.*[15] The only volume of the series *Untersuchungen zur Rassenkunde und menschlichen Erblehre* to be published was entitled *Familienanthropologische Untersuchungen in dem ostschwäbischen Dorfe Marienfeld im Rumänischen Banat* (1942). It was written by Robert Routil, a member of the Anthropology Department of the Museum of Natural History, who had previously taken part in the measurement of detained Jewish men in the Vienna stadium in the Prater, most of whom were subsequently transported to Buchenwald. Routil had also been involved in the measurements at the Kaisersteinbruch and Wolfsberg prisoner of war camps.[16] Family anthropology studies were seen as useful for determining the extent to which the character of an ethnic minority, the "characteristics of a guest nation," was determined biologically, i.e. "through a racial composition differing from the host nation."[17] The Commission for the Publication of Writings on the Study of Race and Human Genetics was dissolved at the first ordinary General Assembly on 22 June 1945. A work by the physiologist of race and fervent Nazi Robert Stigler, originally intended for the series, was published in 1952 in collaboration with full member Eduard Pernkopf under the title *Rassenphysiologische Ergebnisse meiner Forschungsreise in Uganda 1911/12* [Physiological Findings concerning Race from my Uganda Expedition 1911/12] in the series of *Denkschriften* [Proceedings] of the Section for Mathematics and the Natural Sciences (vol. 109,3).[18]

Ethnicity research

The self-mobilization of the Academy could also be observed with regard to the Phonogram Archive, not only in terms of rhetoric – as discussed above – but also of action. An initiative concerning studies in prisoner of war camps makes this

13 AÖAW, Minutes of the General Assembly of 6 February 1942 (A 968). On the activities of this Committee, see Matis (1997), *Anpassung*, pp. 44–5.

14 Meister (1947), *Geschichte*, p. 182.

15 AÖAW, Minutes of the General Assembly of 25 October 1940 (A 957), Annex.

16 See Pawlowsky (2005), *Erweiterung*, pp. 74–9.

17 Geyer (1934), *Anthropologie*, pp. 325–6. Because of the "family structure of such minorities," biometric family anthropology studies promised to provide new findings in connection with this politically relevant objective.

18 AÖAW, Minutes of the meeting of the Section for Mathematics and the Natural Sciences of 11 January 1951 (B 2761).

self-mobilization manifest. The first such initiative was undertaken by the designated archive director Walter Ruth in 1939, the second by the designated deputy chairman of the Phonogram Archive Commission, ordinary member Friedrich Wild, in July 1940, albeit in vain, as was to transpire following protracted negotiations. In the same year, three ordinary members who were or were to become members of the Nazi Party were co-opted into the Phonogram Archive Commission, namely physicist Heinrich Mache, Germanist Dietrich Kralik-Meyrswalden, and Anglicist Friedrich Wild. In 1940 further Nazis, engineer Franz Aigner and Germanist Anton Pfalz, were elected. The long-standing commission chairman Arnold Durig, a "Catholic conservative" considered to be sympathetic to the authoritarian *Ständesstaat* [Corporate State],[19] had offered to resign in April 1938. On 26 April 1940 he applied on the grounds of permanent absence for ordinary member Friedrich Wild to be designated as deputy chairman. Wild was appointed chairman on 7 March 1941,[20] and Ruth was given Leo Hajek's former title "head of the Phonogram Archive" on 25 October 1940. He was definitively appointed head of the archive on 28 November 1941, directly after he had completed his habilitation.

Fig. 65: Walter Ruth

Fig. 66: Friedrich Wild

[19] Soukup (2004), *Durig*, p. 130.

[20] For details of Friedrich Wild, see Pils (2010), *Gelehrter*, pp. 471–85.

Wild and Ruth had urged Academy President Srbik on several occasions since 1939 to apply to the Berlin Supreme Command of the *Wehrmacht* regarding *recordings of speech and singing of different peoples and tribes of the French and British empires, including natives* and of *speech and singing of Polish prisoners of war* in the camps of the *"Ostmark"*.[21] Srbik's applications were rejected[22] because the *Institut für Lautforschung* [Institute of Sound Research] in Berlin had already been authorized to make recordings in prisoner of war camps and *double visits* were to be avoided.[23] The argument that the Archive, on account of the *extensive recordings taken in the* [First] *World War in prisoner of war camps had a good deal of experience in this area*[24] and that *only in wartime did the rare opportunity* present itself again *of making modern electrical recordings of folksongs and dialects of Polish, Ukrainian, and Belarusian prisoners in the prisoner of war camps* was not accepted.[25]

The scientific work initiated and carried out by the Phonogram Archive between 1938 and 1945 included recordings of the most valuable church bells in Austria (1941/42), which were to be melted down to help the wartime economy, speech recordings of South Tyroleans who had resettled in the Reich (1940), and recordings of dialects of Bessarabian and Dobruja Germans resettling in various *Gaue* [highest regional and organizational units of the Nazi Party] of the *"Ostmark"* (1941).[26] The latter enterprise was awarded a subsidy on Srbik's request from the *Vereinigte Grenzlandämter der Gaue Wien und Nieder-Donau* [Unified Offices of the *Gaue* Vienna and Lower Danube].[27] The Phonogram Archive had the latest technology and in, 1940, the Section for Humanities and the Social Sciences approved RM 4,300 for the purchase of a cathode-ray oscillograph.[28] The Phonogram Archive also supported "research […] in the service of Nazi education into pathological speech and its therapy through recordings and examinations."[29] The increase in *tasks resulting from*

[21] AÖAW, Phonogrammarchiv, Box 1, Folder 4, Srbik to Supreme Command of the *Wehrmacht* of 18 July 1940, and ibid., Srbik to Supreme Command of the *Wehrmacht* of 19 December 1940.

[22] See AÖAW, Phonogrammarchiv, Box 1, Folder 4, Supreme Command of the *Wehrmacht* to Academy of Sciences in Vienna of 8 August 1940.

[23] See AÖAW, Phonogrammarchiv, Box 1, Folder 4, Institute for Sound Research of the University of Berlin to Academy of Sciences in Vienna of 7 February 1941.

[24] AÖAW, Phonogrammarchiv, Box 1, Folder 4, Srbik to Supreme Command of the *Wehrmacht* of 19 December 1940; see Lange (2010), *Forschungen*.

[25] See AÖAW, Phonogrammarchiv, Box 1, Folder 4, Ruth to the Ministry of Interior and Cultural Affairs of 3 October 1939.

[26] AÖAW, Phonogrammarchiv, Box 1, Folder 4, activity report of the Phonogram Archive for 1941 of 25 March 1942.

[27] AÖAW, Phonogrammarchiv, Box 1, Folder 4, Minutes of the meeting of the Phonogram Archive Commission of 25 October 1940.

[28] AÖAW, Minutes of the General Assembly of 25 October 1940 (A 957), Annex.

[29] Ruth (1941), *Phonogrammarchiv*, pp. 90–1.

the war[30] and several interventions by members of the Academy's Presiding Committee in the *Wehrmeldeamt* [Military Recruiting Office] did not protect Walter Ruth from being drafted in 1942. After captivity, denazification, and pardon by the Federal President, Ruth resumed his leading position in the Phonogram Archive on 1 October 1948 as an employee of the federal government. Wild was officially listed in the *Almanach* for 1949 as chairman of the Phonogram Archive Commission again following the application approved by the Federal President for exemption from atonement.[31] In 1954 Wild provided a detailed report of the *current activity* of the Phonogram Archive. The research program had barely changed and the continuity in terms of personnel and content were evident. The dialect recordings, which *on account of the content and technical quality* were to provide the basis for further activities of this nature, were the recordings of the South Tyrolean dialects by Josef Schatz, the German dialects of Bessarabia by Anton Pfalz, the dialects of Carinthia, East Tyrol, Upper Austria, and Burgenland by Eberhard Kranzmayer, and those of Styria by Leo Jutz. Schatz, Pfalz, and Kranzmayer had contributed *to the systematic definition of all Austrian dialects* during the Nazi era.[32]

South-eastern research

The Academy profited from the boom in south-eastern research and, during the Nazi era, Vienna increasingly established itself as its center. It focused on applied research so that, as the Viennese cultural geographer Hugo Hassinger wrote in 1942, *science will never again be too late when it comes to political actions.*[33] Vienna was the location of various institutes devoted to south-eastern research. At the Academy, it was carried out by the Balkan Commission, renamed in 1940, divided after 1942 into three departments (linguistic, antiquarian, and scientific) and after 1943 into two departments (humanities and science) under the new name the South-Eastern Commission.[34] The Balkan Commission replaced the Commission for Historical, Archeological, and Philological Ethnographic Research into the Balkan Peninsula established in 1897. The suggestion of establishing a south-eastern institute in the Academy, which, according to the minutes of the Academy meeting, had come from the Office of the *Reichsstatthalter* [Reich Governor], was not taken up by the Section for Humanities and the Social Sciences, but instead the Balkan Commission was upgraded in 1940

---

30 AÖAW, Phonogrammarchiv, Box 1, Folder 4, activity report of the Phonogram Archive for 1941 of 25 March 1942.

31 See AÖAW, PA Walter Ruth, and PA Friedrich Wild; *Almanach* for 1949, 99 (1950), p. 121.

32 AÖAW, Phonogrammarchiv, Box 1, Folder 5, Wild to Presiding Committee of the Academy of Sciences of 16 March 1954. For the activities of Anton Pfalz and Eberhard Kranzmayer during the Nazi era, see Wahlmüller (2010), *Akademie*, pp. 94–9, and Ranzmaier (2010), *Germanistik*.

33 UAW, Papers of Hugo Hassinger, 131.01, Hassinger to Triska of 7 May 1942.

34 Stadtmüller (1942), *Balkankommission*.

to become an intersectional institution.[35] Six of its seventeen members were also members of the Nazi Party. For one of the most highly funded commissions, the scientific output was minimal and at first glance politically harmless. It is to be assumed that the preparations for the Nazi *"Umvolkung"* ["ethnic cleansing"] policy in south-eastern Europe were not carried out at the Academy. The Balkan and South-Eastern Commission were merely part of the south-eastern research complex in Vienna, in which ordinary members Heinrich Srbik, Hugo Hassinger, and Viktor Christian pulled the strings. In 1942 Christian was appointed delegate of the Academy of Sciences in the *Südostgemeinschaft der Wiener Hochschulen (Südosteuropagesellschaft)* [South-Eastern Society of the Vienna Universities (South-Eastern Europe Society)].[36] According to a memorandum by Christian, Srbik was to chair a committee in the *Südosteuropäisches Forschungsinstitut* [South-Eastern Europe Research Institute] planned by Rosenberg's office, whose task it would be *to provide expert opinions on scientific undertakings in south-eastern Europe and to present them to the Reich ministries concerned.*[37] This plan was canceled along with the South-Eastern Europe Research Institute; in Vienna the *Südosteuropagesellschaft*, a *Südostgemeinschaft Wiener Hochschulen* [South-Eastern Community of Vienna Universities], the *Arbeitsgemeinschaft für Raumforschung* [Working Group for Spatial Research], and the *Südostdeutsche Forschungsgemeinschaft* [South-East German Research Council] (SODFG) were active in this area. The main aim of these organizations was the scientific preparation for *"Umvolkung."*[38] The SODFG in particular was involved in Nazi "ethnicity and extermination policy."[39] Ordinary members of the Academy, including historians Hans Hirsch and Otto Brunner, geographer Fritz Machatschek, and the above-mentioned Hugo Hassinger, had leading positions in it.[40] In 1945 all of these organizations were disbanded. The South-East Commission at the Academy was incorporated into the Section for Humanities and the Social Sciences (1948) and renamed the Balkan Commission in 1950. Hugo Hassinger, who had never been a member of the Nazi Party but had carried out ethnicity research in its interests and saw "Vienna's German mission" in the "gradual" shifting of "the cultural divide between West and East" further eastwards[41] was able to continue his research activities without interruption. In 1946 he founded the Commission for Spatial Research and Reconstruction. The following year, on the application of full member Richard Meister, an Austrian Research Community for the South-East and the Orient was established at the

[35] See AÖAW, Minutes of the meeting of the Section for Humanities and the Social Sciences of 27 April 1938 (C 2579).

[36] *Almanach* for 1942, 92 (1942), p. 97.

[37] BAB, BDC, PA Viktor Christian, sheets 137–8, 141–2.

[38] See Beer/Seewann (2004), *Südostforschung*.

[39] Fahlbusch (2000), *Forschungsgemeinschaft*, p. 260.

[40] See Svatek (2010), *Hassinger*, and Svatek (2010), *Wien*.

[41] Hassinger (1942), *Sendung*, and Hassinger (1941), *Lebensraumfragen*.

Austrian Academy of Sciences under Hassinger's chairmanship, which was disbanded in 1950 by order of the occupying powers.[42]

Summary

Various attitudes and actions can be discerned at the Academy of Sciences in Vienna between 1938 and 1945. Most of the research activities were oriented towards opportunistic adaptation, self-mobilization, and self-motivated involvement, as has been examined in this essay. Examples included nuclear research, race research, ethnicity research, and south-eastern research, with a shift from basic to applied research. The self-mobilizing and often young researchers at the Academy thus made use of opportunities to obtain additional financial and symbolic resources through research activities aimed at substantiating political beliefs, no doubt in the hope of climbing the career ladder this way.

Johannes Feichtinger

---

[42] *Die Furche*, 2 July 1950, p. 4.

I. 4. National and International Interconnections

The "national honor" of German Academies

The Vienna Academy caught between national and international academic cooperations

Academies of sciences tend to have a cosmopolitan understanding of science and are not bound by national borders. They cooperate in the widest variety of research projects based on an "international peaceful order."[1] The Cartel of German Academies and Scholarly Societies founded in 1893, to which the Imperial Academy of Sciences in Vienna and the academies of the German Reich belonged, espoused this understanding of science.[2] In 1899, the Cartel participated in the founding of the International Association of Academies (IAA), in which 31 scientific institutions were connected on an interdisciplinary and international basis. The IAA, in which both natural sciences and humanities were represented, was active till the beginning of World War I and "never formally disbanded."[3]

After 1918 an attempt was made to re-establish contact with the international network of academies that had been destroyed in the war. The International Research Council/Conseil International de Recherches (IRC/CIR) for natural sciences and the International Union of Academies/Union Académique International (UAI) for humanities and social sciences were founded at a congress in Brussels on 18 to 28 July 1919 as successors to the IAA.[4] The UAI statutes, unlike those of the IRC, had no exclusion provisions for the former Central Powers, i.e. Germany and its allies during the war.[5] In 1922 and in 1923, the UAI, through the Dutch Academy, approached the Vienna Academy to join the Union and act as a link to the academies in the German Reich. The Vienna Academy did not want to take steps towards joining international organizations without the agreement of the German academies and declined the offer.[6] In a letter of refusal to the Dutch Academy of 23 October 1923, the Acad-

---

[1] Mommsen (2000), *Wissenschaft*, p. 3.

[2] Meister (1947), *Geschichte*, p. 127, and recently Wöckinger (2010), *Akademie*.

[3] Grau (1995), *Wissenschaftsakademien*, pp. 31–2.

[4] See Grau (2000), *Preussische Akademie*, p. 293.

[5] See Grau (2000), *Preussische Akademie*, p. 298.

[6] See Grau (1995), *Wissenschaftsakademien*, p. 35.

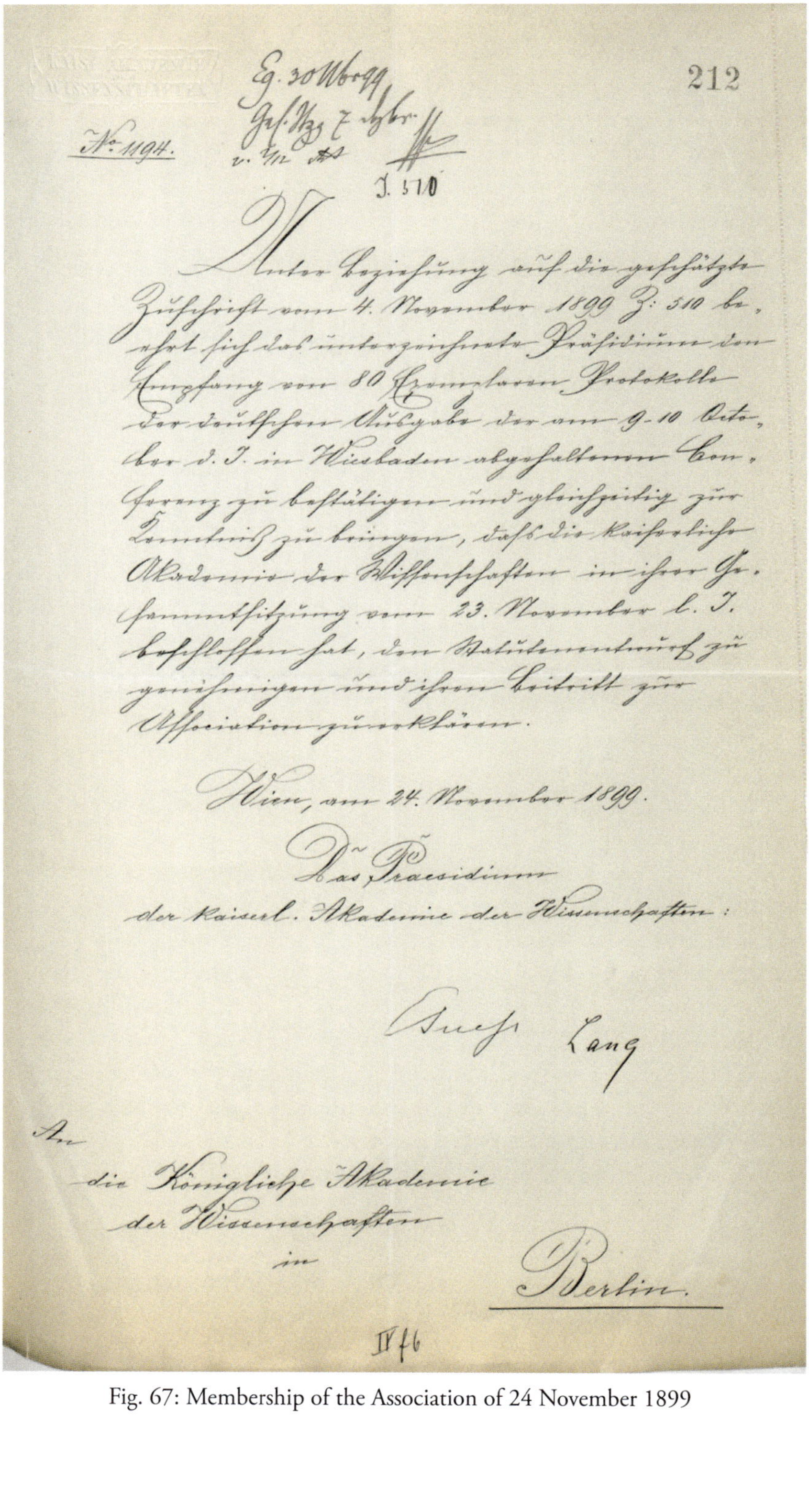

212

№ 1194.

J. 510

Unter Beziehung auf die geschätzte Zuschrift vom 4. November 1899 Z: 510 beehrt sich das unterzeichnete Präsidium den Empfang von 80 Exemplaren Protokolle der deutschen Ausgabe der am 9.-10. October d. J. in Wiesbaden abgehaltenen Conferenz zu bestätigen und gleichzeitig zur Kenntniß zu bringen, daß die Kaiserliche Akademie der Wissenschaften in ihrer Gesammtsitzung vom 23. November l. J. beschlossen hat, den Statutenentwurf zu genehmigen und ihren Beitritt zur Association zu erklären.

Wien, am 24. November 1899.

Das Praesidium
der kaiserl. Akademie der Wissenschaften:

Suess Lang

An
die Königliche Akademie
der Wissenschaften
in
Berlin.

IV f6

Fig. 67: Membership of the Association of 24 November 1899

emy in Vienna referred to the occupation of the Ruhr by France which made it *hardly possible at present that German and French scholars would sit together at the meeting table. Given this lack of prospects of being able to canvas successfully for the entry of our Reich German colleagues in the Union Académique International, the main reason that the Vienna Academy might have considered for distancing itself temporarily from the German academies for tactical reasons also no longer exists.*[7]

When the Cartel joined the UAI in 1935, Redlich expected that all problems *irreconcilable with the national honor of the academies in the Cartel*, would now be solved and that *international cooperation would be possible* [...] *forever.*[8] The philologist Ludwig Radermacher and the historian Heinrich Srbik, who had been Secretary of the Section for Humanities and the Social Sciences since 1933, were elected as delegates to the UAI.[9] However, only Radermacher attended the UAI conferences in Brussels in 1936[10] and in London[11] in 1937.[12]

With the "Anschluss" of Austria to the German Reich in March 1938, the Vienna Academy received letters and telegrams of congratulation from the German academies. Paragraph 1 of the new Provisional Statutes set the task of promoting *science in the service of the German people.*[13] To demonstrate *to the world the absolute unity of German science*,[14] the Academy of Sciences in Vienna joined the *Deutsche Forschungsgemeinschaft* [German Research Foundation] (DFG) in October 1938.[15]

In view of Austria's entry into the Greater German Reich, Srbik and Radermacher resigned their mandates with the UAI.[16] To ensure that the Cartel of German Academies was *duly represented* at the congress in London from 8 to 11 May 1939, Bernhard Rust, Reich Minister of Science, Education, and Culture, selected Johannes Stroux, Prussian Academy of Sciences, and Srbik, Academy of Sciences in Vienna, as representatives of the German Reich.[17] Both attended the UAI congress in London in 1939. Although the working language of the UAI was French, and the representatives of Great Britain and Italy also communicated in that language, Stroux and Srbik submitted a request that German be admitted as an official language in the conviction

[7] Quoted in Grau (1995), *Wissenschaftsakademien*, p. 35.

[8] AÖAW, UAI, 1/A, No. 312/1935, Redlich to the Federal Ministry of Education in Vienna of 1 June 1935.

[9] AÖAW, UAI, 1/A, No. 433/1935, Redlich to Pelseneer of 18 December 1935.

[10] AÖAW, UAI, 1/B, No. 209/1936, Srbik to the Federal Chancellery, Directorate General for Public Safety, of 12 May 1936.

[11] AÖAW, UAI, 1/B, No. 41/1937, Srbik to the UAI Secretary of 27 January 1937.

[12] AÖAW, UAI, 1/B, No. 8/1938, Srbik to the UAI Secretary of 3 March 1938.

[13] Provisional Statutes of the Academy of Sciences in Vienna, in: *Almanach* for 1938, 88 (1939), p. 9.

[14] AÖAW, Allgemeine Akten, No. 363/1938, President of the DFG to the President of the Vienna Academy of Sciences of 30 September 1938.

[15] AÖAW, Allgemeine Akten, No. 363/1938, Srbik to Mentzel of 13 October 1938.

[16] AÖAW, UAI, 1/B, No. 176/1938, Srbik to UAI of 7 May 1938.

[17] AÖAW, UAI, 1/B, No. 184/1939, Rust to Srbik of 3 April 1939.

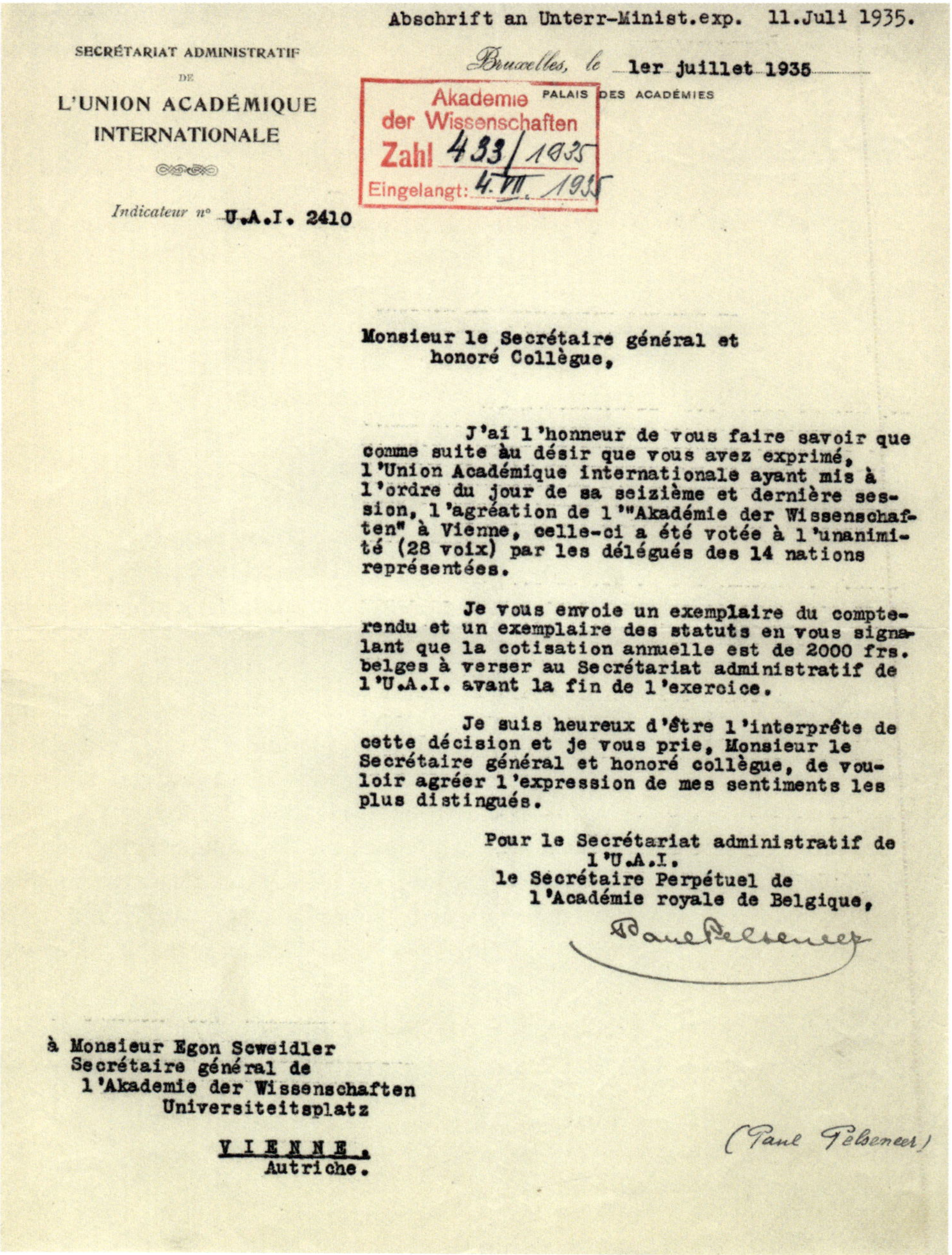

Abschrift an Unterr-Minist.exp. 11.Juli 1935.

SECRÉTARIAT ADMINISTRATIF
DE
L'UNION ACADÉMIQUE
INTERNATIONALE

Bruxelles, le 1er juillet 1935
PALAIS DES ACADÉMIES

Akademie der Wissenschaften
Zahl 433/1935
Eingelangt: 4.VII.1935

Indicateur n° U.A.I. 2410

Monsieur le Secrétaire général et
honoré Collègue,

J'ai l'honneur de vous faire savoir que comme suite au désir que vous avez exprimé, l'Union Académique internationale ayant mis à l'ordre du jour de sa seizième et dernière session, l'agréation de l'"Akadémie der Wissenschaften" à Vienne, celle-ci a été votée à l'unanimité (28 voix) par les délégués des 14 nations représentées.

Je vous envoie un exemplaire du compte-rendu et un exemplaire des statuts en vous signalant que la cotisation annuelle est de 2000 frs. belges à verser au Secrétariat administratif de l'U.A.I. avant la fin de l'exercice.

Je suis heureux d'être l'interprête de cette décision et je vous prie, Monsieur le Secrétaire général et honoré collègue, de vouloir agréer l'expression de mes sentiments les plus distingués.

Pour le Secrétariat administratif de
l'U.A.I.
le Secrétaire Perpétuel de
l'Académie royale de Belgique,

Paul Pelseneer

à Monsieur Egon Scweidler
Secrétaire général de
l'Akademie der Wissenschaften
Universiteitsplatz

VIENNE.
Autriche.

(Paul Pelseneer)

Fig. 68: Letter from the UAI of 1 July 1935

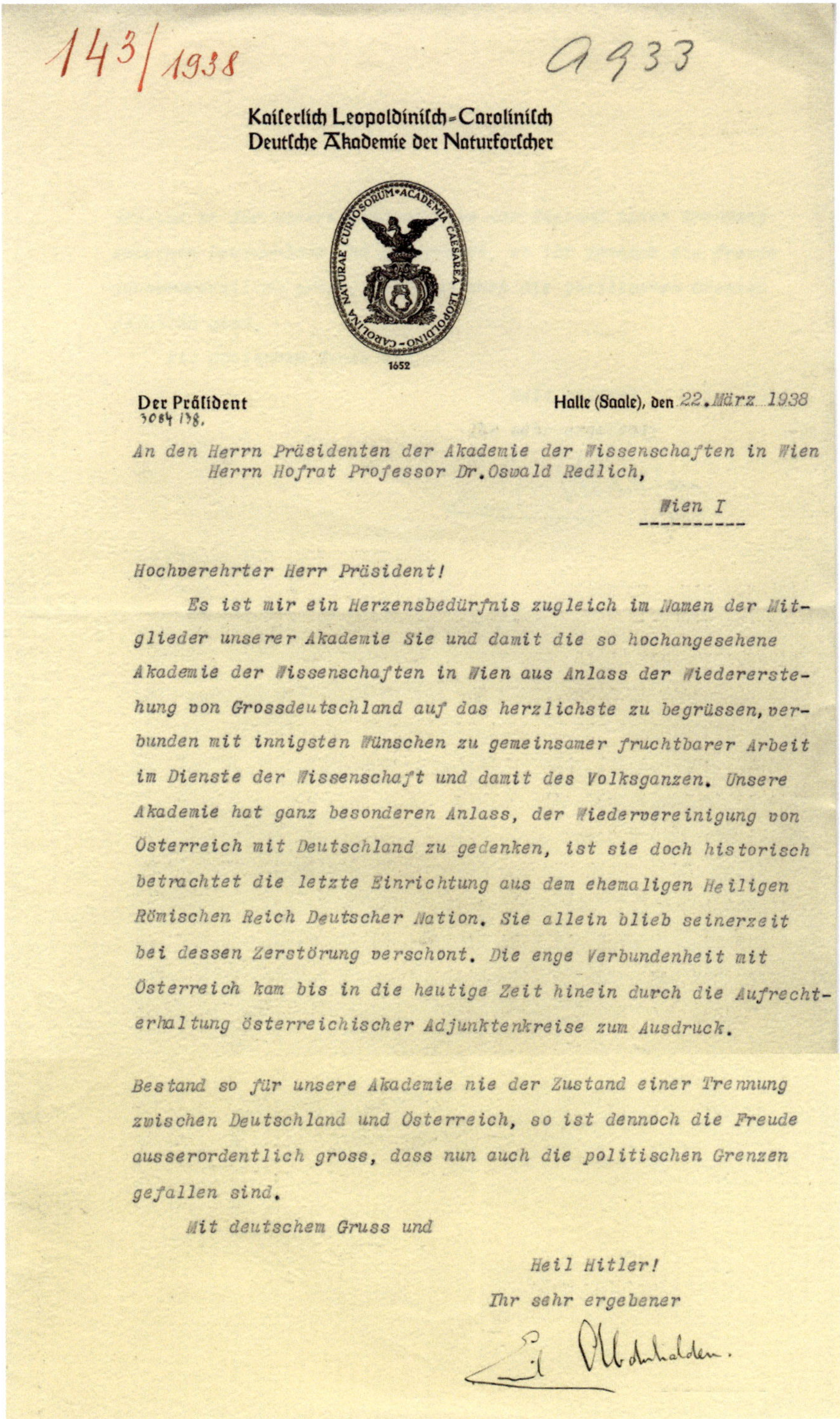

143/1938 a 933

Kaiserlich Leopoldinisch-Carolinisch
Deutsche Akademie der Naturforscher

CAROLINA NATURAE CURIOSORUM ACADEMIA CAESAREA LEOPOLDINO
1652

Der Präsident
3084 138.

Halle (Saale), den 22. März 1938

An den Herrn Präsidenten der Akademie der Wissenschaften in Wien
Herrn Hofrat Professor Dr. Oswald Redlich,
Wien I

Hochverehrter Herr Präsident!

Es ist mir ein Herzensbedürfnis zugleich im Namen der Mitglieder unserer Akademie Sie und damit die so hochangesehene Akademie der Wissenschaften in Wien aus Anlass der Wiedererstehung von Grossdeutschland auf das herzlichste zu begrüssen, verbunden mit innigsten Wünschen zu gemeinsamer fruchtbarer Arbeit im Dienste der Wissenschaft und damit des Volksganzen. Unsere Akademie hat ganz besonderen Anlass, der Wiedervereinigung von Österreich mit Deutschland zu gedenken, ist sie doch historisch betrachtet die letzte Einrichtung aus dem ehemaligen Heiligen Römischen Reich Deutscher Nation. Sie allein blieb seinerzeit bei dessen Zerstörung verschont. Die enge Verbundenheit mit Österreich kam bis in die heutige Zeit hinein durch die Aufrechterhaltung österreichischer Adjunktenkreise zum Ausdruck.

Bestand so für unsere Akademie nie der Zustand einer Trennung zwischen Deutschland und Österreich, so ist dennoch die Freude ausserordentlich gross, dass nun auch die politischen Grenzen gefallen sind.

Mit deutschem Gruss und

Heil Hitler!
Ihr sehr ergebener
E. Abderhalden.

Fig. 69: Welcome letter from Halle of 22 March 1938

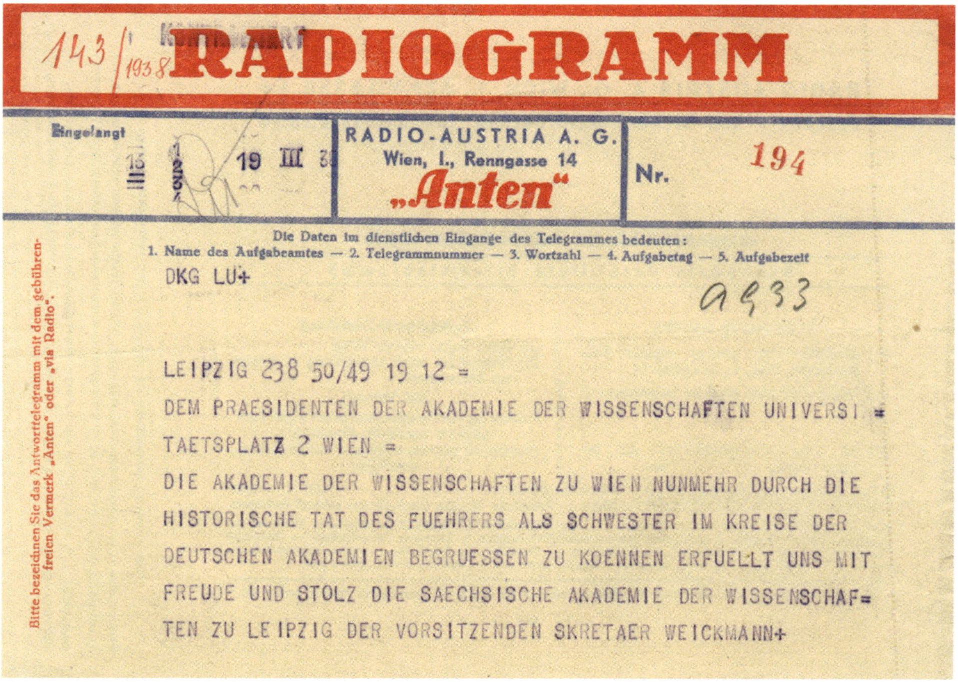
RADIOGRAMM

Eingelangt

RADIO-AUSTRIA A. G.
Wien, I., Renngasse 14
„Anten"

Nr. 194

Die Daten im dienstlichen Eingange des Telegrammes bedeuten:
1. Name des Aufgabeamtes — 2. Telegrammnummer — 3. Wortzahl — 4. Aufgabetag — 5. Aufgabezeit

Bitte bezeichnen Sie das Antworttelegramm mit dem gebührenfreien Vermerk „Anten" oder „via Radio".

DKG LU+

LEIPZIG 238 50/49 19 12 =
DEM PRAESIDENTEN DER AKADEMIE DER WISSENSCHAFTEN UNIVERSI =
TAETSPLATZ 2 WIEN =
DIE AKADEMIE DER WISSENSCHAFTEN ZU WIEN NUNMEHR DURCH DIE
HISTORISCHE TAT DES FUEHRERS ALS SCHWESTER IM KREISE DER
DEUTSCHEN AKADEMIEN BEGRUESSEN ZU KOENNEN ERFUELLT UNS MIT
FREUDE UND STOLZ DIE SAECHSISCHE AKADEMIE DER WISSENSCHAF=
TEN ZU LEIPZIG DER VORSITZENDEN SKRETAER WEICKMANN+

Fig. 70: Welcome telegram from Leipzig of 19 March 1938

that in doing so, they would be helping that language *gain basic recognition.*[18] Stroux and Srbik also reported that *during the entire congress there was no political dissonance among the delegates and that on the contrary, the wish for neutral and open collaboration was felt.*[19]

After the outbreak of war, international correspondence with "enemy" states was greatly reduced. The Société Mathématique in Amsterdam[20] and University College in London[21] still corresponded with the Vienna Academy in 1939, but correspondence with the Agricultural Experiment Station in Rehovot, Palestine,[22] was discontinued. When the director of a Dutch laboratory of phytophysiology ceased correspond-

[18] AÖAW, UAI, 1/B, No. 184/1939, report by Srbik and Stroux on the 20th Congress of the UAI, 8–11 May 1939, of 22 April 1939, pp. 1–2.

[19] Ibid., p. 7.

[20] See AÖAW, Protokollbuch 1939, No. 83, correspondence of the Société Mathématique in Amsterdam with the Academy of Sciences in Vienna of 8 February 1939.

[21] See AÖAW, Protokollbuch 1939, No. 85, correspondence of University College in London with the Academy of Sciences in Vienna of 8 February 1939.

[22] See AÖAW, Allgemeine Akten, No. 86/1939, correspondence of the Agricultural Experiment Station in Rehovot, Palestine, with the Academy of Sciences in Vienna of 10 February 1939.

Union Académique Internationale.

His Majesty's Government in the United Kingdom of Great Britain and Northern Ireland request the honour of the company of Professor Dr. and Frau Professor von Srbik at Dinner at Claridge's Hotel, on Wednesday, the 10th May, 1939, at 8.15 for 8.30 p.m. The Earl De La Warr, President of the Board of Education, will preside.

Evening Dress.
Decorations.
Ballroom Entrance, Brook Street.

An early answer is requested to The Secretary, Government Hospitality, Treasury Chambers, Whitehall, S.W.1. Telephone: Whitehall 1481.

Fig. 71: Invitation to UAI reception in London of 10 May 1939

ing in 1939 with German universities because of the exclusion of Jewish students,[23] Reich Minister Rust gave to understand that the German Reich attached *no value* [...] *to continuing relations with these anti-German circles.*[24] Rust forbade German anthropologists from taking part in the Congress for Anthropology and Prehistoric Archeology in Istanbul in 1939 because the organizer, the Paris Institute of Anthropology, had *a hostile attitude to the German Reich.*[25] By contrast, *cultural relations* were intensified with states like Finland. In January 1939, politically "unencumbered" Finnish scientists were invited by Reich Minister Rust to give lectures in the German Reich.[26] After 1940, visits abroad by German scientists were strictly controlled. The

[23] See AÖAW, Protokollbuch 1939, No. 159, Botanic Institute of the University of Technology, Vienna, to Blaauw, head of the Laboratorium voor Plantenphysilogisch Onderzoek Landbouwhoogeschool, Wageningen, forwarded to the Ministry of Interior and Cultural Affairs, and then to the Academy of Sciences in Vienna, of 6 March 1939.

[24] AÖAW, Protokollbuch 1939, No. 159, Rust to rectors and administrative offices of German universities and educational administrations including Austria of 14 February 1939.

[25] AÖAW, Allgemeine Akten, No. 116/1939, Rust to all academic institutions in the German Reich and administrative offices of 26 January 1939.

[26] See AÖAW, Allgemeine Akten, No. 104/1939, Rust to all academic institutions in the German Reich and all administrative offices of 18 January 1939.

Fig. 72: Reich Minister Bernhard Rust

heads of scientific institutions had to provide a detailed report on the *scientific and social suitability of the applicant.*[27]

For the Vienna Academy, as Herbert Matis has noted, the "coercive breaking of contacts with other countries" was probably the "most serious obstacle to the international exchange of knowledge."[28] When the Academy was reorganized after the Nazi regime had come to an end, the revival of contacts with the international scientific community[29] was seen as one of the most important aims.

Felicitas Seebacher

[27] AÖAW, Allgemeine Akten, No. 276/1940, Rust to Srbik of 18 July 1940.

[28] Matis (1997), *Anpassung*, p. 50.

[29] See the essay in this volume by Heidemarie Uhl, "Centennial anniversary of the Academy of Sciences 1947," pp. 191–9.

"Increase the achievements of German science by all available means"

The National Socialist Project of the Reich Academy of German Sciences

The National Socialist regime also tried to subjugate all Academies of Sciences to the "Führer principle." An important step was the centralization of the Cartel of German Academies, to which the academies of Göttingen, Leipzig, Munich, Berlin, Heidelberg, and Vienna all belonged. Hitherto the seat of the leading academy, the *"Vorort"* [lead site], as it was called, had changed annually. In May 1939 the Prussian Academy of Sciences in Berlin was made the *permanent lead site and administrative headquarters of the Cartel of German Academies.*[1] At the last meeting of the Cartel on 7 to 8 July 1939 in Leipzig, the statutes of the Reich Association of German Academies were drafted. In August 1939 the minutes of the Academy of Sciences in Vienna already had *Reich Association* in parenthesis after *Cartel.*[2] On 21 August 1940 the new Statutes of the Reich Association were approved by Rust[3] and, in this way, the Cartel was officially replaced by the Reich Association of German Academies.

A further change in the relationship of the Vienna Academy to the Berlin headquarters occurred in the same year. Like the Austrian universities, the Academy was subordinated to the Reich Ministry of Science, Education, and Culture in Berlin on 1 February 1940.[4] Academy President Srbik wrote in a letter to Minister Rust of the *great satisfaction* at this step and gave an assurance that the Academy would *meet its commitments in the most conscientious manner.*[5] He wrote to Rudolf Mentzel, head of the Ministry's Science Department, welcoming the *closer connection* henceforth.[6] The German Society of Sciences and Arts in Prague was incorporated into the Reich Association in the same year.[7]

---

1 See AÖAW, Protokollbuch 1939, No. 262, Rust to Srbik of 22 May 1939.

2 AÖAW, Protokollbuch 1939, No. 373, report of the Cartel (Reich Association of German Academies) on the Cartel meeting in Leipzig on 7–8 July 1939 of 24 August 1939.

3 Statute of the Reich Association of German Academies of Sciences, in *Almanach* for 1941, 91 (1941), p. 160.

4 See 6th Regulation on the Transfer of Tasks and Authority of the *Reichsstatthalter* [Reich Governor] in Austria (Austrian regional government) of 11 January 1940 (= Reichsgesetzblatt, Part 1, No. 9), § 7. See Bergmann-Pfleger (2010), *Geschichte*, p. 27. The final liquidation of the Ministry of Education in Vienna took place with effect from 6 November 1940.

5 AÖAW, Allgemeine Akten, No. 30/1940, Rust to Srbik of 2 February 1940.

6 AÖAW, Allgemeine Akten, No. 30/1940, Srbik to Mentzel of 10 February 1940.

7 See AÖAW, Protokollbuch 1940, No. 382, Rust to Srbik on 12 November 1940.

Fig. 73: Karl Theodor Vahlen

Behind this loss of autonomy for the German Academies was Karl Theodor Vahlen (1869–1945), a proponent of anti-Semitic "German" mathematics[8] and a fervent Nazi who had held various positions in the Nazi Party since the 1920s. In December 1938 Reich Minister Rust made Vahlen commissarial head of the Prussian Academy of Sciences, and although he was not confirmed in this position in the subsequent elections in June 1939, he was made President of the Berlin Academy "by decree."

As President of the permanent lead site of the new Reich Association of German Academies, Theodor Vahlen could now officially carry forward his activities. His aim was the creation of a new institution, the Reich Academy of German Sciences. After just two days in office, Vahlen invited the Academy Presidents to a meeting to be held on 2 September 1940, but he only sent out a draft version of the statutes on 3 September.

Paragraph 1 formulated the central task of the Reich Academy as *increasing the achievements of German science by all available means, highlighting outstanding individual achievements, promoting the link between research and the people, and fostering the popular understanding of science*. For that purpose a *day of German science* was to be introduced.[9] This *dies academicus* was deliberately set for 18 January, the date of

[8] Nötzold (2000), *Strategien*, pp. 259–60.

[9] AÖAW, Reichsakademie, No. 296/1940, Vahlen to Srbik of 3 September 1940. Annex "Draft Statutes of the Reich Academy of German Sciences," p. 1.

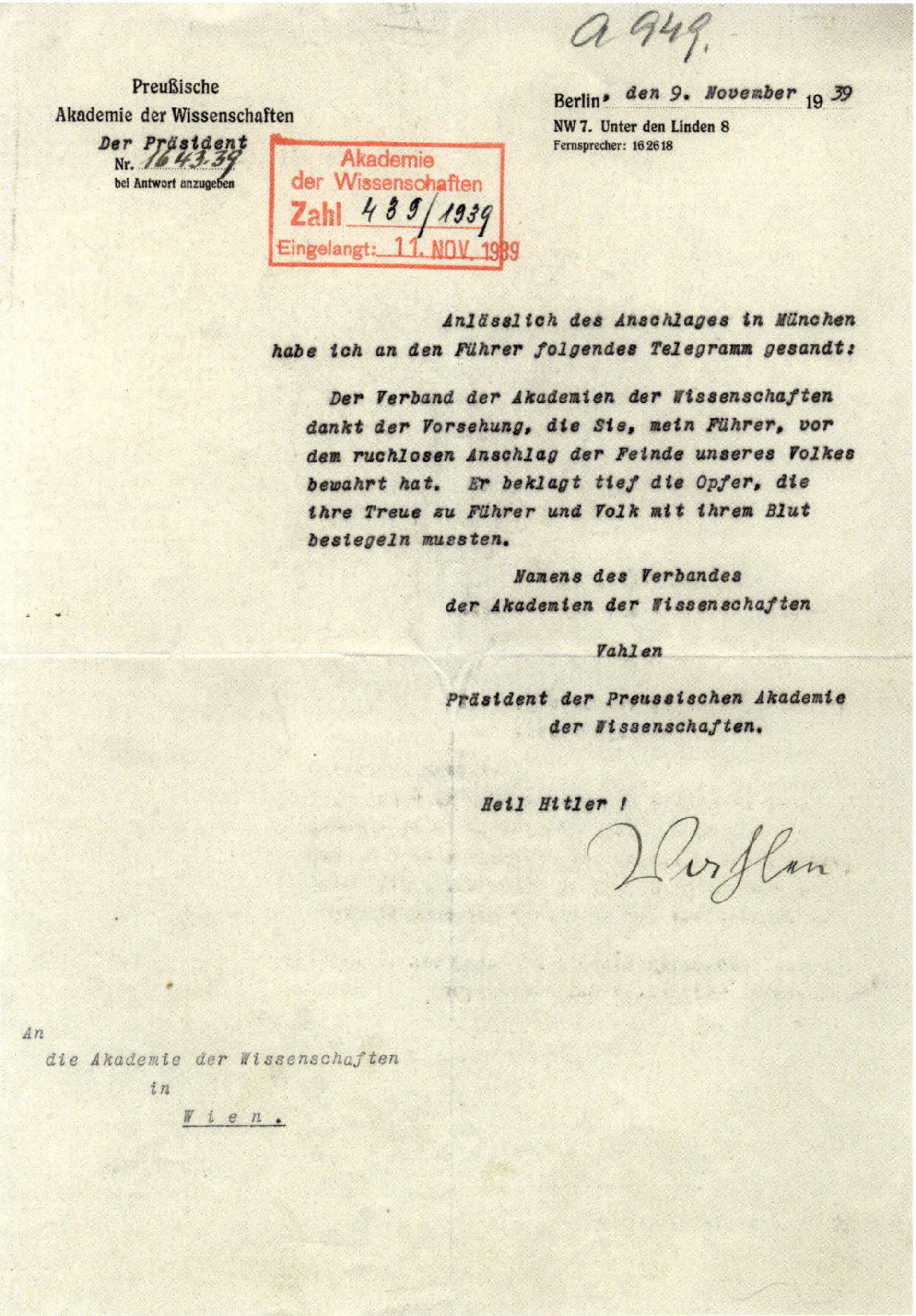

Preußische
Akademie der Wissenschaften
Der Präsident
Nr. 1643.39
bei Antwort anzugeben

Berlin, den 9. November 1939
NW 7. Unter den Linden 8
Fernsprecher: 16 26 18

a 949.

Akademie
der Wissenschaften
Zahl 439/1939
Eingelangt: 11. NOV. 1939

Anlässlich des Anschlages in München habe ich an den Führer folgendes Telegramm gesandt:

Der Verband der Akademien der Wissenschaften dankt der Vorsehung, die Sie, mein Führer, vor dem ruchlosen Anschlag der Feinde unseres Volkes bewahrt hat. Er beklagt tief die Opfer, die ihre Treue zu Führer und Volk mit ihrem Blut besiegeln mussten.

Namens des Verbandes
der Akademien der Wissenschaften

Vahlen

Präsident der Preussischen Akademie
der Wissenschaften.

Heil Hitler !

Vahlen

An
die Akademie der Wissenschaften
in
Wien.

Fig. 74: Letter of the Prussian Academy of 9 November 1939

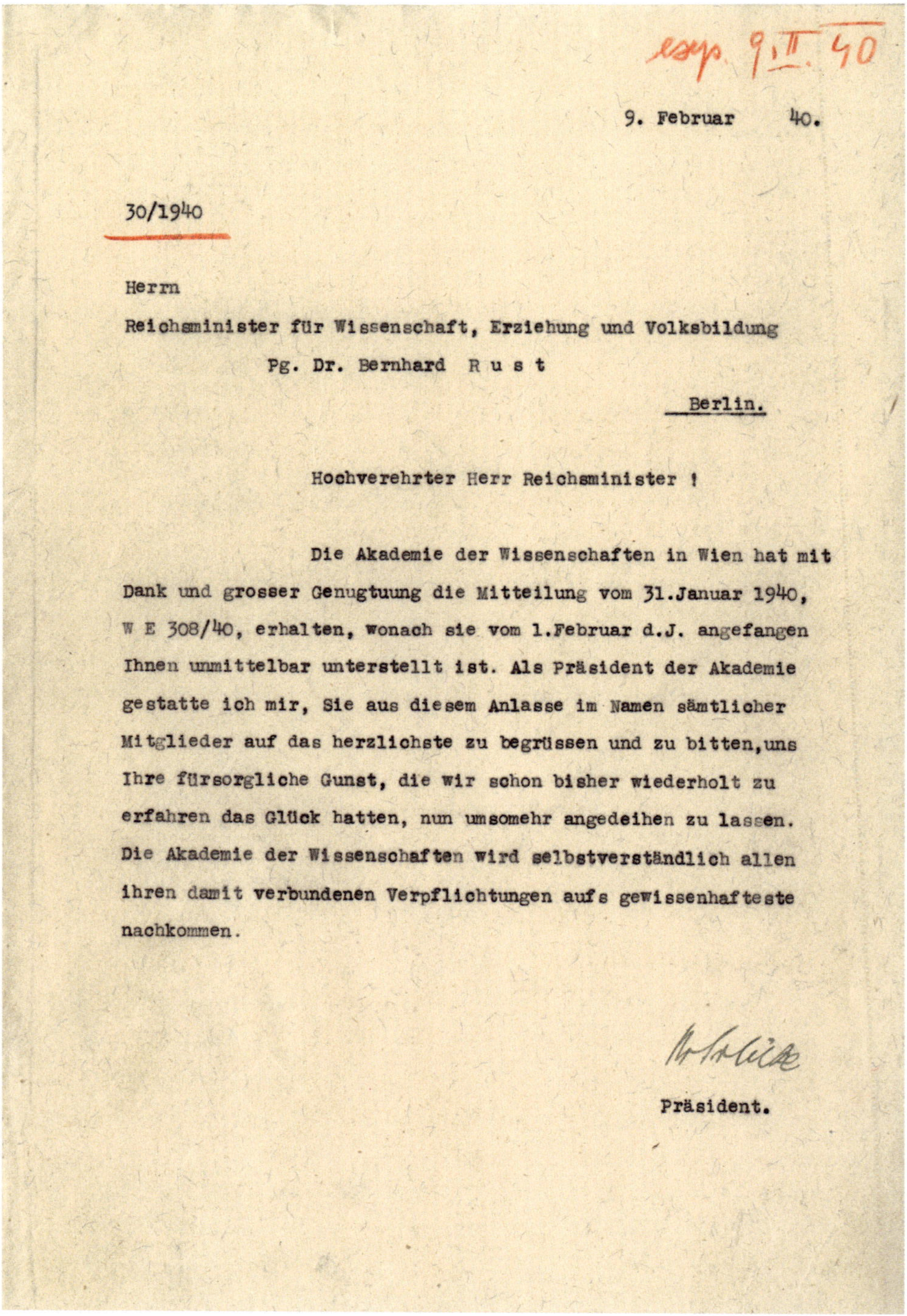

exp. 9.II.40

9. Februar 40.

30/1940

Herrn
Reichsminister für Wissenschaft, Erziehung und Volksbildung
Pg. Dr. Bernhard R u s t
Berlin.

Hochverehrter Herr Reichsminister !

Die Akademie der Wissenschaften in Wien hat mit Dank und grosser Genugtuung die Mitteilung vom 31.Januar 1940, W E 308/40, erhalten, wonach sie vom 1.Februar d.J. angefangen Ihnen unmittelbar unterstellt ist. Als Präsident der Akademie gestatte ich mir, Sie aus diesem Anlasse im Namen sämtlicher Mitglieder auf das herzlichste zu begrüssen und zu bitten,uns Ihre fürsorgliche Gunst, die wir schon bisher wiederholt zu erfahren das Glück hatten, nun umsomehr angedeihen zu lassen. Die Akademie der Wissenschaften wird selbstverständlich allen ihren damit verbundenen Verpflichtungen aufs gewissenhafteste nachkommen.

Präsident.

Fig. 75: Letter from the Academy to Reich Minister Rust of 9 February 1940

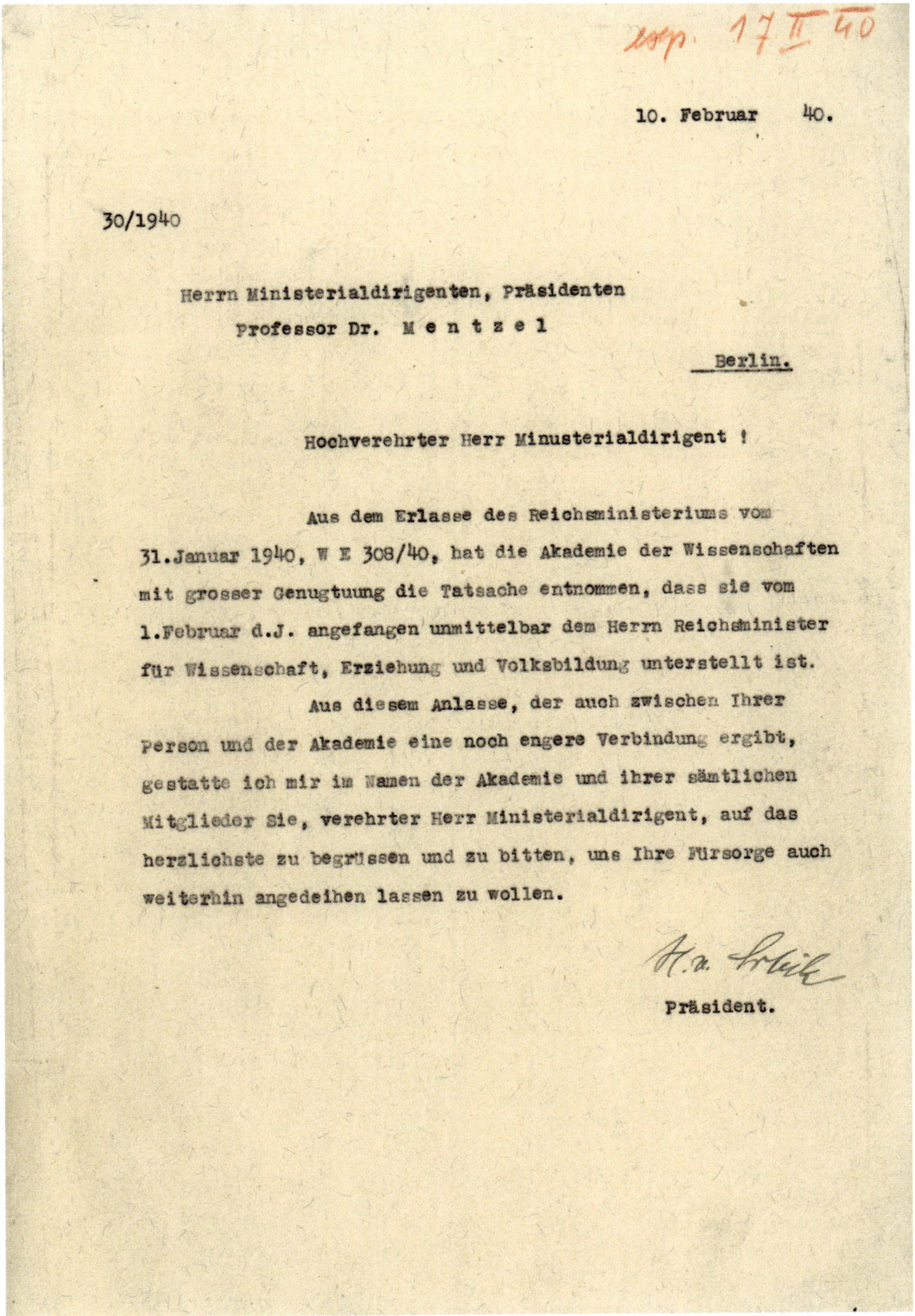

exp. 17 II 40

10. Februar 40.

30/1940

Herrn Ministerialdirigenten, Präsidenten
Professor Dr. M e n t z e l

Berlin.

Hochverehrter Herr Minusterialdirigent !

Aus dem Erlasse des Reichsministeriums vom 31.Januar 1940, W E 308/40, hat die Akademie der Wissenschaften mit grosser Genugtuung die Tatsache entnommen, dass sie vom 1.Februar d.J. angefangen unmittelbar dem Herrn Reichsminister für Wissenschaft, Erziehung und Volksbildung unterstellt ist.

Aus diesem Anlasse, der auch zwischen Ihrer Person und der Akademie eine noch engere Verbindung ergibt, gestatte ich mir im Namen der Akademie und ihrer sämtlichen Mitglieder Sie, verehrter Herr Ministerialdirigent, auf das herzlichste zu begrüssen und zu bitten, uns Ihre Fürsorge auch weiterhin angedeihen lassen zu wollen.

H. v. Srbik

Präsident.

Fig. 76: Letter from the Academy to Rudolf Mentzel of 10 February 1940

the founding of the German Reich in 1871.[10] Above all, the Reich Academy was to carry out *joint work* in those disciplines to which the *National Socialist state* attached *particular importance.*[11] The ordinary members of the Reich Academy were to be Reich German men *of the best age* [and] *and at the height of their powers*. According to paragraph 15, honorary members could also be Reich German women who promoted German scientific research or had put it into practice. Membership could be withdrawn in the event of *unworthiness.*[12] To symbolize the unity of the Reich Academy, the German Academies were to add the designation *Sozietät der Deutschen Reichsakademie* [Society of the German Reich Academies] to their name. They were to consist of three sections, *Mathematics and Physics, Biology,* and *Humanities.*[13]

The draft statutes were to be discussed within twelve days in *extraordinary general assemblies* and then submitted for adoption at a meeting of the Academy Presidents on 19 September 1940. At the same time, Vahlen started a press campaign and at least 37 newspapers reported, mostly on 4 and 5 September, on the founding of the Reich Academy.[14] Minister Rust acted precisely as Vahlen wished: on 13 September, before the deadline for completion of the consultations by the Academies, he elevated the Reich Association to a Reich Academy and put it under the commissarial leadership of the President of the Prussian Academy.

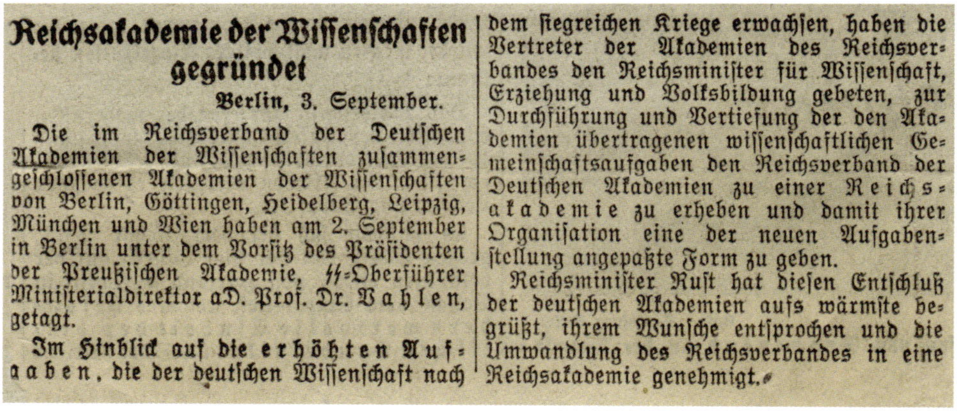

Reichsakademie der Wissenschaften gegründet

Berlin, 3. September.

Die im Reichsverband der Deutschen Akademien der Wissenschaften zusammengeschlossenen Akademien der Wissenschaften von Berlin, Göttingen, Heidelberg, Leipzig, München und Wien haben am 2. September in Berlin unter dem Vorsitz des Präsidenten der Preußischen Akademie, SS-Oberführer Ministerialdirektor aD. Prof. Dr. Vahlen, getagt.

Im Hinblick auf die erhöhten Aufgaben, die der deutschen Wissenschaft nach dem siegreichen Kriege erwachsen, haben die Vertreter der Akademien des Reichsverbandes den Reichsminister für Wissenschaft, Erziehung und Volksbildung gebeten, zur Durchführung und Vertiefung der den Akademien übertragenen wissenschaftlichen Gemeinschaftsaufgaben den Reichsverband der Deutschen Akademien zu einer Reichsakademie zu erheben und damit ihrer Organisation eine der neuen Aufgabenstellung angepaßte Form zu geben.

Reichsminister Rust hat diesen Entschluß der deutschen Akademien aufs wärmste begrüßt, ihrem Wunsche entsprochen und die Umwandlung des Reichsverbandes in eine Reichsakademie genehmigt.

Fig. 77: *Völkischer Beobachter*: founding of the Reich Academy of 8 September 1940

[10] Seidler (1995), *Elite*, p. 19.

[11] AÖAW, Reichsakademie, No. 296/1940, Vahlen to Srbik of 3 September 1940. "Draft Statutes of the Reich Academy of German Sciences," p. 1.

[12] Ibid., pp. 8–9.

[13] Ibid., p. 2.

[14] AÖAW, Reichsakademie, No. 296/1940, Vahlen to Srbik of 20 November 1940. Annex, newspaper cuttings of reports about the Reich Academy of German Sciences.

The draft statutes met with "heavy criticism" in the discussions at the Academies.[15] In the Vienna Academy on 13 September 1940 there was a *lively discussion* on the classification into three sections.[16] The other Academies also had reservations about the planned Reich Academy and proposed several amendments to the statutes.[17] In spite of these reservations the Academy Presidents agreed at a meeting on 19 September 1940 in Berlin on a joint draft version of the statutes of the Reich Academy that differed only in one aspect, albeit an important one, from the original draft: the Reich Association should not be subsumed within the Reich Academy, and the special status of the "old" Academies should be retained.[18]

The Reich Academy now appeared to be taking concrete shape: financial resources amounting to RM 60,000 were earmarked in the 1941 Reich budget, and conversion plans for the rooms in the Royal Palace of Berlin were drawn up. The draft statutes were not dealt with by the Ministry, however, and instead it presented a new version of the statutes for the Reich Academy on 15 April 1941. The commissarial President was requested to "obtain the agreement of the Academies concerned."[19] The changes compared with the draft of October 1940 were so fundamental, however, that the Academies refused to agree to them, and Vahlen was *inundated with massive requests for change*. After discussion of the ministerial draft in a General Assembly of the Prussian Academy, Vahlen took up the requested changes and distributed a revised proposal, which was accepted by the General Assembly of the Berlin Academy. Two days later, on 31 May 1941, he sent this draft to the Academy Presidents for approval.

The other Academies remained *firm in their rejection*, however. It is significant to note that they maintained close contact so as to coordinate their actions. For example, the Viennese President Heinrich Srbik wrote on 6 June 1941 to the Academies in Göttingen, Heidelberg, Leipzig, Munich, and Prague pointing out that Vahlen had *stated clearly for the first time that the Reich Association had ceased to exist*.[20] All of the comments on the draft statutes were also circulated among the Academies. When Srbik informed Vahlen of the results of the sectional meetings of 11 and 19 June, his letter included the requested changes that he had received from the other Academies.[21]

On 9 July 1941 Vahlen was obliged to inform the Ministry that he had been unable to achieve approval of the Reich Academy statutes and that the Academy Presidents wanted a further oral consultation in the presence of a representative of the

---

15 Nötzold (2000), *Strategien*, p. 265.
16 AÖAW, Minutes of the extraordinary General Assembly of 13 September 1940 (A 956), p. 2.
17 See AÖAW, Reichsakademie, No. 296/1940, Saxon Academy of Sciences to Vahlen of 16 September 1940.
18 See Nötzold (2000), *Strategien*, p. 266.
19 Quoted in Nötzold (2000), *Strategien*, p. 268.
20 AÖAW, Reichsakademie, No. 110/1941. Quoted in Nötzold (2000), *Strategien*, p. 269, who in n. 151 refers to the archive signature valid at the time.
21 See AÖAW, Reichsakademie, No. 110/1941, Srbik to Vahlen of 20 June 1941, p. 1.

Reich Ministry. The Ministry refused this request. The plan for a Reich Academy was shelved for the time being on 5 March 1942, when the Reich Ministry informed the Academies that *no Reich funds will be made available again for the fiscal year 1942 for the Reich Academy of German Sciences*. The reason given for the decision was a decree by Hitler saying that *such measures are not vital to the war effort and are to be suspended until further notice*.[22]

In April 1943 Vahlen resigned as President of the Prussian Academy of Sciences; he was replaced by Vice-President Hermann Grapow.[23] Grapow invited the *Presidents of the Reich Academy* to a meeting in Weimar on 22 May 1944.[24] Because of the impending Academy elections and the Ceremonial Session,[25] Srbik only sent the Actuary Wilfried Oberhummer to represent him.[26] Oberhummer reported to the Vienna Academy only that there was no funding for a Reich Academy.[27] A last appeal by Grapow to Reich Minister Rust, the *patron of German science*, was unsuccessful.[28]

Although the designation *Sozietät der Reichsakademie* was still given under the names of the individual Academies in letterheads,[29] Berlin's centralization plan had failed. Evidently the "self-interest of the Academies and their defensive attitude when faced with remote governance from Berlin and an uncontrollable 'Führer President'" had mobilized "considerable resistance."[30] Herbert Matis suggests, however, that this policy succeeded "ultimately, perhaps, thanks to the evident paralysis of state activities from 1941 on account of the war."[31]

Felicitas Seebacher

---

[22] Nötzold (2000), *Strategien*, p. 268.

[23] See Mommsen (2000), *Wissenschaft*, p. 20.

[24] AÖAW, Allgemeine Akten, No. 84/1944, Grapow to Srbik of 4 April 1944.

[25] See AÖAW, Allgemeine Akten, No. 84/1944, Oberhummer to Srbik of 8 April 1944

[26] See AÖAW, Allgemeine Akten, No. 84/1944, Srbik to Grapow of 27 April 1944.

[27] See AÖAW, Allgemeine Akten, No. 84/1944, report by Oberhummer of the meeting of Academy Presidents in Weimar of 22 May 1944, p. 1.

[28] Ibid., p. 5.

[29] AÖAW, Allgemeine Akten, No. 145/1944, Srbik to Knoll of 4 September 1944.

[30] Wennemuth (1995), *Heidelberger Akademie*, p. 123.

[31] Matis (1997), *Anpassung*, p. 60.

II. DEALING WITH NATIONAL SOCIALISM AFTER 1945

Tasks and areas of responsibility of the new Presiding Committee

On 18 May 1945, shortly after the Republic of Austria had been established through the Declaration of Independence of 27 April 1945, thirteen of the ordinary members in Vienna met for an extraordinary General Assembly in the Classical Philology Seminar of the University of Vienna, which was headed by Richard Meister. The meeting did not take place in the Academy building because it was severely damaged. None of those present had been a member of the Nazi Party.[1] The participants had been selected after consultation with the *Staatsamt für Volksaufklärung, für Unterricht und Erziehung und für Kultusangelegenheiten* [State Office for Public Enlightenment, Education, and Cultural Affairs]. The meeting was chaired by full member Ernst Späth, who had been Secretary General of the Academy since 1938.[2] Heinrich Srbik, who had been President of the Academy from 1938 to 1945, had left Vienna for Tyrol, and Vice-President Egon Schweidler had headed for Salzburg. Dietrich Kralik-Meyrswalden, Secretary of the Section for Humanities and the Social Sciences, was a former member of the Nazi Party and had not therefore been invited to attend the meeting. As all of the actions and orders by the Nazi authorities after 13 March 1938 had been declared null and void, Späth and Meister assumed that the *current Presiding Committee* had *thus been rendered inoperative*.[3] The aim of the meeting was therefore to elect interim leaders of the Academy so as to guarantee its restructuring and to convene an extraordinary General Assembly to select a new Presiding Committee. Späth was elected as head and Meister as his deputy. Späth assumed the responsibilities of the Section for Mathematics and the Natural Sciences, and Meister those of the Secretary General and Secretary of the Section for Humanities and the Social Sciences. He was also tasked with restructuring the staff, taking an inventory, and devising a new program. On 23 May 1945, the State Office approved the election of the interim management and their assumption of the responsibilities associated with this function.[4]

---

[1] The archeologist Camillo Praschniker, the only one of five invited Nazi Party members to attend the meeting, had applied for membership to the Nazi Party but had been refused because of a Jewish grandmother. He initially retained his professorship at the University of Vienna but was removed from his position in 1945. For details on Praschniker, see Pfefferle/Pfefferle (2012), *Glimpflich entnazifiziert*, pp. 128–30, and Wlach (2012), *Praschniker*.

[2] See Feichtinger/Uhl (2005), *Akademie*, pp. 313–4.

[3] AÖAW, Minutes of the General Assembly of 18 May 1945 (A 994), Annex, Späth and Meister to *Staatsamt für Volksaufklärung, für Unterricht und Erziehung und für Kultusangelegenheiten* [State Office for Public Enlightenment, Education, and Cultural Affairs] of 19 May 1945.

[4] See Feichtinger/Uhl (2005), *Akademie*, pp. 315–6.

AKADEMIE DER WISSENSCHAFTEN IN WIEN
Wien I., Universitätsplatz 2.

Abschrift

Zl.52/1945. Wien, den 19.Mai 1945.

An das
Staatsamt für Volksaufklärung, für Unterricht und Erziehung
und für Kultusangelegenheiten in W i e n .

Der Unterzeichnete berichtet, daß am Freitag, den 18.Mai 1945, eine Gesamtsitzung der "Akademie der Wissenschaften in Wien" stattgefunden hat, zu der die derzeit in Wien anwesenden ordentlichen Mitglieder mit Ausschluß ehemaliger Angehöriger der NSDAP eingeladen waren, mit der Aufgabe, die nötigen Maßnahmen für die Weiterführung der Akademie zu treffen.

Da die Bestätigung des gegenwärtigen Präsidiums durch das vormalige Reichsministerium für Wissenschaft, Erziehung und Volksbildung im Sinne der Bestimmung über die Ungültigkeit aller seit dem 13.März 1938 vollzogenen Handlungen der früheren Reichsregierung ihre Geltung verloren hat, so erscheint das gegenwärtige Präsidium damit außer Funktion gesetzt.

Die am 18.Mai 1945 versammelten Mitglieder der Akademie haben daher zur vorläufigen Führung der Geschäfte bis zur Wiederwahl eines Präsidiums einen interimistischen Leiter und einen Stellvertreter für diesen gewählt, und zwar

als ersteren Prof.Dr.Ernst S P Ä T H,
als letzteren Prof.Dr.Richard M E IS T E R.

Der Unterzeichnete bittet den Herrn Staatssekretär:

1. die Gewählten mit der Führung der laufenden Agenden der Akademie und deren Leitung bis zur Wiederwahl eines Präsidiums zu betrauen;

2. an Stelle der gegenwärtigen Satzung das Bundesgesetz vom 14.Oktober 1921, B.G.Bl.Nr.569, betreffend die Akademie der Wissenschaften in Wien, sowie die diesem Gesetze zufolge gegebene Satzung und Geschäftsordnung der Akademie wieder in Kraft zu setzen;

3. zu genehmigen, daß die Akademie der Wissenschaften in einem späteren mit dem Staatsamt zu vereinbarenden Zeitpunkte, jedenfalls aber noch im Laufe dieses Jahres, die Wahl des Präsidiums und die Ersatzwahlen wirklicher und korrespondierender Mitglieder auf die erledigten Stellen vornehme.

Als die nächsten Agenden sind anzuführen:

1. Überprüfung des Standes der Mitglieder der Akademie, d.h. Rückberufung der wirklichen und korrespondierenden Mitglieder, die im Zusammenhang mit den politischen Ereignissen des Jahres 1938 ausgetreten sind, und Ausscheidung solcher Mitglieder, die unter besonders belastenden Umständen aus ihrer amtlichen Stellung entfernt wurden oder (wenn pensioniert oder privat) aus gleichen Gründen untragbar sind.

2. Überprüfung des Angestelltenpersonals der Akademie.

3. Sicherung des Eigentums der Akademie (Gebäude, Einrichtung, Institute, Stiftungen, Bibliothek) durch Bestandaufnahme, Wiederinstandsetzung, Rückführung verlagerter Bestände u.s.w.

4. Aufstellung eines Arbeitsplanes für eine möglichst rasche Wiederaufnahme der Forschungstätigkeit und womöglich der Veröffentlichungen der Akademie mit dem Ziele, der Akademie und damit Österreich baldigst einen geachteten Platz in der Wissenschaft der Kulturstaaten zu schaffen.

5. Aufstellung eines Budgetentwurfes der Akademie für die Dauer des laufenden Jahres.

6. Vorbereitung und Durchführung der Wahlen des Präsidiums sowie der Ersatzwahlen wirklicher und korrespondierender Mitglieder der Akademie.

SPÄTH e.h.

Fig. 78: Letter of the Academy to the State Office of 19 May 1945

Among the central agendas of the new Presiding Committee was the restructuring of the staff and institutions of the Academy and their reintegration into international networks. The main precondition for accomplishing these tasks was the restoration of institutional autonomy, which was also confirmed by the State Office on 23 May through the re-entry into force of the Academy Law of 1921 and the Statutes of 1922, replacing the Provisional Statutes. After the first General Assembly of 18 May 1945, steps were taken to review the political affiliations of the members and staff, recall ordinary and corresponding members who had been excluded between 1938 and 1941, and dismiss those members whose political liabilities made them unacceptable. There was also a need to safeguard the Academy's assets, return the material that had been moved elsewhere, elaborate a work plan, draft a budget, and prepare for elections.

The new Presiding Committee

The legal situation of the Academy was defined in the minutes of the first General Assembly: *The legal position invalidating all dispositions made after 13 March 1938 also applies to the appointments to the Presiding Committee of the Academy.*[5] Thus Srbik, Schweidler, Kralik-Meyrswalden, and Späth were all removed from office. The chemist Ernst Späth, who had been rector of the University of Vienna before the "Anschluss", was subsequently re-elected, as mentioned above. He had resigned from this office on 15 March 1938 saying "that the interests of the University of Vienna can be represented only if the office of the rector is held by a man [Fritz Knoll], who is a member of the Party."[6] The same year Späth was elected Secretary General of the Academy, a position he retained until the end of the war.[7] Richard Meister, interim deputy head of the Academy, had had to give up his professorship of education in 1938. Instead he was assigned a tenured professorship in classical philology, the subject of one of his two habilitations.[8] In addition, in 1943 he had been made interim head of the departments of philosophy, psychology, and education, which had been merged to form a large Department of Philosophy. He was not a member of the Nazi Party but belonged to several Nazi associations.[9] In the authoritarian *Ständestaat* [Corporate State], he had represented academic research on the *Bundeskulturat* [Federal Cultural Council] and had belonged to several pan-German associations such as the *Deutscher Klub* [German Club].

---

[5] AÖAW, Minutes of the General Assembly of 18 May 1945 (A 994). The complete invalidation of dispositions made during the Nazi era, such as the confirmation of newly elected members by the Reich Minister for Science, Education, and Culture, was not ultimately effected.

[6] Quoted in Lichtenberger-Fenz (1988), *Hochschulen*, p. 269.

[7] See Feichtinger/Uhl (2005), *Akademie*, p. 314.

[8] See Römer/Schreiner (2010), *Dis-kontinuitäten*, pp. 320–39.

[9] See Feichtinger/Uhl (2005), *Akademie*, pp. 321–2.

Fig. 79: Presiding Committee at the Ceremonial Session of 1947

The interim heads of the Academy, Späth and Meister, were elected definitively as President and Vice-President at the extraordinary General Assembly of 30 October 1945. Josef Keil and Adalbert Prey were elected as the other members of the Presiding Committee. The classical historian Keil was Secretary General and Secretary of the Section for Humanities and the Social Sciences from 1945 to 1959, and the astronomer Prey was Secretary of the Section for Mathematics and the Natural Sciences from 1945 to 1949. Along with Späth and Meister, Prey and Keil were part of the network of Academy members who had started their careers during the authoritarian *Ständestaat* and had survived the Nazi era unscathed. Prey had been elected a full member in 1935, Keil an ordinary member in 1939. After the sudden death of Ernst Späth, the meteorologist Heinrich Ficker was elected Academy President in November 1946. This newly elected Presiding Committee had the responsible task of restructuring the post-war Academy.

Restructuring the Academy staff

After the legal basis for the continuation of the Academy had been established, the Presiding Committee now took steps to recall members and staff who had been dismissed in 1938 and to examine the political background of Academy members and staff in accordance with the *Verbotsgesetz* [law banning re-engagement in National

Fig. 80: Ernst Späth

Fig. 81: Richard Meister

Fig. 82: Josef Keil

Fig. 83: Adalbert Prey

Fig. 84: Heinrich Ficker

Socialist activities] of 8 May 1945.[10] The following section will deal briefly with the political screening of leading staff members: The two highest-placed administrators in the Academy, the Actuaries Viktor Junk and Wilfried Oberhummer, had been members of the Nazi Party. Junk, an illegal Nazi since 1933, had retired on 1 February 1945, Oberhummer (applicant since 1938, member since 1942) initially remained in office by agreement of the Federal Ministry of Education. The political screening of the Academy staff was carried out on the basis of a ministerial decree of 8 March 1946 (No. 1147/Präs/46) under the responsibility of the Special Commission at First Instance of the University of Vienna. The Academy sent its Secretary, Adalbert Prey, to this Commission. Rafael Kaiser, senior gardener of the Institute for Experimental Biology (BVA) (Nazi Party applicant since 1943), and the equally incriminated staff members Franz Köck and Marie Repototschnig no longer worked for the Academy. Oberhummer (member of the *Betriebs-SA* [Academy's internal SA organization for employees] and of the *"Nationalsozialistische Volkswohlfahrt"* ["National Socialist People's Welfare"]) remained in office thanks, amongst other things, to a mitigating letter by Academy President Ernst Späth.[11] Oberhummer became First Actuary and together with Ludmilla Krestan, the Second Actuary who initially had been entrusted

[10] See essay in this volume by Johannes Feichtinger and Dieter J. Hecht, "Denazification at the Academy of Sciences," pp. 163–79.

[11] See AÖAW, PA Wilfried Oberhummer, and AÖAW, Politischer Fragebogen, Mitarbeiter, ad Oberhummer.

by Richard Meister on 3 August 1945 with managing the agendas of both actuaries, was responsible for the agendas of both Sections in the first years after the war.[12]

Institutional restructuring of the Academy

The first activities were designed to safeguard the Academy's material assets, secure funding for its work, and to draft a work plan. The main building of the Academy had been heavily damaged during an air raid in the fall of 1944 and during the fighting in April 1945, and the ceiling fresco in the ceremonial hall was in jeopardy because of humidity. The repair work was started in 1946 with funds from the Federal Ministry of Education and the State and Federal Building Administration of the Republic and completed by the early 1950s. The general assembly was held again in the main building for the first time on 7 December 1945. The inventories that had been moved out of the Academy in wartime had been returned in their entirety by the summer of 1946 and the library was re-established in 1947. A reading room for members of the Academy was set up in the clubroom. The building at Liebiggasse 5, where the Phonogram Archive is still housed today, had also been severely damaged. The large recording room was repaired with the support of the State and Federal Building Administration in 1947/48. The remains of the building of the Institute for Experimental Biology in the Prater, which had been completely destroyed during the fighting in 1945, were sold in April 1947 to the *Prater-Betriebsgesellschaft* [Service Management], with the proceeds going to the Biological Station in Lunz. The buildings in which the Institute for Radium Research and the *Wiener Wörterbuchkanzlei* [Austrian-Bavarian Dictionary Commission] had been housed were intact.

In 1945 the pre-war Academy was also reconstructed symbolically. The Commission for the Publication of Late Latin Texts was renamed Commission for Editing the Corpus of the Latin Church Fathers and the addition in the original "of critically amended texts" was left out. The Prehistoric Commission and South-Eastern Commission, both of which had been renamed between 1938 and 1945, initially retained these names. Starting in December 1945, the reconversion of Academy foundations that had been renamed and/or transformed in 1939 and that had played a central role in the execution of the Academy's projects was addressed. Furthermore, the original fund statutes were restored by deleting racial passages and stipulations of responsibility towards the former German Reich. The Guttenbrunner Foundation was renamed the Gustav Figdor Foundation in 1946; in the Anton Hansgirg Foundation, the words "without discrimination by nation and religion" were added again; the Wagner Jauregg Foundation was given back the name of its founder, the Jewish doctor from Czernowitz Arnold Flinker and was now called again Arnold Flinker and Julius Wagner Jauregg Foundation. In the statutes of the Sederl Foundation, all references to the Nazi era were expunged, and in the statutes of the Matthäus and Rudolf Much

[12] See AÖAW, PA Wilfried Oberhummer, and AÖAW, Minutes of the General Assembly of 25 October 1946 (A 1005).

Prize Foundation the sentence *Prize winners must be ethnic Germans of Aryan descent* and the reference to *"Ahnenerbe"* [Ancestral Heritage] were removed. The statutes of the Grillparzer Prize were redrafted.[13]

The audit of the Academy's annual accounts in December 1945 for the period from 1 April 1945 showed a surplus of RM 160,440.79. This was equivalent to the average amount earmarked annually for the Academy by the Nazi state.[14] The Academy had received no funding from the Republic of Austria between April and October of that year and a total of ÖS 14,300 (RM:ÖS = 1:1) for November and December. Among the commissions that had received the largest share of state subsidies during the Nazi period were the Thesaurus Linguae Latinae, the Egyptian Commission, and the Phonogram Archive. Alongside these, in the decade after the war, the Biological Station in Lunz and the new Commissions for Spatial Research and Reconstruction and the Austrian Biographical Lexicon received increased funding from the state.

The interim heads of the Academy saw their main task as being the speedy resumption of academic work. The first regular General Assembly on 22 June 1945 adopted a decision to dissolve the Commission for Publication of Writings on the Study of Race and Human Genetics established in 1942, to resume the activities of the other commissions, to establish a meeting timetable for 1945, and to restructure the *Verbandkommission* [Commission for the association of Austrian academic institutions], which will be discussed in greater detail below. The resumption of the full publication program was a declared aim in order to show the uninterrupted continuation of the Academy's work. The main program point was *to continue to work in the same spirit of strict scholarship as it had always been done*. According to Meister's speech of 22 June 1945 on the *work program for the near future*, however, *work by authors who, for personal reasons, would evince unnecessary criticism* had to be postponed. Meister therefore emphasized that the content of all publications *would be strictly checked to ensure that no trace of National Socialist ideology had crept in*.[15]

---

[13] AÖAW, Minutes of the General Assembly of 4 June 1946 (A 1003), Annex, report of the Vice-President on the redrafting of the statutes of the foundations. The decision to rename the Wagner Jauregg Foundation is not mentioned in the *Almanachs*.

[14] Between 1939 and 1943 the state subsidy was at around 15 percent, before being reduced to 5 percent in 1944. After 1945 the share of the Academy assets was to be gradually reduced in favor of state subsidies. See the unpublished audit of the annual statements of the Academy from 1938 to 1955 by the economist Johanna Aigner, MS., carried out within the framework of the research project "Continuity and Transformation. The Austrian Academy of Sciences in the 20th Century," run by Institute of Culture Studies and Theatre History and subsidized by the city of Vienna (MA 7).

[15] AÖAW, Minutes of the General Assembly of 22 June 1945 (A 995), report by Richard Meister.

Resistance to restructuring

In June 1945 the Academy was confronted with plans for a fundamental restructuring. They provided for its reorganization into a kind of *Wissenschaftskammer* [professional association of academics] whose task it would be to centrally coordinate academic institutions and bodies in Austria.[16] The shock that these restructuring plans caused was immense and was still being echoed in the official speeches of the members of the Presiding Committee in 1946 and 1947. In his opening speech at the 1946 Ceremonial Session, Ernst Späth referred explicitly to the averted restructuring plans.[17] In his speech at the centennial celebration in 1947, Meister also spoke of "the kind of rash project" that, "as always in revolutionary times," had been suggested for the Academy in 1945, but also of the successful resistance to it.[18] Maintaining the independence of the most important non-university research institution and scholarly society in Austria was justified on two counts: first, on account of its resistance activities during the Nazi era, e.g. the rejection of the founding of a Reich Academy of Sciences with its headquarters in Berlin; and second, on account of the immediate commencement of an extensive program of basic research, which – as Meister informed the full members – *is linked to the problems that have arisen out of Austria's soil and history or* which could be carried out *thanks to the existence of major researchers in the various areas of science and the humanities.*[19] By resisting the attacks on the Academy's independence, Meister took the initiative. On 3 August 1945 he set about the transformation of the *Verbandkommission wissenschaftlicher Körperschaften* [Commission for the association of academic bodies], established in 1892, into the *Verbandkommission österreichischer Wissenschaft* [Commission for the association of Austrian academic institutions], which would act in the future as focal point for the coordination of academic institutions and bodies in Austria. This move – presenting old structures in a new guise – proved to be a successful strategy.

International integration and networking

International networking occurred after 1945 at two levels: the election of corresponding members abroad, and exchange with other academies and participation in conferences. This approach has established itself as a constant feature of Academy policy. After World War I, persons from former enemy countries were rarely elected as Academy members. For the most part the proposals for election were restricted to candidates from the German Reich and neutral states, such as the Scandinavian

---

16 Meister (1947), *Geschichte*, p. 191.

17 Opening speech of the President of the Academy of Sciences, Ernst Späth, in: *Almanach* for 1946, 96 (1948), pp. 35–41.

18 Ceremonial speech by Vice-President Richard Meister, "The history of the Academy of Sciences in Vienna 1847–1947," in: *Almanach* for 1946, 96 (1948), pp. 196–216, here p. 214.

19 AÖAW, Minutes of the General Assembly of 22 June 1945 (A 995), report by Richard Meister.

countries.[20] After 1945, the election of corresponding members from abroad became more international.

Resumption of international relations by the Academy after 1945 was done through Allied institutions, to whom the Academy had to present activity reports.[21] In November 1945, the Soviet Academy of Sciences in Moscow was the first to apply for a resumption of the exchange of papers with the Academy in Vienna and a number of scientific institutions in Austria. The Moscow Academy successfully requested the publications of the Vienna Academy from 1939 to 1945.[22] In late 1945, the British Council invited the Academy to exchange papers with British scientific journals.[23] Further contacts followed in 1946, along with the first trips abroad by Academy members; initially these had to be approved by the authorities. In early 1946, the *Schweizer Naturforschende Gesellschaft* [Swiss Association of the Natural Sciences] invited the Academy to its 200th anniversary celebrations. Späth accepted the invitation, but died in Zurich on 30 September 1946 during his visit.[24] Contacts were also established in the summer of 1946 with German academies, as, for example, through the invitation by the Saxon Academy to its 100th anniversary celebrations,[25] and in the fall of the same year to the meeting of the Academy Cartel in Göttingen.[26] Important steps in building up international relations included the exchange of papers with the Library of Congress in Washington, D.C., from 1949, and the inclusion of Austria in the International Council of Scientific Unions on 19 June 1949. The Academy represented Austria on this Council and sent its President Heinrich Ficker as its delegate to the General Assembly in Copenhagen in September 1949.[27] In March of that year, discussions resumed concerning participation in the Cartel of German Academies. The Vienna Academy adopted a decision stating that it attached *great importance* to having a delegate in the Thesaurus Linguae Latinae Commission, regardless of whether *the Cartel rightly continues to exist today* […] *and even in the event that the Cartel were to be disbanded or temporarily suspended.* The academies in German-speaking countries had formed a Cartel in 1893 with to the aim of editing the *Thesaurus Linguae Latinae*. Following an inquiry by the Federal Ministry of Education in 1949, the Academy decided to participate again in the Cartel of German Academies, arguing that it was not a creation of the Nazi era.[28] The Cartel was not to be revived in its original form, however. Participation by the Academy in the

---

[20] See Graf-Stuhlhofer (1995), *Akademie*, p. 148.
[21] See AÖAW, Minutes of the General Assembly of 25 October 1946 (A 1005).
[22] See AÖAW, Minutes of the General Assembly of 7 December 1945 (A 998).
[23] See AÖAW, Minutes of the General Assembly of 18 January 1946 (A 999).
[24] See AÖAW, Minutes of the General Assembly of 17 May 1946 (A 1002), and AÖAW, Minutes of the General Assembly of 25 October 1946 (A 1005).
[25] See AÖAW, Minutes of the General Assembly of 5 July 1946 (A 1004).
[26] See AÖAW, Minutes of the General Assembly of 25 October 1946 (A 1005).
[27] See AÖAW, Minutes of the General Assembly of 1 July 1949 (A 1028).
[28] See AÖAW, Minutes of the General Assembly of 11 March 1949 (A 1025).

Thesaurus Linguae Latinae and the publication of the *Monumenta Germaniae Historica* was assured by a different approach.

In December 1953, President Meister the annual meeting of the Bavarian Academy of Sciences as a delegate for the first time.[29] After his return, he suggested, unsuccessfully, that gowns be introduced for the Presiding Committee, as was the practice in the Bavarian Academy.[30]

Through its various activities the Academy thus achieved the level of international cooperation and integration that it had enjoyed before 1938.

Johannes Feichtinger/Dieter J. Hecht

[29] See AÖAW, Minutes of the General Assembly of 29 January 1954 (A 1062).

[30] See AÖAW, Minutes of the General Assembly of 30 April 1954 (A 1064), and AÖAW, Minutes of the Election Meeting of the Academy as a Whole of 26 May 1957 (A 1089).

Denazification at the Academy of Sciences

The 22 June 1945 could have been an auspicious day for the Academy, but it was not. On that Friday, nineteen full members (including five members or applicants for membership of the Nazi Party, banned since 8 May 1945) met in the Department of Classical Philology of the University of Vienna for the first regular General Assembly since the end of the war. The meeting was chaired by the interim head Ernst Späth; his deputy Richard Meister reported on the Academy's activities. The most sensitive item was the *political screening of the members of the Academy*,[1] which was discussed in the second part of the meeting from which former members of the Nazi Party or those who had applied for membership were excluded. On 16 June the most senior member of the Academy, Viennese historian Alfons Dopsch,[2] had submitted *proposals for restructuring*.

His most important motion was that *all members who were Party members should automatically be deprived of the honorable position of being a member of the Academy, even if they retain their positions at the university*.[3] The motion, which at this time exceeded the *Sühnefolgen* [atonement] required by law, was defeated because of the resistance of the deputy interim leader and Secretary General of the Academy, Richard Meister,[4] who persuaded the fourteen full members present[5] of the inadmissibility of the *automatic* collective exclusion of members who had been members of the Nazi Party. Dopsch's motion also called for other more extensive changes: all elections between March 1938 and March 1945 should be reviewed, the interim leadership, including Meister as deputy interim leader, should be replaced following new elections as soon as possible, and the type of membership should be made dependent on

1 AÖAW, Minutes of the General Assembly of 22 June 1945 (A 995).

2 For details of Dopsch, see Buchner (2008), *Dopsch*.

3 AÖAW, Minutes of the General Assembly of 22 June 1945 (A 995), Annex, Dopsch to Späth of 16 June 1945.

4 See AÖAW, Minutes of the General Assembly of 22 June 1945 (A 995), report of Richard Meister and his comments on Dopsch's motion.

5 Five full members who had taken part in the General Assembly had to leave the room on account of their membership or application for membership of the Nazi Party (Kralik-Meyrswalden, Kruppa, Mewaldt, Saliger, Wild). Other Nazi Party members (Brunner, Egger, Junker, Mache, Mayrhofer, Praschniker, Sedlmayr) had been invited to the General Assembly but were not in attendance. Members who did not live in Vienna or who were not in Vienna at the time of the meeting (Bauer, Nadler) were not invited, nor were those for whom it was assumed that their continuance in the Academy would be in violation of the Constitutional Law on the Prohibition of the Nazi Party (Knoll, Pernkopf, Christian, Schönbauer). Those members whose professorships had been indefinitely suspended by the *Staatsamt für Volksaufklärung, für Unterricht und Erziehung und für Kultusangelegenheiten* [State Office for Public Enlightenment, Education, and Cultural Affairs] (Schaffernak, Menghin, Srbik) were also not invited.

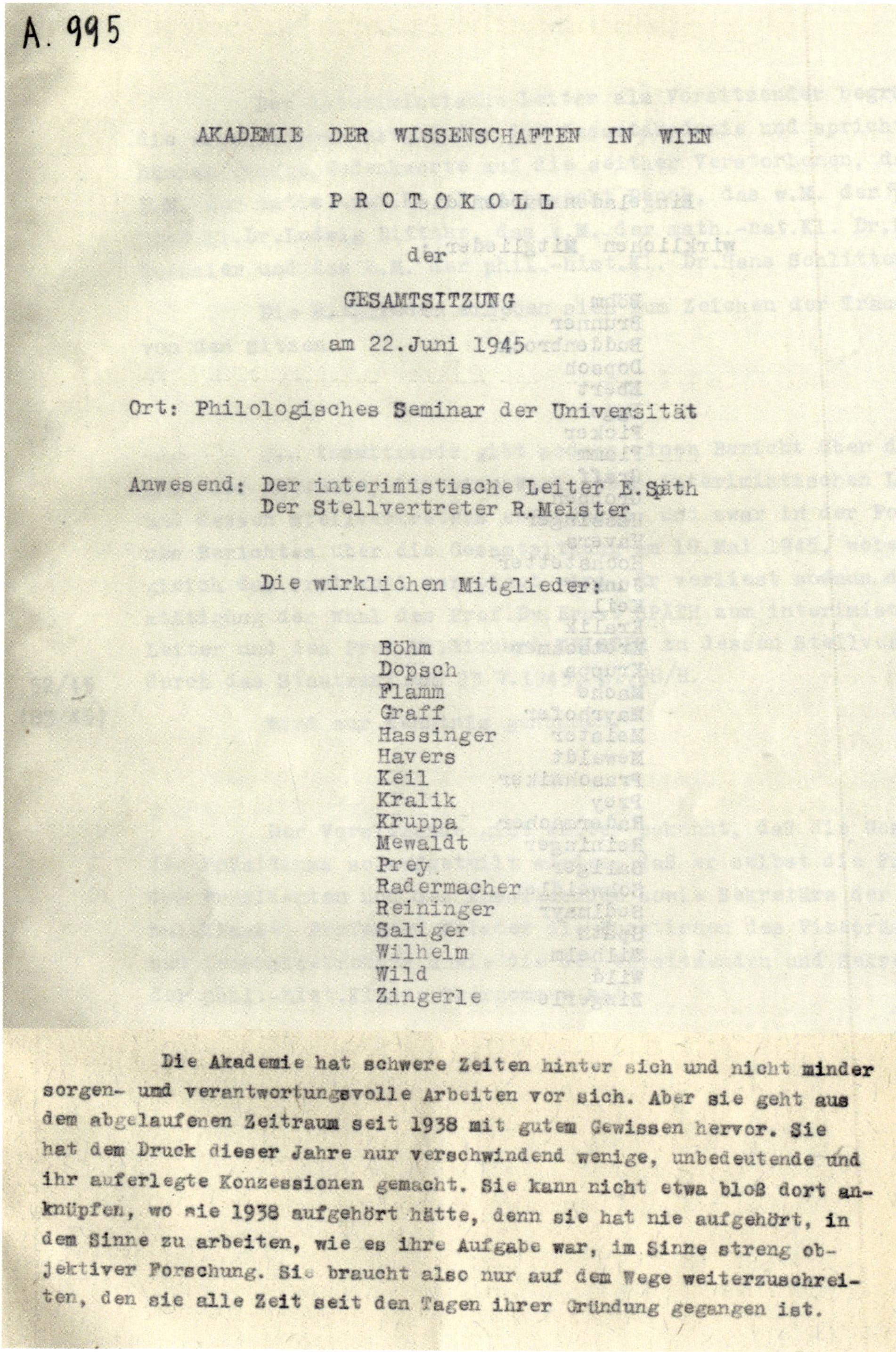

A. 995

AKADEMIE DER WISSENSCHAFTEN IN WIEN

PROTOKOLL

der

GESAMTSITZUNG

am 22.Juni 1945

Ort: Philologisches Seminar der Universität

Anwesend: Der interimistische Leiter E.Späth
Der Stellvertreter R.Meister

Die wirklichen Mitglieder:

Böhm
Dopsch
Flamm
Graff
Hassinger
Havers
Keil
Kralik
Kruppa
Mewaldt
Prey
Radermacher
Reininger
Saliger
Wilhelm
Wild
Zingerle

Die Akademie hat schwere Zeiten hinter sich und nicht minder sorgen- und verantwortungsvolle Arbeiten vor sich. Aber sie geht aus dem abgelaufenen Zeitraum seit 1938 mit gutem Gewissen hervor. Sie hat dem Druck dieser Jahre nur verschwindend wenige, unbedeutende und ihr auferlegte Konzessionen gemacht. Sie kann nicht etwa bloß dort anknüpfen, wo sie 1938 aufgehört hätte, denn sie hat nie aufgehört, in dem Sinne zu arbeiten, wie es ihre Aufgabe war, im Sinne streng objektiver Forschung. Sie braucht also nur auf dem Wege weiterzuschreiten, den sie alle Zeit seit den Tagen ihrer Gründung gegangen ist.

Fig. 85: Minutes of the first ordinary General Assembly of 22 June 1945

the domicile of the member. The full members, according to Dopsch's proposal, should be domiciled in Vienna (so as to guarantee that the meetings were quorate), and the corresponding members should be domiciled outside Vienna. If his motion had been carried, the Academy would have had to exclude half of its full members, including Heinrich Srbik, and three-fifths of its corresponding members inland, and would have had to admit that it – as a scholarly body – had not behaved during the Nazi era in the way that Richard Meister, the architect of political screenings at the Academy, had been claiming was the case at least since June 1945: *The Academy* [...] *can look back on the time since 1938 with a clear conscience. It made only very few, insignificant, and coerced concessions to the pressure of these years.*[6]

Fig. 86: Alfons Dopsch

Meister used a subtle argument to refute Dopsch's motion for a *general solution*[7] regarding *cleansing* of the personnel. He had received the *authorization of the State Office* for the immediate election of a new Presiding Committee, but he regarded Dopsch's motion as a *serious defamation of* and *disdain for* the work of the *provisional Committee.* He skillfully played off Dopsch's motions against one another by linking

[6] AÖAW, Minutes of the General Assembly of 22 June 1945 (A 995); see facsimile on the left side.
[7] Ibid.

them. He rejected the reserving of full membership to persons domiciled in Vienna as *un-Austrian centralism*[8] – but without a quorate General Assembly there would be no election of a definitive Presiding Committee, and without a definitive Presiding Committee there could be no definitive exclusion of the Nazi Party members. The General Assembly rejected the motions for restricting full membership to Viennese members and for the immediate new election of the Presiding Committee, whereupon Dopsch withdrew his motion for the automatic exclusion of Nazi Party members. It is unclear why Dopsch submitted this motion. What is clear is that he was one of the most active members of the Academy between 1938 and 1945 and was the chairman or member of twelve commissions. It may therefore be assumed that in retrospect, he believed that the actions of Nazi Party members were irreconcilable with Academy membership, which he described as the *greatest scientific honor.*[9]

The Academy thus continued the approach chosen by Meister in May 1945 of individual denazification, albeit with a slight change in orientation. In May 1945 the provisional Committee had notified the *Staatsamt für Volksaufklärung, für Unterricht und Erziehung und für Kultusangelegenheiten* [State Office for Public Enlightenment, Education, and Cultural Affairs] of the following steps: *recall of full and corresponding members who left the Academy in connection with the political events of 1938 and exclusion of members who have been removed from their positions under particularly incriminating circumstances or (if retired or private) are unacceptable for the same reasons.*[10] The first step was carried out but the second was delayed – and ultimately abandoned. In the years 1938 to 1941 "racially" and politically persecuted members of the Academy had been excluded regardless of their scholastic excellence.[11] Many free positions had been filled by Nazi Party members. Between 1945 and 1948 the membership of former Nazi Party members was officially held in abeyance. In 1949, however, practically all former Nazi Party members who had had to give up their positions (at least temporarily) at the universities once again appeared in the membership of the Academy of Sciences. How did this happen?

Denazification and its contexts

The upheaval in 1945 offered various political actors an opportunity to interfere with the autonomous position of the Academy that was based on the Academy Law of 1921

[8] With few exceptions, the ordinary members of the Academy of Sciences before 1945 were all from Vienna. In the *Almanach* for 1938, 88 (1939), there were 49 Viennese members compared with just 7 non-Viennese.

[9] AÖAW, Minutes of the General Assembly of 22 June 1945 (A 995), Annex, Dopsch to Späth of 16 June 1945.

[10] AÖAW, Minutes of the General Assembly of 18 May 1945 (A 994), Annex, Späth and Meister to *Staatsamt für Volksaufklärung, für Unterricht und Erziehung und für Kultusangelegenheiten* [State Office for Public Enlightenment, Education, and Cultural Affairs] of 19 May 1945.

[11] Matis (1997), *Anpassung*, and the essay in this volume by Herbert Matis, "Exclusion of members," pp. 53–9.

and the Statutes of 1922–5. Although the State Office had decreed as early as 23 May 1945 that the original Statutes re-enter into force, the political venture aimed at a "complete restructuring" of the Academy as some kind of a *Wissenschaftskammer* [professional association of academics] for Austria had endangered its existence as a scholarly society.[12] Richard Meister managed to repel all efforts to reduce the Academy's re-found autonomy, and he also acted with relative autonomy in the denazification process.

Meister's main strategy was to now use the signs of self-assertion that the Academy had shown during the Nazi era as an argument to ward off the demands of the state and politicians. This applied, for example, to the exclusion of Academy members who had been members of the Nazi party. Meister asserted that *how it was perceived abroad* was not *the major consideration,* but rather that *the retention of members in the Academy should be judged above all with account taken of the need for uninterrupted continuation and intensification, especially in the near future, of the Academy's research work.*[13] In this context he mentioned Heinrich Srbik, whose exclusion from the Academy should not be automatic because *as President of the Academy he had not acted at any time in the spirit of Nazism*, but *had emphasized the Austrian tradition and, in a number of cases, had personally and resolutely opposed unacceptable political demands coming even from the Reich Ministry of Science.* Meister cited numerous examples, giving expression to his conviction that *it* [the Academy][...] *could not simply carry on from where it had left off in 1938 because it had never stopped working according to its tradition of strictly objective research. It needs only continue on the path it had pursued at all times since the days of its establishment.*[14]

To continue on this path, in May 1945 the Academy had received confirmation from the State Office that the Statutes approved on 14 February 1922 on the basis of the Academy Law (Bundesgesetzblatt 569/1921) and the By-Laws adopted on 29 May 1922 had re-entered into force. The Statutes of the Academy did not provide for the cancellation or abeyance of membership. This circumstance alone fostered a "benevolent" denazification process. With the exception of four particularly incriminated illegal Nazis,[15] the Nazi Party members were not excluded, but their membership of the Academy merely held in abeyance.[16] The prospect was held out to some members that even if the screening process was unfavorable, the Academy reserved the right to render their membership active again. By 25 August 1946, screening had revealed that around half of the full members – 26 out of 53 – and three-fifths of the corresponding members inland – 38 out of 66 – had been members or applicants for

[12] Meister (1947), *Geschichte*, p. 191.

[13] AÖAW, Minutes of the General Assembly of 22 June 1945 (A 995), report by Richard Meister.

[14] AÖAW, Minutes of the General Assembly of 22 June 1945 (A 995), p. 5; facsimile on p. 164, Fig. 85.

[15] Viktor Christian, Fritz Knoll, Karl Mayrhofer, and Eduard Pernkopf were deleted from the list of members. More information further down on p. 171.

[16] Between 1948 and 1950, the four excluded full members, Viktor Christian, Fritz Knoll, Karl Mayrhofer, and Eduard Pernkopf, were reinstated as fully fledged members of the Academy.

membership of the Nazi Party.[17] While Otto Brunner, Viktor Christian, Fritz Knoll, Josef Nadler, Oswald Menghin, Eduard Pernkopf, and Heinrich Srbik were not allowed to continue to teach at the university, their Academy membership was reactivated. Christian and Menghin, who did not initially figure in the official list of members, were listed again in 1950 and 1959, respectively, Christian as a full member and Menghin as a corresponding member abroad. Other Nazi Party members among full members, such as the Germanist Dietrich Kralik-Meyrswalden, the mathematician Karl Mayrhofer, the art historian Hans Sedlmayr, and the Anglicist Friedrich Wild, were able to start new university careers.[18]

The interim leadership of the Academy tried initially to sidestep the statutory provisions concerning denazification but had been obliged to comply with them after July 1945. This procedure shows, as Herbert Matis aptly puts it, that "sustained and internal critical engagement with the Nazi era" was neither considered nor, as it will be shown, applied at all at the Academy.[19]

Denazification procedure at the Academy

The denazification measures were carried out on the basis of the *Verbotsgesetz* [law banning re-engagement in National Socialist activities] of 8 May 1945, the decree of the State Office No. 2805/III/4a/45 of 2 August 1945 on the immediate removal from office of all Party members, the amendment to the *Verbotsgesetz* of 15 August 1945, and the 3rd *Verbotsgesetz* Executive Order of 22 August 1945. Späth, the interim head of the Academy, had already sent a letter on 1 June 1945, i.e. before the promulgation of the *Verbotsgesetz* of 8 May (promulgated on 6 June 1945), to the members of the Academy living in Vienna requesting them to *give an account of their attitude* [...] *to the former Nazi Party.*[20] The letter stated that membership of the Academy, a legal entity under the special protection of the state, was irreconcilable with illegal membership of the Nazi Party or Nazi organizations (SS, SA, NSKK, NSFK) or high office in the Party. The members were asked to fill out a form and were informed that refusal to do so would be construed to mean that they did not wish to

[17] Graf-Stuhlhofer (1995), *Akademie*, and Matis (1997), *Anpassung*, have carried out significant preparatory work for a study of the denazification of Academy members. Of the 64 "incriminated" persons, ten full members and 24 corresponding members were initially excluded. The membership of four full members and one corresponding member was "temporarily suspended" (until their degree of incrimination had been determined). Another twelve full members and thirteen corresponding members were classified as "less incriminated," Matis (1997), *Anpassung*, pp. 65–6.

[18] Pfefferle/Pfefferle (2012), *Glimpflich entnazifiziert*, and Rathkolb (2005), *Universität Wien*, pp. 38–53.

[19] Matis (1997), *Anpassung*, p. 67.

[20] AÖAW, Minutes of the General Assembly of 22 June 1945 (A 995), Annex, Späth to members of the Academy of 1 June 1945.

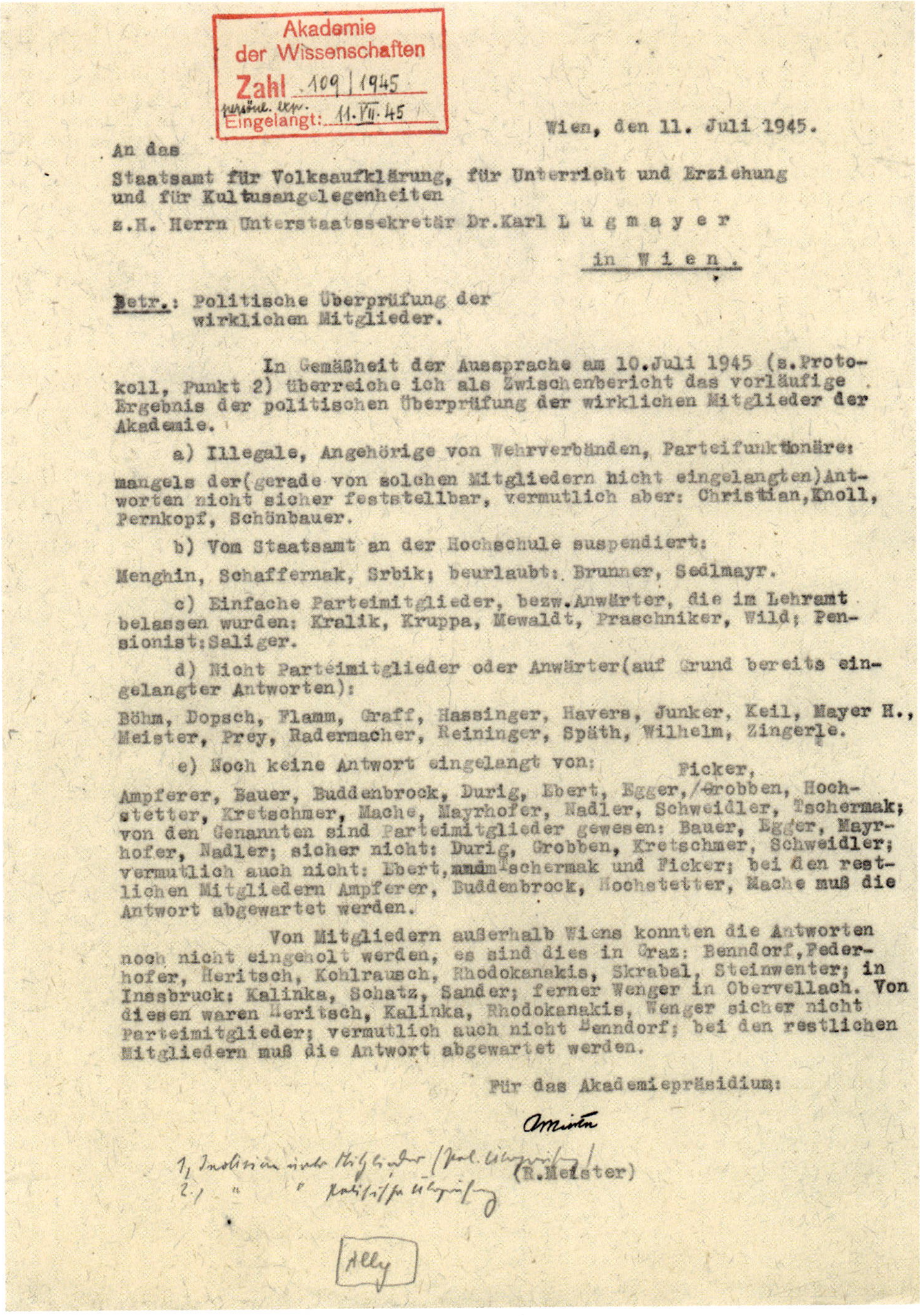

Akademie der Wissenschaften
Zahl 109/1945
Eingelangt: 11.VII.45

Wien, den 11. Juli 1945.

An das
Staatsamt für Volksaufklärung, für Unterricht und Erziehung und für Kultusangelegenheiten
z.H. Herrn Unterstaatssekretär Dr.Karl L u g m a y e r
in W i e n.

Betr.: Politische Überprüfung der wirklichen Mitglieder.

In Gemäßheit der Aussprache am 10.Juli 1945 (s.Protokoll, Punkt 2) überreiche ich als Zwischenbericht das vorläufige Ergebnis der politischen Überprüfung der wirklichen Mitglieder der Akademie.

a) Illegale, Angehörige von Wehrverbänden, Parteifunktionäre:

mangels der(gerade von solchen Mitgliedern nicht eingelangten)Antworten nicht sicher feststellbar, vermutlich aber: Christian,Knoll, Pernkopf, Schönbauer.

b) Vom Staatsamt an der Hochschule suspendiert:

Menghin, Schaffernak, Srbik; beurlaubt: Brunner, Sedlmayr.

c) Einfache Parteimitglieder, bezw.Anwärter, die im Lehramt belassen wurden: Kralik, Kruppa, Mewaldt, Praschniker, Wild; Pensionist:Saliger.

d) Nicht Parteimitglieder oder Anwärter(auf Grund bereits eingelangter Antworten):

Böhm, Dopsch, Flamm, Graff, Hassinger, Havers, Junker, Keil, Mayer H., Meister, Prey, Radermacher, Reininger, Späth, Wilhelm, Zingerle.

e) Noch keine Antwort eingelangt von:

Ampferer, Bauer, Buddenbrock, Durig, Ebert, Egger, Ficker, Grobben, Hochstetter, Kretschmer, Mache, Mayrhofer, Nadler, Schweidler, Tschermak; von den Genannten sind Parteimitglieder gewesen: Bauer, Egger, Mayrhofer, Nadler; sicher nicht: Durig, Grobben, Kretschmer, Schweidler; vermutlich auch nicht: Ebert, Tschermak und Ficker; bei den restlichen Mitgliedern Ampferer, Buddenbrock, Hochstetter, Mache muß die Antwort abgewartet werden.

Von Mitgliedern außerhalb Wiens konnten die Antworten noch nicht eingeholt werden, es sind dies in Graz: Benndorf,Federhofer, Heritsch, Kohlrausch, Rhodokanakis, Skrabal, Steinwenter; in Inssbruck: Kalinka, Schatz, Sander; ferner Wenger in Obervellach. Von diesen waren Heritsch, Kalinka, Rhodokanakis, Wenger sicher nicht Parteimitglieder; vermutlich auch nicht Benndorf; bei den restlichen Mitgliedern muß die Antwort abgewartet werden.

Für das Akademiepräsidium:

(R.Meister)

Fig. 87: Letter of the Academy to the State Office of 11 July 1945

remain in the Academy.[21] The interim leadership conveniently ignored the fact that registration obligation and atonement under the *Verbotsgesetz* applied not just to illegals, members of Nazi organizations, and high Nazi Party officials, but also to persons who had been ordinary members of the Nazi Party after 12 March 1938. Meister had *allowed* this group of *ordinary Party members or applicants to work at the Academy for the time being if there were no concerns on account of conspicuous activity in favor of Nazism.*[22]

In a confidential meeting, Späth and Meister reported on 3 August 1945 that they had had to report on 10 July to Undersecretary of State Karl Lugmayer and *Ministerialrat* [Ministerial Councilor] Otto Skrbensky on account of *suspicions* regarding the continuation of the political screening of Academy members.[23] Following the meeting at the State Office[24] and the decree of 2 August 1945, the Academy was required to act within the meaning of the *Verbotsgesetz* and, analogous to the universities, to exclude Nazi members *in general* from their ranks. Additionally, the Academy was not allowed to reinstate them until a *rehabilitation process* had been carried out on the basis of the questionnaire, which was also applicable to civil servants. A vote as to whether the *Presiding Committee should continue as before or, like the state, should suspend the membership of former Party members* was thus academic. The Academy unanimously resolved to suspend the membership of all former members of the Nazi Party and to inform them thereof.[25] It did not feel obliged, however, to *abide in all cases by the results of the screening by the university.*[26] Following the decision that mem-

---

[21] According to the *Verbotsgesetz* of 8 May 1945, persons with regular domicile in Austria who had belonged to the Nazi Party between 1 July 1933 and 27 April 1945 were subject to registration with the corresponding registration authorities. Membership or application for membership of the Nazi Party entailed atonement, e. g. dismissal or early retirement. The list of persons was to be publicized. Under the law, "illegals," those who had been members of the Nazi Party or one of its organizations before 13 March 1938, were guilty of high treason. Those who had joined afterwards were to be registered as *Mitläufer* [bystanders] but were also subject to atonement. In Austria some 535,000 persons were registered in 1945/46 as former Nazi Party members. Their names were removed from the list by order of the denazification commissions and by the execution of the National Socialist Law of 1947 and of the so-called Amnesty Law of 1948.

[22] AÖAW, Allgemeine Personalakten, Box 3, Folder 16, Official memo on the suspension of membership of the Academy of 4 August 1945.

[23] AÖAW, Minutes of the General Assembly of August 3, 1945 (A 996), annex, confidential meeting [of July 10].

[24] See AÖAW, Allgemeine Akten, No. 108/1945, Minutes of the meeting at the State Office of the interim directors of the Academy of Sciences with Undersecretary of State Dr Karl Lugmayer and Ministerial Councilor Dr Skrbensky of 11 July 1945; also AÖAW, Allgemeine Akten, No. 109/1945, Meister to Lugmayer on political screening of full members of 11 July 1945 [with the comment *delivered in person*]; see facsimile overleaf.

[25] See AÖAW, Minutes of the General Assembly of 3 August 1945 (A 996), Annex, confidential meeting [of 10 July].

[26] Ibid. Only in the case of retirees did Meister recommend the [definitive] *exclusion of former illegals or Party officials.*

bership of all former Nazi Party members or applicants was to be held in abeyance *until rehabilitation by decision of the State Office Examination Commission or rescission of the obligation to register by the State Office of the Interior*, the full members concerned were not invited to the Election Meeting of 30 October 1945.[27] They were informed, however, that this measure would be rescinded immediately "in the event of a favorable outcome" of the screening process.[28] Franz Graf-Stuhlhofer notes that in the letters to members Rudolf Egger and Josef Nadler, the Academy reserved the right to "reverse abeyance on membership" even "in the event of an unfavorable outcome."[29] The first definitive denazification measures consisted in the *termination* of the full membership of Viktor Christian, Fritz Knoll, Karl Mayrhofer, and Eduard Pernkopf, as pronounced at the sectional meetings of 17 and 18 October 1945.[30] As it proved later, this exclusion was not definitive and the memberships were revived in 1948 and 1950. No further measures were taken in 1945.

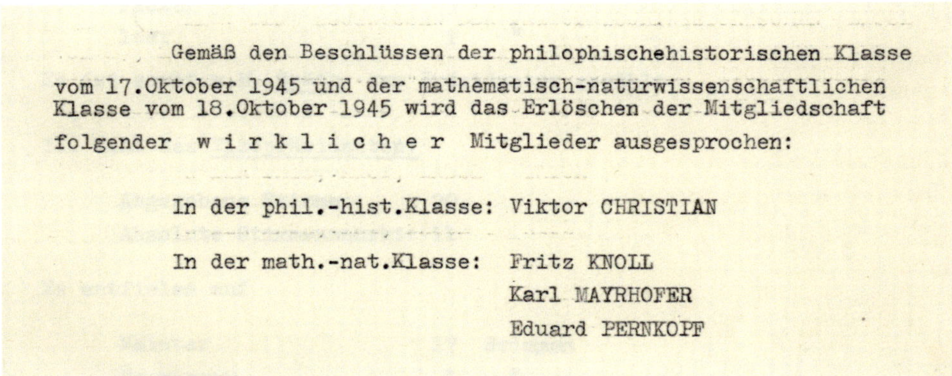

Gemäß den Beschlüssen der philophischehistorischen Klasse vom 17.Oktober 1945 und der mathematisch-naturwissenschaftlichen Klasse vom 18.Oktober 1945 wird das Erlöschen der Mitgliedschaft folgender w i r k l i c h e r Mitglieder ausgesprochen:

In der phil.-hist.Klasse: Viktor CHRISTIAN

In der math.-nat.Klasse: Fritz KNOLL
Karl MAYRHOFER
Eduard PERNKOPF

Fig. 88: Minutes of the General Assembly of 30 October 1945 (extract)

Many of those who had been dismissed or removed from the university and had their Academy membership held in abeyance continued to attend Academy meetings and, after the sudden death of Ernst Späth in November 1946, even took part in the election of the new President Heinrich Ficker. They also appeared on unpublished lists as chairmen or members of the individual commissions.[31] For the years 1945 (after 27 April), 1946, and 1947, the Academy did not publish a list of members in the *Almanach*, despite the fact that, according to the Statutes, it had to contain a list of all members. In those years the problem of political screening of Academy members

[27] AÖAW, extraordinary General Assembly of 30 October 1945 (A 997).

[28] Graf-Stuhlhofer (1995), *Akademie*, p. 147.

[29] Ibid.

[30] AÖAW, Minutes of the General Assembly of 30 October 1945 (A 997).

[31] See AÖAW, Minutes of the General Assembly of 7 December 1945 (A 998), Annex, Commissions (14 November 1945).

was tacitly ignored at the meetings.[32] In contrast, Academy members repeatedly considered the political screening of Academy employees.[33] The Presiding Committee supported the reinstatement not only of Chancellery Secretary Wilfried Oberhummer (Nazi Party member since 1942), who had been responsible for the *centralized management of the chancellery and accounts department* since 21 October 1938[34] and had risen to become First Actuary, but also of the illegal Nazi Party member Walter Ruth as head of the Phonogram Archive, Franz Ruttner as head of the Biological Station in Lunz, as well as other (including illegal) Nazis. Most were able to resume work in their old positions.

The denazification issue appears in the minutes of the Academy meetings again after the promulgation of the National Socialist Law of 17 February 1947. Two paragraphs in this law refer directly to the Academy. Paragraph 18n states that incriminated Academy members were subject to atonement consisting in not being permitted to belong to the Academy as full members or corresponding members inland. Under paragraph 19j, less incriminated persons could not be full members or corresponding members inland until 30 April 1950. Exceptions were made for less incriminated persons over 70 years of age and of invalid class III, and incriminated persons of invalid class IV.[35] The direct impact of the National Socialist Law on Academy members who had not yet been exempted from atonement was that they were not allowed to attend the confidential part of meetings and were not invited to the centennial celebration in 1947.[36] Exceptions were made for full members Hermann Junker, Camillo Praschniker, Heinrich Mache, and honorary member Hans Sperl, who were over 70 and had been classified as less incriminated. The indirect impact of the law can be seen in a report by Meister, which he presented to the General Assembly on 10 October 1947, on the latest *status of denazification*. Only nine of 35 full members of the Section for Humanities and the Social Sciences and six of 32 in the Section for Mathematics and the Natural Sciences were still being held in abeyance, and in both Sections two unnamed members had *departed*. Because of the age limit on

[32] See *Almanachs* for 1945, 95 (1947); 1946, 96 (1948), and 1947, 97 (1948). Only in the General Assembly of October 25, 1946 did Meister refer to the *denazification in the Academy*, reporting: *by order of the Allies notified by telephone on 24 August 1946, a report on denazification had to be provided by 10 a.m. on 25 August 1946.* AÖAW, Minutes of the General Assembly of 25 October 1946 (A 1005). See also AÖAW, Minutes of the General Assembly of 30 October 1945 (A 997).

[33] See the essay in this volume by Johannes Feichtinger and Dieter J. Hecht, "Tasks and areas of responsibility of the new Presiding Committee," pp. 151–61.

[34] AÖAW, Minutes of the General Assembly of 21 October 1938 (A 939).

[35] See Federal Constitutional Law of 6 February 1947 on the treatment of National Socialists (National Socialist Law) published on 17 February 1947, Federal Legal Gazette, No. 25/1947.

[36] See AÖAW, Minutes of the General Assembly of 21 February 1947 (A 1008), and AÖAW, Minutes of the General Assembly of 25 April 1947 (A 1010). In the Minutes of the General Assembly of 21 March 1947 (A 1009) mathematician Erwin Kruppa, botanist Karl Höfler, and geologist Kurt Leuchs are listed as *guests*.

BUNDESGESETZBLATT

FÜR DIE REPUBLIK ÖSTERREICH

Jahrgang 1947 Ausgegeben am 17. Februar 1947 8. Stück

25. Bundesverfassungsgesetz: Nationalsozialistengesetz.

25. Bundesverfassungsgesetz vom 6. Februar 1947 über die Behandlung der Nationalsozialisten (Nationalsozialistengesetz).

Der Nationalrat hat beschlossen:

I. HAUPTSTÜCK.

3. Verbotsgesetznovelle.

Abschnitt I.

Das Verfassungsgesetz vom 8. Mai 1945, St. G. Bl. Nr. 13, über das Verbot der NSDAP (Verbotsgesetz) in der Fassung des Verfassungsgesetzes vom 15. August 1945, St. G. Bl. Nr. 127 (1. Verbotsgesetznovelle), des Verfassungsgesetzes vom 16. November 1945, B. G. Bl. Nr. 16/19… und des Bundesverf… 1946, B. G. Bl. Nr. … folgt:

1. § 3, Abs. (2), … treten folgende Besti…

„§ 3 a. Eines Verb… und wird mit dem … gesamten Vermögens …

1. wer versucht, … nationalsozialistische Organisation aufrechtzuerhalten oder wiederherzustellen oder mit einer solchen Organisation oder einer in ihrem Namen handelnden Person in Verbindung zu treten; als nationalsozialistische Organisationen (§ 1) gelten: die NSDAP, die SS, die SA, das NSKK, das NSFK, der N… ziersbund, alle … NSDAP und die i… sowie jede andere … sation;

2. wer eine Verbin… es ist, durch Betäti… nationalsozialistischen … und Unabhängigkeit … zu untergraben oder … den Wiederaufbau … wer sich in einer Ver… betätigt;

3. wer den Ausbau einer der in der Z. 1 und der Z. 2 bezeichneten Organisationen und Verbindungen durch Anwerbung von Mitgliedern, Bereitstellung von Geldmitteln oder in ähnlicher Weise fördert, die Mitglieder einer solchen Organisation oder Verbindung mit Kampfmitteln, Verkehrsmitteln oder Einrichtungen zur Nachrichtenübermittlung ausrüstet oder in ähnlicher Weise die Tätigkeit einer solchen Organisation oder Verbindung ermöglicht oder unterstützt;

4. wer für eine solche Organisation oder Verbindung Kampfmittel, Verkehrsmittel oder Einrichtungen zur Nachrichtenübermittlung herstellt, sich verschafft oder bereithält.

§ 3 b. Wer an einer Organisation oder Verbindung der in § 3 a bezeichneten Art teilnimmt oder sie durch Geldzuwendungen oder in anderer Weise unterstützt, wird, wenn die …rafbar ist, wegen …erker von 10 bis …erfall des gesam…

…r in den §§ 3 a und …en erlischt, wenn …ntrieb, ehe die Be…hrt, alles, was ihm …r Verbindung und …u einer Zeit, da es noch geheim war und ein Schaden verhütet werden konnte, der Behörde entdeckt.

§ 3 d. Wer öffentlich oder vor mehreren Leuten, in Druckwerken, verbreiteten Schriften oder bildlichen Darstellungen zu einer der nach § 1 oder § 3 verbotenen Handlungen auffor…en sucht, insbe…Ziele der NSDAP, …nahmen verherr…n sich darin nicht …erbrechen darstellt, …0 bis zu 20 Jahren …esamten Vermögens

…hung eines Mordes, …legung, eines Ver…oder 89 des Straf…hens nach § 4 des Sprengstoffgesetzes als Mittel der Betätigung im nationalsozialistischen Sinn mit einem anderen verabredet, wird mit dem Tode und mit dem Verfall des gesamten Vermögens bestraft.

„§ 18. Belastete Personen im Sinne des § 17, Abs. (2), haben die nachstehenden Sühnefolgen zu tragen:

n) Sie können der Akademie der Wissenschaften (der Österreichischen Akademie der Wissenschaften in Wien) weder als wirkliche noch als korrespondierende Mitglieder angehören.

„§ 19. (1) Minderbelastete Personen im Sinne des § 17, Abs. (3), haben die nachstehenden Sühnefolgen zu tragen:

j) Sie können bis zum 30. April 1950 der Akademie der Wissenschaften (der Österreichischen Akademie der Wissenschaften in Wien) nicht als wirkliche Mitglieder angehören; sie können bis zu diesem Zeitpunkt nicht zu korrespondierenden Mitgliedern ernannt werden.

Fig. 89: National Socialist Law of 17 February 1947 (extract)

8. <u>Politische Überprüfung der Akademiemitglieder.</u>

Der Vizepräsident berichtet über den derzeitigen Stand der Mitglieder der Akademie, die ehemals der NSDAP angehört haben:

	w. M.			E.M.		k.M.	
	ph.h.	m.-n.	Ges.	ph.h.	m.-n.	ph.h.	m.n.
Nicht P.G.	2o	22	2	-	1	21	19
Entregistriert	4	3	-	1	-	4	3
Minderbelastet	9	5	-	-	-	7	11
Unbestimmt	-	2	-	-	-	5	7
Vermutlich bel.	1	-	-	-	-	-	-
Belastet	1	-	-	-	-	-	1
Reichsdeutsche	-	-	2	5	2	24	19
Übrige Ausländ.	-	-	-	2	3	17	26
Summe	35	32	4	8	6	78	86.

w.M. <u>Entreg.:</u> Bauer, Junker, Mewaldt, Praschniker - Durig, Mache, Skrabal.
<u>Minderb.:</u> Brunner, Egger, Kralik, Nadler, Schönbauer, Srbik, Sedlmayr, Steinwenter, Wild - Federhofer, Knoll, Kruppa, Mayrhofer, Schaffernak.
<u>Unbest.:</u> Pernkopf, Saliger.
<u>Belastet:</u> Christian, Menghin.

E.M. <u>Nicht PG:</u> Erzh. Eugen, Renner K., Meller
<u>Entreg.:</u> Sperl
<u>Reichsd.:</u> Hoops, Koschaker, Kraus, Meinecke, Panzer - Carathéodory, Prandtl,
<u>Ausland:</u> Jouguet, Murray - Hedin, Hubble, Niggli

k.M. <u>Entreg.</u> Hold, Lach, Lesky, Stolz - Grosser, Oberguggenberger, Toldt
<u>Minderbel:</u> Eichler A., Grohmann, Jutz, Miltner, Pöschl, Rupprich, Schober - Cornelius, Höfler, Kirsch, Klebelsberg, Leuch, Pesta, Patzelt, Richter, Staffe, Stetter, Tertsch
<u>Unbest.:</u> Frauwallner, Günther, Pfalz, Steinacker, Steinhauser - Barrenscheen, Huber, Krames, Ortner, Porsch, Sequenz, Wettstein
<u>Belastet:</u> Kofler

<u>Reichsd.:</u> ph.-h.: ~~Becker~~ Brecht, Brackmann, Dölger, Gamilschegg, Gehlen, Hartmann, Hugelmann (entlastet), Kluckhohn, Koch, Küchler, Lehmann, Littmann, Maull (Mitläufer4), Mayer Th., Mitteis, Müller, San Nicolò, Schäfer, Spranger, Stengel, Übersberger, Vasmer, Vossler, Litt

m.-n.: Abderhalden, Buddenbrock, Fuess, Hahn, Kopff, Korschelt, Kühn, Küster, Kuhn, Lauer, List, Machatschek, Renner O., Schütte, Sommerfeldt, Strubecker, Süring, Tschermak A., Weber

Sudetendeutsche: Überleitung k.M. Inland: Grohmann, Grosser, Richter.

Da in der folgenden Diskussion gegen die Belassung einzelner Mitglieder Einspruch erhoben wurde, hat die Gesamtsitzung beschlossen, eine Liste aller Betroffenen zusammenzustellen und diese an alle wirklichen Mitglieder zu senden mit der Bitte um schriftliche Stellungnahme bis 1. März. - In der Gesamtsitzung am 5. März soll eine Beschlußfassung über diesen Punkt erfolgen. Die Beantwortung dieser Liste ist für jedes wirkliche Mitglied verbindlich, bei einem etwaigen Einspruch mit Angabe der Gründe.

Einstimmig angenommen.

Fig. 90: Minutes of the General Assembly of 9 January 1948 (extract)

atonement, former Nazi Party members or applicants Wilhelm Bauer, Arnold Durig, and Heinrich Mache appeared again in the lists as fully fledged members of the Academy. The abeyance of membership of classical philologists Johannes Mewaldt and Albin Lesky was rescinded as a result of their removal from the list, and Camillo Praschniker was reinstated because he was not obliged to register.[37]

On 9 January 1948 Meister was again able to report to the General Assembly that the following full members were still listed as less incriminated: in the Section for Humanities and the Social Sciences Otto Brunner, Rudolf Egger, Dietrich Kralik-Meyrswalden, Josef Nadler, Ernst Schönbauer, Heinrich Srbik, Hans Sedlmayr, Artur Steinwenter, and Friedrich Wild, and in the Section for Mathematics and the Natural Sciences Fritz Knoll, Erwin Kruppa, Karl Mayrhofer, and the engineers Karl Federhofer and Friedrich Schaffernak, who both were classified as invalid class III. The chemist Anton Skrabal was removed from the list as he was 70 years old. Viktor Christian and Oswald Menghin were still incriminated, and Eduard Pernkopf and the engineer and "Anschluss rector" of the Vienna College of Technology Rudolf Saliger undetermined.[38] In view of the fact that, according to Meister, *a larger number* of the corresponding members inland had *left under the law of 1945 than would have done so under the* [law] *of 1947*, the corresponding members had been requested in the fall of 1947 to provide evidence from the registration authority of their status as less incriminated or of the waiving of their registration obligation so that their membership could again be made permanent.[39]

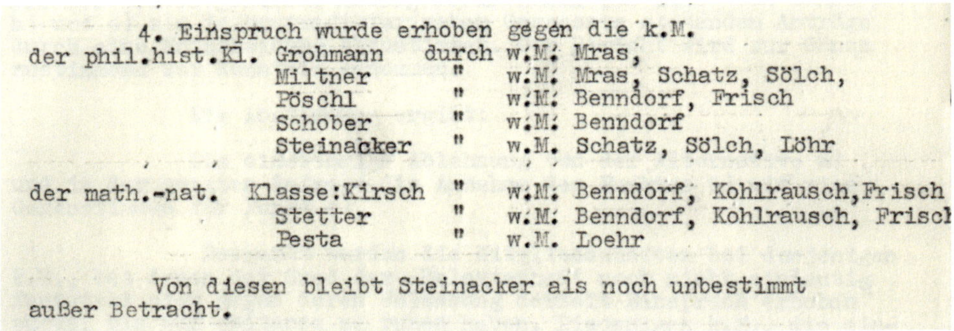
4. Einspruch wurde erhoben gegen die k.M.
der phil.hist.Kl. Grohmann durch w.M. Mras,
Miltner " w.M. Mras, Schatz, Sölch,
Pöschl " w.M. Benndorf, Frisch
Schober " w.M. Benndorf
Steinacker " w.M. Schatz, Sölch, Löhr

der math.-nat. Klasse:Kirsch " w.M. Benndorf, Kohlrausch, Frisch
Stetter " w.M. Benndorf, Kohlrausch, Frisch
Pesta " w.M. Loehr

Von diesen bleibt Steinacker als noch unbestimmt außer Betracht.

Fig. 91: Minutes of the General Assembly of 16 March 1948 (extract)

[37] See AÖAW, Minutes of the General Assembly of 10 October 1947 (A 1013), report by Richard Meister on denazification, pp. 6–7.

[38] See AÖAW, Minutes of the General Assembly of 9 January 1948 (A 1015), political screening of Academy members; see Mikoletzky (2003), *Hort*.

[39] AÖAW, Minutes of the General Assembly of 10 October 1947 (A 1013), report by Richard Meister on denazification.

At the General Assembly of 16 March 1948, the fate of individual corresponding members was decided. Those who had been removed from the list or had reached the age of 70 could – in the words of the Meister giving the report – *at all events* remain members.[40] This group included international jurist Alexander Hold-Ferneck, classical philologist Albin Lesky, musicologist Robert Lach, historian Otto Stolz, physician Otto Grosser, astronomer Viktor Oberguggenberger, and zoologist Karl Toldt. It was decided that the membership of corresponding members with the status of less incriminated or undetermined whose membership of the Academy had been objected to by other full members should not be revoked but remained held in abeyance until further notice.[41] These included Semitist and Arabist Adolf Grohmann,[42] ancient historian Franz Miltner, canonist Arnold Pöschl, archeologist Arnold Schober,[43] historian Harold Steinacker,[44] physicists Gerhard Kirsch[45] und Georg Stetter, and zoologist Otto Pesta. Those less incriminated corresponding members about whom no objections had been made were allowed to retain their Academy membership. These included Anglicist Albert Eichler, Germanists Leo Jutz and Hans Rupprich, geologist Hans Peter Cornelius, botanist Karl Höfler, geologist and paleontologist Raimund Klebelsberg, geologist Kurt Leuchs, histologist Viktor Patzelt, botanist Oswald Richter, zoologist Adolf Staffe, and mineralogist Hermann Tertsch. The decision on a group whose degree of incrimination was still *undetermined* at the time was deferred. This applied to Indologist Erich Frauwallner, economist Adolf Günther, Germanist Anton Pfalz, historian Harold Steinacker, Germanist Walter Steinhauser, chemist Hermann Barrenscheen, mathematicians Anton Huber and Josef Krames, physicist Gustav Ortner, botanist Otto Porsch, engineer Heinrich Sequenz, and zoologist Otto Wettstein-Westersheimb.

Since Richard Meister had informed the General Assembly of the danger that *public opinion* […] *might object to less incriminated members being allowed to remain members*, the full members voted to reject two options as to how such persons should be dealt with. One was favored by Secretary General Josef Keil *that less incriminated members should not be expunged at all*, and the other that a *procedure* be established *regarding the continued membership* of less incriminated members. A third option was adopted. Meister reported: the membership of those whose level of incrimination had not yet been determined and against whom an objection existed *at the moment* would remain held in abeyance. *Those corresponding members who were clearly less incriminated*

[40] AÖAW, Minutes of the General Assembly of March 16, 1948 (A 1017), report by Richard Meister on the decision on membership of corresponding members inland who had been members of the Party.

[41] Ibid.

[42] Wentker (2012), *Grohmann.*

[43] Pesditschek (2012), *Miltner*; Steirische Gesellschaft für Kulturpolitik (1985), *Grenzfeste*, p. 92 (on Pöschl), and Mindler (2011), *Schober*, p. 86 (on Schober).

[44] See Spreitzer (2008), *Steinacker.*

[45] See Pfefferle/Pfefferle (2012), *Glimpflich entnazifiziert*, pp. 118–9.

and whose continued membership had not been objected to will be informed of their continued membership and, where this has not yet occurred, will receive all publications since 1945 until further notice. Although Meister announced in this context that printing a membership list in the 1947 *Almanach* was *unavoidable*,[46] this did not occur. The Academy was apparently hesitant because of the threat of public criticism.

The turning point came ultimately with the Amnesty Law of 21 April 1948.[47] It marked the definitive *conclusion of the political screening of full, honorary, and corresponding members in Austria who had been* [less incriminated] *members of the Party*.[48] In the confidential part of the General Assembly of 2 July 1948, President Ficker reported that after *the President of the Constitutional Court, full member of the Section for Humanities and the Social Sciences Univ.-Prof. Dr. Ludwig Adamovich, had obtained an expert opinion from both Sections* [...], *a unanimous decision* [was] *adopted to invite all full members who had not been able to belong to the Academy because of that provision* [...] *to resume their membership* [...] [and] *to refrain from any objections in general to the continued membership of corresponding members*.[49] All of those invited to rejoin the Academy accepted the invitation, while Viktor Christian, Oswald Menghin, Eduard Pernkopf, and the pharmacognosist Ludwig Kofler remained suspended.[50] The Federal Ministry of Education was merely *informed* of this measure and no authorization was requested.[51] With a few exceptions, the holding in abeyance of memberships was thereby ended. Christian returned to the Academy as full member in 1950, and Menghin, who was now living in Argentina, became a corresponding member abroad in 1959. Ludwig Kofler, who had been elected as a corresponding member inland in 1941, died before he could be readmitted. Other corresponding members who had been dismissed from their professorships in 1945, such as Heinrich Sequenz, Anton Pfalz, and Anton Huber, were included in the official lists again in 1949. The members list for 1949 also included Rudolf Saliger as a full member, despite the efforts of full members Friedrich Hopfner and Ernst Melan, and corresponding member inland Karl Wolf to prevent this.

---

46 AÖAW, Minutes of the General Assembly of 16 March 1948 (A 1017).

47 Federal Constitutional Law on the early conclusion of the atonement provided for in the National Socialist Law for less incriminated persons, published on 5 June 1948, BGBl., No. 88/1948.

48 AÖAW, Minutes of the General Assembly of 2 July 1948 (A 1020), Conclusion of political screening of full, honorary, and corresponding members inland.

49 Ibid.

50 The corresponding members Erich Frauwallner and Anton Pfalz of the Section for Humanities and the Social Sciences and Hermann Barrenscheen, Anton Huber, Otto Porsch, and Heinrich Sequenz in the Section for Mathematics and the Natural Sciences did not initially benefit from the Amnesty Law.

51 AÖAW, Ministerium 1948–1950, Presiding Committee of the Academy to Federal Ministry of Education of 8 July 1948.

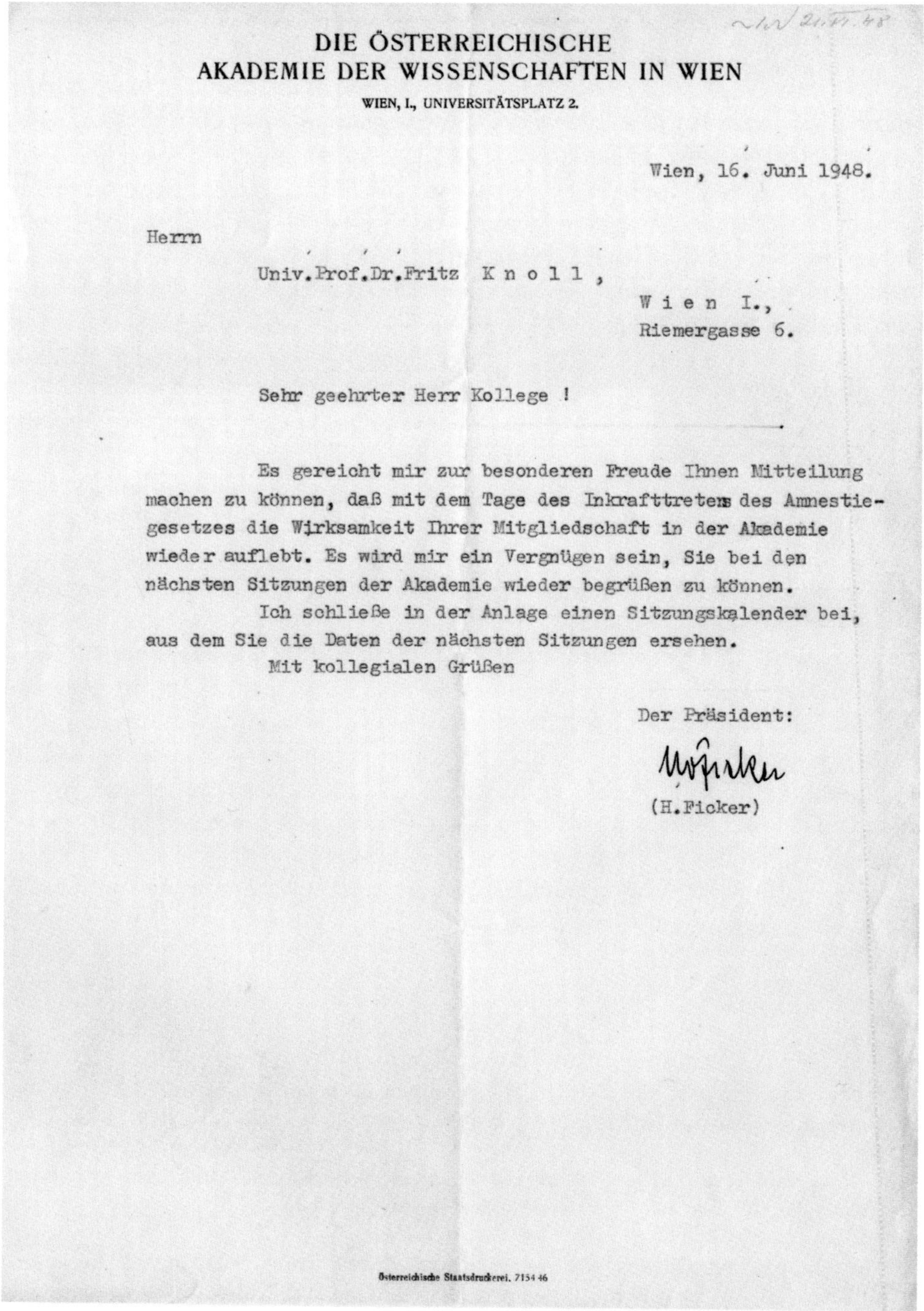

DIE ÖSTERREICHISCHE
AKADEMIE DER WISSENSCHAFTEN IN WIEN
WIEN, I., UNIVERSITÄTSPLATZ 2.

Wien, 16. Juni 1948.

Herrn

Univ.Prof.Dr.Fritz K n o l l ,

W i e n I.,
Riemergasse 6.

Sehr geehrter Herr Kollege !

Es gereicht mir zur besonderen Freude Ihnen Mitteilung machen zu können, daß mit dem Tage des Inkrafttretens des Amnestiegesetzes die Wirksamkeit Ihrer Mitgliedschaft in der Akademie wieder auflebt. Es wird mir ein Vergnügen sein, Sie bei den nächsten Sitzungen der Akademie wieder begrüßen zu können.

Ich schließe in der Anlage einen Sitzungskalender bei, aus dem Sie die Daten der nächsten Sitzungen ersehen.

Mit kollegialen Grüßen

Der Präsident:

(H.Ficker)

Österreichische Staatsdruckerei. 7154 46

Fig. 92: Letter of the Academy to Knoll of 16 June 1948

In 1948, over a third of the reactivated members of the Academy had been members of the Nazi Party, and they were to have a decisive influence on the future composition of the Academy through their behavior in voting for new members. Richard Meister had taken charge of the denazification question in April 1945 and never relinquished control. In 1951 he was elected President of the Academy and remained in office until 1963. During his Presidency and thereafter, former Nazis were also rehabilitated symbolically. Erwin Kruppa was Vice-President from 1957 to 1960, Fritz Knoll was Secretary General from 1959 to 1964 and Secretary of the Section for Mathematics and the Natural Sciences from 1957 to 1959, and Albin Lesky was Secretary from 1959 to 1963.

Johannes Feichtinger/Dieter J. Hecht

1945 and after. One break and two continuities

On 19 May 1945, in a letter by the interim heads of the Academy, Ernst Späth and Richard Meister, to the *Staatsamt für Volksaufklärung, für Unterricht und Erziehung und für Kultusangelegenheiten* [State Office for Public Enlightenment, Education, and Cultural Affairs], the following was considered as a future agenda item: *Verification of the status of members of the Academy, i.e. recall of full and corresponding members who left in connection with the political events of 1938, and exclusion of members who have been removed from their official positions or (if retired or private) have become unacceptable because of particularly incriminating circumstances.*[1]

One break ...

On 22 June 1945, the interim leadership of the Academy announced as a first staff measure that the *suspension of membership* on the basis of racial laws or for political reasons was invalid.[2] On this day Meister reported the *recall* of members excluded after 1938, which he described as *reparation*[3] or an "act of reparation."[4] Stefan Meyer, August Loehr, Josef Weninger, Walther Brecht, Karl Bühler, Emil Abel, Viktor Moritz Goldschmidt, Victor Franz Hess, Hermann Franz Mark, Wolfgang Pauli, Ernst Peter Pick, and Erwin Schrödinger were invited to resume their membership.[5]

After the fall and winter of 1945, radium researcher Stefan Meyer, historian and museum director August Loehr, and anthropologist Josef Weninger took part regularly and actively in Academy meetings and activities.[6] In 1945, Loehr (corresponding member since 1933) and Weninger (corresponding member since 1937) were

---

[1] AÖAW, Minutes of the General Assembly of 18 May 1945 (A 994), Annex, Späth and Meister to the *Staatsamt für Volksaufklärung, für Unterricht und Erziehung und für Kultusangelegenheiten* [State Office for Public Enlightenment, Education, and Cultural Affairs] of 19 May 1945.

[2] AÖAW, Minutes of the General Assembly of 22 June 1945 (A 995); see also report by Richard Meister on the restructuring of the Academy personnel after 27 April 1945 in the *Almanach* for 1945, 95 (1947), pp. 89–91, here p. 90.

[3] AÖAW, Minutes of the General Assembly of 22 June 1945 (A 995), report by Richard Meister.

[4] Meister (1947), *Geschichte*, p. 188.

[5] See AÖAW, Minutes of the General Assembly of 22 June 1945 (A 995), report by Richard Meister. Full members Hans Horst Meyer, Berthold Hatschek, Franz Eduard Suess, and corresponding members Alfred Francis Přibram, Eduard Norden, Richard Willstätter, Ernst Theodor Brücke, Franz Boas, and Alfred Hettner had died in the meantime. At the same time, the election of Hans Mayer as an ordinary member and George Shull as a corresponding member abroad, which had not been confirmed by the Reich Minister, were declared valid. Those ordinary members who had lived outside the borders of Austria between 1938 and 1945 became corresponding members abroad (Fritz Machatschek, Karl Terzaghi, Hermann Weber). See Feichtinger/Uhl (2005), *Akademie*, p. 316.

[6] Meyer and Loehr had been "racially" persecuted after the "Anschluss", and Weninger forced into retirement because of his Jewish wife. He also lost his Academy membership.

elected full members. Thanks to Stefan Meyer, the expelled physicist Karl Przibram also returned as full professor to the Department of Physics II of the University of Vienna in 1946. He was elected into the Academy as a corresponding member in the same year and as a full member in 1950. Other Academy members excluded after the "Anschluss" no longer played a significant role in the Academy because they were abroad. Physics Nobel Prize winner Victor Franz Hess was teaching in New York, Erwin Schrödinger in Dublin. Schrödinger was elected a full member on his return in 1956. In 1970, the work of the eminent Viennese researcher Hermann Franz Mark in New York was also recognized through his election as an honorary member of the Austrian Academy of Sciences. The first expelled scientist living abroad to become a corresponding member abroad (in 1947) was the Viennese international jurist Hans Kelsen, now professor at the University of California, Berkeley. The first woman to become a corresponding member abroad (in 1948) was the physicist Lise Meitner, now teaching in Stockholm.[7] In 1950, the mathematician Paul Funk, persecuted during the Nazi era on "racial" grounds, was elected a full member. After liberation from the Nazi Theresienstadt concentration camp in 1945 he had been appointed professor at the Vienna College of Technology. Other returnees like the Viennese chemist Engelbert Broda, who had worked at the Cavendish Laboratory in Cambridge during World War II, did not become members of the Academy.[8]

… and two continuities

Former supporters of the authoritarian *Ständestaat* [Corporate State] took charge at the Academy and the university in 1945. As conservatives with German national or Greater German sympathies, most of them had been able to safeguard their positions at the university and the Academy after the "Anschluss" with the aid of Nazi supporters.[9] After 1948, the pre-1938 elite made it possible for former Nazi Party members, after a period of denazification, i.e. the removal from their posts and the abeyance of their Academy membership, to resume their old positions at the university and the Academy of Sciences.

In 1945, Richard Meister was already supporting the *retention of members in the Academy* because of the *need for uninterrupted* […] *intensive continuation of research work*. This point of view appeared to him as *more important* than *how it was perceived abroad*.[10] Meister and the other protagonists clearly assumed that the exclusion of half of the full members would probably have made the Academy ineffective and increased the chances of it being transformed into a kind of *Wissenschaftskammer* [professional association of academics] in Austria. At the General Assembly of 3 August 1945 it

[7] See AÖAW, Minutes of the General Assembly of 13 May 1947 (A 1011), and AÖAW, Minutes of the General Assembly of 25 May 1948 (A 1019). For details on Hans Kelsen, see Feichtinger (2009), *Vernetzungen*, pp. 327–35, and for Lise Meitner, see Sexl/Hardy (2002), *Meitner*.

[8] See Oberkofler (2012), *Bemerkungen*, p. 1, and Oberkofler (2005), *Mathematiker*, pp. 200–17.

[9] See Heiss (2005), *Wendepunkt*, pp. 27–8.

[10] AÖAW, Minutes of the General Assembly of 22 June 1945 (A 995), report by Richard Meister.

was therefore decided that Academy members who had belonged to the Nazi Party should not be excluded but merely have their membership held in abeyance.[11] On the basis of sectional decisions of 17 and 18 October 1945, full members Viktor Christian, Fritz Knoll, Karl Mayrhofer, and Eduard Pernkopf, who had been dismissed from the university, were initially excluded.[12] Further measures were taken only after the adoption of the National Socialist Law in 1947, and the continuation of the political screening of members was not discussed at the General Assemblies.[13] Following the Amnesty Law of 21 April 1948, most Academy memberships held in abeyance were officially reinstated.

Within the Academy, Ernst Späth, Richard Meister, and Josef Keil had already supported the reintegration of former Nazis in 1945. Späth and Meister intervened on behalf of, amongst others, the deposed Academy President Heinrich Srbik and full member Oswald Menghin, who was listed as a war criminal.[14] Other Academy members like the Anglicist Friedrich Wild, who had been dismissed from the university, were able to count on the new Presiding Committee. According to unofficial lists, in November 1945 Wild was already chairman of the Phonogram Archive Commission again.[15] On 14 February 1948 Secretary General Keil wrote on behalf of the Presiding Committee in support of Wild's application to Federal President Karl Renner in which he requested that his atonement be rescinded. Wild's application was approved on 22 May 1948 and his Academy membership was officially reinstated on 24 May 1948.[16] The Presiding Committee also actively supported the reinstatement of Walter Ruth who, "on account of his merits during the prohibition period," had been put in provisional charge of the Phonogram Archive in May 1938.[17] Keil intervened successfully on behalf of the ex-Nazi Ruth after his return from detention as a prisoner of war.[18] Josef Keil and Richard Meister also intervened several times with the State

[11] See the essay in this volume by Johannes Feichtinger and Dieter J. Hecht, "Denazification at the Academy of Sciences," pp. 163–79, especially p. 171.

[12] See AÖAW, Minutes of the General Assembly of 30 October 1945 (A 997). The minutes state that the *extinction of the membership* of these full members was *decreed*.

[13] See the essay in this volume by Johannes Feichtinger and Dieter J. Hecht, "Denazification at the Academy of Sciences," pp. 163–79.

[14] See AÖAW, PA Heinrich Srbik, and AÖAW, PA Oswald Menghin, and UAW, PA Oswald Menghin, PH PA 2617/161. See also UAW, Papers of Richard Meister, Box 324, correspondence of Meister with Oswald Menghin.

[15] See AÖAW, Minutes of the General Assembly of 7 December 1945 (A 998), Annex, Commissions (14 November 1945).

[16] See AÖAW, PA Friedrich Wild.

[17] AÖAW, Phonogrammarchiv, Box 1, Folder 4, No. 92/1939. See essay in this volume by Marlene Wahlmüller, "Consequences for the academic staff. The case of Leo Hajek," pp. 69–76.

[18] AÖAW, Ministry 1948–1950, 1948. Keil was listed in the *Almanachs* for 1946 to 1948 as deputy chairman of the Phonogram Archive Commission. In the *Almanach* for 1948, 98 (1949), p. 91, Wild is named as a member of the Phonogram Archive Commission, but there is no chairman listed, with only Keil as deputy chairman. In the *Almanach* for 1949, 99 (1950), p. 121, Wild is again listed as chairman.

Office to secure the retention of the staff of the Biological Station in Lunz, all of whom had been illegal members of the Nazi Party before 1938. In 1947 Meister warned Minister Felix Hurdes that he would resign as Vice-President if the staff issues in Lunz were not resolved to his satisfaction by the end of the year.[19] All of the staff in Lunz were able to stay and were offered new employment contracts. Against this background, the transfer from the Institute for Experimental Biology in the Prater of the budgeted position of its head and the proceeds from the sale of its destroyed buildings to the Biological Station in Lunz appears particularly questionable.[20]

Fig. 93: Biological Station in Lunz

The Federal Ministry of Education did not approve at all of the blanket reinstatement of former Nazi Party members. This can be seen in the inquiry of 2 September 1948 sent by Section Head Otto Skrbensky to the Academy.[21] He asked whether the Academy really wanted to reinstate those members who had just been exempted from

[19] This warning is described in a letter by Ludmilla Krestan to Franz Ruttner of 15 November 1947. AÖAW, Biologische Station in Lunz, Folder "Diverses 1923–1950."

[20] See the essays in this volume by Klaus Taschwer, "Expelled, burnt, sold, forgotten, and suppressed, pp. 101–11, and by Johannes Feichtinger and Dieter J. Hecht, "Tasks and areas of responsibility of the new Presiding Committee," pp. 151–61.

[21] AÖAW, Ministerium 1948–1950, No. 1389/1948, Skrbensky to Ficker of 2 September 1948 (received on 8 October).

Fig. 94: Participants of the Centennial anniversary visiting Lunz, May 1947

atonement. As a key figure in the denazification process at the university, Skrbensky was not averse to former Nazis,[22] provided they shared his conservative Christian values. His argument to the Academy was that there was no entitlement to membership and that the reintegration of persons such as Nadler or Srbik would compromise Austria and the Academy, particularly as the Academy was accepting persons who had been removed from the university because of their Nazi past. In his reply, President Ficker countered Skrbensky, emphasizing that the Academy had always acted in accordance with the law and that incriminated members had not lost their membership because the atonement had been for a limited period only. Regarding the removal of the persons concerned from the university, he claimed that there they had an influence on young people, which was not the case with the work at the Academy.[23] This attitude can also be seen in a letter by Meister to Ficker the same day, in which he supports Srbik's request to give a lecture at the Academy with the succinct comment:

[22] For the role of Skrbensky, see Pfefferle/Pfefferle (2012), *Glimpflich entnazifiziert*, pp. 25–48.
[23] AÖAW, Ministerium 1948–1950, No. 1389/1948, Ficker to Skrbensky of 9 October 1948.

If there are people in the Academy who object to a lecture by Srbik, then so be it. It is time once and for all to put an end to these things.[24]

This attitude by the Academy Presiding Committee towards its Nazi past was also criticized in the press. On 15 July 1951 an article in *Der Neue Vorwärts. Wochenblatt für fortschrittliche Sozialisten in Österreich* attacked Richard Meister upon his election as President of the Academy: "The members of the 'Academy of Sciences,' as the entity designated to represent Austria's scientific elite, are in their majority still the old protected children of the Fascist era. There is Nadler, Knoll, Christian, Pernkopf, and the rest, who deported themselves like fanatical Nazis while their Jewish colleagues were being gassed. That they were not flushed out in 1945 and after is the dubious work of a man whom we have already presented in *Der Neue Vorwärts* as Austria's black-brown behind-the-scenes eminence: Richard Meister, who, for over twenty years, has been intriguing at universities and wherever else the opportunity arose against everything that smells of democracy and has been endeavoring to retain everything that will ensure his own survival even in a crisis."[25]

Restorative renewal

With the comprehensive reactivation of memberships held in abeyance in 1945, the Academy was not in line with the radical democratic renewal demanded, inter alia, by the occupying forces, but it did act on the basis of the laws of the Second Republic. Actors from the time of the authoritarian *Ständestaat* returned to office at the Academy and the universities. With their assistance, many Nazi Party members were able to come back after a short period of having their membership held in abeyance or dismissal. One difference was that university professors retired on reaching a certain age, while Academy members were elected for life and were frequently active until their death. It is therefore to be assumed that, from the late 1940s onwards, the way generations succeed one another meant that the Academy of Sciences was mainly composed of former members of the authoritarian *Ständestaat* and the Nazi Party. Election practice after 1945 did not mark a fundamental break because following the amnesty for less incriminated cases in 1948, corresponding members who had been classified as (less) incriminated were elected full members from the early 1950s onwards. Former Nazi Party members who had not been Academy members before 1945 were also elected in both Sections. It is significant that in 1955, the year of the Austrian State Contract, the proportion of newly elected former Nazi Party members or applicants was particularly large. In that year the Section for Humanities and the Social Sciences elected Indologist Erich Frauwallner and philosopher Friedrich Kainz as full members, and the Section for Mathematics and the Natural Sciences accepted

[24] AÖAW, PA Heinrich Ficker, Meister to Ficker of 9 October 1948.
[25] AÖAW, PA Richard Meister, Folder 2.

paleontologist Othmar Kühn.[26] Apparently, the election of former Nazis as new members of the Academy was conditional on their rehabilitation at the university, however:[27] Kainz and Kühn were already full professors at the University of Vienna when they were elected; Kainz was appointed an extraordinary professor in 1949 and a full professor in 1950, Kühn in 1951. Erich Frauwallner, an illegal Nazi Party member, was appointed an extraordinary professor at the University of Vienna in March 1955, immediately before his election as a full member. He became full professor at the University of Vienna in 1960.[28]

Other (less) incriminated corresponding members also became full members in the 1950s: classical philologist Albin Lesky in 1950, botanist Karl Höfler in 1951, and astronomer Viktor Oberguggenberger in 1954. Franz Ruttner, head of the Biological Station in Lunz, was elected into the Academy in 1952 as a corresponding member. In the 1950s the ancient historian and heavily exposed Nazi Fritz Schachermeyr, who succeeded Josef Keil as full professor at the University of Vienna in 1952 after having been banned from university teaching for several years, became a member of the Austrian Academy of Sciences (corresponding member in 1954 and full member in 1957).[29] Between 1945 and 1955, the Section for Humanities and the Social Sciences elected 26 full members, of whom four, or 15.4 percent of all new members, were former Nazi Party members or applicants. During this period the Section for Mathematics and the Natural Sciences elected 25 new full members, of whom 5, or 20 percent, were former Nazi Party members or applicants.

In the 1960s and 1970s further (less) incriminated corresponding members became full members: among others, Semitist and Arabist Adolf Grohmann, mathematician Josef Krames, ethnologist Richard Wolfram, Germanists Otto Höfler, Eberhard Kranzmayer and Hans Rupprich, and physicists Gustav Ortner and Georg Stetter. The illegal Nazi Gustav Ortner had been nominated director of the Institute for Radium Research in 1938 and dismissed from the university in 1945. In the mid-1950s he returned to Vienna after having taught in Cairo for several years. He was allowed to teach again in 1955. The Federal Ministry of Education entrusted him

---

[26] Details of Nazi Party membership are based on research in the ÖStA-AdR, the Vienna City Archives, and the files in the BDC. See also AÖAW, Minutes of the General Assembly of 17 May 1955 (A 1073).

[27] Those whose membership had been held in abeyance or persons whose membership had been cancelled in 1945 were also reinstated as Academy members even without prior rehabilitation at the university. This was the case with full members Viktor Christian, Fritz Knoll, Karl Mayrhofer, and Eduard Pernkopf. The mathematician Mayrhofer, an illegal Nazi Party member, appeared again in the list of members in the *Almanach* for 1948, 98 (1949), p. 17. The 46-year-old had been dismissed from the university in May 1945 and was not allowed to teach again until 1954. In 1957 he returned to the University of Vienna as a full professor. Pfefferle/Pfefferle (2012), *Glimpflich entnazifiziert*, p. 93.

[28] Stuchlik (2009), *Ansatz*; Pfefferle/Pfefferle (2012), *Glimpflich entnazifiziert*, p. 84, and Pollock (2002), *Ex Oriente Nox*, pp. 359–62.

[29] For details on Schachenmeyr, see Pesditschek (2009), *Barbar, Kreter, Arier*.

Fig. 95: Friedrich Ruttner

initially with planning the Austrian university reactor. In 1960 he was appointed full professor of technical nuclear physics at the Vienna College of Technology and later became director of the Atomic Institute of the Austrian Universities.[30] Like Ortner, Stetter, who had been a member of the Nazi Party before 1938, was elected a full member of the Academy. With his deputy Ortner he had directed the Four-Year Plan Institute for Neutron Research from 1943 and, after being authorized to teach again, he was appointed full professor at the University of Vienna in 1953. In 1964, at the age of 88, Harold Steinacker, the "Anschluss rector" of the University of Innsbruck, was made an honorary member of the Academy, in part at the instigation of Rudolf Egger.[31] Objections had been lodged in 1947 against the membership of all three.[32]

After the 1950s, denazified Nazi Party members were once again able to occupy important positions at the Academy and the university. During the Academy presidency of Richard Meister (1951–63) they were also elected to the Presiding Committee.[33] Thus the classical philologist Albin Lesky, for example, managed to build a notable career at the Academy in the 1960s: from 1959 to 1963 he was Secretary of the Section for Humanities and the Social Sciences, from 1963 to 1969 Vice-

[30] See Pfefferle/Pfefferle (2012), *Glimpflich entnazifiziert*, pp. 127–8.

[31] See Feichtinger/Uhl (2005), *Akademie*, pp. 335–6.

[32] See the essay in this volume by Johannes Feichtinger und Dieter J. Hecht, "Denazification at the Academy of Sciences," pp. 161–79.

[33] Ibid.

President, and from 1969 to 1970 President. Lesky, who was also rector of the University of Vienna from 1963 to 1964, was able to make the credible assertion that he had only joined the Nazi Party out of concern for his professional prospects.[34]

The rehabilitation of former Nazi Party members and their reintegration in the academic community were no exceptions. On the contrary, they were typical of the Austrian attitude to Nazism at the time.[35] Christian Fleck coined the phrase "autochthonous provincialization" to describe the development of the academic community in the decades after the war.[36]

As in other Austrian scientific institutions the effects of the staffing policy during the *Ständestaat* dictatorship and Nazi era were felt long after 1945. Continuity is reflected in the attitude to scholarship and practice and, not least, in the composition of the Academy membership and, as a consequence, research policies.

Johannes Feichtinger/Dieter J. Hecht

[34] See Goller/Oberkofler (2003), *Universität*, p. 27. In 1994, a street in the 22nd district was named for him and his wife Erna Lesky, who had also been a member of the Nazi Party, and in 1998 a gateway on the University of Vienna campus. See Feichtinger/Uhl (2005), *Akademie*, p. 335.

[35] See Uhl (2011), *Opfer*, pp. 27–46.

[36] See Fleck (2012), *Provinzialisierung*; Fleck (1996), *Provinzialisierung*, and Reiter (2006), *Naturwissenschaften*.

Centennial anniversary of the Academy of Sciences 1947

Austrian identity – new positioning in the international scientific community – suppression of the Nazi era

A chance anniversary offered the Academy of Sciences the opportunity, two years after the end of the Nazi era, to present itself to the public in a positive way as a traditional stronghold of "pure," ostensibly apolitical scholarship that had not been contaminated by Nazism and as therefore able to take up its place in the international academic community again.

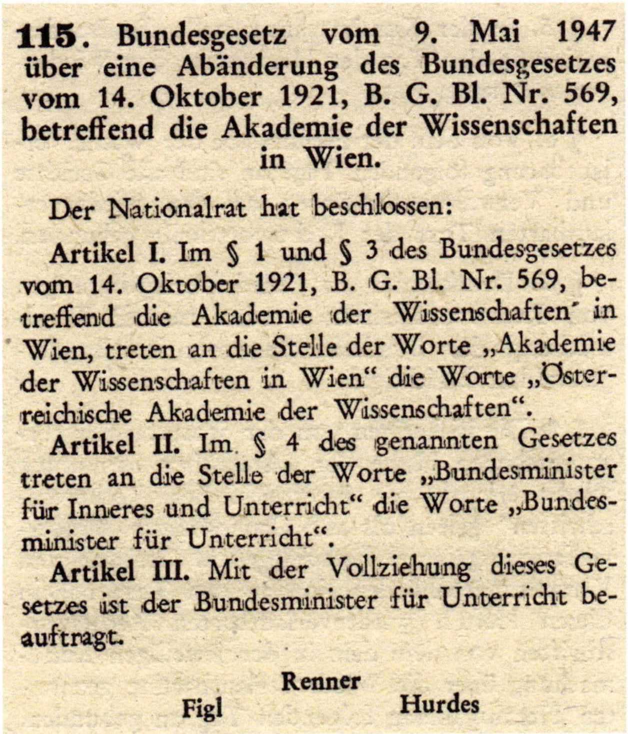

115. Bundesgesetz vom 9. Mai 1947 über eine Abänderung des Bundesgesetzes vom 14. Oktober 1921, B. G. Bl. Nr. 569, betreffend die Akademie der Wissenschaften in Wien.

Der Nationalrat hat beschlossen:

Artikel I. Im § 1 und § 3 des Bundesgesetzes vom 14. Oktober 1921, B. G. Bl. Nr. 569, betreffend die Akademie der Wissenschaften in Wien, treten an die Stelle der Worte „Akademie der Wissenschaften in Wien" die Worte „Österreichische Akademie der Wissenschaften".

Artikel II. Im § 4 des genannten Gesetzes treten an die Stelle der Worte „Bundesminister für Inneres und Unterricht" die Worte „Bundesminister für Unterricht".

Artikel III. Mit der Vollziehung dieses Gesetzes ist der Bundesminister für Unterricht beauftragt.

Renner

Figl **Hurdes**

Fig. 96: Federal Law 1947

A desire to position itself historically on a line of Austrian continuity formed the new framework in which the Academy again sought to legitimize its academic and institutional activities after 1945. The intersectional *Verbandkommission österreichischer Wissenschaft* [Commission for the association of Austrian academic institutions] had already been established in August 1945. As President Späth stressed at the

Ceremonial Session of 5 June 1946, this Commission placed the Academy "in the services of the present day."[1] Of particular symbolic value was the change of name to the Austrian Academy of Sciences, proposed at the General Assembly of 22 February 1946 by full member Leopold Wenger and promulgated in the Federal Law of 9 May 1947 "regarding the Academy of Sciences in Vienna."[2] The intersectional Commission for the Elaboration of an Austrian Biographical Encyclopedia was established in October 1946. Its aim was to complement the *Neue Österreichische Biographie* started in 1917 with a new biographical encyclopedia.[3]

The Academy also put itself in the service of strengthening Austrian identity at the national celebrations to mark "950 years of Austria." The first documented mention of the name *Ostarrîchi* provided the occasion for a large-scale state offensive aimed at redefining and publicly communicating a still uncertain Austrian identity. The new Austria styled itself as a major cultural player: two years after the end of the war, its achievements in art, science and scholarship were to re-establish its reputation internationally, above all with respect to the occupying powers. The Academy opened "a series of events celebrating Austrian scholarship" with an extraordinary Ceremonial Session on 21 October 1946. In his opening address, Vice-President Meister saw it as the Academy's role to pay fitting tribute to the "traditional foundations" and "historic significance" of the anniversary. He said that the document from the year 996 indicated that "Austria was already known and generally recognized as a special area, demonstrated by the existence of a specific popular name."[4] Thereupon Raoul Aslan, director of the *Burgtheater*, recited Anton Wildgans's speech about Austria. The ceremonial address on "the document of 996 and the conditions for the establishment of an independent state in the area of Austria" was given by the historian Alphons Lhotsky,[5] who referred to the "natural and historical factors that have always contributed to Austria's character and special status." He said that looking back over "around two thousand years" of Austrian history, it could be concluded that the

[1] *Almanach* for 1946, 96 (1948), p. 37. At the constituting session of the *Verbandkommission österreichischer Wissenschaft* on 22 August 1945, plans for the publication of a yearbook of Austrian science were discussed. Five volumes of the yearbook appeared between 1948 and 1965. The publication of a series entitled *Austria. Darstellungen aus Natur, Geschichte und Kultur Österreichs* was also planned.

[2] BGBl., No. 115/1947. The proposal was adopted by the General Assembly of 4 June 1946. The name change proposed here however was "Austrian Academy of Sciences in Vienna." AÖAW, Minutes of the General Assembly of 22 February 1946 (A 1000). See also AÖAW, Minutes of the General Assembly of 4 June 1946 (A 1003).

[3] Meister (1947), *Geschichte*, pp. 201, 289. As chairman of the Commission, the proposer, historian Leo Santifaller, was appointed. The first initiative came from the owner of the Amalthea publishing house, however, who had approached Vice-President Meister in early 1946 with the suggestion that the *Neue Österreichische Biographie* be reactivated. Santifaller (1957), Foreword, p. VIII.

[4] *Almanach* for 1946, 96 (1948), pp. 192–3.

[5] *Almanach* for 1946, 96 (1948), pp. 192–3; see also Lhotsky (1947), *Ostarrîchi*.

Das Referat über den gegenwärtigen Stand der Angelegenheit erscheint durch die vorstehenden Ausführungen erstattet. Ich erlaube mir weiterhin dazu folgendes zu berichten:

Die Bearbeitung eines "Biographischen Lexikons" aller bedeutender Oesterreicher für den Zeitraum von 1815 bis zur Gegenwart, welches nach dem Vorbilde des deutschen und englischen Werkes kurze, streng wissenschaftlich-systematisch gearbeitete und mit allen erforderlichen Quellen- und Literaturangaben versehene

Biographien enthalten sollte, entspricht einem dringenden Bedürfnis der Wissenschaft und des praktischen Lebens des In- und des Auslandes. Dieses bedeutsame österreichische Wissenschaftunternehmen ist daher der tatkräftigen Förderung der österreichischen Akademie der Wissenschaften in jeder Hinsicht würdig. Ohne die Hilfe einer grösseren wissenschaftlichen Körperschaft erscheint die Fertigstellung des Werkes überhaupt kaum durchführbar. Ich stelle daher zur Erwägung, ob die hohe Akademie das "Biographische Lexikon" als Unternehmen der Historischen Kommission erklären oder für die Betreuung desselben eine eigene Kommission einsetzen solle; eventuell würde es auch genügen, wenn die Hohe Akademie das "Biographische Lexikon" finanziell unterstützen und in ihren Schutz nehmen würde.

Wien, 23. Okt. 1946 Leo Santifaller

Fig. 97: Proposal by Santifaller of 23 October 1946 for establishing the Austrian Biographical Encyclopedia (extracts)

country had repeatedly “managed successfully to resist being absorbed completely in a larger overriding structure.” There were “inevitable conditions”, “constant, far-reaching historical forces” that had enabled Austria “always to find itself again.”[6]

---

[6] *Almanach* for 1946, 96 (1948), p. 195.

Lhotsky's remarks thus reflected the ideas that the Vice-President had expressed at the General Assembly of 29 March 1946 regarding the Academy's participation in the Austria celebrations. Namely, that in view of its importance for the establishment of *the independent state of Austria in the Danube region*, the 996 document should be *interpreted* within the context of the *geopolitical and historical situation.*[7]

The emphasis on Austria and the reclaimed importance of the Academy as an academic institution of international caliber were also the focuses of the centennial celebrations from 11 to 16 May 1947 in Vienna. The events were aimed at academic and political audiences and the public in Austria, but particularly at the international scientific community, as Richard Meister's report indicates: "The links with the international scientific community were broken by the war," and the celebration now offered the opportunity "to demonstrate to the public in Austria and elsewhere [...] that it had retained its old working energy and determination to celebrate further accomplishments in the future. In this regard, it is making every effort to re-establish links with academies and scholarly bodies throughout the world."[8] This aim was manifestly achieved. Representatives of prestigious academies and scientific institutions from nine countries – Belgium, Czechoslovakia, France, Hungary, Poland, Sweden, Switzerland, the United Kingdom, and the Vatican[9] – followed the invitation to *sister academies*,[10] which was also translated into the languages of the occupying powers.

The guests were informed that the celebration could *only be modest in view of Austria's current situation*, but that *the Academy of Sciences would endeavor to receive its guests with the greatest hospitality and to make their visit to Vienna worthwhile and pleasant.*[11] In the event, the program was anything but modest. The foreign participants in particular were shown not only the Academy but also the best of Austrian countryside, culture, and cuisine. The opening of the elaborate accompanying program was a welcome evening for full and corresponding members and representatives of foreign academies and scholarly bodies on 11 May in the *Johannessaal* of the Academy, together with the exhibition on the Academy's history in the Meeting Room.[12] After the Ceremonial Session of the Section for Humanities and the Social Sciences on 12 May, there was a guided tour of the *Kunsthistorisches* [Art History] Museum and, in the evening, an invitation by the federal government to a *Burgtheater* production of Hugo von Hofmannsthal's *Jedermann* in the Ronacher Theater.[13] On 13 May the Ceremonial Session of the Section for Mathematics and the Natural Sciences was held, followed by guided tours of the Museum of Natural History and the Institute for Radium Research. The evening of the Ceremonial Session on 14 May was also the

[7] AÖAW, Minutes of the General Assembly of 29 March 1946 (A 1001).
[8] *Almanach* for 1947, 97 (1948), pp. 65–6.
[9] *Almanach* for 1947, 97 (1948), pp. 65–6.
[10] AÖAW, Feierliche Sitzungen, Box 2, Folder "1947," Invitation.
[11] AÖAW, Feierliche Sitzungen, Box 2, Folder "1947," Invitation.
[12] *Almanach* for 1947, 97 (1948), p. 67.
[13] See *Almanach* for 1947, 97 (1948), p. 116.

highpoint of the celebrations. The participants and "a number of guests from scientific circles" were received by the Federal President and the government in the *Hofburg* [former imperial residence], and the State Opera performed Mozart's *Marriage of Figaro* in the *Redoutensaal*. The "magnificent performance was received with great enthusiasm by the guests," reported the Vice-President.[14] 15 May was devoted to a visit to the Biological Station in Lunz, followed by a reception at Melk Abbey. On 16 May the participants visited the *Prunksaal* [ceremonial hall] of the National Library and saw an exhibition of precious manuscripts and early prints compiled specially for the Academy celebration. At the ensuing lunch on the Kahlenberg by invitation of the city of Vienna, Mayor Theodor Körner welcomed the guests and was followed by the delegate of the British Academy, Sir Charles Webster, who thanked the mayor and the Academy on behalf of the visitors, "expressing the great satisfaction at the organization of the celebration and at the demonstration of the genuine willingness of the Austrian academic world to rebuild."[15]

Fig. 98: Auditorium at the centennial celebration in 1947
(from l. to r.: Renner, Innitzer, Figl, and Schärf)

The "actual ceremonial act to mark the centennial" was the Ceremonial Session at which Academy President Heinrich Ficker, Federal President Karl Renner, Federal Chancellor Leopold Figl, and Minister of Education Felix Hurdes all spoke. The positions they represented give an indication of the political context and outlook for the academic field two years after the end of the Nazi era and at the start of the Cold War. President Ficker invoked to this "High Ceremonial Assembly," – full and corresponding members, representatives of foreign academies, the Federal President and Federal Chancellor, Cardinal Theodor Innitzer, members of the federal government, the

[14] *Almanach* for 1947, 97 (1948), p. 215.
[15] *Almanach* for 1947, 97 (1948), p. 220.

mayor of Vienna and other heads of state and society, and representatives of the high commissioners of the Allied powers – the "glorious" hundred-year past of the institution, which had withstood the year of revolution in 1848 and the "most destructive storm [...] that has ever raged over the earth." "We stand here in the ruins left by the storm, and it is enough that we can say: We are still alive and working again!" It was precisely the Academy's tradition that now lent it the task of generating respect for the "little republic" in the world, because "even if we are and will remain a small and politically powerless state, we aspire to be a m a j o r p o w e r [spacing in the original] in culture, art, and science." In view of the inadequate financial resources, as Ficker pointed out, this called above all for the provision of appropriate funds from the public sector.

However, Ficker continued, it was not the lack of funds that was "the worst thing for science and research." "The most stifling [...] for science" were the "parties and ideologies that claimed totality and once in power ruthlessly pursued this aim." "We experienced this '*Gleichschaltung*' [alignment/ consolidation] in the years before the end of the war," Ficker explained, and not only "historians, philosophers, and jurists had their work controlled and obstructed during the Nazi era. No one was spared!" The natural sciences were affected too, as Ficker illustrated with reference to "world ice theory," as it was called, that was intended as a component of the National Socialist world view. Freedom in research and teaching were "the basis for what we understand by scholarship." Ficker closed with the appeal: "Free research and free teaching in a free Austria!"[16]

Federal President Karl Renner, who had just been elected as an honorary member of the Academy, expressed his thanks for "the highest recognition that the Academy can give," and described it as a "solemn message" that Austria's academic elite professed its "unreserved commitment to a free and democratic people's state."[17] Nazism and the "terrible catastrophe of the Second World War that surpassed all past conceptions" had "intellectually and morally deprived" the "cognitive world" of an entire generation. Renner's appeal turned to the future: "Get ready, gentlemen, for the future and come to terms with the past."[18] What counts now are "internationalism, democracy, and socialism as the basic orientation of intellectual work. This gives the Academy, which has lost so much ground, new and larger scope on the threshold of

---

[16] *Almanach* for 1947, 97 (1948), pp. 152–61. The Academy President was even clearer the day before in his welcome speech at the Ceremonial Session of the Section for Mathematics and the Natural Sciences when he said: "At a time in which the struggle for a new social order is well under way, in which the entire economy is dominated by the contrast between private and planned economies, at such a time there is an even greater danger than before that the idea of steering and appropriating science will take on greater significance." (Ibid., p. 117). The academies, he continued, had "always been a symbol of the unity of all sciences," unity and freedom of science "had always been the true cornerstones of academic activity and should also remain so for our Academy." (Ibid., p. 119)

[17] *Almanach* for 1947, 97 (1948), pp. 162–3.

[18] *Almanach* for 1947, 97 (1948), pp. 172–5.

Fig. 99: Federal President Renner as guest speaker at the centennial celebration in 1947

its second century of existence: it has twice lost the empire in which it worked but is in the process of acquiring a world, the whole world, as its field of activity."[19]

Renner's claim that "the book of the past was closed"[20] was in line, two years after the end of Nazi rule, with the way Austrian society was dealing with former Nazis. Thus, the fact that Academy members had also belonged to the Party that had been responsible for the "stifling" *"Gleichschaltung"* of the sciences (Heinrich Ficker) was, naturally, not mentioned. An intimation in this regard can be found in the activity report of Secretary General Josef Keil for the period from 5 June 1946 to May 1947, although the remark is designed more to conceal the fact that the political screening of Academy members is still ongoing: Keil stated that "precise information about the

[19] *Almanach* for 1947, 97 (1948), p. 177.

[20] *Almanach* for 1947, 97 (1948), p. 177.

Fig. 100: Commemorative medal, recto and verso

current status of members of the Academy cannot be given at the moment because of some as yet unclear points."[21]

In view of the various efforts by the Academy to accommodate those members subject to the 1945 *Verbotsgesetz* [law banning the re-engagement in National Socialist activities], the choice of the inscription for the centennial medal is significant: MULTI PERTRANSIERUNT ET PERTRANSIBUNT | AUCTA EST ET AUGEBITUR SCIENTIA (Many went there and will go there, knowledge was and will be increased). This motto may be interpreted as a symbolic amnesty. The idea was that regardless of their individual political involvement, all members had contributed to the progress of knowledge. The cogency of this interpretation is illustrated by the closing words of Richard Meister's ceremonial speech on the history of the Academy of Sciences in Vienna from 1847 to 1947: "Thus the Academy stands before you today and can say of itself that through all of the checkered times it has never been unfaithful to the law of strictest objectivity applicable to all research. Every person in this house without exception has served this law and all members of the Academy and the Academy as a whole will continue to serve this law in future. All human activity is subject to change over time but one area of culture after another rises from it with works that [...] may be described as lasting."[22]

The striving for acceptance and recognition in the international scientific community was a determining factor in the post-war Academy of Sciences. The election of Lise Meitner as the first female member of the Section for Mathematics and the Natural Sciences in 1948 can also be seen in this light. However, among the elected members, scholars who held high-ranking positions in the Nazi era crop up again and

[21] *Almanach* for 1947, 97 (1948), p. 71.
[22] *Almanach* for 1947, 97 (1948), pp. 202, 216.

again.[23] The accommodation of former National Socialists that prevailed in society and in (party) politics was also reflected in the Academy of Sciences. Further analysis is required to establish whether the Academy was in the mainstream of Austrian political culture or went even further.[24]

The Academy took the first step towards thematizing its own role on the occasion of the 150th anniversary celebrations in 1997. The *Festschrift* published on this occasion included an essay by Herbert Matis entitled *Akademie der Wissenschaften 1938 bis 1945*.[25] This marked the start by the Academy of Sciences, albeit later than the Austrian universities, which had embarked on this research in the 1980s, to come to terms with the history of a period in which the attempt had been made "to place science in the service of a criminal regime contemptuous of human life."[26] In an in-depth analysis entitled *Zwischen Anpassung und Widerstand. Die Akademie der Wissenschaften in den Jahren 1938–1945* [Between Accommodation and Resistance. The Academy of Sciences in the Years 1938–1945], Matis sums up the situation after 1945 thus: "Because the problem of 'denazification' was dealt with at a purely legal level, there was no sustained and internal confrontation with Nazism."[27]

Heidemarie Uhl

---

[23] See the essay in this volume by Johannes Feichtinger and Dieter J. Hecht, "1945 and after. One break and two continuities," pp. 181–9.

[24] One example is the election of the historian Harold Steinacker, President of the University of Innsbruck 1938–1942, as an honorary member of the Section for Humanities and the Social Sciences in 1964. See also the obituary of Franz Huter in the *Almanach* for 1965, 155 (1966), pp. 306–35.

[25] Matis (1997), *Akademie*, pp. 21–34.

[26] Matis (1997), *Anpassung*, p. 7.

[27] Matis (1997), *Anpassung*, p. 67.

III. SHORT BIOGRAPHIES

Short Biographies

The following entries contain brief biographical information about the members of the Academy mentioned in the articles of this publication, both in Austria and abroad, and about Academy employees. Information is provided about their scholarly careers and the type of Academy membership they held.

With regard to the information about the Nazi past of particular persons, the following must be noted: Since it was not always possible to ascertain what type of membership an individual held in the various Nazi organizations, the only information that is included is what is currently known about their membership of the Nazi Party, SS or SA. Mention is made in all cases when the respective individual was officially required to register under the *Verbotsgesetz* of 8 May 1945, the law banning the Nazi Party and re-engagement in Nazi activities. This law applied to persons living in Austria "who between 1 July 1933 and 27 April 1945 were members of the Nazi Party [NSDAP] or one of its military organizations (SS, SA, NSKK, NSFK)," and "all aspiring party members and persons who had applied to become members of the SS (Schutzstaffel)."

The biographical details are based on *Almanach* obituaries (for the members), the personnel files held in the AÖAW (for members and employees), the denazification *Politischen Fragebögen der Mitglieder* [Political Questionnaires of Members concerning denazification] held in the AÖAW, the *Österreichisches Biographisches Lexikon*, and the works cited in the bibliography.

Emil **Abel** (2 June 1875–2 April 1958)

Emil Abel was from Vienna, where he studied chemistry at the Vienna College of Technology. He received his doctorate in 1900 at the University of Göttingen. He then worked in Vienna as an industrial chemist. He completed a habilitation in 1905 at the College of Technology and another in 1910 at the University of Vienna. In 1911 he became an associate professor at the Vienna College of Technology and, in 1923, full professor of physical chemistry and department head. In 1938 he was removed from his post on "racial" grounds. Abel was able to emigrate to England in 1939, where he worked at University College London and in private industry. After 1945 he resumed contact with the Vienna College of Technology and held guest lectures. Abel became a corresponding member in Austria (c.m.i.) of the Academy in 1929. In 1945, since he lived in London, his membership was re-designated as corresponding member abroad (c.m.a.). He resigned from the Academy on 4 January 1939 and thus was never officially excluded.

Othenio **Abel** (20 June 1875–4 July 1946)

Othenio Abel was born in Vienna. He studied law and natural sciences and received his doctorate in 1899. In 1902 he finished his habilitation and in 1907 was appointed associate professor of paleontology at the University of Vienna. He was appointed full professor of paleontology in 1912 and full professor of paleobiology in 1917. In 1928 the two chairs were combined into a single department, which he then headed. In 1927/28 Abel held the post of dean at the University of Vienna and in 1932/33, that of rector. In the early 1920s he set up a network whose goal was to prevent academics who were Jewish or Social Democrats from finishing their habilitations or receiving professorships. In 1934 he was pensioned off because of his Nazi leanings. In 1935 he accepted an appointment as professor in Göttingen. After his retirement, he moved to Salzburg to head the *Institut für Lebensgeschichte* [Institute of Life History], a newly founded institution that was part of the SS *"Ahnenerbe"* [Ancestral Heritage] research organization. In 1945 he was subject to registration as a member of the Nazi Party. Abel was elected a corresponding member (c.m.i.) by the Academy in 1921.

Leopold **Adametz** (11 November 1861–27 January 1941)
Leopold Adametz was from Feldsberg, which at that time was part of Lower Austria. He studied zoology at the College of Natural Resources and Life Sciences in Vienna and at the University of Leipzig. He received his doctorate in 1886 and, after working for a short time as a farmer, became an assistant to the Chair of animal husbandry at the College of Natural Resources and Life Sciences. Adametz completed his habilitation in 1888 and became an associate professor in Vienna in 1890. From 1891 he taught as an associate professor at the University of Cracow, before accepting an appointment in 1898 as full professor at the College of Natural Resources and Life Sciences. In 1901/02 he was rector of the College. Adametz became a corresponding member (c.m.i.) of the Academy in 1931 and a full member (f.m.) in 1937.

Ludwig **Adamovich** (30 April 1890–23 September 1955)
Ludwig Adamovich was born in Esseg (Osjiek)/Croatia; he studied law at the University of Vienna. After finishing his doctorate in 1913, he began to work in 1920 for the Constitutional Service of the Austrian Federal Chancellery. Adamovich completed his habilitation in 1924 at the University of Vienna. In 1927 he became an associate professor at the German University in Prague. In 1928 he was appointed full professor of public and administrative law at the University of Graz and in 1934 he accepted an appointment at the University of Vienna. From 1930 he was a member of the Austrian Constitutional Court. He was Minister of Justice in the final Schuschnigg Cabinet (1938); after the "Anschluss" he was forced to retire. From 1945 to 1947 he was rector of the University of Vienna. In 1945 he was Vice-President of the Constitutional Court and President from 1946 to 1955. In 1945 Adamovich was elected a full member (f.m.) of the Academy.

Franz **Aigner** (13 May 1882–19 July 1945)
Franz Aigner was born in St. Pölten/Lower Austria; he studied physics at the University of Vienna. He received his Ph.D. in 1906 and completed his habilitation in 1918. In 1925 he became an associate professor and, in 1930, full professor of high frequency telecommunications at the Vienna College of Technology. In 1937/38 he held the post of dean at the Vienna College of Technology. The Academy elected him as a corresponding member (c.m.i.) in 1939.

Otto **Ampferer** (1 December 1875–9 July 1947)
Otto Ampferer was born in Hötting near Innsbruck; he studied mathematics, physics, and geology at the University of Innsbruck, finishing his studies in 1899 with a doctorate. In 1901 he began to work for the Imperial and Royal (k.k.) Geological Survey in Vienna. He was the director of the Federal Geological Survey in Vienna from 1935 to 1937. Ampferer was elected by the Academy as a corresponding member (c.m.i.) in 1925 and as an ordinary member (o.m.) in 1939.

Hermann **Barrenscheen** (19 November 1887–3 November 1958)
Hermann Barrenscheen was born in Stuttgart. After studying medicine, he turned to applied medical chemistry, physiological chemistry, and medical biochemistry. After working as an assistant physician at the University Medical Clinic II, he became a full professor at the Uni-

versity of Vienna in 1941. From 1933 or 1934, Barrenscheen was an illegal member of the Nazi Party and the *Sturmabteilung* (SA), and from 1938 held the rank of *Sturmbannführer*. In 1943 he was not conferred the position of university dean due to opposition from within the faculty. In 1945 he was subject to registration as a member of the Nazi Party and was dismissed from the University of Vienna. After 1945, Barrenscheen worked as a physician at the Salzburg Regional Hospital. In 1941 he was elected by the Academy as a corresponding member (c.m.i.); he was one of very few who no longer appeared in the registries of Academy members after 1945.

Wilhelm **Bauer** (31 May 1877–23 November 1953)
Wilhelm Bauer was born in Vienna, where he studied history and attended the training course at the Institute for Austrian Historical Research. He received his Ph.D. in 1902. He completed his habilitation at the University of Vienna in 1907 and was conferred the title associate professor in 1916. In 1919 he became an associate professor and in 1923 was conferred the title full professor. In 1930 he became a full professor of general contemporary history and co-director of the Department of History at the University of Vienna. In 1945 he was subject to registration as a member of the Nazi Party and in the same year was removed from his position at the University of Vienna and banned from teaching. In 1946 he was forced to retire permanently. The Academy elected Bauer a corresponding member (c.m.i.) in 1931 and an ordinary member (o.m.) in 1938. In 1945 his Academy membership was held in abeyance. The Amnesty Law of April 1948 permitted his membership to be reinstated; his name appears again in the 1948 registry of members.

Hans **Benndorf** (13 December 1870–11 February 1953)
Hans Benndorf was from Zurich; he studied physics at the Universities of Vienna, Heidelberg, and Berlin. He received his doctorate in 1895 and completed his habilitation in 1899 at the University of Vienna. In 1904 he became an associate professor, and a full professor of experimental physics at the University of Graz in 1910. He held the post of dean at the University of Graz in 1920, and in 1933/34 that of rector. He was forced to retire in 1936 but, from 1945 to 1947, he taught at the University of Graz as an honorary professor. Benndorf was a corresponding member (c.m.i.) of the Academy from 1914 and a full member (f.m.) from 1927.

Franz **Boas** (9 July 1858–21 December 1942)
Franz Boas was from Minden/Westphalia; he studied mathematics, physics, and geography at the Universities of Heidelberg, Bonn, and Kiel. He received his doctorate in 1881 in Kiel, completed his habilitation in 1886 at the University of Berlin, and moved the same year to the United States. In 1892 he became an assistant professor of anthropology at Clark University in Worcester, Massachusetts. From 1896 he held a directorship position at the American Museum of Natural History in New York, and in 1899 became a professor at Columbia University, New York. He taught there until retiring in 1934. Boas was a corresponding member abroad (c.m.a.) of the Academy from 1923. He was excluded from the Academy on 3 October 1940.

Leopold Karl **Böhm** (11 November 1886–11 September 1958)
Leopold Karl Böhm was from Vienna. After finishing his Ph.D. in 1910, he worked first as an assistant at the College of Veterinary Medicine in Vienna in the Departments of Fish Biology and Pathology, and of General Zoology and Parasite Studies. He finished his habilitation in 1920, and worked from 1927 as an associate professor and head of the newly established Department of General Zoology. He was appointed full professor in 1938. Since he was not a member of the Nazi party, he remained in this position in 1945. From 1948 to 1950, Böhm

was the rector of College of Veterinary Medicine in Vienna. Böhm was elected a corresponding member (c.m.i.) of the Academy in 1939 and an ordinary member (o.m.) in 1941.

Walther **Brecht** (31 August 1876–1 July 1950)
Walther Brecht was born in Berlin. He studied history and German philology in Freiburg im Breisgau, Bonn, and Göttingen. He received his doctorate in 1902, completed his habilitation in 1906 at the University of Göttingen, and in 1910 accepted a professorship at the Royal Academy in Posen (Poznan). From 1913 to 1925 he was a full professor at the University of Vienna. In 1926 he moved to Breslau (Wrocław) and, from 1927 to 1937, was a full professor of German language and literature at the University of Munich. Brecht was a corresponding member in Austria (c.m.i.) of the Academy from 1916 and a full member (f.m.) from 1919. In 1926 his status was re-designated as corresponding member abroad (c.m.a.), in 1938 as ordinary member (o.m.), and from 1945 again as corresponding member abroad (c.m.a.). He was excluded from the Academy on 3 October 1940.

Ernst Theodor **Brücke** (8 October 1880–12 June 1941)
Ernst Theodor Brücke was born in Vienna and studied medicine both there and at the University of Leipzig. He received his doctorate in 1904 in Vienna and completed his habilitation in 1908. From 1913 he bore the title associate professor. In 1916 he was appointed full professor of physiology at the University of Innsbruck. In 1938 he was removed from his post on "racial" grounds. In 1939 he emigrated to the United States, where he then worked in the laboratory of A. Forbes at Harvard University in Cambridge, Massachusetts. Brücke was a corresponding member (c.m.i.) of the Academy from 1922. He was excluded from the Academy on 20 February 1939.

Franz Theodor **Brücke** (15 January 1908–25 March 1970)
Franz Theodor Brücke was born in Leipzig; he studied medicine at the Universities of Innsbruck, Vienna, Berlin, and Leipzig. After finishing his doctorate in Innsbruck in 1931, he did research for several years in Berlin, Graz, and Vienna. In 1934 he took an assistant position in the Department of Pharmacology at the University of Vienna. In 1941 he completed his habilitation and in 1948 he was appointed full professor of pharmacology at the University of Vienna, a position he then held until his death. In the years 1954/55 Brücke held the post of dean. He was elected a corresponding member (c.m.i.) of the Academy in 1957 and a full member (f.m.) in 1959.

Otto **Brunner** (21 April 1898–12 June 1982)
Otto Brunner was born in Mödling/Lower Austria; in Vienna he studied history and geography, later also art history, German legal history, and governmental sciences. In addition, he completed the training course at the Institute for Austrian Historical Research. From 1923 he worked as an archivist and completed his habilitation in 1929 at the University of Vienna, where he then became an associate professor in 1931. In 1940 Brunner took over the directorship of the Institute for Austrian Historical Research, and in 1941 became a full professor. In 1945 he was subject to registration as a member of the Nazi Party. In the same year, Brunner was dismissed from the University of Vienna and banned from teaching; he was permanently pensioned off in 1948. In 1954 he accepted an appointment as full professor of history at the University of Hamburg, where in 1957/58 he held the post of dean and 1959/60 that of rector. Brunner was a corresponding member (c.m.i.) of the Academy from 1939 to 1944, and from 1944 to 1954 an ordinary member (o.m.) and then full member (f.m.). In 1954 his status was re-designated as corresponding member abroad (c.m.a.). In 1945 his membership was held in

abeyance. The Amnesty Law of April 1948 permitted his membership to be reinstated; his name appears again in the 1948 registry of members.

Karl **Bühler** (27 May 1879–24 October 1963)
Karl Bühler was from Meckesheim/Baden. He studied medicine at the University of Freiburg im Breisgau, and psychology at the University of Straßburg (Strasbourg). He received his doctorate in 1903 and finished his habilitation in 1907 in Würzburg, whereupon he moved to the University of Bonn. From 1913 to 1918 Bühler worked as an associate professor at the University of Munich, and in 1918 received an appointment as full professor at Dresden College of Technology. In 1922 he became a full professor of philosophy and psychology at the University of Vienna; in 1938 he was removed from his post on "racial" grounds. He emigrated the same year to Oslo and in 1939 to the United States. He initially worked there as a professor of psychology at the College of St. Scholastica in Duluth and, from 1940, at St. Thomas College in St. Paul, Minnesota. From 1945 to 1955 he was visiting clinical professor of psychiatry at the University of Southern California in Los Angeles. Bühler was elected a corresponding member (c.m.i.) of the Academy in 1934 and in 1939 was re-designated a corresponding member abroad (c.m.a.). On 3 October 1940 he was excluded from the Academy.

Viktor **Christian** (30 March 1885–28 May 1963)
Viktor Christian was from Vienna, where he studied to be a history and geography teacher and also studied Semitic languages. He continued his education at the University of Berlin, eventually returning to Vienna where he took over the academic directorship of the Urania Adult Education Center in 1922. In 1923 he finished his habilitation at the University of Vienna, where he became an associate professor in 1924. In 1930 he was appointed full professor of Early Semitic philology and Oriental archeology. From 1934 to 1936 he was suspended from his post but, from 1938 to 1943, he was then the dean of the University of Vienna's Faculty of Philosophy. Christian, a member of the Nazi Party and an SS member holding the rank of *Hauptsturmführer*, was the head of the Viennese *Lehr- und Forschungsstätte für den vorderen Orient* [Education and Research Center of the Near East] of the SS's *"Ahnenerbe"* [Ancestral Heritage] research association. In 1945 he was subject to registration as a member of the Nazi Party and in the same year was dismissed from the University of Vienna. In 1950 he was permanently retired. Christian did not return to university. He became a corresponding member (c.m.i.) of the Academy in 1938 and an ordinary member (o.m.) in 1939. In 1945 his membership at the Academy was deemed terminated; his name appears again in the registry of members for the year 1950.

Hans Peter **Cornelius** (29 September 1888–2 April 1950)
Hans Peter Cornelius was born in Munich; he studied mineralogy and petrography first there and then at the Zurich Institute of Technology. From 1928 to 1945 he worked at the Federal Geological Survey in Vienna. In 1945 he was subject to registration as an illegal Nazi. Cornelius became a corresponding member (c.m.i.) of the Academy in 1941. In 1945 his Academy membership was held in abeyance. The Amnesty Law of April 1948 permitted his membership to be reinstated; his name appears again in the 1948 registry of members. His election to full membership (f.m.) was under discussion before he passed away.

Alfons **Dopsch** (14 June 1868–1 September 1953)
Alfons Dopsch came from Lobositz (Lovosice) in northern Bohemia (Czech Republic). He studied geography, history, and art history at the University of Vienna. From 1889 to 1891 he took the training course at the Institute for Austrian Historical Research. After his habilitation in 1893, Dopsch became an associate professor, and then from 1900 to 1937 held a position

as full professor of general and Austrian history at the University of Vienna. In 1920/21 he was rector of the University of Vienna. Dopsch was a member of the Academy from 1903, first as a corresponding member (c.m.i.) and then, from 1909, as a full member (f.m.).

Arnold **Durig** (12 November 1872–18 October 1961)
Arnold Durig was born in Innsbruck, where he studied medicine at the University. Receiving his doctorate in 1898, in the same year he began to work as a junior physician and volunteer in various clinics in Innsbruck. In 1902 he finished his habilitation at the University of Vienna; he was then appointed associate professor at the College of Natural Resources and Life Sciences in Vienna in 1904 and full professor in 1905. In 1918 he took over the chair of physiology at the University of Vienna. In 1938 he was forced to retire for political reasons. According to his own testimony, he joined the Nazi Party in 1941 or 1942. In 1945, he was subject to registration as a member of the Nazi Party. Durig became a corresponding member (c.m.i.) of the Academy in 1911 and a full member (f.m.) in 1915. In 1945 his membership was held in abeyance. The Amnesty Law of April 1948 permitted his membership to be reinstated; his name appears again in the 1948 registry of members.

Josef Maria **Eder** (16 March 1855–18 October 1944)
Josef Maria Eder came from Krems/Lower Austria; he studied chemistry and physics in Vienna at both the University and the College of Technology. In 1880 he finished his habilitation at the Vienna College of Technology, and from 1882 he taught at the *Staatsgewerbeschule* [State Vocational School] in Vienna. In 1888, Eder became the director of the *Graphische Lehr- und Versuchsanstalt* (the old *Lehranstalt für Photographie und Reproduktionsverfahren*) [Federal Training and Research Institute for Graphic Art – formerly the Training Institute for Photography and Reproduction Techniques] in Vienna, which he founded and headed until 1922. In 1892 he became an associate professor. From 1902 to 1925 he held the post of full professor of photochemistry at the Vienna College of Technology. Eder was elected a corresponding member (c.m.i.) of the Academy in 1903 and a full member (f.m.) in 1916.

Rudolf **Egger** (11 April 1882–7 May 1969)
Rudolf Egger was born in Bruck a.d. Mur/Styria; he studied classical philology, ancient history, epigraphy, and German language and literature at the University of Vienna before entering the teaching profession as a high school teacher. In 1917 he finished his habilitation at the University of Vienna. In 1923 he became an associate professor at the University of Vienna and, in 1929, a full professor. In 1935 he became co-director of the Austrian Archaeological Institute. In 1945 he was subject to registration as a member of the Nazi Party. Banned in the same year from teaching and dismissed from the University of Vienna, in 1947 he was pensioned off permanently. He continued to be active at the Austrian Archaeological Institute. Egger was a member of the Academy as a corresponding member (c.m.i.) from 1929, and as a full member (f.m.) from 1937. In 1945 his membership was held in abeyance. The Amnesty Law of April 1948 permitted his membership to be reinstated; his name appears again in the 1948 registry of members.

Albert **Ehrhard** (17 October 1845–23 September 1940)
Albert Ehrhard came from Lower Alsace. He was ordained a Catholic priest in 1885. He was appointed a professor at the Straßburg (Strasbourg) Seminary in 1889, and then at the University of Würzburg in 1892. In 1898 he was appointed full professor at the University of Vienna, where he held the post of dean in 1899. In 1902 he became a professor at the University of Freiburg im Breisgau, moving in 1903 to the University of Straßburg, where he held the post of rector in 1911/12. From 1920 to 1927 he worked at the University of Bonn. Erhard was

elected by the Academy as a corresponding member (c.m.i.) in 1900 and as a full member (f.m.) in 1901. In 1902 his membership was re-designated as corresponding member abroad (c.m.a.) and, in 1938, as ordinary member (o.m.).

Albert **Eichler** (26 April 1879–8 December 1953)
Albert Eichler was born in Vienna, where he studied English and German language and literature. After receiving his doctorate in 1902, he took the examinations for the teaching profession and became a high school teacher. He completed his habilitation in 1908 at the University of Vienna, and in 1912 became an associate professor at the University of Graz. In 1918 Eichler was appointed full professor in Graz. In 1925/26 he held the post of dean. From 1938 to 1944 Eichler was the pro-rector of the University of Graz. In 1945, he was subject to registration as a member of the Nazi Party; in 1946, due following a negative ruling by the denazification committee, he was dismissed from his teaching post. Eichler did not return to university work. He was a corresponding member (c.m.i.) of the Academy from 1944. In 1945 his membership was held in abeyance. The Amnesty Law of April 1948 permitted his membership to be reinstated; his name appears again in the 1948 registry of members.

Friedrich **Emich** (5 September 1860–22 January 1940)
Friedrich Emich came from Graz, where he studied chemistry at the College of Technology. After his studies, he worked first at a high school for girls in Graz. He completed his habilitation in 1888, becoming an associate professor at Graz College of Technology in 1889, and a full professor in 1894. He held the posts of dean and rector several times. Emich retired in 1931. He was elected by the Academy as a corresponding member (c.m.i.) in 1917 and as a full member (f.m.) in 1928.

Friedrich **Engel-Janosi** (18 February 1893–7 March 1978)
Friedrich Engel-Janosi was born in Vienna; at the University of Vienna he first studied law (1919 Dr. iur.), and then history (Ph.D. 1921). He completed his habilitation in 1929 at the University of Vienna and held the title of associate professor from 1935. From 1924 he directed the family company, a wood and parquet flooring factory in Vienna-Heiligenstadt. Persecuted on "racial" grounds, Engel-Janosi emigrated to England in 1939 and, in 1940, to the United States, where he worked at the Johns Hopkins University in Baltimore. From 1942 to 1959 he was a professor at the Catholic University of America in Washington, D.C. After having returned from exile, he took over the chair of contemporary history at the University of Vienna in 1959. Engel-Janosi was a corresponding member (c.m.i.) of the Academy from 1963.

Karl **Federhofer** (5 July 1885–6 November 1960)
Karl Federhofer came from Knittelfeld/Styria; he studied civil engineering at Graz College of Technology, receiving his Ph.D. in 1909. He worked for the Austrian State Railways and the Public Building Services of the Styrian provincial government before finishing his habilitation in 1913 at Leoben College of Mining. In 1920 he was appointed full professor at Brno College of Technology. In 1923 he returned to Graz College of Technology as a full professor of technical mechanics, working there until his retirement in 1956. From 1925 to 1927 he held the post of dean of the civil engineering school at Graz College of Technology; in 1928/29 he was the Institute's rector. In 1945, he was subject to registration as a member of the Nazi Party; in 1946, after a positive ruling by the denazification committee, he was allowed to continue teaching. Federhofer was a corresponding member (c.m.i.) of the Academy from 1935, and elected an ordinary member (o.m.) in 1939. In 1945 his membership was held in abeyance. The Amnesty Law of April 1948 permitted his membership to be reinstated; his name appears again in the 1948 registry of members.

Heinrich **Ficker** (22 November 1881–29 April 1957)

Heinrich Ficker was born in Munich; he studied at the Universities of Vienna and Innsbruck. In 1906 he received his doctorate at the University of Innsbruck, and in 1909 finished his habilitation. In 1911 he became an associate professor at the University of Graz. In 1919 he was appointed full professor in Graz. In 1923 he accepted an appointment as full professor at the University of Berlin and became director of the Prussian Meteorological Institute. Ficker, as acting Secretary of the Prussian Academy of Sciences in Berlin, was involved in the exclusion of Albert Einstein from the Academy in 1933. From 1937 until his retirement in 1953 he worked as a full professor of geophysics at the University of Vienna and directed the Central Institute for Meteorology and Geodynamics. Ficker became a corresponding member (c.m.i.) of the Academy in 1922; in 1923 his status was re-designated as corresponding member abroad (c.m.a.). In 1937 his status was again re-designated as corresponding member in Austria (c.m.i.), and in 1939 he was elected an ordinary member (o.m.). Ficker was the President of the Academy from 1946 to 1951, and then Vice-President until his death.

Ludwig **Flamm** (29 January 1885–4 December 1964)

Ludwig Flamm was born in Vienna, where he studied physics at the University. He received his doctorate in 1909, completed his habilitation at the University of Vienna in 1916, and became an associate professor at the Vienna College of Technology in 1919. From 1922 until his retirement in 1956, Flamm was a full professor of physics and head of the Department of Physics II at the Vienna College of Technology. From 1929 until 1931 he held the post of dean at the Vienna College of Technology and was its rector during the academic year 1930/31. Flamm was a corresponding member (c.m.i.) of the Academy from 1928 and became an ordinary member (o.m.) in 1940.

Erich **Frauwallner** (28 December 1898–5 July 1974)

Erich Frauwallner came from Vienna, where he studied classical philology, Indology, and Iranian studies. He received his Ph.D. in 1921. He initially worked as a high school teacher, and then completed his habilitation in 1928 at the University of Vienna. In 1939, a letter from Hitler announced Frauwallner's appointment as associate professor. In 1945 Frauwallner was subject to registration as an illegal Nazi. Removed from his post at the University of Vienna the same year, banned from teaching, and permanently pensioned off in 1948, in 1955 he again became an associate professor at the University of Vienna and head of the Department of Indology. In 1960 he finally became a full professor. He was elected a corresponding member (c.m.i.) of the Academy in 1940 and a full member (f.m.) in 1955. In 1945 his membership was held in abeyance. The Amnesty Law of April 1948 permitted his membership to be reinstated; his name appears again on the 1948 registry of members.

Lucia **Freiberg** (* 3 December 1926)

Lucia Freiberg was employed by the Academy as a war-time replacement worker when she was not yet sixteen. She worked as a mid-level bookkeeper in the accounting department. She was recruited because the chief accountant, Leopold Liegler, had become seriously ill. In 1947 she finished the external general upper secondary exams, whereupon she became an upper grade civil servant. In 1949 she passed an exam in public auditing. In 1962 Freiberg succeeded Leopold Svajda as director of the accounting department; she retired in 1983.

Paul **Funk** (14 April 1886–3 June 1969)

Paul Funk was born in Vienna; he studied mathematics and physics in Tübingen, Vienna, and Göttingen. He received his doctorate in 1911 in Göttingen. In 1915 he finished his habilitation at the German University in Prague, where in 1921 he became an associate professor. In

1928 he was appointed full professor at the same university. When Czechoslovakia was occupied in 1939, Funk was forced to retire; he was later deported to Theresienstadt concentration camp, from which he was liberated in 1945. In the same year he accepted an appointment as professor of mathematics at the Vienna College of Technology; he also taught as an honorary professor at the University of Vienna. He was elected a full member of the Academy in 1950.

Philipp **Furtwängler** (21 April 1869–19 May 1940)
Philipp Furtwängler came from Elze near Hannover; he studied mathematics at the University of Göttingen. He received his doctorate in 1895. From 1899 he worked as an assistant at the Geodesy Institute in Potsdam before being appointed full professor at the Agricultural Academy in Bonn in 1904. In 1907 he moved to Aachen College of Technology, returning to the Agricultural Academy in Bonn in 1910. From 1912 to 1940 he was a full professor of mathematics at the University of Vienna. Furtwängler was a member of the Academy as a corresponding member (c.m.i.) from 1916, and from 1927 as a full member.

Viktor Moritz **Goldschmidt** (27 January 1888–20 March 1947)
Viktor Goldschmidt was born in Zurich; he studied mineralogy, geology, and chemistry at the University of Oslo, where he received his Ph.D. in 1911. In 1914 he became a professor at his *alma mater*, becoming director of its Department of Geology and Mineralogy. In 1929 he accepted an appointment as professor of mineralogy at the University of Göttingen. He left the German Reich in 1935 because of "racial" persecution. He then worked again in Oslo as a full professor, institute director, and director of the state committee for natural resources. After the *Wehrmacht* [armed forces] occupied Norway in 1940, Goldschmidt was able to remain until 1942. After being temporarily interned, he was able to flee to the United Kingdom via Sweden. Goldschmidt was a corresponding member of the Academy (c.m.a.) from 1928. He was excluded from the Academy on 12 February 1941.

Roland **Grassberger** (26 November 1867–4 December 1956)
Roland Grassberger came from Salzburg; he studied medicine in Vienna. He received his doctorate in 1892 and, after several years of working as a pathologist, became an assistant at the Department of Hygiene at the University of Vienna in 1897. After finishing his habilitation, he became an associate professor at the University of Vienna in 1906. In 1917 he was conferred the title of full professor and in 1924 was appointed full professor of hygiene. In 1937 Grassberger was elected as a corresponding member (c.m.i.) of the Academy.

Karl **Grobben** (27 August 1854–13 April 1945)
Karl Grobben came from Brünn (Brno)/Moravia (Czech Republic); he studied natural sciences in Vienna, majoring in zoology. He received his doctorate in 1877, finished his habilitation in 1879, became an associate professor in 1884, and accepted an appointment as full professor of zoology at the University of Vienna in 1893. He was director of the Department of Zoology I at the University of Vienna from 1896 until his retirement in 1925. Grobben was elected a corresponding member (c.m.i.) in 1891 and a full member (f.m.) in 1895. Following the death in 1937 of Hans Molisch, Vice-President of the Academy, Grobben was elected his temporary successor at the end of January 1938. He resigned from this post on 18 March 1938.

Adolf **Grohmann** (1 March 1887–21 September 1977)
Adolf Grohmann was from Graz; he studied Semitic philology and Egyptology at the University of Vienna, receiving his doctorate in 1911. He completed his habilitation in 1916 in Vienna and, in 1921, became an associate professor at the German University in Prague. There, in 1923, he was appointed full professor of Semitic philology, Islamic studies, and Arabian

papyrology. In 1930 he was dean. In Prague he was head of the "Oriental Institute" of the Reinhard Heydrich Foundation, established in 1942. In 1945 he was subject to registration as a member of the Nazi Party. Driven out of Prague in 1945, from 1949 to 1962 he gave lectures as an honorary professor at the University of Innsbruck. From 1949 to 1956 he held a position as professor of Muslim history and archaeology at the University of Cairo. The Academy elected Grohmann as a corresponding member (c.m.i.) in 1937 and as a full member (f.m.) in 1961. In 1945 his membership was held in abeyance. The Amnesty Law of April 1948 permitted his membership to be reinstated; his name appears again in the 1948 registry of members.

Otto **Grosser** (21 November 1873–23 March 1951)

Otto Grosser was born in Vienna, where he studied medicine. He received his doctorate in 1899, completed his habilitation in 1902, and held the title of associate professor from 1907. From 1909 he was head – now a full professor of anatomy – of the Department of Anatomy at the German University in Prague. Grosser held the post of dean at the German University in Prague from 1913 to 1915, 1922/23 and 1936/37, and of rector in 1928/29 and 1934/35. From 1918 he was the chairman of the German Association of Sciences and Arts, which in 1941 was converted into the German Academy of Sciences in Prague. In 1945, Grosser was subject to registration as a member of the Nazi Party. He was elected by the Academy as a corresponding member abroad (c.m.a.) in 1937. In 1945 his membership was held in abeyance. The Amnesty Law of April 1948 permitted his membership to be reinstated; his name appears again in the 1948 registry of members. As he was now living in Austria, his status was redesignated as corresponding member in Austria (c.m.i.).

Adolf **Günther** (21 March 1881–14 January 1958)

Adolf Günther came from Munich; he studied philosophy, law, and governmental sciences in Munich, Kiel, and Erlangen. He completed his habilitation in 1910 at the University of Berlin. In 1920 he accepted an appointment at the Nuremberg *Handelshochschule* [School of Commerce], where he held the post of rector in 1921/22. In 1923 Günther was appointed full professor at the University of Innsbruck, where he also held the post of dean in 1924/25 and 1930/31, in 1927/28 he was the rector. In 1938/39 he was again dean. He was given the rank of SA-*Sturmführer*. In 1940 he was appointed full professor of economics and sociology at the University of Vienna. In 1945, he was subject to registration as a member of the Nazi Party and was dismissed from his teaching post in 1946 following a negative ruling by the denazification committee. In 1948 he was pensioned off permanently from the University of Vienna. He was a corresponding member (c.m.i.) of the Academy from 1941. In 1945 his membership was held in abeyance. The Amnesty Law of April 1948 permitted his membership to be reinstated; his name appears again in the 1948 registry of members.

Martin **Gusinde** (29 October 1886–20 October 1969)

Martin Gusinde was born in Breslau (Wrocław); he studied theology in St. Gabriel near Mödling. In 1911 he was ordained a missionary priest. In 1912 he went to Santiago/Chile, where he worked as a teacher and at the ethnological museum. In 1917 he accepted an appointment as professor at the Universidad Católica in Santiago/Chile. Between 1918 and 1924 he carried out research expeditions to Tierra del Fuego, which resulted in his well-known, multi-volume work on the native population of Tierra del Fuego. Gusinde received his doctorate in 1926 from the University of Vienna. After working at the Lateran Museum in Rome from 1925 to 1927, he became a member of the Anthropos Institute in St. Gabriel in 1930. In 1949 he was appointed professor of ethnology at the Catholic University of America in Washington, D.C., where he worked until his retirement in 1957. Gusinde was a corresponding member (c.m.i.) of the Academy from 1967.

Leo **Hajek** (8 January 1887 – July 1975)

Leo Hajek was born in Prague; he studied to be a teacher of mathematics and physics at the University of Vienna. After working for a short time as a high school teacher, in 1913 he began to work at the Phonogram Archive Commission of the Academy, first as an associate academic assistant and from 1921 as a full assistant. In 1928 he took over the directorship of the Phonogram Archive and, in 1937, finally received the title of *Kustos* 1st Class. After the "Anschluss", Hajek was persecuted on "racial" grounds, suspended from his job and, in 1939, dismissed from public service. He was able to emigrate to the United States in the same year. Later he lived in Israel.

Günther **Hamann** (12 October 1924–13 October 1994)

Günther Hamann was born in Vienna. He studied history at the University of Vienna and completed the training course at the Institute for Austrian Historical Research. He finished his habilitation in 1961, became associate professor in 1964, and full professor of modern history at the University of Vienna in 1971. Hamann was elected a corresponding member (c.m.i.) of the Academy in 1970, and a full member (f.m.) in 1974.

Friedrich **Hartmann** (29 March 1876–16 January 1945)

Friedrich Hartmann was from Troppau (Opava); he studied civil engineering at Brno College of Technology. Between 1902 and 1916 he was employed as a design and structural engineer by various railway companies and plants in Vienna and northern Bohemia (Czech Republic). During World War I, he accepted an appointment as full professor of bridge engineering at the Vienna College of Technology. He stayed in this position until his death in 1945. Between 1922 and 1924 he held the post of dean at the Vienna College of Technology, and in 1928/29 that of rector. Hartmann was one of the first engineers to be elected a full member (f.m.) of the Academy (1925).

Hugo **Hassinger** (8 November 1877–13 March 1952)

Hugo Hassinger was born in Vienna, where he studied geography, history, and geology at the University. He received his doctorate in 1902 and obtained a teaching certificate in 1903, whereupon he worked as a high school teacher. He completed his habilitation in 1914 at the University of Vienna. In 1918 he became an associate professor and then was appointed full professor at the University of Basel. In 1924/25 he held the post of dean. From 1927 to 1930 he worked as a full professor at the University of Freiburg im Breisgau, returning in 1931 as a full professor of cultural geography at the University of Vienna. In 1931 Hassinger was instrumental in founding the Viennese *Südostdeutsche Forschungsgemeinschaft* [Southeast German Research Council], which he headed until 1934. Hassinger was a corresponding member (c.m.i.) of the Academy from 1931 and a full member (f.m.) from 1934.

Berthold **Hatschek** (3 April 1854–18 January 1941)

Berthold Hatschek came from Kirwein (Skrbeň)/Moravia; he studied medicine and natural sciences at the Universities of Vienna and Leipzig. From 1885 to 1896 he worked as a full professor at the German University in Prague. In 1896 he was appointed full professor of zoology at the University of Vienna, where he directed the Department of Zoology II until 1925. After 1938, Hatschek was persecuted on "racial" grounds, dying in Vienna before the major deportations began. Hatschek was a corresponding member (c.m.i.) of the Academy from 1896 and a full member (f.m.) from 1932. He resigned from the Academy on 31 December 1938 and thus was not officially excluded.

Franz **Heritsch** (26 December 1882–17 April 1945)
Franz Heritsch was from Graz, where he studied geology at the University. He received his doctorate in 1906, and after his habilitation in 1909, worked first as a visiting lecturer. In 1921 he became an associate professor at the University of Graz, and in 1924 was appointed full professor, holding the chair for geology and paleontology. Heritsch was a corresponding member (c.m.i.) of the Academy from 1935 and a full member (f.m.) from 1941.

Marie **Hesch** (28 October 1888 – December 1970)
Marie Hesch was born in Lechwitz (Lechovice), near Znaim (Znojmo) in southern Moravia, where she went to elementary school. Until the age of eighteen, she worked on a farm. In 1906 she moved to Vienna and worked as a cook for various employers until 1933. After her marriage to the Academy's janitor, Emerich Hesch (1877–1939), she supported him in his work, taking over his position after he died in 1939. On reaching retirement age in 1953, her employment as a cleaning woman was terminated. However, she continued to work as the Academy's janitor. Marie Hesch retired in 1956 on health grounds.

Victor Franz **Hess** (24 June 1883–17 December 1964)
Victor Franz Hess was born in Deutschfeistritz/Styria. He studied physics at the University of Graz. He received his doctorate in 1906 and finished his habilitation in 1910. He worked until 1919 as an assistant in the Department of Physics II at the University of Vienna, and the Institute for Radium Research at the Academy of Sciences. In 1919 he was conferred the title of associate professor. In 1920 he became an associate professor at the University of Graz, but shortly thereafter went to the United States for two years to take part in developing the research laboratory of the Radium Corporation. In 1925 he was appointed full professor of experimental physics at the University of Graz. In 1929/30 he held the post of dean. In 1931 he accepted an appointment at the University of Innsbruck. In 1936 he received the Nobel Prize in Physics for his discovery of cosmic rays in 1912. In 1937 he was again appointed full professor at the University of Graz. In the authoritarian *Ständestaat* [Corporate State], Hess had sat as representative of science on the *Bundeskulturrat* [Federal Cultural Council]. In 1938 he was dismissed from his position as professor, imprisoned, and released. Hess then emigrated to the United States with his Jewish wife, where he took a position as professor in the Department of Physics at Fordham University in New York. Hess was a corresponding member of the Academy from 1933 (c.m.i.); his status was re-designated as a corresponding member abroad (c.m.a.) in 1938. He was excluded from the Academy on 3 October 1940.

Alfred **Hettner** (6 August 1859–31 August 1941)
Alfred Hettner was born in Dresden. He studied geography at the Universities of Halle, Bonn, and Straßburg (Strasbourg). He received his doctorate in 1881, completed his habilitation in 1887 at the University of Leipzig and, in 1897, became an associate professor at the University of Tübingen. In 1899 he moved to the University of Heidelberg, where in 1906 he took over the chair for geography, remaining in this position until retiring in 1928. Hettner was elected as a corresponding member (c.m.a.) of the Academy in 1930. He was excluded from the Academy on 3 October 1940.

Karl **Hillebrand** (26 December 1861–10 January 1939)
Karl Hillebrand was born in Vienna; he studied astronomy, theoretical physics, and mathematics at the University of Vienna. He received his doctorate in 1890, worked from 1892 as an assistant at the Vienna Observatory and, from 1897, was a visiting lecturer at the University of Vienna. In 1902 he became an associate professor at the University of Graz. From 1911 until 1933 he presided over the Graz University Observatory as a full professor of astronomy.

Hillebrand was a corresponding member (c.m.i.) of the Academy from 1926 and a full member (f.m.) from 1936.

Alfred **Himmelbauer** (6 February 1884–18 April 1943)
Alfred Himmelbauer was born in Vienna, where he studied natural sciences at the University, specializing in mineralogy and petrography. He received his doctorate in 1906, and after finishing his habilitation in 1908, taught from 1910 at the University of Vienna as a visiting lecturer. In 1921 he was appointed full professor of geognosy at the College of Natural Resources and Life Sciences in Vienna. From 1927 until his death, he was the head of the Department of Mineralogy and Petrography at the University of Vienna. In 1937/38 he held the post of dean. Himmelbauer was a corresponding member (c.m.i.) of the Academy from 1929 and a full member (f.m.) from 1931.

Hans **Hirsch** (27 December 1878–20 August 1940)
Hans Hirsch was born in Zwettl/Lower Austria; he studied history at the University of Vienna. He received his doctorate in 1903 and, after completing his habilitation in 1908, became an associate professor at the University of Vienna in 1913. In 1918 he was appointed full professor at the German University in Prague. In 1923/24 he held the post of dean. In 1926 he returned to the University of Vienna as a full professor of medieval history and historical auxiliary sciences, taking over as head of the Institute for Austrian Historical Research. From 1934 he headed the *Südostdeutsche Forschungsgemeinschaft* [Southeast German Research Council] in Vienna and was in charge of its early development. In 1936/37 he held the post of dean at the University of Vienna, and from 1939 he was the pro-rector. Hirsch was elected a corresponding member (c.m.i.) of the Academy in 1927, and a full member (f.m.) in 1931. Between 1938 and his death, he served as Secretary of the Academy.

Ferdinand **Hochstetter** (5 February 1861–10 November 1954)
Ferdinand Hochstetter came from Hruschau (Hrušov)/Austrian Silesia (Czech Republic); he was known as an expert in the field of comparative and systematic anatomy and comparative embryology. He finished his habilitation in 1888. In 1892 he became an associate professor at the University of Vienna, and in 1896 accepted an appointment as full professor at the University of Innsbruck. In 1908 he returned to Vienna as head of the Department of Anatomy II, where he worked until his retirement in 1932. Hochstetter was elected by the Academy as a corresponding member (c.m.i.) in 1900 and a full member (f.m.) in 1911.

Karl **Höfler** (11 May 1893–22 October 1973)
Karl Höfler was from Vienna, where he studied natural sciences, mathematics, physics, and chemistry. He received his doctorate in 1919 and completed his habilitation in 1925 at the University of Vienna. In 1935 he took over as temporary head of the Department of Botany and Plant Physiology at the University. In 1937 he became the head of the department as associate professor, and in 1940 was appointed full professor of botanical anatomy and physiology. In 1945, he was subject to registration as a member of the Nazi Party, was removed from his post at the University of Vienna and banned from teaching. In 1949, Höfler was again appointed full professor at the University of Vienna. Höfler was a corresponding member (c.m.i.) of the Academy from 1942. In 1945 his membership was held in abeyance. The Amnesty Law of April 1948 permitted his membership to be reinstated; his name appears again in the 1948 registry of members. In 1951 he became a full member (f.m.) of the Academy.

Otto **Höfler** (10 May 1901–25 August 1987)

Otto Höfler was born in Vienna, where he studied German and Scandinavian languages and literature, and philosophy, receiving his doctorate in 1926. He completed his habilitation in 1931. In 1935 he was appointed full professor of Germanic *Altertumskunde* [archeology] and philology at the University of Kiel and, in 1938, full professor of Germanic philology and ethnology at the University of Munich. From 1943 Höfler headed the *Deutsches Wissenschaftliches Institut* [German Scientific Institute] in Copenhagen. In 1945 he was removed from these posts and, because of his membership in the Nazi Party, was banned from teaching. In 1950 he was given permission to teach Scandinavian languages and literature again. In 1954, after having proven his political integrity, he was appointed associate professor of Nordic philology and Germanic archeology in Munich. In 1957 he was appointed chair of German language and literature at the University of Vienna. He retired in 1971. Höfler was elected a corresponding member abroad (c.m.a.) of the Academy in 1956 and a full member (f.m.) in 1964.

Alexander **Hold-Ferneck** (10 October 1875–25 January 1955)

Alexander Hold-Ferneck was born in Vienna. He studied law at both the University of Vienna and the University of Innsbruck. He received his doctorate in 1899 and completed his habilitation in 1903 at the University of Vienna, where he became an associate professor in 1912. In 1919/20 he was the substitute chair for criminal law at the German University in Prague. In 1922 he was appointed full professor of international law and philosophy of law at the University of Vienna. In 1929/30 he was dean at the University of Vienna and in 1934/35, its rector. In 1945, he was subject to registration as a member of the Nazi Party and, in the same year, was sent into permanent retirement from the University of Vienna. Hold-Ferneck was a corresponding member (c.m.i.) of the Academy from 1940. In 1945 his membership was held in abeyance. The Amnesty Law of April 1948 permitted his membership to be reinstated; his name appears again in the 1948 registry of members.

Friedrich **Hopfner** (28 October 1881–5 September 1949)

Friedrich Hopfner was born in Trautenau (Trutnov) in Bohemia (Czech Republic); he studied mathematics, physics, astronomy, and geophysics at the German University in Prague and in Munich. He received his doctorate in 1905 in Prague and then worked at the meteorological institutes in Berlin, Innsbruck, and Vienna and in the Imperial and Royal (k.k.) Naval Observatory in Trieste. In 1921 he became chief astronomer for scientific surveying and mapping in the *Bundesamt für Eich- und Vermessungswesen* [Federal Office for Calibration and Measurement] in Vienna. In 1936 he was appointed full professor of higher geodesy and spherical astronomy at the Vienna College of Technology. In 1938 he was removed from his post at the Institute. In 1945 he was given back his chair and became dean. In 1948/49 he was rector of the Vienna College of Technology. Hopfner was elected a full member (f.m.) by the Academy in 1945.

Anton **Huber** (24 January 1897–31 August 1975)

Anton Huber was born in Teufelhof near St. Pölten; he studied mathematics and related fields at the University of Vienna and at the Vienna College of Technology. In 1922 he passed the exams for a teaching certificate, received his doctorate in 1924 and completed his habilitation in 1927 at the College of Natural Resources and Life Sciences in Vienna. In 1928 he became an associate professor and in 1933 accepted an appointment as full professor at the University of Fribourg in Switzerland. In 1938 he was appointed full professor of applied mathematics at the University of Vienna. In 1945 he was subject to registration as an illegal Nazi and, in the same year, was dismissed from the University of Vienna and banned from teaching. From 1952 he worked as a mathematical consultant at the nitrogen plants in Linz. Huber was a corresponding member (c.m.i.) of the Academy from 1941. In 1945 his membership was held in abeyance; his name appears again in the 1949 registry of members.

Johan **Huizinga** (7 December 1872–1 February 1945)
Johan Huizinga was born in Groningen/Netherlands, where he began to study Dutch philology, history, and geography. He received his doctorate in 1897 and from 1903 taught ancient Indian literature and art history at the University of Amsterdam. In 1905 he took over the chair for general and Dutch history at the University of Groningen and in 1915 obtained the chair for general history at the University of Leiden. From 1927 to 1931 he was dean of the University of Leiden and in 1932/33, its rector. He remained a full professor of history until the University was closed in 1942. After being interned by the German occupying forces in the summer of 1942 and forbidden from returning to Leiden, he took up residence in Arnheim. In 1937, he was elected by the Academy as a corresponding member abroad (c.m.a.).

Adolf **Jarisch** (23 February 1891–31 August 1965)
Adolf Jarisch was from Innsbruck and studied medicine in Graz. He received his doctorate in 1914 and from 1919 worked at the Department of Pharmacology at the University of Graz. He completed his habilitation in 1922 and was appointed professor at the University of Innsbruck in 1923. In 1930 he accepted an appointment at the University of Düsseldorf but returned to Innsbruck as the chair for pharmacology in 1931, remaining there until his retirement in 1958. Jarisch was a corresponding member (c.m.i.) of the Academy from 1951.

Viktor **Junk** (18 April 1875–5 April 1948)
Viktor Junk was born in Vienna, where he studied German language and literature at the University. He received his doctorate in 1899 and completed his habilitation in 1906 at the University of Vienna. In 1926 he was conferred the title of associate professor. In 1900 Junk became a *Konzeptsbeamter* [paralegal secretary] at the Academy, bearing the title First Chancellery Clerk. His title was changed in 1903 to Second Actuary. Junk was an illegal Nazi; in 1945 he retired.

Hermann **Junker** (29 November 1877–9 January 1962)
Hermann Junker was born in Bendorf am Rhein/Germany; in 1896 he entered the seminary in Trier, where he studied Catholic theology. After being ordained, he became a chaplain in Ahrweiler. At the same time he studied Egyptology, Semitic languages, and Sanskrit at the Universities of Bonn and Berlin. He received his doctorate in 1903 in Berlin and, after his habilitation 1907, became an associate professor at the University of Vienna in 1909. In 1912 he was appointed full professor in Vienna, where he headed the Department of Egyptology and African Studies, which had been established for him. Junker directed the excavations in Gizeh. As head of the German Archaeological Institute in Cairo, he taught and carried out research at the Universities of Vienna and Cairo until 1939. In 1945 he was subject to registration as a member of the Nazi Party. Having been pensioned off in 1945, he taught as an honorary professor at the University of Vienna from 1948 until being made emeritus professor in 1953. He was elected a corresponding member (c.m.i.) of the Academy in 1914, and a full member (f.m.) in 1919. In 1945 his membership was held in abeyance. The Amnesty Law of April 1948 permitted his membership to be reinstated; his name appears again in the 1948 registry of members.

Leo **Jutz** (3 March 1889–6 December 1962)
Leo Jutz was born in Frastanz/Voralberg; he studied German and Romance languages and literature at the University of Innsbruck. He received his doctorate in 1914 and, after completing

his teaching certificate, began to work as a high school teacher in 1918. In 1923 he took a job as an academic librarian. He completed his habilitation in 1926 at the University of Innsbruck and, in 1932, was conferred the title associate professor. In 1936 he became an associate professor at the University of Graz and in 1940 was appointed full professor of German language and literature. In 1945 Jutz was subject to registration as a member of the Nazi Party. In 1946, following a positive ruling by the denazification committee, he was allowed to continue teaching, which he did in Graz until his retirement. In 1941 the Academy elected Jutz a corresponding member (c.m.i.). In 1945 his membership was held in abeyance. The Amnesty Law of April 1948 permitted his membership to be reinstated; his name appears again in the 1948 registry of members. In 1961 he was elected a full member (f.m.) of the Academy.

Friedrich **Kainz** (4 July 1897–1 July 1977)
Friedrich Kainz was born in Vienna, where he studied philosophy, psychology, German language and literature, and art history. He also studied history and musicology. He received his doctorate in 1921 and in 1923 became a lecturer at the Teachers' Training College of the City of Vienna. Kainz completed his habilitation in 1925 at the University of Vienna. From 1931 he was conferred the title of associate professor and, in 1939, received an associate professor position. In 1945 Kainz was subject to registration as an aspiring member of the Nazi Party and in the same year was relieved of his duties at the University of Vienna. In 1949 he was again appointed associate professor and in 1950, full professor of philosophy. From 1950 to 1954 he was the head of the Department of Dramatics. In 1950 he was elected a corresponding member (c.m.i.) of the Academy and in 1955, a full member (f.m.)

Rafael **Kaiser** (6 July 1892 – ?)
Rafael Kaiser was born in Vienna. After completing elementary school, he did an apprenticeship as a gardener and then worked as a gardening assistant in various commercial and private gardens. In 1920 he was employed by the Institute for Experimental Biology (BVA) as a gardener and, in 1921, received civil servant status. In 1945 Kaiser was subject to registration as a member of the Nazi Party and in the same year lost his civil servant status, whereupon he left his job at the Institute. In 1946 he was permanently pensioned off.

Josef **Keil** (13 October 1878–13 December 1963)
Josef Keil was from Reichenberg (Liberec) in northern Bohemia (Czech Republic); he studied classical philology, archeology, ancient history, and epigraphy at the University of Vienna. He received his doctorate in 1903. From 1904 to 1914 he was Secretary of the Austrian Archaeological Institute in Smyrna (Izmir). After finishing his habilitation in 1920, he became an extraordinary associate professor at the University of Vienna in 1925. From 1927 to 1935, Keil worked as a full professor at the University of Greifswald. In 1936 he returned to the University of Vienna as a full professor of Greek history, archeology, and epigraphy, remaining in this post until his retirement in 1951. In 1946 he was temporarily removed from his position but was allowed to return after one month. Keil was a corresponding member (c.m.i.) of the Academy from 1938 and an ordinary member (o.m.) from 1939. He was the Academy's General Secretary from 1945 to 1959.

Hans **Kelsen** (11 October 1881–19 April 1973)
Hans Kelsen was born in Prague; he studied law at the University of Vienna. He received his doctorate in 1906, completed his habilitation in 1911, and in 1915 was conferred the title associate professor. In 1918 he became an associate professor and in 1919 was appointed full professor of constitutional and administrative law at the University of Vienna. From 1919 to 1930 he was a member of the Austrian Constitutional Court. From 1930 to 1933 he was a full

professor of international law at the University of Cologne, and from 1933 to 1940 at the Institut universitaire de hautes études internationales in Geneva. In addition, from 1936 to 1938 he was a guest professor at the German University in Prague. From 1940 to 1941 he worked as a lecturer at Harvard University in Cambridge, Mass., and also as a guest professor at Wellesley College. From 1942 he was guest professor and then lecturer at the University of California, Berkeley, where he was appointed full professor in 1945. He retired in 1951. The Academy elected him as a corresponding member abroad (c.m.a.) in 1947.

Gerhard **Kirsch** (21 June 1890–15 September 1956)
Gerhard Kirsch was born in Vienna, where he studied physics and geology. After receiving his doctorate in 1920, Kirsch was employed at the Institute for Radium Research and as an assistant at the Department of Physics II. He completed his habilitation in 1925 at the University of Vienna and from 1932 had the title of assistant professor. In 1938 he became commissarial head of the Department of Physics III at the University of Vienna and was also in charge of the Gastein Research Institute. In 1939 he became an extraordinary professor and, in 1941, was appointed full professor of physics and director of the Department of Physics I at the University of Vienna. In 1945 he was subject to registration as an illegal Nazi, was dismissed from the University of Vienna in the same year, and in 1947 was pensioned off permanently. Kirsch did not return to university. From 1940 he was a corresponding member (c.m.i.) of the Academy. In 1945 his membership was held in abeyance. The Amnesty Law of April 1948 permitted his membership to be reinstated; his name appears again in the 1948 registry of members.

Josef **Kisser** (19 September 1899– 28 July 1984)
Josef Kisser was born in Vienna, where he studied chemistry and botany at the University. He completed his habilitation in 1927 and in 1930 moved to the Institute for Experimental Biology. In 1934 he was conferred the title associate professor and became an employee of the Museum of Natural History in Vienna. In 1936 he became an associate professor and headed the Department of Botany at the College of Natural Resources and Life Sciences in Vienna. He was dismissed in 1938 for political reasons, whereupon he worked until 1941 at the Institute for Experimental Biology. In 1945 he temporarily took over the directorship of the Department of Botany and Gardens at the University of Vienna. In the same year he again became head of the Department of Botany at the College of Natural Resources and Life Sciences. In 1946 he was appointed full professor of botany. He retired in 1971. Kisser was the rector of the College of Natural Resources and Life Sciences eight times. He was a corresponding member (c.m.i.) of the Academy from 1968.

Raimund **Klebelsberg** (14 December 1886–6 June 1967)
Raimund Klebelsberg was from Brixen (Bressanone); he studied geology and paleontology at the Universities of Munich and Vienna. He received his doctorate in 1910 and completed his habilitation in 1915. He became an associate professor at the University of Innsbruck in 1921. In 1925 he became full professor and head of the Department of Geology and Paleontology. In 1933/34 and from 1942 to May 1945, Klebelsberg presided over the University of Innsbruck as rector. In 1945 he was subject to registration as a member of the Nazi Party. In 1946 he was dismissed from his post as professor and banned from teaching. In 1949 he was rehabilitated and again appointed full professor. Klebelsberg was elected a corresponding member (c.m.i.) of the Academy in 1942. His membership was held in abeyance in 1945. The Amnesty Law of April 1948 permitted his membership to be reinstated; his name appears again in the 1948 registry of members. In 1950 he was elected a full member (f.m.).

Fritz **Knoll** (21 October 1883–24 February 1981)

Fritz Knoll was born in Gleisdorf/Styria; he studied natural sciences at the University of Graz, majoring in zoology and botany. He received his doctorate in 1906 and finished his habilitation in 1912 in Graz. He then became an assistant in the Department of Botany at the University of Vienna in 1913. In 1922 he was conferred the title of associate professor. The same year he became an associate professor at the German University in Prague and director of the Department of Botany and Gardens. In 1926 he was appointed full professor. In 1930 he held the post of dean. In 1933 Knoll was appointed full professor at the University of Vienna, where he headed the Department of Botany and the Botanical Gardens. In 1938 he was named commissarial rector of the University of Vienna, remaining in this post until 1943. In 1938 he was also charged with safeguarding *the interests of the regional administration of the Nazi party in Austria at* the Academy of Sciences. In 1945 Knoll was subject to registration as an illegal Nazi. In 1945 he was dismissed from the University of Vienna and, in 1947, permanently pensioned off. He never returned to the University. Knoll was a corresponding member (c.m.i.) of the Academy from 1934, and an ordinary member (o.m.) from 1939. His membership was deemed terminated in 1945. The Amnesty Law of April 1948 permitted his membership to be reinstated; his name appears again in the 1948 registry of members. From 1957 to 1959 he served as Secretary of the Academy and, from 1959 to 1964, was its General Secretary.

Rudolf **Köstler** (15 June 1878–11 February 1952)

Rudolf Köstler was born in Mödling/Lower Austria; he studied law at the Universities of Czernowitz, Vienna, and Bonn. He received his doctorate in 1901 and completed his habilitation in 1908 at the University of Czernowitz, where he was appointed associate professor in 1912. In 1913 he became an associate professor at the University of Vienna and in 1923 was appointed full professor of ecclesiastical and German law. He held the post of dean in 1928/29 and 1946/47. The Academy elected him as a corresponding member (c.m.i.) in 1941, but this was not confirmed until 1943. He was a full member (f.m.) from 1947.

Ludwig **Kofler** (30 November 1891–23 August 1951)

Ludwig Kofler was born in Dornbirn/Vorarlberg; he studied botany and pharmacology at the University of Vienna, and later also medicine. Finishing his habilitation in 1922, he was appointed associate professor at the University of Innsbruck in 1925. He also took over the directorship of the Department of Pharmacognosy. In 1929 he was appointed full professor of pharmacology. In 1934/35 he was dean and 1935/36 rector of the University of Innsbruck. In 1938 he was appointed *Gaudozentenführer* [*Gau* head of the Nazi Association for university teachers]. In 1945 he was subject to registration as an illegal Nazi. In 1946, following a negative ruling by the denazification committee, he was dismissed from his post and banned from teaching. He did not work again in higher education. Kofler was a corresponding member (c.m.i.) of the Academy from 1941. In 1945 his membership was held in abeyance; he died before his foreseeable reinstatement.

Fritz **Kohlrausch** (6 July 1884–17 September 1953)

Fritz Kohlrausch was from Gstettenhof/Lower Austria; he studied physics and mathematics at the University of Vienna. He received his doctorate in 1907 and worked from 1908 to 1920 as an assistant at the Department of Physics II at the University of Vienna. He completed his habilitation in 1911. He was a lecturer at the Vienna Music Academy and, from 1917/18 to 1920, taught at the *Kunstgewerbeschule* [College of Applied Arts] and the *Graphische Lehr- und Versuchsanstalt* [Federal Training and Research Institute for Graphic Art] in Vienna. From 1920 he held the title of associate professor. In the same year he was appointed full professor of physics at Graz Institute of Technology. Kohlrausch was dean of the Institute in 1922/23 and from 1946 to 1948, and in 1923/24, he held the post of rector. The Academy elected Kohlrausch a corresponding member (c.m.i.) in 1929 and an ordinary member (o.m.) in 1939.

Erwin **Kolbenheyer** (30 December 1878–12 April 1962)
Erwin Kolbenheyer was born in Budapest; he studied zoology and philosophy in Vienna. After his studies he turned to writing and the art of poetry. From 1919 he lived in Tübingen; in 1932 he moved to Munich, where he cultivated a lively career giving lectures. He was a member of the Nazi Party and received numerous awards for his support of Nazi cultural efforts. In 1948 the denazification tribunals classified him as "incriminated" and later as a "follower." The Academy elected him an honorary member in 1941. In 1947 he resigned from the Academy.

Dietrich **Kralik-Meyrswalden** (15 August 1884–27 December 1959)
Dietrich Kralik-Meyrswalden was from Vienna; he studied German language and literature at the University of Vienna. He received his doctorate in 1907 and finished his habilitation in 1914. He was appointed full professor at the University of Würzburg in 1923. He returned in 1924 as a full professor of German language and literature to the University of Vienna, where he then worked until retiring in 1957. In 1934/35 he held the post of dean. In 1945 Kralik-Meyrswalden was subject to registration as a member of the Nazi Party and, in the same year, was dismissed from his teaching position. In 1949 he was again appointed full professor. The Academy elected him a corresponding member (c.m.i.) in 1925 and a full member (f.m.) in 1935. From 1941 to 1945 he held the post of Secretary at the Academy. In 1945 his membership was held in abeyance. The Amnesty Law of April 1948 permitted his membership to be reinstated; his name appears again in the 1948 registry of members.

Josef **Krames** (7 October 1897–30 August 1986)
Josef Krames was from Vienna; he studied for a teaching certificate in mathematics and descriptive geometry, and civil engineering at the Vienna College of Technology. He received his doctorate in 1920, completed his habilitation in 1924, and in 1929 became an associate professor at Brno College of Technology. In 1932 he was appointed full professor of descriptive geometry at Graz College of Technology, where he was also dean and pro-rector in 1938/39. In 1939 he took over the Department of Descriptive Geometry II at the Vienna College of Technology. In 1945 he was subject to registration as a member of the Nazi Party and, in the same year, was dismissed from his university position. He was then employed from 1948 to 1956 at the *Bundesamt für Eich- und Vermessungswesen* [Federal Office for Calibration and Measurement] in Vienna. In 1957 he became a full professor and the head of the Department of Geometry I at the Vienna College of Technology. There he also held the post of rector in 1961/62. He retired in 1969. The Academy elected Krames a corresponding member (c.m.i.) in 1942. In 1945 his membership was held in abeyance. The Amnesty Law of April 1948 permitted his membership to be reinstated; his name appears again in the 1948 registry of members. In 1962 he was elected a full member (f.m.).

Eberhard **Kranzmayer** (15 May 1897–13 September 1975)
Eberhard Kranzmayer was born in Klagenfurt; he studied linguistics and Germanic *Altertumskunde* [archeology] in Vienna and Innsbruck. He received his doctorate in 1925 and joined the staff of the Academy's *Wiener Wörterbuchkanzlei* [Austrian-Bavarian Dictionary Commission]. He completed his habilitation in 1933. In 1940 he became an associate professor at the University of Munich and, in 1942, at the University of Graz. In the same year, Kranzmayer was appointed head of the Institute for Carinthian Archeological Research, which was part of the SS's *"Ahnenerbe"* [Ancestral Heritage] research organization. In 1945 he was subject to registration as a member of the Nazi Party and was dismissed from his position as professor. After

returning to Vienna, his teaching credentials were reinstated in 1949. In 1959 Kranzmayr became an associate professor and in 1961 a full professor of German language and medieval German literature at the University of Vienna. The Academy elected him a corresponding member (c.m.i.) in 1951 and a full member (f.m.) in 1967.

Ludmilla **Krestan** (10 May 1911–3 October 1998)
Ludmilla Krestan was born in Vienna, where she studied classical philology and Romance languages and literature. After receiving her teaching certificate in 1935, she was initially employed as a schoolteacher. From 1938 she worked as an academic assistant at the Commission for Editing the Corpus of critically amended texts of the Latin Church Fathers and, from 1941, she also worked for other commissions of the Academy. From 1945 to 1976 she was the second Actuary of the Academy. In 1950 she was conferred the title of *Kustos* 2nd Class and received civil servant status. In 1954 she received the title of *Kustos* 1st Class.

Paul **Kretschmer** (2 May 1866–9 March 1956)
Paul Kretschmer was born in Berlin, where he studied linguistics and archeology. He received his doctorate in 1889 and completed his habilitation in 1891 at the University of Berlin, where he then taught until 1896. In 1897 he became an associate professor at the University of Marburg. In 1899 he continued his academic career at the University of Vienna as a full professor of comparative linguistics. He stayed in this position until retiring in 1936. The Academy elected Kretschmer a corresponding member (c.m.i.) in 1902 and a full member (f.m.) in 1909.

Erwin **Kruppa** (11 August 1885–26 January 1967)
Erwin Kruppa was born in Bielitz-Biala (Bielsko-Biała)/Silesia; he studied civil engineering, mathematics, and descriptive geometry in Graz and Vienna. He received his doctorate in 1911 in Graz and completed his habilitation in the same year at the University of Czernowitz. In 1921 he was conferred the title of associate professor at the Vienna College of Technology. In 1929 he was appointed a full professor there and headed the College's Department of Descriptive Geometry I until his retirement. Kruppa was dean from 1933 to 1935 and then again from 1940 to 1945. In 1945 he was subject to registration as a member of the Nazi Party. In 1953/54 he was rector of Vienna College of Technology. Kruppa was a corresponding member (c.m.i.) of the Academy from 1935 and a full member (f.m.) from 1937. In 1945 his membership was held in abeyance. The Amnesty Law of April 1948 permitted his membership to be reinstated; his name appears again in the 1948 registry of members. Between 1957 and 1960 he held the post of Vice-President of the Academy.

Othmar **Kühn** (5 November 1892–26 March 1969)
Othmar Kühn was born in Vienna, where he studied botany and paleontology. He received his doctorate in 1919, whereupon he worked first as a high school teacher and then in the Geological-Paleontological Department at the Museum of Natural History Vienna. In 1944 he was conferred the title of *Kustos* 1st Class and in 1949 became director of the Geological-Paleontological Department. In 1945 he was subject to registration as a member of the Nazi Party. In 1951 he accepted an appointment as full professor of paleontology at the University of Vienna, where in 1956/57 he held the post of dean and, in 1960/61, that of rector. Kühn retired in 1964. Kühn was a corresponding member (c.m.i.) of the Academy from 1952 and a full member (f.m.) from 1955.

Robert **Lach** (29 January 1874–11 September 1958)
Robert Lach was from Vienna, where he studied first law and then musicology. He received his doctorate in 1902 at the German University in Prague and completed his habilitation in 1915 at the University of Vienna. He directed the music collection of the Imperial and Royal (k.k.) Court Library from 1912 to 1920. In 1920 he became an associate professor at the University of Vienna and in 1927 was appointed full professor and head of the Department of Musicology. He directed the Department until his retirement in 1939. In addition he worked as a professor at the Vienna Music Academy from 1924 to 1945. In 1945, Lach was subject to registration as an illegal Nazi. The Academy elected him a corresponding member (c.m.i.) in 1918. In 1945 his membership was held in abeyance. The Amnesty Law of April 1948 permitted his membership to be reinstated; his name appears again in the 1948 registry of members.

Viktor **Lang** (2 March 1838–3 July 1921)
Viktor Lang was from Wiener Neustadt; he studied physics at the Universities of Vienna, Heidelberg, and Giessen, where he received his doctorate in 1858. He completed his habilitation in 1861 at the University of Vienna and became an associate professor at the University of Graz in 1864. In 1865 he was appointed full professor of physics at the University of Vienna. In 1870 he held the post of dean and in 1884 and 1889, that of rector. He retired in 1908. Lang was a corresponding member (c.m.i.) of the Academy from 1866 and a full member (f.m.) from 1867. From 1898 he was charged with the post of Secretary and from 1899, with that of General Secretary. From 1911 to 1915 Lang was the Vice-President of the Academy and from 1915 to 1919 he presided over the Academy as its President.

Max **Layer** (17 September 1866–24 January 1941)
Max Layer was born in Graz; he studied law at the Universities of Graz, Vienna, and Heidelberg. He received his doctorate in 1889 and completed his habilitation in 1902 at the University of Graz. In 1903 he became an associate professor at the University of Vienna. In 1908 he was appointed full professor of public law and, for a time, ecclesiastical law at the University of Graz, where in 1912/13 and 1924/25 he held the post of dean. From 1924 to 1929 he was a member of the Austrian Constitutional Court. In 1928 he was appointed full professor of constitutional and administrative law at the University of Vienna. In 1933 he was forced to retire because of having initiated nationwide protests against the dissolution of the Constitutional Court. Layer was a corresponding member (c.m.i.) of the Academy from 1934 and a full member (f.m.) from 1940.

Albin **Lesky** (7 July 1896–28 February 1981)
Albin Lesky was from Graz, where he studied classical philology. After successfully completing his Ph.D. and teaching certificate exams (both in 1920), he taught high school. He completed his habilitation in 1924. In 1932 he became an associate professor at the University of Vienna. In 1936 he was appointed professor at the University of Innsbruck, where in 1937/38 he was also dean, and in 1942 pro-rector. In 1945 he was subject to registration as a member of the Nazi Party. In 1946, based on a positive ruling by the denazification committee, he was allowed to continue teaching and in 1949 was appointed full professor of classical philology at the University of Vienna. He held the post of dean there in 1958/59 and of rector in 1963/64. He was a corresponding member (c.m.i.) of the Academy from 1942. In 1945 his membership was held in abeyance. The Amnesty Law of April 1948 permitted his membership to be reinstated; his name appears again in the 1948 registry of members. In 1950 he was elected a full member (f.m.). He was Secretary of the Academy from 1959 to 1963, Vice-President from 1963 to 1969, and President in 1969/70.

Kurt **Leuchs** (14 September 1881–7 September 1949)
Kurt Leuchs was from Nuremberg; he studied natural sciences at the University of Munich, in particular geology and paleontology. He received his doctorate in 1906, completed his habilitation in 1912 in Munich, and was conferred the title of associate professor in 1919. From 1925 he taught at the University of Frankfurt. In 1936 he accepted an appointment as a full professor at the University of Ankara, where he also held the post of dean in 1938/39. In 1939 he moved to the University of Vienna and from 1940 headed its Department of Geology. In 1945 he was subject to registration as an illegal Nazi and, in the same year, was dismissed from the University of Vienna. From 1948 he worked again in his former department. In 1943 he was elected a corresponding member (c.m.i.) of the Academy. In 1945 his membership was held in abeyance. The Amnesty Law of April 1948 permitted his membership to be reinstated; his name appears again in the 1948 registry of members.

Alphons **Lhotsky** (8 May 1903–21 June 1968)
Alphons Lhotsky was born in Vienna, where he studied history and art history, and also completed the training course at the Institute for Austrian Historical Research. He received his doctorate in 1925. In 1927 he was employed at the Office for Adult Education at the Federal Ministry of Education, where in 1937 he received the status of civil servant. In 1938 he became an advisor for historical matters at the *Kunsthistorisches* [Art History] Museum of Vienna. In 1945 he completed his habilitation at the University of Vienna, where he was appointed associate professor in 1946 and, in 1951, full professor of Austrian history. Lhotsky was a corresponding member (c.m.i.) of the Academy from 1946 and a full member (f.m.) from 1950.

Leopold **Liegler** (30 June 1882–8 October 1949)
Leopold Liegler was from Vienna. From 1899 he worked in the billing department of the Imperial and Royal (k.k.) Ministry of Finance. In 1913 he became an assistant accountant at the Academy and, from 1914, worked as a billing assistant. His application in 1924 to become the successor of Kohl as First Actuary failed. In 1925 he became the successor of the accountant Streicher. From August 1942, Liegler could no longer serve as the head of the accounting department for health reasons. He was pensioned off in 1946.

August **Loehr** (31 March 1882–11 July 1965)
August Loehr was from Vienna; he studied history, art history, classics, and geography there and in Heidelberg and Grenoble. Later he also studied law. He completed the training course at the Institute for Austrian Historical Research. He received his doctorate in 1911 and, in 1913, took over the directorship of the numismatic collection at the *Kunsthistorisches* [Art History] Museum in Vienna. In 1929 he became an honorary professor at the University of Vienna. He was retired in 1938. In 1945, Loehr became the first director of the *Kunsthistorisches* [Art History] Museum and resumed lecturing at the University of Vienna. In addition, he served as director general of the Cultural History Collections of the Federal Republic. Loehr was a corresponding member (c.m.i.) of the Academy from 1933; he became a full member (f.m.) in 1945. He was excluded from the Academy on 29 March 1939.

Karl **Luick** (27 January 1865–20 September 1935)
Karl Luick was born in Vienna. He studied English language and literature at the University of Vienna, received his doctorate in 1889, and completed his habilitation there in 1890. In 1891 he was appointed associate professor of English at the University of Graz and, in 1898, full professor. In 1908 he accepted an appointment as full professor at the University of Vienna. Luick held the post of dean in 1920/21 and, in 1925/26, that of rector. From 1909 he was

corresponding member (c.m.i.) of the Academy and from 1915, a full member (f.m.). In 1926 Luick took over the post of chairman of the Academy's Phonogram Archive Commission.

Fritz **Machatschek** (22 September 1876–25 September 1957)
Fritz Machatschek was from Wischau (Vyškov)/Moravia; he studied geography at the University of Vienna before becoming a high school teacher in Vienna and Brno. He completed his habilitation in 1906 and in 1915 accepted an appointment as full professor at the German University in Prague. From 1924 he headed the Department of Geography at Zurich Institute of Technology. He then obtained a position at the University of Vienna in 1928. Machatschek helped establish the *Südostdeutsche Forschungsgemeinschaft* [Southeast German Research Council] in Vienna and was a board member. He was suspended from his position in 1934, whereupon he accepted an appointment in 1935 as full professor of physical geography at the University of Munich, where he worked until 1946. From 1949 to 1951 he worked at the University of Tucumán in Argentina and then returned to Munich. He was elected a full member (f.m.) of the Academy in 1929; in 1936 his membership was re-designated as corresponding member abroad (c.m.a.) and in 1938, ordinary member (o.m.). From 1945 he was again a corresponding member abroad (c.m.a.).

Heinrich **Mache** (27 April 1876–1 September 1954)
Heinrich Mache was born in Prague; he studied physics and astronomy in Prague and at the University of Vienna. He received his doctorate in 1898. After finishing his habilitation in 1901, in 1906 he became an associate professor at the University of Innsbruck. In 1908 he became an associate professor of physics at the Vienna College of Technology and then, in 1911, full professor. From 1916 to 1918 Mache held the post of dean at the Vienna College of Technology and, in 1925/26, that of rector. In 1945 he was subject to registration as a member of the Nazi Party. Mache was a corresponding member (c.m.i.) of the Academy from 1924 and a full member (f.m.) from 1927. In 1945 his membership was held in abeyance. The Amnesty Law of April 1948 permitted his membership to be reinstated; his name appears again in the 1948 registry of members.

Hermann Franz **Mark** (3 May 1895–6 April 1992)
Hermann Franz Mark was from Vienna, where he studied chemistry and physics. From 1922 he carried out research at the Kaiser Wilhelm Institute for Fiber Chemistry in Berlin. Mark completed his habilitation in 1925 and, in the same year, became department head. In 1927 Mark moved to Ludwigshafen to become deputy director of the I.G. Farben company. At the same time he taught as an extraordinary professor at Karlsruhe College of Technology. In 1932 Mark returned to the University of Vienna to become a full professor of physical chemistry. He was expelled from his post in 1938, whereupon Mark emigrated to Canada. In Ontario he worked as a head of research in a large company. In 1940 Mark became an associate professor at the Polytechnic Institute of New York in Brooklyn and, in 1942, full professor. In 1944 he founded the Institute of Polymer Research in New York, which he headed until 1964. The Academy elected Mark as a corresponding member (c.m.i.) in 1934 and as a full member (f.m.) in 1935. He was excluded from the Academy on 3 October 1940. In 1945 he was reinstated as a corresponding member abroad (c.m.a.) and in 1970 he was finally elected an honorary member.

Hans **Mayer** (7 February 1879–27 October 1955)
Hans Mayer was from Vienna, where he studied law and governmental sciences at the University. While working at the Imperial and Royal (k.k.) Finance Administration, he completed his habilitation. In 1912 he became an associate professor at the University of Fribourg in

Switzerland. In 1914 he was appointed to the newly established chair of political economics at the German Polytechnic Institute in Prague. Due to the war, he only returned to this post in 1919. In 1921 he accepted an appointment as full professor at the University of Graz. From 1923 to 1950 he taught as a full professor of political economics at the University of Vienna. There Mayer held the post of dean in 1927/28 and, in 1945/46, that of pro-dean. From 1932 Mayer was a corresponding member (c.m.i.) of the Academy and from 1941 he was ordinary member (o.m.) and then full member (f.m.).

Karl **Mayrhofer** (24 March 1899–24 July 1969)
Karl Mayrhofer was from Kastelruth/South Tyrol; he studied mathematics and physics at the Universities of Innsbruck and Munich and at the Colleges of Technology in Munich and in Vienna. In Innsbruck he received his doctorate in 1922 and finished his habilitation in 1927. He did research in 1927/28 at the University of Hamburg, whereupon he became a lecturer at the University of Tübingen. From 1929 he was an assistant at the University of Vienna. In 1935 he was conferred the title associate professor. He was appointed full professor of mathematics at the University of Vienna in 1936. In 1945 he was subject to registration as an illegal Nazi; in the same year he was dismissed from his post and banned from teaching. In 1947 he was permanently pensioned off. In 1954 his teaching credentials were reinstated and in 1957 he returned to the University of Vienna as a full professor. The Academy elected Mayrhofer as a corresponding member (c.m.i.) in 1937 and as an ordinary member (o.m.) in 1941. In 1945 his Academy membership was deemed terminated. The Amnesty Law of April 1948 permitted his membership to be reinstated; his name appears again in the 1948 registry of members.

Richard **Meister** (5 February 1881–11 July 1964)
Richard Meister was born in Znaim (Znojmo)/Moravia; he studied Indo-Germanic languages and literature, classical archeology, philosophy, and education at the University of Vienna. He received his doctorate in 1904 and a high school teaching certificate in 1905. Before he began teaching in Austria, he was sent by the Academy of Sciences in Vienna in 1906/07 to work with the team producing the *Thesaurus Linguae Latinae* at the University of Munich. In 1918 he became associate professor of classical philology at the University of Graz and in 1920 he returned to the University of Vienna to take the same position. There he was appointed full professor of education in 1923. In 1930/31 he held the post of dean. Before and during the period of the authoritarian *Ständestaat* [Corporate State], Meister was a member of various organizations promoting Greater Germany. From 1934 to 1938 he had sat as representative of science on the *Bundeskulturrat* [Federal Cultural Council]. Relieved of all his political functions, he was transferred in 1938 to the chair for classical philology. In 1945 Meister returned to his position as professor of education (expanded to include cultural philosophy), where he remained until his retirement in 1956. In 1945 he was pro-rector and, in 1949/50, rector of the University of Vienna. The Academy elected him as a corresponding member (c.m.i.) in 1931 and as a full member (f.m.) in 1934. In the years 1945 to 1951 he served as Vice-President of the Academy and from 1951 to 1963 as its President.

Lise **Meitner** (7 November 1878–27 October 1968)
Lise Meitner was born in Vienna, where she studied physics and mathematics. She received her doctorate in 1906; the second women to do so in physics at the University of Vienna. She also completed a teaching certificate. In 1907 she moved to Berlin and in 1912 became an assistant to Max Planck. In the same year she was taken on as a guest research fellow in the Hahn Section of the Kaiser Wilhelm Institute for Chemistry. She completed her habilitation in 1922 at the University of Berlin and in 1926 – as the first woman to hold this position in the German Reich – she became an associate professor. In 1933 Meitner's teaching qualifications were taken

away on "racial" grounds. As an Austrian citizen, she was allowed to keep her professional position. Because of the "Anschluss" in 1938 she was forced to emigrate to Sweden, where she continued to carry out research at the Nobel Institute. In 1946 she was a guest professor at the Catholic University of America in Washington, D.C. From 1947 until her retirement in 1960 she worked at the Department of Physics at the Stockholm Institute of Technology, where she directed the research unit for nuclear physics. In 1948 Meitner was the first woman to be elected a corresponding member (c.m.i.) of the Academy.

Ernst **Melan** (16 November 1890 –10 December 1963)
Ernst Melan was born in Brünn (Brno)/Moravia (Czech Republic); he studied civil engineering at the German Polytechnic Institute in Prague. He received his doctorate in 1917, whereupon he worked as a construction engineer. He completed his habilitation in 1922 at the Vienna College of Technology. In 1923 he became an associate professor of structural mechanics and the mechanics of material strengths at the German Polytechnic Institute in Prague. In 1925 he returned to the Vienna College of Technology as a full professor of structural engineering, where he remained until his retirement in 1962. From 1946 to 1948 he held the post of dean at the Vienna College of Technology and, in 1952/53, that of rector. The Academy elected him as a full member (f.m.) in 1945.

Max **Mell** (10 November 1882–12 December 1971)
Max Mell was born in Marburg (Maribor). He studied art history and German language and literature at the University of Vienna, receiving his doctorate in 1906. He then worked as a poet, playwright, and author. Although he resigned from the P.E.N. Club in 1933 in protest at the book burning in the German Reich, he headed the *Bund Deutscher Schriftsteller Österreichs* [Association of German Authors in Austria], which was sympathetic to the Nazis and, after 1938, published in Nazi anthologies. Mell is considered one of the most important post-1945 Catholic Austrian authors. He became an honorary member of the Academy in 1956.

Oswald **Menghin** (19 April 1888–29 November 1973)
Oswald Menghin was from Meran (Merano); he studied prehistoric archeology at the University of Vienna. He also completed the training course at the Institute for Austrian Historical Research. He received his doctorate in 1910 and finished his habilitation in 1913. In 1918, he became an associate professor and, in 1922, full professor at the Department of Prehistory at the University of Vienna. He headed the Department until 1945. In 1928/29 Menghin held the post of dean at the University of Vienna and, in 1935/36, that of rector. Also at this time he was a member of the *Siebzehnerausschuss* [Committee of Seventeen], which tried to integrate illegal members of the Nazi Party into the political life of the authoritarian *Ständestaat* [Corporate State]. After the "Anschluss" Menghin served as Minister of Education in the cabinet of Seyss-Inquart. In this function, he was responsible for the "racial" and political "cleansing" of the universities. In 1945 he was subject to registration as a member of the Nazi Party and, in the same year, was dismissed from the University of Vienna. In December of 1945 he was placed on the so called "*erste Kriegsverbrecherliste*" [first list of war criminals]. He was imprisoned until 1947 by the U.S. occupation forces. In 1948 he fled to Argentina, where he taught at the Universities of Buenos Aires and La Plata. In 1957 Menghin was permanently pensioned off from the University of Vienna. From 1927 he was a corresponding member (c.m.i.) of the Academy; after several unsuccessful attempts, he was finally elected a full member (f.m.) of the Academy in 1936. In 1945 his Academy membership was held in abeyance. Following a decision taken by the Academy, Menghin was again listed as a corresponding member abroad (c.m.a.) from October 1959.

Johannes **Mewaldt** (29 April 1880–1 May 1964)

Johannes Mewaldt was born in Posen (Poznan); he studied classical philology and medicine in Berlin. Finishing his habilitation in 1907, he worked as a lecturer at the University of Berlin before accepting an associate professor position at the University of Greifswald in 1909. In 1914 he was appointed full professor at the University of Marburg. In 1916 he returned to the University of Greifswald and in 1923 received an appointment at the University of Königsberg (Kaliningrad). From 1927 to 1931 he worked at the University of Tübingen and in 1931 finally became a full professor of classical philology at the University of Vienna. In 1945 he was subject to registration as a member of the Nazi Party; in the same year he was dismissed from the University of Vienna and was permanently pensioned off in 1946. In 1932 Mewaldt became a corresponding member (c.m.i.) of the Academy and, in 1937, a full member (f.m.). In 1945 his membership was held in abeyance. The Amnesty Law of April 1948 permitted his membership to be reinstated; his name appears again in the 1948 registry of members.

Hans Horst **Meyer** (17 March 1853–6 October 1939)

Hans Horst Meyer was from Insterburg (Chernyakhovsk)/East Prussia; he studied medicine in Königsberg (Kaliningrad), Leipzig and Berlin. He received his doctorate in 1877, completed his habilitation in 1881 in Straßburg (Strasbourg), and in 1882 accepted an appointment as full professor of pharmacology, dietetics, and the history of medicine at the University of Dorpat (Tartu, Estonia). From 1884 to 1904 he headed the Department of Pharmacology as a full professor at the University of Marburg. Meyer was twice dean at the University of Marburg and, in the year 1900, rector. In 1904 he took the chair for pharmacology at the University of Vienna, where he remained until his retirement in 1924. After the "Anschluss", Meyer was persecuted on "racial" grounds. He was a member of the Academy from 1905, first as a corresponding member (c.m.i.) and, from 1920, as a full member (f.m.). He declared his resignation from the Academy on 13 December 1938 and thus was never officially excluded.

Stefan **Meyer** (27 April 1872–29 December 1949)

Stefan Meyer was born in Vienna; he studied physics, mathematics, and chemistry in Vienna and at the University of Leipzig. He attended courses in engineering at the Vienna College of Technology. He received his doctorate in 1896 from the University of Vienna. In 1897 he became an assistant at the Department of Physics at the University, working for Ludwig Boltzmann. He completed his habilitation in 1899 at the University of Vienna. From 1908 he took over the planning and unofficial directorship of the Academy's Institute for Radium Research. The Institute, the first scientific institution devoted to research on radioactivity, was opened in 1910. In 1911 Meyer became an associate professor at the University of Vienna, in 1915 received the title of full professor, and in 1920 he was appointed full professor at the University of Vienna. At this time he also became the official director of the Institute for Radium Research. Immediately after the "Anschluss", Meyer requested his retirement. Meyer was persecuted on "racial" grounds but survived the Nazi era by living in seclusion in his summer residence in Bad Ischl. The Academy elected Meyer as a corresponding member (c.m.i.) in 1921 and as a full member (f.m.) in 1932. He declared his resignation from the Academy on 24 November 1938 and thus was never officially excluded.

Franz **Miltner** (28 October 1901–23 July 1959)

Franz Miltner was from Vienna, where he studied classical antiquity. He received his doctorate in 1925, completed his habilitation in 1932, and in 1933 became an associate professor of ancient history, including the history of the ancient Orient, at the University of Innsbruck. In 1939, as associate professor, he was appointed dean (holding this post until 1943). In 1940 he was appointed full professor of ancient history and in 1941 became director of the Institute for

Ancient History and Epigraphy. In 1945 he was subject to registration as an illegal Nazi and, in the same year, was dismissed from the University. In 1947 he was pensioned off. In 1950 he was admitted into the Asia Minor Commission and the Limes Commission at the Academy. In 1954 Miltner was again given a position with civil servant status at the Austrian Archaeological Institute, where he headed the excavations in Ephesus as "State Archeologist 1st Class." Miltner was elected a corresponding member (c.m.i.) of the Academy in 1943. In 1945 his membership was held in abeyance. The Amnesty Law of April 1948 permitted his membership to be reinstated; his name appears again in the 1948 registry of members.

Hans **Molisch** (6 December 1856–8 December 1937)
Hans Molisch was from Brünn (Brno)/Moravia (Czech Republic); he studied natural sciences in Vienna, receiving his doctorate in 1879 and finishing his habilitation in 1885. In 1889 he became an associate professor at the Graz College of Technology. From 1894 to 1909 he worked as a full professor at the German University in Prague. From 1909 until his retirement in 1928, Molisch was a full professor of plant anatomy and physiology and head of the Department of Plant Physiology at the University of Vienna. In 1922/23 he was dean and, in 1926/27, rector. Molisch was a corresponding member (c.m.i.) of the Academy from 1894 and a full member (f.m.) from 1908. Between 1931 and 1937 he served as Vice-President of the Academy.

Josef **Nadler** (23 May 1884–14 January 1963)
Josef Nadler was born in Neudörfl (Nová Veská)/Bohemia (Czech Republic); he studied German language and literature, and classical philology at the German University in Prague. He received his doctorate in 1908 and in 1912 became an associate professor (without having written a habilitation, but based on the first volume of his *Literaturgeschichte der deutschen Stämme und Landschaften* [Literary History of the German Tribes and Regions] at the University of Fribourg in Switzerland, where he became a full professor in 1914. From 1925 he was full professor at the University of Königsberg (Kaliningrad). In 1931 he accepted an appointment as full professor of German language and literature at the University of Vienna. From 1941 to 1945 Nadler was director of the Department of German Studies at the University of Vienna. In 1945 he was subject to registration as a member of the Nazi Party; in the same year he was dismissed from his post at the University of Vienna and banned from teaching. In 1947 he was permanently pensioned off. He was a corresponding member (c.m.i.) of the Academy from 1933 and a full member (f.m.) from 1934. In 1945 his membership was held in abeyance. The Amnesty Law of April 1948 permitted his membership to be reinstated; his name appears again in the 1948 registry of members.

Emma **Neumann** (30 April 1900–1 April 1974)
Emma Neumann, daughter of the former Actuary of the Academy Emil Kohl (1862–1924), was born in Vienna and graduated from the *Handelsschule des Schulvereines für Beamtentöchter* [Commercial College of the School Association for Daughters of Civil Servants]. In 1924 she was employed as a clerk at the Academy. From 1928 she worked full time as a Chancellery Clerk but was not given a contract with civil servant status. In 1938 she received an employment contract from the Academy; she left her job in August 1945. From 1946 she was employed by the Department of Mechanical Technology at the Vienna College of Technology, where she worked as an administrator until retiring in 1965.

Eduard **Norden** (21 September 1868–13 July 1941)
Eduard Norden was from Emden/Germany; he studied classical philology at the University of Bonn. He received his doctorate in 1891 and completed his habilitation in 1892 at the

University of Straßburg (Strasbourg). In the following year he became an associate professor at the University of Greifswald, where in 1895 he was appointed full professor of classical philology. This was followed by appointments at the University of Breslau (Wrocław) in 1898 and at the University of Berlin in 1906. In 1927/28 Norden was rector of the University of Berlin. After 1933 Norden was persecuted on "racial" grounds and in 1935 his teaching qualifications were withdrawn. He was able to emigrate to Switzerland in 1939. Norden was a corresponding member abroad (c.m.a.) of the Academy from 1923. He declared his resignation from the Academy on 20 December 1938 and thus was never officially excluded.

Viktor **Oberguggenberger** (3 February 1893–2 March 1963)

Viktor Oberguggenberger was born in Innsbruck, where he studied physics, mathematics, and astronomy. He received his doctorate in 1921, completed his habilitation in 1926, and worked from 1929 as an associate professor at the University of Innsbruck. In 1945 Oberguggenberger was subject to registration as a member of the Nazi Party; in 1946, following a positive ruling by the denazification committee, he was allowed to continue teaching. He retired in 1956. Oberguggenberger was a corresponding member (c.m.i.) of the Academy from 1940. In 1945 his membership was held in abeyance. The Amnesty Law of April 1948 permitted his membership to be reinstated; his name appears again in the 1948 registry of members. In 1954 he was elected a full member (f.m.).

Wilfried **Oberhummer** (2 April 1900–26 March 1982)

Wilfried Oberhummer was born in Munich; he studied chemistry at the Universities of Vienna and Berlin. After completing his Ph.D. in 1923, he gained his teaching qualifications in 1936. In 1937 Oberhummer started working for the Academy as an Actuary. He was Second Actuary until 1945, whereupon he became First Actuary. In 1945 he was subject to registration as a member of the Nazi Party. In 1966 he was awarded the *Goldenes Ehrenzeichen für Verdienste um die Republik Österreich* [Grand Decoration of Honor in Gold for Services to the Republic of Austria] by the Federal President, and from 1971 he bore the title *Hofrat* [Court Councilor]. In 1972 the Academy awarded him a golden "Bene Merito" medal.

Gustav **Ortner** (31 July 1900–24 November 1984)

Gustav Ortner was born in Haus im Ennstal/Styria; he studied mathematics and physics at the University of Vienna. He received his doctorate in 1923, completed his habilitation in 1931, and in 1938 took over provisional directorship of the Academy's Institute for Radium Research. From 1939 Ortner was a scheduled associate professor and he remained the Institute's head until 1945. In 1945 he was subject to registration as an illegal Nazi; in the same year he was dismissed from the University of Vienna and banned from teaching. From 1950 to 1955 he was a full professor at the University of Cairo. In 1960 he was appointed full professor of nuclear physics at the Vienna College of Technology. In 1961 he became chairman of the Atomic Institute of the Austrian Universities. He remained in both positions until his retirement in 1970. He was a corresponding member (c.m.i.) of the Academy from 1941. In 1945 his membership was held in abeyance. The Amnesty Law of April 1948 permitted his membership to be reinstated; his name appears again in the 1948 registry of members. In 1964 he was elected a full member (f.m.).

Viktor **Patzelt** (8 July 1887–17 September 1956)

Viktor Patzelt was born in Prague; he studied medicine there and in Freiburg im Breisgau and in Graz. He received his doctorate in 1913 at the University of Graz and finished his habilitation in 1923. In 1928 he became an associate professor and took over – now as a full professor – the Department of Histology and Embryology at the University of Vienna. In 1945 he was subject to registration as a member of the Nazi Party. In the same year he was pardoned and, since there was no one who could replace him, he remained in his post. In 1950 he was again appointed full professor. Patzelt was a corresponding member (c.m.i.) of the Academy from 1940. In 1945 his membership was held in abeyance. The Amnesty Law of April 1948 permitted his membership to be reinstated; his name appears again in the 1948 registry of members.

Wolfgang **Pauli** (11 September 1869–4 November 1955)
Wolfgang Pauli was from Prague, where he studied medicine at the German University. He received his doctorate in Prague in 1893 and moved in the same year to Vienna, where he completed his habilitation in 1899 at the University of Vienna. Pauli worked as a physician in various departments at the University of Vienna, as well as at the Rudolf Hospital and the General Polyclinic of Vienna. In 1907 he was conferred the title of associate professor. In 1913 he was appointed associate professor at the University of Vienna and, in 1922, full professor of biological-physical chemistry. In 1934 he retired due to age but continued to teach. After the "Anschluss" he was forbidden to teach in any way. Persecuted on "racial" grounds, he emigrated the same year to Zurich, where he was able to work at the Department of Chemistry at the university. Pauli was elected a corresponding member (c.m.i.) of the Academy in 1935. After his emigration, his membership was re-designated as corresponding member abroad (c.m.a.) in 1938. On 28 January 1939 Pauli was excluded from the Academy.

Eduard **Pernkopf** (24 November 1888–17 April 1955)
Eduard Pernkopf was born in Rappottenstein/Lower Austria; he studied medicine at the University of Vienna. He received his doctorate in 1912 and completed his habilitation in 1921. In 1927 he was conferred the title associate professor. In 1929 he was appointed associate professor at the University of Vienna and, in 1933, full professor of anatomy and embryology. From 1938 to 1943 Pernkopf was dean of the Medical Faculty and, from 1943 to 1945, rector of the University of Vienna. He was an illegal member of the Nazi Party from 1933 and from 1934 a member of the SA. In 1938 he was given the rank of *SA-Obersturmbannführer*. In 1945 he was subject to registration as an illegal Nazi and, in the same year, was dismissed from the University of Vienna. He was then imprisoned in the Glasenbach internment camp until 1947. In 1949 he was permanently pensioned off. The Academy elected Pernkopf as a corresponding member (c.m.i.) in 1939 and as an ordinary member (o.m.) in 1940. In 1945 his Academy membership was deemed terminated. The Amnesty Law of April 1948 permitted his membership to be reinstated; his name appears again in the 1948 registry of members.

Otto **Pesta** (8 June 1885–5 April 1974)
Otto Pesta was born in Innsbruck, where he studied zoology and botany. He also obtained a teaching certificate for natural history, with physics and mathematics as subsidiary subjects. He received his doctorate in 1907 and then became an assistant at the Imperial and Royal (k.k.) Court Museum of Natural History in Vienna. In 1922 he received a teaching position at the College of Natural Resources and Life Sciences in Vienna and in 1933 he was conferred the title of associate professor of zoology. He completed his habilitation in 1937 at the University of Vienna. In 1938 he was named commissarial head of the Museum of Natural History and continued to teach at the University of Vienna. In 1945 he was subject to registration as an illegal Nazi and, in the same year, was banned from teaching. Pesta was a corresponding member (c.m.i.) of the Academy from 1939. In 1945 his membership was held in abeyance. The Amnesty Law of April 1948 permitted his membership to be reinstated; his name appears again in the 1948 registry of members.

Anton **Pfalz** (4 December 1885–11 November 1958)

Anton Pfalz was from Deutsch-Wagram/Lower Austria; he studied German language and literature and related subjects at the University of Vienna. He received his doctorate in 1910, completed the exams for a teaching certificate in 1911, and finished his habilitation in 1919 at the University of Vienna. He became an associate professor there in 1931. From 1912 Pfalz also worked as first assistant at the Academy's newly established *Wiener Wörterbuchkanzlei* [Austrian-Bavarian Dictionary Commission]; he took over its directorship in 1920. In 1945 Pfalz was subject to registration as an illegal Nazi; he was dismissed from the University of Vienna and banned from teaching. In 1949 he was permanently pensioned off. He did not return to the university. He was a corresponding member (c.m.i.) of the Academy from 1939. In 1945 his membership was held in abeyance. His name appears again in the 1949 registry of members.

Ernst Peter **Pick** (18 May 1872–1 January 1960)

Ernst Peter Pick was born in Jermer (Jaroměř)/Bohemia (Czech Republic); he studied medicine at the German University in Prague. There he received his doctorate in 1896, whereupon he worked as a researcher for three years in the Department of Physiological Chemistry at the University of Straßburg (Strasbourg). In 1899 Pick joined the staff of the state Serotherapeutic Institute in Vienna. He completed his habilitation in 1904 at the University of Vienna, where he became an associate professor in 1912. In 1924 he was appointed full professor of pharmacology and applied medical chemistry at the University of Vienna. He also became head of the Department of Pharmacology and director of the Pharmacological Experimental Research Institute. In 1932/33 he held the post of dean and, from 1933 to 1937, that of vice-dean. In 1938 Pick was forced to retire on "racial" grounds and was temporarily imprisoned. He was finally able to emigrate to the United States, where from 1939 to 1946 he worked as a clinical professor at Columbia University, at the Mount Sinai Hospital in New York, and at the Merck Research Institute. Pick was a corresponding member (c.m.i.) of the Academy from 1931. He declared his resignation from the Academy on 1 January 1939 and thus was never officially excluded.

Theodor **Pintner** (5 September 1857–9 September 1942)

Theodor Pintner was from Brünn (Brno)/Moravia (Czech Republic); he studied zoology at the University of Vienna, where he received his doctorate in 1888. From 1885 to 1887 he worked at the Department of Mineralogy and Geology at Brno College of Technology, and then as a prosector at the Department of Zoology at the University of Graz. In 1894 he became a conservator in the Department of Zoological Comparative Anatomy at the University of Vienna. Following his habilitation in 1897, he became an associate professor in 1905. In 1913 he was appointed full professor of zoology at the University of Vienna. From 1925 until his retirement he was the head of the Department of Zoology I at the University of Vienna. Pintner was a corresponding member (c.m.i.) of the Academy from 1920 and a full member (f.m.) from 1937.

Otto **Porsch** (12 September 1875–1 January 1959)

Otto Porsch was born in Vienna, where he studied zoology and botany. He received his doctorate in 1901 and completed his habilitation in 1906 at the University of Vienna. From 1909 he headed the Department of Botany at the College of Veterinary Medicine in Vienna. In 1911 he became an associate professor at the University of Czernowitz, where he was appointed full professor of botany in 1914. In 1920 he moved as a full professor of botany to the College of Natural Resources and Life Sciences in Vienna. There, in 1932 and 1939–1941, he held the post of rector. In 1945 he was subject to registration as an illegal Nazi and was pensioned off in the same year. The Academy elected him a corresponding member (c.m.i.) in 1940. In 1945 his membership was held in abeyance. The Amnesty Law of April 1948 permitted his membership to be reinstated; his name appears again in the 1948 registry of members.

Arnold **Pöschl** (14 May 1880–15 October 1959)
Arnold Pöschl was born in Graz, where he studied law. Later he continued his education in Graz, Vienna and Bonn, studying mathematics and history. Pöschl completed his habilitation in 1908 in Graz and in 1909 became an associate professor. In 1915 he received an appointment there as full professor of ecclesiastical law. In the years 1920, 1930, 1938, and 1939 he was dean at the University of Graz and, in 1927/28, rector. From 1934 to 1938 Pöschl was forced to retire. In 1938 he was again given a post as associate professor. In 1945 Pöschl was subject to registration as an illegal Nazi and in 1946, following a negative ruling by the denazification committee, he was dismissed from his teaching post. Pöschl was elected a corresponding member (c.m.i.) of the Academy in 1920. In 1945 his membership was held in abeyance. The Amnesty Law of April 1948 permitted his membership to be reinstated; his name appears again in the 1948 registry of members.

Camillo **Praschniker** (13 October 1884–1 October 1949)
Camillo Praschniker was born in Vienna; he studied classical antiquity at the University of Innsbruck. He received his doctorate in 1908 in Graz and completed his habilitation in 1914 at the University of Vienna. In 1923, after having been conferred the title of associate professor, Praschniker took a professorship at the German University in Prague. In 1930 he accepted an appointment at the University of Jena; in 1931 he returned to University of Vienna as an associate professor. In 1934 he was appointed full professor of classical archeology and in 1935 he became the director of the Austrian Archaeological Institute. In 1945 Praschniker was subject to registration as an aspiring member of the Nazi Party and he was dismissed in the same year from the University of Vienna. In 1948 he was again named full professor. The Academy elected Praschniker as a corresponding member (c.m.i.) in 1932 and as a full member (f.m.) in 1937. In 1945 his membership was held in abeyance. The Amnesty Law of April 1948 permitted his membership to be reinstated; his name appears again in the 1948 registry of members.

Adalbert **Prey** (16 October 1873–22 December 1949)
Adalbert Prey was born in Vienna, where he studied physics, mathematics, and astronomy at the University. He received his doctorate in 1896 and, in the same year, became an assistant at the Vienna University Observatory. In 1900 he became an assistant at the Austrian Bureau of Geodesy. In 1902 he finished a habilitation at the University of Vienna and, in 1906, at the Vienna College of Technology. In 1909 Prey was conferred the title of associate professor and he became head of the Innsbruck Observatory. In 1911 he became an associate professor. In 1917 he moved to the German University in Prague, taking a position as full professor of astronomy. In 1930 he returned to the University of Vienna, where he worked in the Department for Theoretical Astronomy until his retirement in 1939. Nevertheless he acted as chair until 1945 and continued to work as an honorary professor until shortly before his death. Prey was a corresponding member (c.m.i.) of the Academy from 1929 and a full member (f.m.) from 1935. From 1945 to 1949 he was Secretary of the Academy.

Alfred Francis **Přibram** (1 September 1859–7 May 1942)
Alfred Francis Přibram was born in London; he studied history at the University of Vienna and completed the training course at the Institute for Austrian Historical Research in Vienna. He received his doctorate in 1882 and became a lecturer in 1887. In 1893 he was conferred the title of associate professor and, in 1900, that of full professor. In 1913 he was appointed full

professor of medieval and modern history at the University of Vienna. After the "Anschluss" he was persecuted on "racial" grounds. In 1939 he emigrated to the United Kingdom, where he taught at the London School of Economics until his death. Přibram was a corresponding member (c.m.i.) of the Academy from 1919. He resigned from the Academy in December 1938 and thus was never officially excluded.

Hans **Przibram** (7 July 1874–20 May 1944)
Hans Przibram was born in Lainz near Vienna; he studied zoology at the Universities of Vienna, Leipzig, and Straßburg (Strasbourg). He received his doctorate in 1899 from the University of Vienna and finished his habilitation in 1903. In 1913 he was conferred the title of associate professor and, in 1921, became an associate professor at the University of Vienna. In 1903 Przibram and the botanists Leopold Portheim and Wilhelm Figdor bought the Vivarium, an exhibition aquarium in the Prater in Vienna. They transformed the building into a research institute for experimental biology; this private research institution was called the Institute for Experimental Biology (BVA). In 1914 the founders presented the Institute to the Academy. Przibram was the director of the zoology department, which he had founded. He was dismissed in 1938 on "racial" grounds, whereupon he emigrated to Amsterdam. In 1943 he and his wife were deported to Theresienstadt concentration camp, where they both perished in 1944.

Karl **Przibram** (21 December 1878–10 August 1973)
Karl Przibram was born in Vienna; he studied physics, chemistry, and mathematics there and at the University of Graz. He received his doctorate in 1901 in Graz and completed his habilitation in 1905. In 1912 he started work at the Institute for Radium Research, first as a private scholar and from 1920 as an assistant. In 1927 he became an associate professor at the University of Vienna. In 1938 he was forced to retire on "racial" grounds. Having lived in exile in Brussels from 1940 to 1946, he was appointed associate professor of physics in 1946 and, in 1947, was named a full professor. He headed the Department of Physics II at the University of Vienna until his retirement in 1951. The Academy elected Przibram as a corresponding member (c.m.i.) in 1946 and as a full member (f.m.) in 1950.

Ludwig **Radermacher** (31 October 1867–28 June 1952)
Ludwig Radermacher was from Siegburg/Germany. At the University of Bonn he studied first medicine and then classical philology and German language and literature, receiving his doctorate in 1891. He then taught high school before returning to the University of Bonn to complete his habilitation in 1897. In 1903 he became an associate professor at the University of Greifswald. In 1906 he moved to the University of Münster as an associate professor and finally, in 1909, to Vienna, where he took over the chair for classical philology. In 1936 he retired. The Academy elected Radermacher as a corresponding member (c.m.i.) in 1914 and as a full member (f.m.) in 1915. From 1918 to 1929 he served as Secretary of the Academy and from 1929 to 1933 as its General Secretary.

Oswald **Redlich** (17 September 1858–20 January 1944)
Oswald Redlich was born in Innsbruck; he studied history and geography both there and in Vienna, and he completed the training course at the Institute for Austrian Historical Research. He received his doctorate in 1881, and in 1887 and in 1890 finished the habilitation in historical subsidiary sciences and Austrian history at the University of Innsbruck. In 1893 he became an associate professor at the University of Vienna, where from 1897 until his retirement in 1929 he was a full professor of history and historical auxiliary sciences. In 1908/09 he held the position of dean at the University of Vienna and, in 1911/12, that of rector. From 1926 to 1929 he was director of the Institute for Austrian Historical Research. From 1918 to

1924 he worked as the Archival Commissioner of the Republic of Austria. Redlich was a corresponding member (c.m.i.) of the Academy from 1899 and a full member (f.m.) from 1900. In 1915 he was the Academy's Vice-President and, in 1919 and 1938, served as its President.

Karl **Renner** (14 December 1870–31 December 1950)
Karl Renner was born in Unter-Tannowitz (Dolní Dunajovice)/Moravia (Czech Republic); he studied law and governmental sciences at the University of Vienna. He received his doctorate in 1898. From 1895 he worked as a librarian at the *Reichsrat* [National Council] Library and from 1907 he represented the Social Democrats in the National Council. Upon the founding of the First Republic in 1918, he took over the office of State Chancellor, which he held until 1920. From 1920 to 1934 Renner was a representative in the National Assembly and, from 1931 to 1933, the Assembly's President. In 1938 he affirmed the "Anschluss" in the referendum of 10 April. During the Nazi era he stayed in Gloggnitz/Lower Austria, where he undertook scholarly and writing activities. On 27 April 1945, Renner was appointed Chancellor of the provisional state government. In the same year, he was elected the first Federal President of the Second Republic of Austria by the National Assembly. He served in this office until his death in 1950. Renner is considered one of the founders of the First and Second Republics. The Academy elected him an honorary member in 1947.

Marie **Repototschnig**, née Calabek (14 July 1895–30 October 1953)
Marie Repototschnig, née Calabek, was born in Žižkov near Prague. She graduated from the *Handelsschule des Schulvereines für Beamtentöchter* [Commercial College of the School Association for Daughters of Civil Servants] in Vienna. From 1911 to 1915 she worked at the Academy, first as an assistant in the chancellery, then as a chancellery officiant and finally, from 1925, as an accounting assistant. She retired in 1941 for health reasons.

Oswald **Richter** (8 June 1878–8 April 1955)
Oswald Richter was born in Prague; he studied botany at the German University in Prague, where he received his doctorate in 1903 and completed his habilitation in 1906. He completed another habilitation in 1908 at the German Polytechnic Institute in Prague. From 1898 he was an assistant at the Department of Plant Physiology at the German University in Prague. In 1910 he became an assistant at the identically named department at the University of Vienna. In 1912 he became associate professor. In 1920 he was appointed full professor at Brno College of Technology, where he was dean in 1925/26 and rector in 1927/28. In 1938 he was also professor of botany at the German University in Prague. In 1941 Hitler appointed Richter full professor and director of the Department of Botany, Commodity Sciences, and Technical Microscopy at the German Technical University in Brno. In 1945 he was expelled from Czechoslovakia with his family. He took up residence in 1948 in Hannover, where he received a guest professorship at the College of Veterinary Medicine. Pensioned off in 1951, he continued to teach. Richter was a corresponding member abroad (c.m.a.) of the Academy from 1926. In 1938 his membership was re-designated as corresponding member in Austria (c.m.i.). In 1945 his membership was held in abeyance. The Amnesty Law of April 1948 permitted his membership to be reinstated; his name appears again – as a corresponding member abroad (c.m.a.) – in the 1948 registry of members.

Richard **Rössler** (7 June 1897–4 May 1945)
Richard Rössler was from Ebensee/Upper Austria; he studied medicine at the University of Innsbruck. He received his doctorate in 1922 and became an assistant in the Department of Pharmacology at the University of Vienna in 1924. After a two-year research sojourn in Cambridge, Oxford, and London, he completed his habilitation in 1931 at the University of

Vienna. In 1934 Rössler was conferred the title associate professor. In 1938 he was given the position of full professor of pharmacology and director of the Department of Pharmacology at the University of Vienna, taking over these posts from his advocate Ernst Peter Pick, who had been persecuted on "racial" grounds and dismissed. Rössler was elected a corresponding member (c.m.i.) of the Academy in 1941.

Hans **Rupprich** (28 October 1898–4 January 1972)
Hans Rupprich was born in Alt-Ruppersdorf/Lower Austria; he studied German language and literature, and history at the University of Vienna. He received his doctorate in 1924, completed his habilitation in 1929, and in 1939 became an associate professor. In 1945 he was subject to registration as a member of the Nazi Party and, in the same year, was dismissed from the University of Vienna. In 1949 he was again named associate professor and worked from 1952 until his retirement in 1970 as a full professor of German language and literature at the University of Vienna. Rupprich was elected a corresponding member (c.m.i.) of the Academy in 1944. In 1945 his membership was held in abeyance. The Amnesty Law of April 1948 permitted his membership to be reinstated; his name appears again in the 1948 registry of members. In 1969 he was elected a full member (f.m.).

Walter **Ruth** (25 September 1905–23 July 1956)
Walter Ruth was born in Waidhofen an der Thaya/Lower Austria; he studied English, German language and literature, and experimental phonetics at the University of Vienna. From 1928 he worked as an academic assistant in the Phonogram Archive Commission of the Academy; he received his doctorate in 1937. In 1938 he started teaching courses in experimental phonetics at the University of Vienna, which were expanded in 1940 to include English phonetics. In 1938 he took over provisional directorship of the Phonogram Archive from Leo Hajek, who had been suspended (and was later dismissed) on "racial" grounds. Ruth completed his habilitation in 1941. He received a position as lecturer in phonetics and was given civil servant status at the Academy in 1942. In 1945 he was subject to registration as an illegal Nazi. After returning from a prisoner of war camp in Yugoslavia in 1946, he was again appointed head of the Phonogram Archive. He held this position until his death.

Franz **Ruttner** (12 May 1882–17 May 1961)
Franz Ruttner was born in Kalk-Podol (Vápený Podol)/Bohemia (Czech Republic); he studied natural sciences at the German University in Prague, receiving his doctorate in 1906. In the same year he became an assistant at the Biological Station in Lunz and, in 1908, its deputy director. He held the position of director from 1924 until his retirement in 1957. Finishing his habilitation in 1925, he was conferred the title of associate professor in 1927. In 1945 he was subject to registration as a member of the Nazi Party. He was a corresponding member (c.m.i.) of the Academy from 1952.

Rudolf **Saliger** (1 February 1873–31 January 1958)
Rudolf Saliger was born in Spachendorf (Leskovec ned Moravici) near Troppau (Opava) in Austrian Silesia (Czech Republic); he studied civil engineering at the Vienna College of Technology. He worked initially in the bridge building office of the Imperial and Royal (k.k.) Austrian Southern Railway. This was followed by several spent in the German Reich, Belgium, and France for study or work. In 1908/09 he became an associate professor at the German Polytechnic Institute in Prague and in 1909 accepted an appointment at the Vienna College of Technology, where he worked until his retirement in 1939 as full professor of reinforced concrete building and structural engineering. He was dean at the Vienna College of Technology from 1920 until 1922, and rector in 1924/25 and 1938. In addition he worked as a building

advisor for the City of Vienna. In 1945 he was subject to registration as a member of the Nazi Party. Saliger was elected as an ordinary member (o.m.) of the Academy in 1939. In 1945 his membership was held in abeyance; his name appears again in the 1949 registry of members.

Leo **Santifaller** (24 July 1890–5 September 1974)
Leo Santifaller was from Kastelruth/South Tyrol; he initially studied astronomy and natural sciences at the University of Vienna and then history. He received his Ph.D. in history in 1919. He completed the training course at the Institute for Austrian Historical Research and finished his habilitation in 1928 at the University of Berlin. In 1929 he became a full professor at the University of Breslau (Wrocław) and, in 1943, moved to the University of Vienna. In 1945 he took over the directorship of the Institute for Austrian Historical Research. In 1946 he was temporarily banned from teaching but was returned to his position in the same year by order of the ministry. In 1952/53 he served as dean. In addition, from 1945 he was director general of the Austrian State Archives. The Academy elected Santifaller as a corresponding member (c.m.i.) in 1943 and as a full member (f.m.) in 1945.

Fritz **Schachermeyr** (10 January 1895–26 December 1987)
Fritz Schachermeyr was from Urfahr near Linz; he studied ancient history, history, and geography at the Universities of Graz, Berlin, Vienna and Innsbruck. He received a Ph.D. in ancient history in 1920 at the University of Innsbruck. From 1921 to 1931 he taught at the *Städtisches Mädchenrealgymnasium* [State Girls' High School] in Innsbruck. He completed his habilitation in 1928. In 1931 he was appointed full professor of ancient history in Jena, in 1936 in Heidelberg, and in 1941 in Graz. In 1945 he was subject to registration as an illegal Nazi; he was dismissed from the University of Graz in the same year and was retired in 1946. He continued work at the department and was appointed full professor of Greek history, archeology, and epigraphy at the University of Vienna in 1952. He retired in 1966. The Academy elected Schachermeyr as a corresponding member (c.m.i.) in 1954 and as a full member (f.m.) in 1957.

Josef **Schaffer** (13 October 1861–27 April 1939)
Josef Schaffer was from Trient (Trento)/Italy; he studied medicine at the University of Graz. He received his doctorate in 1886 and completed his habilitation in 1889 at the University of Vienna. In 1894 he was conferred the title of associate professor. From 1899 he headed the Department of Embryology at the University of Vienna. In 1908 he was granted the title of full professor. In 1911 he was appointed full professor at the University of Graz. From 1913 until his retirement in 1933, Schaffer was a full professor of histology at the University of Vienna. The Academy elected Schaffer as a corresponding member (c.m.i.) in 1906 and as a full member (f.m.) in 1923.

Friedrich **Schaffernak** (27 April 1881–12 March 1951)
Friedrich Schaffernak was born in Windischgraz (Slovenj Gradec)/Lower Styria (Slovenia); he studied civil engineering at the Graz College of Technology. He received his doctorate in 1914, whereupon he was employed by the Styrian Provincial Public Works. He had already been working since 1909 at the Department for Hydroelectric Power Stations in the Imperial and Royal (k.k.) Ministry of Public Works in Vienna. He completed his habilitation in 1917 at the Vienna College of Technology, where he was appointed full professor of hydraulic engineering in 1919. In 1929/30 he held the post of rector of the Vienna College of Technology and, in 1930/31 and 1938, was its pro-rector. In 1945 he was subject to registration as a member of the Nazi Party; in the same year he was dismissed and, in 1947, was retired. The Academy elected Schaffernak as a corresponding member (c.m.i.) in 1927 and as a full member (f.m.) in

1934. In 1945 his membership was held in abeyance. The Amnesty Law of April 1948 permitted his membership to be reinstated; his name appears again in the 1948 registry of members.

Josef **Schatz** (3 March 1871–23 March 1950)
Josef Schatz was from Imst in Tyrol; he studied German language and literature, classical philology, and comparative linguistics at the University of Innsbruck. He received his doctorate in 1895 and completed his habilitation in 1897. For a short period he carried out research at the University of Leipzig before becoming an associate professor at the University of Lemberg (Lwiw)/Galicia (Ukraine) in 1905. In 1911 he was conferred the title of full professor, whereupon he returned to the University of Innsbruck in 1912 as a full professor of German language and literature. In 1917/18 Schatz was dean at the University of Innsbruck and, in 1922/23, its rector. He retired in 1939 but was re-employed from 1943 to 1945. The Academy elected Schatz as a corresponding member (c.m.i.) in 1920 and as an ordinary member (o.m.) in 1939.

Ferdinand **Scheminzky** (17 February 1899–9 June 1973)
Ferdinand Scheminzky was born in Vienna, where he studied medicine. He received his doctorate in 1925 and his habilitation in 1927. He became an assistant at the University of Vienna in 1929. In 1933 he was conferred the title associate professor. In 1942 he became an associate professor in the Department of Physiology at the University of Innsbruck; in 1944 he was appointed full professor of physiology. From 1936 to 1938, and again from 1945, he held a second position as head of the Research Institute of Balneology in Gastein. In 1952 Scheminzky took over the directorship of the newly founded Department of Balneology in Innsbruck. He was dean at the University of Innsbruck in 1945/1946 and from 1951 to 1953. He was a corresponding member (c.m.i.) of the Academy from 1946 and a full member (f.m.) from 1952.

Wilhelm **Schlenk** (22 March 1879–29 April 1943)
Wilhelm Schlenk grew up in Munich; he initially studied philology at the University of Munich and then chemistry. He received his doctorate in 1905, began to work as an industrial chemist, but then returned to Munich and completed his habilitation in 1910. In 1913 he was appointed associate professor at the University of Jena; in 1918 he became a full professor at the University of Vienna. In 1921 he went to Berlin as the successor to Emil Fischer. In 1935, because of his democratic convictions, he was transferred for disciplinary reasons to the University of Tübingen, where he took over as head of the Department of Chemistry. The Academy elected Schlenk as a corresponding member abroad (c.m.a.) in 1917 and as a full member (f.m.) in 1918. In 1921 his membership was re-designated as corresponding member (c.m.i.) and in 1938 as ordinary member (o.m.).

Wilhelm **Schmidt** (16 February 1868–10 February 1954)
Wilhelm Schmidt was born in Hörde near Dortmund. When still a youth, he became a member of the German Catholic *Societas Verbi Divini* [Society of Divine Work Missionaries]. He became an ordained priest in 1892. From 1893 to 1895, Schmidt studied Semitic languages at the University of Berlin. In 1895 he moved to the mission house St. Gabriel near Mödling in Lower Austria. In 1921 he completed his habilitation at the University of Vienna. In 1924 he was conferred the title associate professor. In the same year, by order of Pope Pius XI, he took part in the development of the Museo Missionario-Etnologico in the Vatican, whereupon Schmidt was the museum's acting director from 1926 to 1938. After the "Anschluss" Schmidt was temporarily interned by the Nazis and his teaching qualifications were rescinded. He was able to emigrate to Switzerland by way of Rome; he also transferred the Anthropos Institute, which he had founded, to Switzerland. From 1939 he taught at the University of Fribourg/

Switzerland, as full professor from 1942 to 1948 and as an honorary professor from 1949. Schmidt was a corresponding member (c.m.i.) of the Academy from 1906; after his emigration in 1941, his membership was re-designated as corresponding member abroad (c.m.a.).

Arnold **Schober** (16 April 1886–15 August 1959)

Arnold Schober was born in Windisch-Landsberg (Podčetrtek)/Lower Styria (Slovenia); he studied art history and archeology in Graz, Berlin, Munich, and Vienna. He received his doctorate in 1909 in Graz. From 1912 was an assistant at the University of Vienna, where he completed his habilitation in 1921 and became an associate professor in 1927. In 1935 he was appointed associate professor and chairman of the Department of Archeology at the University of Graz. In 1940 he became a full professor. In 1945 he was subject to registration as a member of the Nazi Party; in the same year he was permanently pensioned off. In 1946, following to a negative ruling by the denazification committee, he was dismissed from his teaching post. He was elected a corresponding member (c.m.i.) of the Academy in 1940. In 1945 his membership was held in abeyance. The Amnesty Law of April 1948 permitted his membership to be reinstated; his name appears again in the 1948 registry of members.

Ernst **Schönbauer** (29 December 1885–3 May 1966)

Ernst Schönbauer was born in Windigsteig/Lower Austria; he studied classical philology in Vienna and German language and literature and law in Prague, where he received his Ph.D. in 1911 and, in 1915, his Dr. iur. As a member of the Austrian Constituent National Assembly, he was part of the Austrian delegation at the peace negotiations in St. Germain in 1919. He resigned his mandate at the National Assembly in 1930. After finishing his habilitation in 1919 at the University of Vienna, Schönbauer became an associate professor of Roman and civil law in 1924 and a full professor in 1929. He was dean of the Law Faculty of the University of Vienna from 1938 to 1943. In 1945 he was subject to registration as a member of the Nazi Party and, in the same year, was permanently pensioned off by the University of Vienna. He was a corresponding member (c.m.i.) of the Academy from 1933 and an ordinary member (o.m.) from 1939. In 1945 his membership was held in abeyance. The Amnesty Law of April 1948 permitted his membership to be reinstated; his name appears again in the 1948 registry of members.

Erwin **Schrödinger** (12 August 1887–4 January 1961)

Erwin Schrödinger was born in Vienna, where he studied mathematics and physics. He received his doctorate in 1910 and completed his habilitation in 1914 at the University of Vienna. In 1920 he became an associate professor at the University of Jena but moved the same year to the Stuttgart College of Technology and the University of Breslau (Wrocław). In 1921 he took over a full professorship for theoretical physics at the University of Zurich, before accepting the appointment in 1927 of the chair for theoretical physics at the University of Berlin (as the successor to Max Planck). In 1933 he received the Nobel Prize in Physics. In the same year Schrödinger, who was an opponent of National Socialism, left the German Reich and took a position at Magdalen College in Oxford. In 1936 he became a full professor at the University of Graz. In 1938, after a short stopover as a guest professor in Ghent, he emigrated to Ireland, where he was director of the School of Theoretical Physics in Dublin from 1940. He returned to Vienna in 1956 and taught at the Department of Theoretical Physics at the University of Vienna. He was a corresponding member (c.m.a.) of the Academy from 1928. His membership was re-designated corresponding member abroad (c.m.i.) in 1936. Schrödinger was excluded from the Academy in October 1940. In 1945 his membership was again re-designated, this time as corresponding member abroad (c.m.a.). He was a full member (f.m.) of the Academy from 1956.

Siegmund **Schumacher-Marienfrid** (26 January 1872–31 May 1944)
Siegmund Schumacher-Marienfrid was from Innsbruck; he studied medicine at the Universities of Innsbruck, Munich, and Vienna. He received his doctorate in 1898 in Vienna, completed his habilitation in 1904 at the same university, and in 1908 was conferred the title associate professor. In 1912 he became an associate professor at the College of Veterinary Medicine in Vienna and, the next year, at the University of Innsbruck. In 1916 he became full professor of histology and embryology. In 1918/19 he was dean. In 1937 Schumacher-Marienfrid was sent into early retirement. The Academy elected him as a corresponding member (c.m.i.) in 1933 and as an ordinary member (o.m.) in 1941.

Egon **Schweidler** (10 February 1873–12 February 1948)
Egon Schweidler was from Vienna, where he studied physics and mathematics. He received his doctorate in 1895 and finished his habilitation in 1899. In 1911 he became an associate professor at the University of Vienna. From 1911 to 1926 he headed the Department of Experimental Physics at the University of Innsbruck, where in 1923 he was also dean and, in 1925/26, rector. In 1926 he returned to the University of Vienna as a full professor and chairman of the Department of Physics I; in 1938 he took over as head of the Department of Physics II, holding this post until his retirement in 1939. The Academy elected Schweidler as a corresponding member (c.m.i.) in 1921 and as a full member (f.m.) in 1925. From 1929 to 1933 he served as Secretary of the Academy, from 1933 to 1938 as General Secretary, and from 1938 to 1945 as Vice-President.

Hans **Sedlmayr** (18 January 1896–9 July 1984)
Hans Sedlmayr was from Hornstein/Burgenland; he studied architecture at the Vienna College of Technology and art history, physics, and law at the University of Vienna. He received his doctorate in 1923 from the University of Vienna in the field of art history. In 1933 he completed a first habilitation at the College of Technology and, in 1934, another at the University of Vienna. In 1936 he accepted an appointment as full professor of art history at the University of Vienna. Sedlmayr became a member of the Nazi Party in 1930 but declared his resignation in 1932. From 1938 to 1945 he was again a member of the Party. In 1945 he was subject to registration as a member of the Party; in the same year he was dismissed from his post at the University of Vienna and banned from teaching. In 1946 he was permanently pensioned off by the University of Vienna. In 1951 he was appointed full professor at the University of Munich. From 1965 to 1969 he was a guest professor in the Department of Art History at the University of Salzburg. Sedlmayr was a corresponding member (c.m.i.) of the Academy from 1939 and an ordinary member (o.m.) from 1941. In 1945 his membership was held in abeyance. The Amnesty Law of April 1948 permitted his membership to be reinstated; his name appears again in the 1948 registry of members. In 1951 his membership was re-designated as corresponding member abroad (c.m.a.) and, in 1966, as full member (f.m.).

Heinrich **Sequenz** (13 January 1895–11 May 1987)
Heinrich Sequenz was born in Vienna; he studied engineering, mathematics, and physics at the University of Vienna, Vienna College of Technology, and Karlsruhe College of Technology. He received doctorates in various fields (1927 Vienna College of Technology, 1938 University of Vienna) and completed his habilitation in 1932 at the Vienna College of Technology. In 1937 he accepted an appointment at Stuttgart College of Technology. In 1939 he was appointed full professor of electrical machines at the Vienna College of Technology. From 1942 to 1945 he served there as rector. In 1945 Sequenz was subject to registration as a suspected illegal member of the Nazi Party. In the same year he was dismissed from the Vienna College of Technology

and he was banned from teaching or publishing. He was held in various internment camps by the U.S. occupation forces (including Glasenbach) until 1947. In 1952 his teaching credentials were reinstated and in 1954 was again appointed full professor and charged with the directorship of the Department of Electrical Installations at the Vienna College of Technology. Sequenz was a corresponding member (c.m.i.) of the Academy from 1941. In 1945 his membership was held in abeyance; his name appears again in the 1949 registry of members.

George Harrison **Shull** (15 April 1874–29 September 1954)
George H. Shull was born in Clark County, Ohio. After working for several years as a teacher, he studied at Antioch College. He then worked for various governmental agencies, including the United States Bureau of Forestry, the National Herbarium in Washington, D.C., and the Bureau of Plant Industry of the U.S. Department of Agriculture. In addition he studied plant physiology at the University of Chicago. From 1915 until his retirement in 1942 he taught at Princeton University. Shull was elected a corresponding member abroad (c.m.a.) of the Academy in 1939.

Anton **Skrabal** (12 April 1877–4 November 1957)
Anton Skrabal was born in Schwechat/Lower Austria; he studied chemistry at the Vienna College of Technology. He received his doctorate in 1903, worked for a time in a mining and smelting company and then completed his habilitation in 1905. In 1911 he was conferred the title associate professor. He was appointed associate professor at the University of Graz in 1912. In 1917 Skrabal became a full professor of chemistry and head of the Department of Chemistry in Graz. He stayed in these posts until his retirement in 1943. In 1927/28 he held the post of dean. In 1945 he was subject to registration as a member of the Nazi Party. The Academy elected Skrabal as a corresponding member (c.m.i.) in 1919 and as a full member (f.m.) in 1924. In 1945 his membership was held in abeyance. The Amnesty Law of April 1948 permitted his membership to be reinstated; his name appears again in the 1948 registry of members.

Josef **Soukup** (13 January 1866–4 May 1942)
Josef Soukup was from Gmunden/Upper Austria. In 1903 he began to serve as the Academy's janitor and concierge. In 1914 he took over the administration of the publication archive, which was separate from the administration of the chancellery and library. Due to his indispensability he was exempted from military service during World War I. After Emerich Hesch became the Academy's janitor in 1922, Soukup became more involved in the administration of the library and the publication archive. In 1933 he was honored with the Silver Medal for Services to the Republic of Austria. Despite having reached pension age, his indispensability meant Soukup only retired in 1941.

Ernst **Späth** (14 May 1886–30 September 1946)
Ernst Späth was born in Bärn (Moravský Beroun)/Moravia; he studied natural sciences at the University of Vienna, majoring in chemistry. He received his doctorate in 1910, completed his habilitation in 1917, and in 1921 became an associate professor at the University of Vienna. From 1924 until his retirement in 1944 he headed the Department of Chemistry II at the University of Vienna as full professor of chemistry. In 1932/33 he held the post of dean at the University of Vienna and, in 1937/38, that of rector. Späth was a corresponding member (c.m.i.) of the Academy from 1925 and a full member (f.m.) from 1926. From 1938 to 1945 he served as General Secretary of the Academy and from 1945 to 1946 he presided as the Academy's President.

Othmar **Spann** (1 October 1878–8 July 1950)

Othmar Spann was born in Vienna; he studied philosophy, economics, and social studies at the University of Vienna, and at the Universities of Zurich, Bern, and Tübingen. He received his doctorate in science of state in 1903 in Tübingen. In 1907 he completed his habilitation at the German Technical University in Brno. From 1908/09 to 1910 he headed the preparations for the population census of 1910 at the Central Commission for Statistics in Vienna. In 1909 he became an associate professor at Brno College of Technology. From 1911 to 1919 he was employed there as a full professor of economics and statistics. From 1919 to 1938 Spann was a full professor of economics and sociology at the University of Vienna. Immediately after the "Anschluss" Spann, who was a theoretician for the authoritarian *Ständestaat* [Corporate State], was dismissed, arrested, and imprisoned for four months in Munich. After this, he moved back to his home in Neustift in Burgenland. In 1945 Spann's post was not reactivated; he was given leave and, in 1949, was pensioned off. Spann was elected a corresponding member (c.m.i.) of the Academy in 1933.

Hans **Sperl** (13 November 1861–3 March 1959)

Hans Sperl was born in Weyer/Upper Austria and studied law at the University of Graz. He received his doctorate in 1884 and finished his habilitation in 1895. In 1899 he became an associate professor in Graz and accepted an appointment in 1900 as full professor of law and governmental sciences at the University of Vienna. He remained there until his retirement in 1933 but resumed teaching during World War II. In 1903/04, 1913/14, and 1923/24 he held the post of dean at the University of Vienna and, in 1924/25, that of rector. Sperl also taught at the Austrian Consular Academy. In 1945 he was subject to registration as a member of the Nazi Party and in the same year was finally pensioned off. He was an honorary member of the Academy from 1942. In 1945 his membership was held in abeyance. The Amnesty Law of April 1948 permitted his membership to be reinstated; his name appears again in the 1948 registry of members.

Heinrich **Srbik** (10 November 1878–16 February 1951)

Heinrich Srbik was from Vienna, where he studied history. He received his doctorate in 1902 and became a research fellow at the Commission for Modern Austrian History. In 1907 he completed his habilitation in Austrian history in Vienna, and in 1910 his teaching credentials were expanded to include general history. In 1912 he became an associate professor of general history at the University of Graz. In 1917 he accepted a full professorship of modern history and economic history. In 1922 Srbik became a full professor of history at the University of Vienna. From 1929 to 1930, he was Minister of Education in the third cabinet of Schober. Returning to the University, Srbik served as dean in 1932/33. In April 1938 he was elected President of the Academy and in the same month was named a member of the Greater German Reichstag. In 1945 Srbik was subject to registration as a member of the Nazi Party and, in the same year, was dismissed from the University of Vienna and banned from teaching. In 1948 he was permanently pensioned off by the University of Vienna. Srbik was a corresponding member (c.m.i.) of the Academy from 1919 and a full member (f.m.) from 1923. Between 1933 and 1938 he held the post of Secretary of the Academy and, from 1938 to 1945, he was the Academy's President. In 1945 his membership was held in abeyance. The Amnesty Law of April 1948 permitted his membership to be reinstated; his name appears again in the 1948 registry of members.

Adolf **Staffe** (2 November 1888–9 March 1958)

Adolf Staffe was born in Klantendorf (Kujavy)/Moravia; he studied animal husbandry at the College of Natural Resources and Life Sciences in Vienna, receiving his doctorate in 1913. He first worked as a farming supervisor on a number of properties and was also politically active. In 1920 Staffe completed his habilitation at the College of Natural Resources and Life Sciences, where in 1928 he became an associate professor. In 1932 he was conferred the title of full professor and in 1938 became a full professor of animal husbandry and dairy farming. From 1941 to 1944 he served as rector of the College of Natural Resources and Life Sciences. In 1945 he was subject to registration as an illegal Nazi and, in the same year, was released from his post. He took a position first at the Agricultural College in Zurich and, in 1951, went to Bogotá/Columbia. Staffe was a corresponding member (c.m.i.) of the Academy from 1941. In 1945 his membership was held in abeyance. The Amnesty Law of April 1948 permitted his membership to be reinstated; his name appears again in the 1948 registry of members.

Eugen **Steinach** (27 January 1861–14 May 1944)
Eugen Steinach was born in Hohenems/Vorarlberg; he initially studied chemistry and zoology at the University of Geneva and later medicine at the Universities of Vienna and Innsbruck. He received his doctorate in 1886 from the University of Innsbruck. From 1886 to 1888 he was an assistant in the Department for Physiology in Innsbruck, and then at the German University in Prague, where he completed his habilitation in 1890. He became an associate professor there in 1895 and, in 1906, a full professor and the first chairman of his newly founded Laboratory for General and Comparative Physiology. In 1912 he established the Department of Physiology at the Institute for Experimental Biology (BVA) in Vienna, which he directed until 1932. In 1919 Steinach was appointed full professor of physiology at the University of Vienna. He retired in 1932. After the "Anschluss" Steinach was persecuted on "racial" grounds. In 1938 he did not return to Vienna again from a lecture series in Switzerland.

Harold **Steinacker** (26 May 1875–29 January 1965)
Harold Steinacker was born in Budapest; he studied ancient history and classical philology at the University of Vienna, and also completed the training course at the Institute for Austrian Historical Research. He received his doctorate in 1898, whereupon he began to study law. He completed his habilitation in 1905 at the University of Vienna and in 1909 became an associate professor at the University of Innsbruck. In 1917 Steinacker accepted an appointment as full professor of historical auxiliary sciences in the German University in Prague. He returned in 1918 to Innsbruck where he had been appointed full professor of medieval history and historical auxiliary sciences. In 1924/25 he held the post of dean at the University of Innsbruck and, from 1938 to 1942, that of rector. In 1945 he was subject to registration as an illegal Nazi. In 1946, following a negative ruling by the denazification committee, he was dismissed from his teaching post. The Academy elected Steinacker as a corresponding member (c.m.i.) in 1932. In 1945 his membership was held in abeyance. The Amnesty Law of April 1948 permitted his membership to be reinstated; his name appears again in the 1948 registry of members. In 1964 he was elected an honorary member.

Walter **Steinhauser** (7 February 1885–3 August 1980)
Walter Steinhauser was born in Vienna, where he studied German language and literature. In 1934 he was appointed associate professor and, from 1935 to 1945, was a full professor of Germanic language history and archeology at the University of Vienna. In 1945 he was subject to registration as an illegal Nazi and, in the same year, was dismissed from the University of Vienna and banned from teaching. In 1947 he was permanently pensioned off by the University of Vienna. His chair was abolished. Steinhauser was a corresponding member (c.m.i.) of the Academy from 1940. In 1945 his membership was held in abeyance. The Amnesty Law of April 1948 permitted his membership to be reinstated; his name appears again in the 1948 registry of members.

Artur **Steinwenter** (17 May 1888–15 March 1959)

Artur Steinwenter was born in Marburg (Maribor)/Lower Styria (Slovenia) and studied law at the University of Graz. In 1914 he completed his habilitation, becoming an associate professor in Graz in 1918 and in 1926 was appointed full professor of Roman law. In 1930/31, 1947/48, and 1949/50 he held the post of dean at the University of Graz. In 1945 he was subject to registration as a member of the Nazi Party. In 1946, following a positive ruling by the denazification committee, he was allowed to continue teaching. In 1958 he went into retirement. He was a corresponding member (c.m.i.) of the Academy from 1935 and an ordinary member (o.m.) from 1943. In 1945 his membership was held in abeyance. The Amnesty Law of April 1948 permitted his membership to be reinstated; his name appears again in the 1948 registry of members.

Georg **Stetter** (23 December 1895–14 July 1988)

Georg Stetter was born in Vienna, where he began his studies in mechanical and electrical engineering at the Vienna College of Technology. After World War I he continued his studies at the University of Vienna. He received his doctorate in 1922 and became an assistant at the Department of Physics II. In 1928 he completed his habilitation at University of Vienna, was conferred the title of professor in 1934, and in 1939 became a full professor and head of the Department of Physics II. In 1943 he took over the directorship of the newly established Four-Year Plan Institute for Neutron Research in Vienna. In 1945 he was subject to registration as an illegal Nazi and, in the same year, was dismissed from the University of Vienna. In 1953 he was again appointed full professor and head of the Department of Physics I. He was a corresponding member (c.m.i.) of the Academy from 1940. In 1945 his membership was held in abeyance. The Amnesty Law of April 1948 permitted his membership to be reinstated; his name appears again in the 1948 registry of members. In 1962 he was elected a full member (f.m.).

Otto **Stolz** (31 March 1881–4 November 1957)

Otto Stolz was from Innsbruck, where he studied geography and history and also completed the training course at the Institute for Austrian Historical Research in Vienna. He received his doctorate in 1905 and completed his habilitation in 1912 while working as an archivist in Innsbruck. In 1923 he was conferred the title of associate professor and in 1926 became a full professor of history and archival sciences the University of Innsbruck. He was concurrently also the head of the *Statthaltereiarchiv* [Archives of the Governor's Office] (1932–1946) in Innsbruck. In 1945 he was subject to registration as a member of the Nazi Party. In 1946, following a positive ruling by the denazification committee, he was allowed to continue teaching. He was a corresponding member (c.m.i.) of the Academy from 1935. In 1945 his membership was held in abeyance. The Amnesty Law of April 1948 permitted his membership to be reinstated; his name appears again in the 1948 registry of members.

Franz Eduard **Suess** (7 October 1867–25 January 1941)

Franz Eduard Suess was from Vienna, where he studied natural sciences, majoring in geology. He received his doctorate in 1891 and then worked as an assistant in the Department of Mineralogy and Geology at the German Polytechnic Institute in Prague. From 1893 to 1908 he worked at the Imperial Geological Institute in Vienna. In 1898 he completed his habilitation at the University of Vienna, in 1905 he was conferred the title of associate professor, and in 1908 he became associate professor at the University of Vienna. In 1911 he accepted an appointment as full professor of mineralogy and geology at the German Polytechnic Institute in Prague but moved the same year to the University of Vienna, where he worked as a full professor of geology until his retirement in 1936. In 1923/24 Suess held the post of dean. After the "Anschluss" he was persecuted on "racial" grounds, being classified a "'Mischling' of the second degree." Suess was a corresponding member (c.m.i.) of the Academy from 1911 and a full member (f.m.) from 1915. He was excluded from the Academy on 2 December 1939.

Leopold **Svajda** (8 October 1896 – August 1976)
Leopold Svajda was born in Vienna, where he studied law at the University. From 1920 he worked at the Ministry of Finance, first in the chancellery, from 1925 in the planning and billing department, and finally as deputy head of the chancellery. He was the head of the chancellery from 1934 until the dissolution of the Ministry of Finance in 1940. He then took on a position at the Academy. In 1941 he was appointed tax commissioner and seconded to the Registrar of academic institutions of higher education in Vienna, where he was transferred to Section P of the *Oberfinanzpräsidium* [Higher Revenue Office]. From 1942 he was effectively the only person responsible for the Academy's accounting office and in 1946 he took over this position officially. In 1945 Svajda received the title *Amtssekretär* and in 1955 that of *Wirklicher Amtsrat*. He retired in 1961.

Hermann **Tertsch** (19 February 1880–14 December 1962)
Hermann Tertsch was from Alt-Petrain (Starý Petříň)/Moravia; he studied natural sciences at the University of Vienna. He received his doctorate in 1903 and after completing his teaching certificate he worked as a high school teacher until 1920. He completed his habilitation at the University of Vienna in 1910, where he taught from 1921 to 1933. In 1922 he was conferred the title associate professor. In 1943/44 he stood in temporarily as chair of the Department of Mineralogy at the University of Vienna. In 1945 Tertsch was subject to registration as a member of the Nazi Party. He was a corresponding member (c.m.i.) of the Academy from 1931. In 1945 his membership was Held in abeyance. The Amnesty Law of April 1948 permitted his membership to be reinstated; his name appears again in the 1948 registry of members.

Karl **Terzaghi** (2 October 1883–25 October 1963)
Karl Terzaghi was born in Prague; he studied mechanical and civil engineering and geology at Graz College of Technology, where he received his doctorate in 1912. He then worked as an engineer in Austria and abroad before taking a professorship at the Engineering College in Istanbul in 1916. In 1919 he continued his career at Robert College in Istanbul and from 1925 was a professor at the Massachusetts Institute of Technology in the United States. From 1929 to 1938 he taught hydraulic engineering at the Vienna College of Technology. Terzaghi was an opponent of Nazism and emigrated to the United States in 1938. He then taught at Harvard University in Cambridge, Mass., where he retired in 1953. Terzagi was a corresponding member (c.m.i.) of the Academy from 1932 and a full member (f.m.) from 1937. In 1945 his membership was re-designated as corresponding member abroad (c.m.a.).

Rudolf **Thiel** (2 March 1902–2 June 1972)
Rudolf Thiel went to elementary school in Vienna and was apprenticed as a bookbinder, although he did not finish the trade examinations. From 1922 he worked as a clerk or assistant in various firms, including Brown-Boveri in Vienna. In between were periods of unemployment, sometimes lasting several years (for example, 1932–38). In 1940 he replaced Ferdinand Weiss, who had been drafted, at the Academy, where he worked as an assistant until his own conscription in 1942. After the war, Thiel returned to Vienna and took over supervision of the Academy's library and its publication archive. He retired in 1967.

Karl **Toldt** (7 January 1875–25 January 1961)
Karl Toldt was from Vienna, where he studied zoology and chemistry. He received his doctorate in 1899 and then became a academic with civil servant status at the Imperial and Royal (k.k.) Court Museum of Natural History. In 1923 he became deputy director of the Museum's zoology department. After retiring in 1925, he moved to Innsbruck, where he took over as academic director of the zoological collection of the Ferdinandeum Museum, an honorary post. In 1945 Toldt was subject to registration as a member of the Nazi Party; in 1946, following a positive ruling by the denazification committee, he was allowed to remain in his post. Toldt was a corresponding member (c.m.i.) of the Academy from 1942. In 1945 his membership was held in abeyance. The Amnesty Law of April 1948 permitted his membership to be reinstated; his name appears again in the 1948 registry of members.

Erich **Tschermak-Seysenegg** (15 November 1871–11 October 1962)
Erich Tschermak-Seysenegg was born in Vienna; he studied agricultural sciences at the College of Natural Resources and Life Sciences in Vienna and at the University of Halle, and biology at the University of Vienna. In 1896 he received his doctorate in Halle. After finishing his habilitation in 1900 he was conferred the title of associate professor at the College of Natural Resources and Life Sciences in Vienna in the year 1903. In 1906 he was appointed associate professor. At the same time, he took over the directorship of the newly founded Department of Plant Breeding. He was appointed full professor of plant breeding in 1909 and in the following years he established numerous research laboratories in Moravia, Bohemia (Czech Republic), Western Hungary, and Lower Austria. He worked as a full professor at the College of Natural Resources and Life Sciences until his retirement in 1941. The Academy elected him as a corresponding member (c.m.i.) in 1926 and as a full member (f.m.) in 1930.

Hans **Voltelini** (31 July 1862–25 June 1938)
Hans Voltelini was from Innsbruck. He studied history at the Universities of Innsbruck and Vienna and completed the training course at the Institute for Austrian Historical Research. He received a Ph.D. in history in 1887, whereupon he studied law at the University of Vienna, receiving a doctorate in 1892 and completing his habilitation in 1899. In 1900 he was appointed associate professor at the University of Innsbruck and, in 1902, full professor. In 1908 he returned to the University of Vienna as a full professor of German law and Austrian imperial history, remaining in this position until his retirement in 1934. Voltelini was a corresponding member (c.m.i.) of the Academy from 1903 and a full member (f.m.) from 1909.

Adam **Wandruszka** (6 August 1914–9 July 1997)
Adam Wandruszka was born in Lemberg (Lwiw)/Galicia (Ukraine); he studied history, art history, and German language and literature at the University of Vienna and completed the training course at the Institute for Austrian Historical Research. He received his doctorate in 1936. In World War II he served in the *Wehrmacht* [armed forces] and was held as a prisoner of war by the U.S. forces. In 1945 he was subject to registration as a member of the Nazi Party. From 1949 to 1958 he worked as a journalist at the Austrian daily *Die Presse*. He completed his habilitation in 1955 at the University of Vienna. In 1959 he accepted an appointment as full professor of medieval and modern history at the University of Cologne. In 1963/64 he served as dean. From 1969 to 1984 he was a full professor of Austrian history at the University of Vienna. Wandruszka was a corresponding member (c.m.i.) of the Academy from 1969 and a full member (f.m.) from 1970.

Friedrich **Weber** (22 May 1886–28 October 1960)

Friedrich Weber was born in Salzburg; he studied natural sciences at the University of Vienna, majoring in botany. He completed his habilitation in 1918 at the University of Graz, where he became an associate professor in 1929. In 1936 he was appointed full professor of plant anatomy and physiology in Graz; he remained in this post until his retirement in 1957. The Academy elected him as a corresponding member (c.m.i.) in 1935 and as a full member (f.m.) in 1955.

Hermann **Weber** (27 November 1899–18 November 1956)

Hermann Weber was from Bretten/Baden (Germany); he studied natural sciences and physics at Stuttgart College of Technology and at the University of Tübingen. He received his doctorate in 1922 and became a lecturer at the University of Bonn in 1928. From 1930 to 1935 he was an associate professor at Danzig (Gdansk) College of Technology. In 1935/36 he stood in for the chair of Forest Zoology in Freiburg im Breisgau. From 1936 to 1939 he worked as a full professor of zoology and comparative anatomy at the University of Münster. He then worked from 1940 to 1941 as a professor at the University of Vienna and, from 1941 to 1944, as a full professor of zoology at the Reich University of Straßburg (Strasbourg). In 1945 he was retired from the University of Vienna and banned from teaching. From 1951 to 1956 Weber was a full professor and head of the Department of Zoology at the University of Tübingen. He was elected as an ordinary member (o.m.) of the Academy in 1940; in 1945 his membership was re-designated as corresponding member abroad (c.m.a.).

Albert **Weiser** (17 May 1909 – April 1995)

Albert Weiser was born in Vienna. After elementary school, he completed three years at the Technical School for Precision Engineering, completing his trade exams as a technician in 1929. From 1932 to 1934 he attended further training courses at the Technical College for Electrical and Mechanical Engineering in Vienna. In 1935, as successor to his father Albert Weiser and on a temporary contract, he became an official staff member at the Institute for Experimental Biology (BVA), where he had worked since 1932. Weiser continued to work there from 1935 to 1946 as a laboratory technician; he was released from his post by the Academy in 1945. He then worked as a state employee at the Chemical Laboratory II of the University of Vienna as a laboratory technician.

Ferdinand **Weiss** (15 January 1905 – January 1996)

Ferdinand Weiss was from Mödling/Lower Austria. After attending a trade school, he became an apprentice as a shoemaker, receiving a journeyman's certificate in 1922. Between 1922 and 1939 he worked, with interruptions, as a horsehair sorter in various Viennese firms. In 1939 Weiss was employed by the Academy as an errand boy and attendant. In 1942 Weiss gained civil servant status. Held as a prisoner of war by the U.S. forces, after returning in May 1945 he again took up his post in the publication archive. In 1960 Weiss was named head supervisor. He retired in 1969. In the same year he was honored with the Silver Medal for Services to the Republic of Austria.

Leopold **Wenger** (4 September 1874–21 September 1953)

Leopold Wenger was born in Obervellach/Carinthia; he studied law at the Universities of Graz and Leipzig. He received his doctorate in 1897 at the University of Graz and completed his habilitation in 1901. In 1902 he became an associate professor. From 1904 he taught at the Universities of Vienna (1904), Graz (1905–8), Heidelberg (1908/09), and Munich (1909–34). In Munich he founded the Department of Papyrology and Ancient Law History. He also served there in 1924/25 as rector. In between, in 1926/27, he also held a full professorship in

Vienna. In 1935 he accepted an appointment as full professor of Roman law and ancient law history at the University of Vienna. He retired in 1938. Wenger was a corresponding member (c.m.i.) of the Academy from 1926 and a full member (f.m.) from 1935.

Josef **Weninger** (15 May 1886–28 March 1959)
Josef Weninger was born in Salzburg; he initially studied civil engineering at the Vienna College of Technology before studying archeology, folklore and ethnology, anthropology, and geography at the University of Vienna. From 1918 to 1927 he worked at the State Historic Monuments Office as a monument conservationist and secretary. In 1926 he completed his habilitation at the University of Vienna, becoming associate professor and head of the Vienna Anthropological Institute in 1927. From 1934 to 1938 he headed the Institute as full professor. Weninger was relived of his professorship after the "Anschluss" because his wife was Jewish. Thanks to the influential dean and SS-member Viktor Christian, who had helped Weninger to advance, he was given a job at the Academy during the Nazi era, where he analyzed anthropological samples collected from prisoner-of-war camps by his teacher Rudolf Pöch. In 1945 Weninger was returned to his post, from which he retired in 1955. Weninger was a corresponding member (c.m.i.) of the Academy from 1937. He was excluded from the Academy on 3 May 1939. In 1945 he was elected a full member (f.m.).

Otto **Wettstein-Westersheimb** (7 August 1892–10 July 1967)
Otto Wettstein-Westersheimb was born in Vienna, where he studied zoology at the University. He received his doctorate in 1915, working from the same year at the Imperial and Royal (k.k.) Court Museum of Natural History, and from 1918 to 1945 as curator of the reptile department at the Museum of Natural History. In 1945 he was subject to registration as an illegal Nazi and, in the same year, was pensioned off. He continued to teach and carry out research as an independent scholar. In 1954 he was conferred the title associate professor. He was elected a corresponding member (c.m.i.) of the Academy in 1940. In 1945 his membership was held in abeyance. The Amnesty Law of April 1948 permitted his membership to be reinstated; his name appears again in the 1948 registry of members.

Friedrich **Wild** (11 November 1888–5 April 1966)
Friedrich Wild was from Vienna, where he studied German, English, and Romance languages and literature. He received his doctorate in 1913. After completing his teaching certificate in 1912, he worked as a high school teacher. He completed his habilitation in 1918 at the University of Vienna, was conferred the title of associate professor in 1927 and full professor in 1931. In 1935 he became a full professor of English philology at the University of Vienna. In 1945 he was subject to registration as a member of the Nazi Party; in the same year he was dismissed from the University of Vienna and, in 1948, permanently pensioned off. From 1949 Wild took on teaching assignments and in 1955 returned as a full professor of English and American language and literature at the University of Vienna. He retired in 1960. The Academy elected him as a corresponding member (c.m.i.) in 1937 and as an ordinary member (o.m.) in 1938. In 1945 his membership was held in abeyance. The Amnesty Law of April 1948 permitted his membership to be reinstated; his name appears again in the 1948 registry of members.

Richard **Willstätter** (13 August 1872–3 August 1942)
Richard Willstätter was born in Karlsruhe; he studied natural sciences at the University of Munich. He received his doctorate in 1894, completed his habilitation in 1896, and became an associate professor and chairman of the Department of Organic Chemistry at the Institute of Chemistry at the University of Munich in 1902. In 1905 he accepted an appointment as full

professor of general chemistry at Zurich Institute of Technology. From 1912 to 1916 he headed the Kaiser Wilhelm Institute for Chemistry in Berlin-Dahlem, after which he was appointed professor of chemistry at the University of Munich in 1916. In 1915 he was awarded the Nobel Prize in Chemistry. In 1924 he resigned from his position as professor in protest at the growing anti-Semitism, whereupon he worked as an industrial chemist. From 1933 Willstätter was persecuted on "racial" grounds. In 1939 he emigrated to Switzerland, where he worked as an industrial chemist. He was elected a corresponding member abroad (c.m.a.) of the Academy in 1920. He was excluded from the Academy on 28 January 1939.

Moriz **Wlassak** (20 August 1854–24 April 1939)
Moriz Wlassak was from Brünn (Brno)/Moravia (Czech Republic); he studied law at the University of Vienna. He received his doctorate in 1877 and, following his habilitation (1879), taught at the Universities of Czernowitz (1879), Graz (1882), Breslau (Wrocław) (1884), and Straßburg (Strasbourg) (1895). He held the post of professor of Roman law at the University of Vienna from 1900 to 1926. The Academy elected Wlassak as a corresponding member (c.m.i.) in 1909 and as a full member (f.m.) in 1914.

Karl **Wolf** (13 November 1886–10 January 1950)
Karl Wolf was born in Bielitz (Bielsko)/Austrian Silesia (Czech Republic); he studied to be a teacher of physics and mathematics at the University of Vienna. In 1909 he received a teaching certificate and in 1910 finished his Ph.D. In 1911 he became an assistant at the Department for Pure Mechanics at the Vienna College of Technology. In 1915 he completed his habilitation. In 1922 he became an associate professor and was appointed head of the Department of Mechanics and Graphic Statics at the Vienna College of Technology. In 1924 he was appointed full professor of mechanics. He was dismissed from his position at the Institute in 1938 on political grounds. In 1945 his professorship was reinstated and he stayed in this position until his death. In 1948 he became President of the Urania Adult Education Center in Vienna. In 1945 he was dean at the Vienna College of Technology and, in 1946/47, its rector. Wolf was a corresponding member (c.m.i.) of the Academy from 1946.

Richard **Wolfram** (16 September 1901–30 May 1995)
Richard Wolfram was born in Vienna, where he studied German and Scandinavian language and literature, art history, and English. He received his doctorate in 1926. Finishing his habilitation in 1936, in 1939 he was appointed associate professor and first chair for Germanic-German Folklore at the University of Vienna. From 1938 to 1945 Wolfram was head of the *Lehr- und Forschungsstätte for germanisch-deutsche Volkskunde* [Teaching and Research Institute for Germanic-German Folklore] at the *Außenstelle Süd-Ost* [South-East Branch] of the SS *"Ahnenerbe"* [Ancestral Heritage] research organization in Vienna and Salzburg. He was also a member of a commission that recorded the cultural heritage of the South Tyrolean German-speaking population before their resettlement. In 1945 he was subject to registration as a member of the Nazi Party; in the same year he was dismissed from his post at the University of Vienna and banned from teaching. The Institute was dissolved. In 1954 his teaching credentials were reinstated. In 1959 Wolfram again became an associate professor and in 1963 was appointed full professor of Austrian and comparative European Folklore. He founded the Department of Folklore at the University of Vienna and served as its head from 1961. Wolfram retired in 1972. The Academy elected him a corresponding member (c.m.i.) in 1968 and as a full member (f.m.) in 1971.

Konrad **Zwierzina** (29 March 1864–20 March 1941)
Konrad Zwierzina was born in Vienna, where he studied German language and literature, classical philology, and philosophy. He received his doctorate in 1886 and completed his habilitation in 1897, whereupon he became a lecturer at the University of Graz. In 1899 he took over a position as full professor of German philology at the University of Fribourg in Switzerland. In 1906 he moved to the University of Innsbruck, and finally returned to the University of Graz in 1912, where he worked until his retirement in 1934. In 1930/31 he was rector of the University of Graz. Zwierzina was elected a corresponding member (c.m.i.) of the Academy in 1917 and as a full member (f.m.) in 1925.

Silke Fengler
(together with Maximilian Kral and the Editors)

IV. APPENDIX

Abbreviations

AdR	Archiv der Republik / Archive of the Republic (Dept. of ÖStA)
AÖAW	Archiv der Österreichischen Akademie der Wissenschaften, Wien / Austrian Academy of Sciences Archives, Vienna
BAB	Bundesarchiv Berlin-Lichterfelde / Federal Archives, Berlin-Lichterfelde
BDC	Berlin Document Center
BGBl.	Bundesgesetzblatt / Federal Law Gazette
BVA	Biologische Versuchsanstalt (der Akademie der Wissenschaften in Wien) / Institute for Experimental Biology (of the Academy of Sciences in Vienna)
c.m.i.	corresponding member in Austria
c.m.a.	corresponding member abroad
DFG	Deutsche Forschungsgemeinschaft / German Research Foundation
f.m.	full member
IAA	Internationale Assoziation der Akademien / International Association of Academies
IFÖG	Institut für Österreichische Geschichtsforschung / Institute for Austrian Historical Research
K	Kronen / Austro-Hungarian krone
k.k.	kaiserlich-königlich / Imperial and Royal (referring to authorities and state institutions of the western/Cisleithanian part of the Austro-Hungarian monarchy)
NSDAP	Nationalsozialistische Deutsche Arbeiter-Partei / National Socialist German Workers' Party (Nazi Party)
NSKK	Nationalsozialistisches Kraftfahrerkorps / National Socialist Motor Corps
NSFK	Nationalsozialistisches Fliegerkorps / National Socialist Flyers Corps
o.m.	ordinary member
ÖAW	Österreichische Akademie der Wissenschaften / Austrian Academy of Sciences
ÖBL	Österreichisches Biographisches Lexikon / Austrian Biographical Dictionary
ÖNB	Österreichische Nationalbibliothek / Austrian National Library
ÖStA	Österreichisches Staatsarchiv / Austrian State Archives
ÖS	Österreichischer Schilling / Austrian schilling
PA	Personalakte / personnel file
Pg.	Parteigenosse / member of the NSDAP
RM	Reichsmark / Reich's mark
RGBl.	Reichsgesetzblatt / Reich Law Gazette
SODFG	Südostdeutsche Forschungsgemeinschaft / Southeast German Research Council
SA	Sturmabteilung / Storm Detachment (original paramilitary wing of the Nazi Party)
SS	Schutzstaffel / Protection Squadron (paramilitary organization of the Nazi Party)
SVD	Societas Verbi Divini / Society of the Divine Word (Divine Word Missionaries)
UAI	Union Académique Internationale / International Union of Academies
UAW	Archiv der Universität Wien / Vienna University Archive

Bibliography

Almanach, Akademie der Wissenschaften in Wien [since 1947: Österreichische Akademie der Wissenschaften] for 1918–[2011], vols. 68–[161], (Vienna, et al., 1918–[2012]).

Mitchell G. Ash, "Wissenschaft und Politik als Ressourcen für einander," in Rüdiger vom Bruch, Brigitte Kaderas (eds.), *Wissenschaften und Wissenschaftspolitik. Bestandsaufnahmen zu Formationen, Brüchen und Kontinuitäten im Deutschland des 20. Jahrhunderts* (Stuttgart, 2002), pp. 32–51.

Mitchell G. Ash, "Wissenschaftswandlungen in politischen Umbruchszeiten. 1933, 1945 und 1990 im Vergleich," in *Vorträge und Abhandlungen zur Wissenschaftsgeschichte 2000/2001* (2004) (= Acta historica Leopoldina 39), pp. 75–95.

Mitchell G. Ash, "Wissenschaftswandlungen und politische Umbrüche im 20. Jahrhundert. Was hatten sie miteinander zu tun?" in Rüdiger vom Bruch, Uta Gerhardt, Aleksandra Pawliczek (eds.), *Kontinuitäten und Diskontinuitäten in der Wissenschaftsgeschichte des 20. Jahrhunderts* (Stuttgart, 2006), pp. 19–37.

Mitchell G. Ash, "Wissenschaft und Politik. Eine Beziehungsgeschichte im 20. Jahrhundert," in *Archiv für Sozialgeschichte*, vol. 50 (2010), pp. 11–46.

Wilhelm Bauer, "Heinrich Srbik," in *Almanach f.d.J. 1951*, vol. 101 (1951), pp. 327–71.

Mathias Beer, Gerhard Seewann (eds.), *Südostforschung im Schatten des Dritten Reiches. Institutionen, Inhalte, Personen* (Munich, 2004) (= Südosteuropäische Arbeiten 119).

Bereichsstudentenführung Süd-Ost (ed.), *Jahrbuch der Deutschen Studentenschaft an den Ostmarkdeutschen Hochschulen* (University of Vienna, 1938).

Margit Berner, "'Die haben uns behandelt wie Gegenstände.' Anthropologische Untersuchungen an jüdischen Häftlingen im Wiener Stadion während des Nationalsozialismus," in Margit Berner, Anette Hoffmann, Britta Lange (eds.), *Sensible Sammlungen. Aus dem anthropologischen Depot* (Hamburg, 2011), pp. 147–67.

Laetitia Boehm, "Langzeitvorhaben als Akademieaufgabe. Geschichtswissenschaft in Berlin und in München," in Wolfram Fischer (ed.), *Die Preußische Akademie der Wissenschaften zu Berlin 1914–1945* (Berlin, 2000) (= Forschungsberichte interdisziplinärer Arbeitsgruppen. Berlin-Brandenburgische Akademie der Wissenschaften 8), pp. 391–434.

Klaus E. Bohnenkamp, "Hofmannsthals Egeria. Elsa Prinzessin Cantacuzène, später verheiratete Bruckmann, im Briefwechsel mit dem Dichter vom 24. November 1893 bis zum 10. Januar 1894 in Wien," in Hofmannsthal, *Jahrbuch zur europäischen Moderne*, vol. 18 (2010), pp. 9–104.

Gerhard Botz, *Nationalsozialismus in Wien. Machtübernahme, Herrschaftssicherung, Radikalisierung 1938/39*, revised and enlarged edition (Vienna, 2008).

Thomas Buchner, "Alfons Dopsch (1868–1953). Die 'Mannigfaltigkeit der Verhältnisse,'" in Karel Hruza (ed.), *Österreichische Historiker 1900–1945*, vol. 1 (Vienna, 2008), pp. 191–223.

Evan Burr Bukey, *Hitler's Austria. Popular Sentiment in the Nazi Era, 1938–1945* (Chapel Hill, London, 2000).

Deborah R. Coen, "Living Precisely in Fin-de-Siècle Wien," in *Journal of the History of Biology* vol. 39 (2006), pp. 493–523.

Ute Deichmann, *Biologen unter Hitler. Porträt einer Wissenschaft im NS-Staat* (Frankfurt/Main, 1995).

Paulus Ebner, *Politik und Hochschule. Die Hochschule für Bodenkultur 1914–1955* (Vienna, 2002).

Rudolf Ebneth, *Die österreichische Wochenschrift "Der Christliche Ständestaat"* (Mainz, 1976) (= Veröffentlichungen der Kommission für Zeitgeschichte. Reihe B: Forschungen 19).

Friedrich Ehrendorfer, "Fritz Knoll," in *Almanach f.d.J. 1982*, vol. 132 (1983), pp. 289–92.

Friedrich Ehrendorfer, "Fritz Knoll 1883–1981," in *Berichte der Deutschen Botanischen Gesellschaft*, vol. 97 (1984), pp. 497–503.

Richard J. Evans, *Das Dritte Reich*, vol. 3, *Krieg* (Munich, 2010).

Michael Fahlbusch, "Die Südostdeutsche Forschungsgemeinschaft. Politische Beratung und NS-Volkstumspolitik," in Winfried Schulze, Otto Gerhard Oexle (eds.), *Deutsche Historiker im Nationalsozialismus* (Frankfurt/Main, 2000), pp. 241–64.

Johannes Feichtinger, "Transatlantische Vernetzungen. Der Weg Hans Kelsens und seines Kreises in die Emigration," in Werner Ogris, Thomas Olechowski, Robert Walter (eds.), *Hans Kelsen. Leben – Werk – Wirksamkeit* (Vienna, 2009) (= Schriftenreihe des Hans Kelsen-Instituts 32), pp. 315–32.

Johannes Feichtinger, Heidemarie Uhl, "Die Österreichische Akademie der Wissenschaften nach 1945. Eine Gelehrtengesellschaft im Spannungsfeld von Wissenschaft, Politik und Gesellschaft," in Margarete Grandner, Gernot Heiss, Oliver Rathkolb (eds.), *Zukunft mit Altlasten. Die Universität Wien 1945 bis 1955* (Innsbruck, Vienna, 2005), pp. 313–37.

Silke Fengler, "'Wüstentrockenheit auf dem Gebiet der Atomzertrümmerung.' Zur politischen Ökonomie der österreichischen Kernforschung in der Zwischenkriegszeit," in Silke Fengler, Carola Sachse (eds.), *Kernforschung in Österreich. Wandlungen eines interdisziplinären Forschungsfeldes. 1900–1978* (Vienna, 2012) (= Wissenschaft, Macht und Kultur in der modernen Geschichte 1), pp. 73–108.

Charles Fenwick, "Editorial Comment: Fuit Austria," in *American Journal of International Law*, vol. 32 (1938), pp. 312–4.

Festgabe der Österreichischen Akademie der Wissenschaften zur Feier des 100. Geburtstages von Oswald Redlich: Akademie-Festreden des Präsidenten Oswald Redlich 1916–1937 mit dem Festvortrag von Leo Santifaller (Vienna, 1958).

Christian Fleck, "Arisierung der Gebildeten. Vergleich zweier aus Österreich emigrierter Wissenschaftlergruppen im Kontext," in Friedrich Stadler (ed.), *Österreichs Umgang mit dem Nationalsozialismus* (Vienna, 2004), pp. 229–54.

Christian Fleck, "Autochthone Provinzialisierung der Wissenschaft," at http://science.orf.at/science/news/134822 (accessed on 1 November 2012).

Christian Fleck, "Autochthone Provinzialisierung," in *Österreichische Zeitschrift für Geschichtswissenschaft*, vol. 7 (1996), pp. 67–92.

Norbert Frei, "Führerbilderwechsel. Hitler und die Deutschen nach 1945," in Hans-Ulrich Thamer, Simone Erpel (eds.), *Hitler und die Deutschen. Volksgemeinschaft und Verbrechen. Eine Ausstellung der Stiftung Deutsches Historisches Museum, Berlin, 15. Oktober 2010 bis 6. Februar 2011* (Dresden, 2010), pp. 142–7.

Norbert Frei (ed.), *Martin Broszat, der "Staat Hitlers" und die Historisierung des Nationalsozialismus* (Göttingen, 2007).

Ute Frevert, "Auch Gefühle haben ihre Geschichte," in *Neue Zürcher Zeitung*, 26/27 July 2008, p. 31.

Richard Germann, *Die "Österreicher" in Ost- und Südosteuropa im Zweiten Weltkrieg* (Vienna, unpublished dissertation, 2006).

Eberhard Geyer, "Anthropologie und Nationalitätenforschung," in *Nation und Staat*, vol. 7 (1934), pp. 323–6.

Sander Gliboff, "The Case of Paul Kammerer: Evolution and Experimentation in the Early 20th Century," in *Journal of the History of Biology*, vol. 39 (2006), pp. 525–63.

Peter Goller, Gerhard Oberkofler, *Universität Innsbruck. Entnazifizierung und Rehabilitation von Nazikadern (1945–1950)* (Innsbruck, 2003).

Franz Graf-Stuhlhofer, "Die Akademie der Wissenschaften in Wien im Dritten Reich," in Eduard Seidler (ed.), *Die Elite der Nation im Deutschen Reich. Das Verhältnis von Akademien und ihrem wissenschaftlichen Umfeld zum Nationalsozialismus* (Leipzig, 1995) (= Acta historica Leopoldina 22), pp. 133–59.

Franz Graf-Stuhlhofer, "'Heil Hitler!' am Schluß von Briefen. Beobachtungen am Schriftverkehr der Wiener Akademie der Wissenschaften," in *Österreich in Geschichte und Literatur*, vol. 40 (1996), pp. 125–8.

Franz Graf-Stuhlhofer, "Opportunisten, Sympathisanten und Beamte. Unterstützung des NS-Systems in der Wiener Akademie der Wissenschaften, dargestellt am Wirken Nadlers, Srbiks und Meisters," in *Wiener Klinische Wochenschrift*, vol. 110, no. 4–5 (1998), pp. 152–7.

Conrad Grau, "Die Wissenschaftsakademien in der deutschen Gesellschaft: Das 'Kartell' von 1893 bis 1940," in Eduard Seidler (ed.). *Die Elite der Nation im Deutschen Reich. Das Verhältnis von Akademien und ihrem wissenschaftlichen Umfeld zum Nationalsozialismus* (Leipzig, 1995) (= Acta historica Leopoldina 22), pp. 31–53.

Thomas R. Grischany, *The Austrians in the German Wehrmacht, 1938–1945* (Chicago, 2007).

Hermann Hakel, *Dürre Äste – Welkes Gras. Begegnungen mit Literaten. Bemerkungen zur Literatur* (Vienna, 1991).

Hermann Hakel, *Von denen ich weiß. Wahrnehmungen eines Literaten* (Vienna, 2011).

Günther Hamann, "Kriegs- und Nachkriegserinnerungen eines Studenten an Heinrich Ritter von Srbik," in *Anzeiger der phil.-hist. Kl. der ÖAW*, vol. 115 (1978), pp. 366–95.

Ernst Hanisch, *Der lange Schatten des Staates. Österreichische Gesellschaftsgeschichte im 20. Jahrhundert* (Vienna, 1994) (= Herwig Wolfram (ed.), *Österreichische Geschichte 1890–1990*).

Hugo Hassinger, *Wiens deutsche Sendung im Donauraum. Wien 1942* (= Mitteilungen der Geographischen Gesellschaft Wien in der Deutschen Geographischen Gesellschaft 85.1–2).

Hugo Hassinger, "Lebensraumfragen der Völker des europäischen Südostens," in K. H. Dietzel, O. Schmieder, H. Schmitthenner (eds.), *Lebensraumfragen Europäischer Völker*, vol. 1: *Europa* (Leipzig, 1941), pp. 588–613.

Gernot Heiss, "Wendepunkt und Wiederaufbau. Die Arbeit des Senats der Universität Wien in den Jahren nach der Befreiung," in Margarete Grandner, Gernot Heiss, Oliver Rathkolb (eds.), *Zukunft mit Altlasten. Die Universität Wien 1945 bis 1955* (Innsbruck, Munich, 2005), pp. 9–37.

Raul Hilberg, *Die Vernichtung der europäischen Juden*, vol. 3, revised and enlarged edition (Frankfurt/Main, 1990).

Albrecht Hirschmüller, "Paul Kammerer und die Vererbung erworbener Eigenschaften," in *Medizinhistorisches Journal*, vol. 26 (1991), pp. 26–77.

Lothar Höbelt, *Von der vierten Partei zur dritten Kraft. Die Geschichte des VdU* (Graz, 1999).

Veronika Hofer, "Rudolf Goldscheid, Paul Kammerer und die Biologen des Prater-Vivariums in der liberalen Volksbildung der Wiener Moderne," in Mitchell G. Ash, Christian H. Stifter (eds.), *Wissenschaft, Politik und Öffentlichkeit. Von der Wiener Moderne bis zur Gegenwart* (Vienna, 2002), pp. 149–84.

Hans Hübner, *Geschichte im Drama. Matthäus von Collin. Der Babenbergerzyklus (1808–1817). Hanns Sassmann. Die österreichsche Trilogie (1929–1932)* (Vienna, unpublished dissertation, 1991).

Johan Huizinga, *Briefwisseling*, vol. 3: *1934–1945*, edited by Léon Hanssen, W. E. Krul, Anton van der Lem (Utrecht, Antwerp, 1991).

Ludwig Jedlicka (ed.), *Das Juliabkommen von 1936. Vorgeschichte, Hintergründe und Folgen. Protokoll des Symposiums in Wien am 10. und 11. Juni 1976* (Vienna, 1977) (= Wissenschaftliche Kommission zur Erforschung der Österreichischen Geschichte der Jahre 1918 bis 1938: Veröffentlichungen/ Wissenschaftliche Kommission des Theodor-Körner-Stiftungsfonds und des Leopold-Kunschak-Preises zur Erforschung der Österreichischen Geschichte 1927 bis 1938, no. 4).

William M. Johnston, *Österreichische Kultur- und Geistesgeschichte. Gesellschaft und Ideen im Donauraum 1848 bis 1938*, 4th edition (Vienna, Cologne, Weimar, 2006).

Jürgen Kämmerer (ed.), *Heinrich Ritter von Srbik. Die wissenschaftliche Korrespondenz des Historikers 1912–1945* (Boppard am Rhein, 1988) (= Deutsche Geschichtsquellen des 19. und 20. Jahrhunderts 55).

Ian Kershaw, *Das Ende. Kampf bis in den Untergang. NS-Deutschland 1944/45*, 3rd edition (Munich, 2011).

Ian Kershaw, *Hitler: 1889–1936* (Stuttgart, 1998).

Ian Kershaw, *Hitler 1936–1945* (Stuttgart, 2000).

Wolfgang Knierzinger, "Das Forschungsinstitut Gastein in der Forschungslandschaft des 'Ständestaats' und des 'Dritten Reiches'," in Silke Fengler, Carola Sachse (eds.), *Kernforschung in Österreich. Wandlungen eines interdisziplinären Forschungsfeldes. 1900–1978* (Vienna, 2012) (= Wissenschaft, Macht und Kultur in der modernen Geschichte 1), pp. 109–29.

Fritz Knoll, *Die Wissenschaft im Neuen Deutschland. Vortrag, gehalten im Rahmen der Vorträge des Deutschen Wissenschaftlichen Instituts in Bukarest am 23. Mai 1941* (Vienna, 1942) (= Wiener wissenschaftliche Vorträge und Reden 1).

Arthur Koestler, *Der Krötenküsser. Der Fall des Biologen Paul Kammerer*, translated from English by Krista Schmidt (Vienna, 2010) (= Bibliothek der Erinnerung 12).

Hedwig Kopetz, *Die Österreichische Akademie der Wissenschaften. Aufgaben, Rechtsstellung, Organisation* (Wien, Graz, 2006).

Christian Krumm, Johan Huizinga, *Deutschland und die Deutschen. Begegnung und Auseinandersetzung mit dem Nachbarn* (Münster, New York, Munich, Berlin, 2011) (= Studien zur Geschichte und Kultur Nordwesteuropas 23).

Birthe Kundrus, "Der Holocaust. Die 'Volksgemeinschaft' als Verbrechensgemeinschaft?" in Hans-Ulrich Thamer, Simone Erpel (eds.), *Hitler und die Deutschen. Volksgemeinschaft und Verbrechen. Eine Ausstellung der Stiftung Deutsches Historisches Museum, Berlin, 15. Oktober 2010 bis 6. Februar 2011* (Dresden, 2010), pp. 130–5.

Britta Lange, *Die Wiener Forschungen an Kriegsgefangenen 1915–1918. Anthropologische und ethnografische Verfahren im Lager* (Vienna, 2013) (= ÖAW. Sitzungsberichte der phil.-hist. Kl. 838 = Veröffentlichungen zur Sozialanthropologie 17).

Irene Maria Leitner, "'Bis an die Grenzen des Möglichen': Der Dekan Viktor Christian und seine Handlungsspielräume an der Philosophischen Fakultät 1938–1943," in Mitchell G. Ash, Wolfram Nieß, Ramon Pils (eds.), *Geisteswissenschaften im Nationalsozialismus. Das Beispiel der Universität Wien* (Göttingen, Vienna, 2010), pp. 49–77.

Anton van der Lem, *Johan Huizinga, Leven en werk in beelden & documenten* (Amsterdam, 1993).

Alphons Lhotsky, *Ostarrîchi. Vortrag in der Festsitzung der Österreichischen Akademie der Wissenschaften am 21. Oktober 1946* (Vienna, 1947).

Brigitte Lichtenberger-Fenz, "Österreichs Hochschulen und Universitäten und das NS-Regime," in Emmerich Tálos, Ernst Hainisch, Wolfgang Neugebauer (eds.), *NS-Herrschaft in Österreich 1938–1945* (Vienna, 1988), pp. 269–82.

Brigitte Lichtenberger-Fenz, "'Es läuft alles in geordneten Bahnen.' Österreichs Hochschulen und Universitäten und das NS-Regime," in Emmerich Tálos (ed.), N*S-Herrschaft in Österreich. Ein Handbuch* (Vienna, 2000), pp. 549–69.

Friedrich Lorenz, *Sieg der Verfemten. Forscherschicksale im Schatten des Riesenrades*, novel (Vienna, 1952).

Walter Manoschek, Roman Pfefferle, Hans Pfefferle, *Glimpflich entnazifiziert. Die Professorenschaft des Sommersemesters 1944 der Universität Wien in den Nachkriegsjahren*, unpublished final report of the research project "Entnazifizierung an der Universität Wien nach 1945. Kontinuitäten und Diskontinuitäten universitärer Wissenschaftseliten" (Vienna, 2012) [print pending].

Peter Markl, "Keimzelle der modernen Biologie," in *Wiener Zeitung*, 11 October 2002.

Albert Massiczek, "Die Situation an der Universität Wien März/April 1938," in Albert Massiczek (ed.), *Wien 1938* (Vienna, 1978) (= Forschungen und Beiträge zur Wiener Stadtgeschichte 2), pp. 216–29.

Herbert Matis, "Die Akademie der Wissenschaften 1938 bis 1945," in Otto Hittmair, Herbert Hunger (ed.), *Akademie der Wissenschaften. Entwicklung einer österreichischen Forschungsinstitution* (Vienna, 1997), pp. 21–34.

Herbert Matis, *Zwischen Anpassung und Widerstand. Die Akademie der Wissenschaften 1938–1945* (Vienna, 1997).

Richard Meister, *Geschichte der Akademie der Wissenschaften in Wien 1847–1947* (Vienna, 1947) (= Österreichische Akademie der Wissenschaften. Denkschriften der Gesamtakademie 1).

Juliane Mikoletzky, *"Von jeher ein Hort starker nationaler Gesinnung". Die Technische Hochschule in Wien und der Nationalsozialismus* (Vienna, 2003) (= Veröffentlichungen des Universitätsarchivs der TU Wien 8).

Wolfgang J. Mommsen, "Wissenschaft, Krieg und die Berliner Akademie der Wissenschaften. Die Preußische Akademie der Wissenschaften in den beiden Weltkriegen," in Wolfram Fischer (ed.), *Die Preußische Akademie der Wissenschaften zu Berlin 1914–1945* (Berlin, 2000) (= Forschungsberichte interdisziplinärer Arbeitsgruppen. Berlin-Brandenburgische Akademie der Wissenschaften 8), pp. 3–23.

Kurt Mühlberger, *Vertriebene Intelligenz 1938. Der Verlust geistiger und menschlicher Potenz an der Universität Wien von 1938 bis 1945* (Vienna, 1993).

Albert Müller, "Dynamische Adaptierung und 'Selbstbehauptung.' Die Universität Wien in der NS-Zeit," in Dieter Langewiesche (ed.), *Universitäten im nationalsozialistisch beherrschten Europa* (Göttingen, 1997) (= Geschichte und Gesellschaft 23.4), pp. 592–617.

Anne Christine Nagel, *Hitlers Bildungsreformer. Das Reichsministerium für Wissenschaft, Erziehung und Volksbildung 1934–1945 (Frankfurt/Main, 2012).*

Wolfgang Neugebauer, "Das NS-Terrorsystem," in Emmerich Tálos, Ernst Hanisch, Wolfgang Neugebauer (eds.), *NS-Herrschaft in Österreich 1938–1945* (Vienna, 1988), pp. 163–83.

Peter Nötzoldt, "Strategien der deutschen Wissenschaftsakademien gegen Bedeutungsverlust und Funktionsverarmung," in Wolfram Fischer (ed.), *Die Preußische Akademie der Wissenschaften zu Berlin 1914–1945* (Berlin, 2000) (= Forschungsberichte interdisziplinärer Arbeitsgruppen. Berlin-Brandenburgische Akademie der Wissenschaften 8), pp. 237–77.

Michael Joseph Oakeshott, *Rationalism in Politics and Other Essays*, new and expanded edition (Indianapolis, 1991).

Gerhard Oberkofler, "Politische Stellungnahmen der Akademie der Wissenschaften in Wien in den Jahren der NS-Herrschaft," in Helmut Konrad, Wolfgang Neugebauer (eds.), *Arbeiterbewegung – Faschismus – Nationalbewusstsein. Festschrift zum 20-jährigen Bestand des Dokumentationsarchivs des österreichischen Widerstandes und zum 60. Geburtstag von Herbert Steiner* (Vienna, Munich, Zurich, 1983, pp. 115–26 [with notes on pp. 446–8].

Gerhard Oberkofler, *Franz Huter (1899–1997). Soldat und Historiker Tirols* (Innsbruck, Vienna, 1999).

Gerhard Oberkofler, "Der Mathematiker Paul Funk wird mit der 'Vergangenheitsbewältigung' der Österreichischen Akademie der Wissenschaften konfrontiert," in *Dokumentationsarchiv des Österreichischen Widerstandes. Jahrbuch 2005*, pp. 200–17.

Gerhard Oberkofler, *Nikolaus Grass. Einige wissenschaftshistorische Miniaturen aus Briefen und seine Korrespondenz mit dem Prager Juden Guido Kisch* (Innsbruck, Vienna, Bolzano, 2008).

Gerhard Oberkofler, *Ludwig Spiegel und Kleo Pleyer. Deutsche Misere in der Biografie zweier sudetendeutscher Intellektueller* (Innsbruck, Vienna, Bolzano, 2012).

Gerhard Oberkofler, "Bemerkungen zur Wahlpolitik der Österreichischen Akademie der Wissenschaften nach 1945," in *Mitteilungen der Alfred-Klahr-Gesellschaft*, vol. 19, no. 3 (2012), pp. 1–10.

Österreichische Akademie der Wissenschaften (ed.), *Österreichische Naturforscher und Techniker* (Vienna, 1951).

Österreichisches Biographisches Lexikon 1815–1950, vols. 1-[13] (Vienna, 1957–[2010]).

Verena Pawlowsky, "Erweiterung der Bestände. Die Anthropologische Abteilung des Naturhistorischen Museums 1938–1945," in *Zeitgeschichte*, vol. 32, no. 2 (2005), pp. 69–90.

Martina Pesditschek, "Heinrich (Ritter von) Srbik (1878–1951). 'Meine Liebe gehört bis zu meinem Tod meiner Familie, dem deutschen Volk, meiner österreichischen Heimat und meinen Schülern'," in Karel Hruza (ed.), *Österreichische Historiker. Lebensläufe und Karrieren 1900–1945*, vol. 2 (Vienna, 2012), pp. 263–328.

Martina Pesditschek, "Franz Miltner (1901–1959)," in Gunnar Brands, Martin Maischberger (eds.), *Lebensbilder. Klassische Archäologen und der Nationalsozialismus* (Rahden/Westfalen, 2012), pp. 177–91 (= Menschen – Kulturen – Traditionen. ForschungsCluster 5.2 no. 1).

Ramon Pils, "'Ein Gelehrter ist kein Politiker.' Die Professoren der Wiener Anglistik im Kontext des Nationalsozialismus," in Mitchell G. Ash, Wolfram Nieß, Ramon Pils (eds.), *Geisteswissenschaften im Nationalsozialismus. Das Beispiel der Universität Wien* (Göttingen, Vienna, 2010), pp. 455–95.

Sheldon Pollock, "Ex Oriente Nox. Indologie im nationalsozialistischen Staat," in Sebastian Conrad, Shalini Randeria (eds.), *Jenseits der Eurozentrismus. Postkoloniale Perspektiven in den Geschichts- und Kulturwissenschaften* (Frankfurt/Main, New York, 2002), pp. 335–71.

Karl Przibram, "Hans Przibram," in *Neue Österreichische Biographie*, vol. 13 (Vienna, 1959), pp. 184–91.

Irene Ranzmaier, "Germanistik. Kontinuitätsstiftende Ansätze der Wissenschaft und die Bedeutung kollegialer Unterstützung," in Mitchell G. Ash, Wolfram Nieß, Ramon Pils (eds.), *Geisteswissenschaften im Nationalsozialismus. Das Beispiel der Universität Wien* (Göttingen, Vienna, 2010), pp. 427–53.

Oliver Rathkolb, "Die Universität Wien und die 'Hohe Politik'," in Margarete Grandner, Gernot Heiss, Oliver Rathkolb (eds.), *Zukunft mit Altlasten. Die Universität Wien 1945 bis 1955* (Innsbruck, Vienna, 2005), pp. 38–53.

Walter Rauscher, *Karl Renner. Ein österreichischer Mythos* (Vienna, 1995).

Wolfgang Reiter, "Österreichische Wissenschaftsemigration am Beispiel des Instituts für Radiumforschung der Österreichischen Akademie der Wissenschaften," in Friedrich Stadler (ed.), *Vertriebene Vernunft. Emigration und Exil österreichischer Wissenschaft*, vol. 2, no. 2 (Vienna, Munich, 1988, Münster [2]2004), pp. 709–29.

Wolfgang L. Reiter, "Zerstört und vergessen. Die Biologische Versuchsanstalt und ihre Wissenschaftler/innen," in *Österreichische Zeitschrift für Geschichtswissenschaften*, vol. 10, no. 4 (1999), pp. 585–614.

Wolfgang L. Reiter, "Stefan Meyer und die Radioaktivitätsforschung in Österreich," in *Anzeiger der phil.-hist. Kl. der ÖAW*, vol. 135 (2000), pp. 105–43.

Wolfgang L. Reiter, "Naturwissenschaften und Remigration," in Sandra Wiesinger-Stock, Erika Weinzierl, Konstantin Kaiser (eds.), *Vom Weggehen. Zum Exil von Kunst und Wissenschaft* (Vienna, 2006), pp. 177–218.

Franz Römer, Sonja Martina Schreiner, "Dis-kontinuitäten. Die Klassische Philologie im Nationalsozialismus," in Mitchell G. Ash, Wolfram Nieß, Ramon Pils (eds.), *Geisteswissenschaften im Nationalsozialismus. Das Beispiel der Universität Wien* (Göttingen, Vienna, 2010), pp. 317–42.

Robert W. Rosner, Brigitte Strohmaier (eds.), *Marietta Blau. Sterne der Zertrümmerung. Biographie einer Wegbereiterin der modernen Teilchenphysik* (Vienna, Cologne, Weimar, 2003).

Dirk Rupnow, "Brüche und Kontinuitäten. Von der NS-Judenforschung zur Nachkriegsjudaistik," in Mitchell G. Ash, Wolfram Nieß, Ramon Pils (eds.), *Geisteswissenschaften im Nationalsozialismus. Das Beispiel der Universität Wien* (Göttingen, Vienna, 2010), pp. 79–110.

Walther Ruth, "Das Phonogrammarchiv der Akademie der Wissenschaften in Wien und seine Aufgaben," in *Anzeiger der phil.-hist. Kl. der Akademie der Wissenschaften in Wien*, vol. 78 (1941), pp. 87–98.

Leo Santifaller, "Vorwort," in Leo Santifaller (ed.), *Österreichisches Biographisches Lexikon 1815–1950*, vol. 1: *A – Glä* (Graz, Cologne, 1957), pp. VII–IX.

Norbert Schausberger, "Der Anschluß und seine ökonomische Relevanz," in *Anschluß 1938. Protokoll des Symposiums in Wien am 14. und 15. März 1978* (Vienna, 1981) (= Wissenschaftliche Kommission des Theodor-Körner-Stiftungsfonds und des Leopold-Kunschak-Preises zur Erforschung der österreichischen Geschichte der Jahre 1927 bis 1938. Veröffentlichungen 7), pp. 244–70.

Erwin A. Schmidl, *März 38. Der deutsche Einmarsch in Österreich* (Vienna, 1987).

Kurt von Schuschnigg, *Ein Requiem in Rot-Weiß-Rot. "Aufzeichnungen des Häftlings Dr. Auster"* (Zurich, 1946).

Eduard Seidler, "Die akademische Elite und der neue Staat," in Eduard Seidler (ed.), *Die Elite der Nation im Deutschen Reich. Das Verhältnis von Akademien und ihrem wissenschaftlichen Umfeld zum Nationalsozialismus* (Leipzig, 1995) (= Acta historica Leopoldina 22), pp. 15–28.

Maren Seliger, *Scheinparlamentarismus im Führerstaat. „Gemeindevertretung" im Austrofaschismus und Nationalsozialismus. Funktionen und politische Profile Wiener Räte und Ratsherren 1934–1945 im Vergleich* (Vienna, 2010) (= Politik und Zeitgeschichte 6).

Hannelore Sexl, Anne Hardy, *Lise Meitner* (Reinbek bei Hamburg, 2002).

R. Werner Soukup, "Arnold Durig 1872–1961," in R. Werner Soukup, *Die wissenschaftliche Welt von gestern. Die Preisträger des Ignaz L. Lieben-Preises 1865–1937 und des Richard Lieben-Preises 1912–1928. Ein Kapitel österreichischer Wissenschaftsgeschichte in Kurzbiografien* (Vienna, Cologne, Weimar, 2004) (= Beiträge zur Wissenschaftsgeschichte und Wissenschaftsforschung 4), pp. 128–32.

Alexander Spitzmüller, *"... und hat auch Ursach, es zu lieben"* (Vienna, Munich, Stuttgart, Zurich, 1955.

Renate Spreitzer, "Harold Steinacker (1875–1965). Ein Leben für 'Volk und Geschichte'," in Karel Hruza (ed.), *Österreichische Historiker 1900–1945*, vol. 1 (Vienna, 2008), pp. 191–223.

Heinrich von Srbik, "Die Wiener Revolution des Jahres 1848 in sozialgeschichtlicher Beleuchtung," in *Schmollers Jahrbuch für Gesetzgebung, Verwaltung und Volkswirtschaft im Deutschen Reiche*, vol. 43, no. 3 (1919), pp. 19–58.

Heinrich von Srbik, *Metternich. Der Staatsmann und der Mensch*, vols. 1–2 (Munich, 1925).

Heinrich von Srbik, *Metternich. Der Staatsmann und der Mensch*, vol. 3: *Quellenveröffentlichungen und Literatur. Eine Auswahlübersicht von 1925–1952* (Munich, 1954).

Heinrich von Srbik, *Deutsche Einheit. Idee und Wirklichkeit vom Heiligen Reich bis Königgrätz*, 4 vols. (Munich, 1935–42).

Heinrich von Srbik, *Mitteleuropa. Das Problem und die Versuche seiner Lösung in der deutschen Geschichte* (Weimar, 1937, ^{2}1938).

Friedrich Stadler, *Vertriebene Vernunft. Emigration und Exil österreichischer Wissenschaft 1930–1940*, 2 vols. (Vienna, Munich, 1987/1988, Münster ^{2}2004).

G[eorg] St[adtmüller], "Die Balkankommission der Akademie der Wissenschaften in Wien," in *Leipziger Vierteljahresschrift für Südosteuropa*, vol. 6 (1942), pp. 198–200.

Zara S. Steiner, *The Triumph of the Dark. European International History 1933–1939* (Oxford, 2011).

Steirische Gesellschaft für Kulturpolitik (ed.), *Grenzfeste deutscher Wissenschaft. Über Faschismus und Vergangenheitsbewältigung an der Universität Graz* (Vienna, 1985).

Heiko Stoff, *Ewige Jugend. Konzepte der Verjüngung vom späten 19. Jahrhundert bis ins Dritte Reich* (Cologne, Weimar, Vienna, 2004).

Christoph Strupp, *Johan Huizinga. Geschichtswissenschaft als Kulturgeschichte* (Göttingen, 2000).

Jakob Stuchlik, *Der arische Ansatz. Erich Frauwallner und der Nationalsozialismus* (Vienna, 2009) (= Sitzungsberichte der phil.-hist. Kl. der ÖAW 797).

Petra Svatek, "Hugo Hassinger und Südosteuropa. Raumwissenschaftliche Forschungen in Wien (1931–1945)," in Carola Sachse (ed.), *"Mitteleuropa" und "Südosteuropa" als Planungsraum. Wirtschafts- und Kulturpolitische Expertisen im Zeitalter der Weltkriege* (Göttingen, 2010), pp. 290–311.

Petra Svatek, "'Wien als Tor nach dem Südosten.' Der Beitrag Wiener Geisteswissenschaftler zur Erforschung Südosteuropas während des Nationalsozialismus," in Mitchell G. Ash, Wolfram Nieß, Ramon Pils (eds.), *Geisteswissenschaften im Nationalsozialismus. Das Beispiel der Universität Wien* (Göttingen, Vienna, 2010), pp. 111–39.

Emmerich Tálos, Ernst Hanisch, Wolfgang Neugebauer (eds.), *NS-Herrschaft in Österreich 1938–1945* (Vienna, 1988).

Klaus Taschwer, "Andenken an eine völlig vergessene Forscherin. Vor genau siebzig Jahren wurde die österreichische Biologin Leonore Brecher ermordet. Eine späte Würdigung der tragisch Gescheiterten," in *Der Standard*, 23 September 2012.

Klaus Taschwer, "Geheimsache Bärenhöhle. Wie eine antisemitische Professorenclique der Universität Wien nach 1918 wissenschaftliche Exzellenz vertrieb," in *Alma mater antisemitica. Akademisches Milieu, Juden und Antisemitismus an den Universitäten Europas zwischen 1918 und 1939. Veröffentlichung zur Tagung vom 15.–16. Juni 2012* (Vienna, [print pending]).

Maria Teschler-Nicola, Margit Berner, "Die anthropologische Abteilung des Naturhistorischen Museums in der NS-Zeit. Berichte und Dokumentation von Forschungs- und Sammlungsaktivitäten 1938–1945," in *Untersuchungen zur anatomischen Wissenschaft in Wien 1938–1945. Senatsprojekt der Universität Wien* (Vienna, ^{2}1998), pp. 333–58.

Hans-Ulrich Thamer, Simone Erpel (eds.), *Hitler und die Deutschen. Volksgemeinschaft und Verbrechen. Eine Ausstellung der Stiftung Deutsches Historisches Museum, Berlin, 15. Oktober 2010 bis 6. Februar 2011* (Dresden, 2010).

Hans-Ulrich Thamer, *Verführung und Gewalt. Deutschland 1933–1945* (Berlin, 1986) (= Siedler deutsche Geschichte. Die Deutschen und ihre Nation, vol. 5).

Walter Thomas, *Bis der Vorhang fiel. Nach Aufzeichnungen aus den Jahren 1940 bis 1945* (Dortmund, 1947).

Georg Traska, Christoph Lind, *Hermann Leopoldi, Hersch Kohn. Eine Biographie* (Vienna, 2012).

Heidemarie Uhl, "Vom 'ersten Opfer' zum Land der unbewältigten Vergangenheit: Österreich im Kontext der Transformationen des europäischen Gedächtnisses," in Volkhard Knigge, Hans-Joachim Veen, Ulrich Mählert, Franz-Josef Schlichting (eds.), *Arbeit am europäischen Gedächtnis. Diktaturerfahrungen und Demokratieentwicklung* (Cologne, Weimar, Vienna, 2011) (= Schriften der Stiftung Ettersberg 17), pp. 27–46.

Otto H. Urban, "Die Urgeschichte an der Universität Wien vor, während und nach der NS-Zeit," in Mitchell G. Ash, Wolfram Nieß, Ramon Pils (eds.), *Geisteswissenschaften im Nationalsozialismus. Das Beispiel der Universität Wien* (Göttingen, Vienna, 2010), pp. 371–94.

Marlene Wahlmüller, *Die Akademie der Wissenschaften in Wien. Kontinuitäten und Diskontinuitäten 1938–1945* (Vienna, unpublished master's thesis, 2010).

Sonja Walch, *Sexualhormone in der Laborpraxis: Eugen Steinachs Experimente und seine Kooperation mit Schering (1910–1938)* (Vienna, unpublished dissertation, 2011).

Peter Th. Walther, "'Arisierung,' Nazifizierung und Militarisierung. Die Akademie im 'Dritten Reich'," in Wolfram Fischer (ed.), *Die Preußische Akademie der Wissenschaften zu Berlin 1914–1945* (Berlin, 2000) (= Forschungsberichte interdisziplinärer Arbeitsgruppen. Berlin-Brandenburgische Akademie der Wissenschaften, vol. 8), pp. 87–118.

Adam Wandruszka, "Heinrich Ritter von Srbik. Leben und Werk," in *Anzeiger der phil.-hist. Kl. der ÖAW*, vol. 115 (1978), pp. 352–65.

Josef Wastl, "Anthropologische Untersuchungen an belgischen und französischen Kriegsgefangenen," in *Anzeiger der math.-nat. Klasse der Akademie der Wissenschaften in Wien*, vol. 78 (1941), pp. 103–6.

Hans-Ulrich Wehler, *Deutsche Gesellschaftsgeschichte*, vol. 4: *Vom Beginn des Ersten Weltkriegs bis zur Gründung der beiden deutschen Staaten 1914–1949*, 3rd edition (Munich, 2008).

Willi Weinert, "Die Maßnahmen der reichsdeutschen Hochschulverwaltung im Bereich des österreichischen Hochschulwesens nach der Annexion 1938," in Helmut Konrad, Wolfgang Neugebauer (eds.), *Arbeiterbewegung, Faschismus, Nationalbewusstsein* (Vienna, 1983), pp. 127–34.

Werner Welzig (ed.), with Hanno Biber and Claudia Resch, *"Anschluss." März/April 1938 in Österreich* (Vienna, 2010) (= ÖAW. Denkschriften der phil.-hist. Kl. 404 = Kulturforschungen 1).

Udo Wennemuth, "Heidelberger Akademie der Wissenschaften im Dritten Reich," in Eduard Seidler (ed.), *Die Elite der Nation im Deutschen Reich. Das Verhältnis von Akademien und ihrem wissenschaftlichen Umfeld zum Nationalsozialismus* (Leipzig, 1995) (= Acta historica Leopoldina 22), pp. 113–30.

Sibylle Wentker, "Adolf Grohmann (1887–1977). Orientalist und Historiker," in Karel Hruza (ed.), *Österreichische Historiker 1900–1945*, vol. 2 (Vienna, 2012), pp. 379–410.

Maurice Williams, *Gau, Volk und Reich. Friedrich Rainer und der österreichische Nationalsozialismus. Eine politische Biographie nach Selbstzeugnissen*, German version by Ulfried Burz and Claudia Fräss-Ehrfeld (Klagenfurt, 2005) (= Archiv für vaterländische Geschichte und Topographie 90).

Maria Wirth, *Christian Broda. Eine politische Biographie* (Göttingen, 2011) (= Zeitgeschichte im Kontext 5).

Gudrun Wlach, "Camillo Praschniker (1884–1949)," in Gunnar Brands, Martin Maischberger (eds.), *Lebensbilder. Klassische Archäologen und der Nationalsozialismus* (Rahden/Westfalen, 2012), pp. 75–89. (= Menschen – Kulturen – Traditionen. ForschungsCluster 5.2, no. 1).

Andreas Wöckinger, *Die Akademie der Wissenschaften im Kartell der deutschsprachigen Akademien* (Vienna, unpublished master's thesis, 2010).

Matthias Zimmer, *Moderne, Staat und internationale Politik* (Wiesbaden, 2008).

Stefan Zweig, *Die Welt von Gestern. Erinnerungen eines Europäers*, unabridged edition (Frankfurt/Main, Hamburg, 1970).

Table of figures

Fig. 1: ÖNB-Bildarchiv, Sign. OEGZ_S60_47
Fig. 2: ÖNB-Bildarchiv, Sign. 153332B
Fig. 3: AÖAW, Allgemeine Akten, No. 143/1938
Fig. 4: AÖAW, Wahlen, Box 4, Folder "1938"
Fig. 5: AÖAW, Bildarchiv, P-1975-C
Fig. 6: *Almanach* for 1948, 98 (1949), between p. 236 and 237
Fig. 7: AÖAW, Bildarchiv, P-1906-C
Fig. 8: AÖAW, Bildarchiv, P-0783-B
Fig. 9: AÖAW, Minutes of the extraordinary General Assembly of 1 April 1938 (A 934)
Fig. 10: AÖAW, Bildarchiv, P-0868-B
Fig. 11: ÖNB-Bildarchiv, Sign. OEGZ_S177_48
Fig. 12: ÖNB-Bildarchiv, Sign. OEGZ_P1553_2
Fig. 13: ÖAW, Library
Fig. 14: AÖAW, Urkundensammlung, No. 10
Fig. 15: AÖAW, PA Jan Huizinga
Fig. 16: AÖAW, Papers of Fritz Knoll, Box 4, Folder 18a
Fig. 17, 18: AÖAW, Papers of Fritz Knoll, Box 1, Folder 1
Fig. 19: ÖNB-Bildarchiv, Sign. PORT_00017995_01, Drawing by Robert Fuchs 1935
Fig. 20: AÖAW, Bildarchiv, P-1449-A
Fig. 21: AÖAW, Bildarchiv, P-0222-B
Fig. 22: AÖAW, Bildarchiv, P-0109-B
Fig. 23: AÖAW, Bildarchiv, P-1185-B
Fig. 24: AÖAW, Bildarchiv, P-1476-B
Fig. 25: AÖAW, Bildarchiv, P-1586-B
Fig. 26: AÖAW, Bildarchiv, P-1327-B
Fig. 27: AÖAW, Bildarchiv, P-0466-B
Fig. 28: *Almanach* for 1943, 93 (1943), p. 85
Fig. 29: AÖAW, Bildarchiv, P-1526-B
Fig. 30: AÖAW, Allgemeine Akten, No. 357/1938
Fig. 31: ÖNB-Bildarchiv, Sign. PORT_00013479_01, Drawing by Robert Fuchs 1935
Fig. 32: ÖNB-Bildarchiv, Sign. Pf49158B1
Fig. 33-35: AÖAW, Allgemeine Personalakten, Box 2, Folder 9, No. 145/1939
Fig. 36, 37: ÖAW, Phonogrammarchiv
Fig. 38: AÖAW, PA Wilfrid Oberhummer
Fig. 39: AÖAW, Bildarchiv, E-0294-B
Fig. 40: AÖAW, Bildarchiv, P-2303-B
Fig. 41: AÖAW, PA Walter Ruth
Fig. 42: AÖAW, Siegelsammlung
Fig. 43: AÖAW, PA Marie Hesch
Fig. 44: AÖAW, Fragebögen der Mitarbeiter, Marie Hesch
Fig. 45: ÖNB-Bildarchiv, Sign. L32608C
Fig. 46: *Almanach* for 1937, 87 (1937), p. 13
Fig. 47: *Almanach* for 1938, 88 (1939), p. 12
Fig. 48: AÖAW, Wahlen, Box 4, Folder "1938"
Fig. 49: Replica of a bust in bronze by Fritz Bahn 1948/49, on permament loan to the ÖAW, Inv.-No. F03, Photo and montage: Stefan Sienell
Fig. 50: AÖAW, Bildarchiv, E-0482-B
Fig. 51: *Almanach* for 1942, 92 (1942), p. 169
Fig. 52: AÖAW, Papers of Fritz Knoll, Box 1, Folder 2, Postkartensammlung
Fig. 53: AÖAW, Papers of Fritz Knoll, Box 1, Folder 2, "Fotoalbum 1931"
Fig. 54: AÖAW, Papers of Fritz Knoll, Box 1, Folder 2, "Foto 1936"
Fig. 55, 56: AÖAW, Papers of Fritz Knoll, Box 1, Folder 2, "Akten (1935)1938"
Fig. 57: ÖNB, Bildarchiv, Sign. 430257B
Fig. 58: Meister (1947), *Geschichte*, Board 15
Fig. 59: AÖAW, Institut für Radiumforschung, Box 1, Folder "B. Personalangelegenheiten 1938-1940," No. 189/1938
Fig. 60: AÖAW, Institut für Radiumforschung, Box 2, Folder "C 1938," No. 190/1938
Fig. 61: AÖAW, Sonnblick-Verein, Folder 7
Fig. 62-64: AÖAW, Subventionen, Box 11, No. 264/1940
Fig. 65: AÖAW, PA Walter Ruth
Fig. 66: *Almanach* for 1966, 116 (1967), between p. 288 and 289
Fig. 67: Archive of the Berlin-Brandenburg Academy of Sciences, PAW II, Sign.: II-XII-18, p. 212
Fig. 68: AÖAW, UAI, Box 1, Folder A

Fig. 69, 70: AÖAW, Allgemeine Akten, No. 143/1938
Fig. 71: AÖAW, UAI, Box 1, Folder "B 1939"
Fig. 72: ÖNB-Bildarchiv, Sign. OEGZ_P394_1
Fig. 73: Ullstein-Bild, Berlin
Fig. 74: AÖAW, Allgemeine Akten, No. 439/1939
Fig. 75: AÖAW, Allgemeine Akten, No. 30/1940
Fig. 76: AÖAW, Reichsakademie, Folder 1, No. 296/1940
Fig. 77: AÖAW, Reichsakademie, Folder 7, Cutting from the *Völkischer Beobachter* of 8 September 1940
Fig. 78: AÖAW, Minutes of the General Assembly of 18 May 1945 (A 994), Annex
Fig. 79: AÖAW, Bildarchiv, E-0414-F2
Fig. 80: ÖAW, Inv.-No. B 040, Painting by Ekke Ozlberger (1944), Photo by Robert Herbst
Fig. 81: ÖAW, Inv.-No. B 014, Painting by Sergius Pauser (1961), Photo by Robert Herbst
Fig. 82: *Almanach* 114 (1964), between p. 248 and 249
Fig. 83: AÖAW, Bildarchiv, P-1501-B
Fig. 84: AÖAW, Bildarchiv, E-0423-F2
Fig. 85: AÖAW, Minutes of the General Assembly of 22 June 1945 (A 995)
Fig. 86: *Almanach* for 1953, 103 (1954), between p. 304 and 305
Fig. 87: AÖAW, Allgemeine Akten, No. 109/1945
Fig. 88: AÖAW, Minutes of the General Assembly of 30 October 1945 (A 997)
Fig. 89: ÖAW, Library
Fig. 90: AÖAW, Minutes of the General Assembly of 9 January 1948 (A 1015)
Fig. 91: AÖAW, Minutes of the General Assembly of 16 March 1948 (A 1017)
Fig. 92: AÖAW, Papers of Fritz Knoll, Box 1, Folder 1
Fig. 93: AÖAW, Bildarchiv, A-0018-B
Fig. 94: AÖAW, Bildarchiv, E-0420-F2
Fig. 95: Hydrobiologia 20.2 (1962), p. 191
Fig. 96: ÖAW, Library
Fig. 97: AÖAW, ÖBL, Box 1
Fig. 98: AÖAW, Bildarchiv, E-0415-F2
Fig. 99: AÖAW, Bildarchiv, E-0416-F2
Fig. 100: AÖAW, Medaillensammlung, No. 76

Index of names

Notes on contributors

Johannes **Feichtinger**, PD Mag. Dr. phil., historian at the Institute for Culture Studies and Theatre History at the Austrian Academy of Sciences. Research interests: Austrian history, cultural history, history of science, cultural theory. Co-leader of the research project *Continuity and Transformation. The Austrian Academy of Sciences in the 20th Century.*

Silke **Fengler**, Dr. phil., Dipl.-Vw., M.A., freelance historian. Research interests: history of science and technology, economic history, history of the 20th century.

Dieter J. **Hecht**, Mag. Dr. phil., associated staff member at the Institute for Culture Studies and Theatre History at the Austrian Academy of Sciences. Research interests: Jewish history of the 19th and 20th centuries, gender studies, provenance research with a focus on restitution. Collaborator on the project *Continuity and Transformation. The Austrian Academy of Sciences in the 20th Century.*

Herbert **Matis**, Dr. phil., Emeritus Professor of Economic and Social History at the Vienna University of Economics and Business. Research interests: history of currency, banking and industry, general economic history of the 18th to the 20th century.

Martina **Pesditschek**, Mag. Dr. phil., staff member at the Institute for Ancient History and Ancient World Studies, Papyrology and Epigraphy at the University of Vienna. Research interests: intellectual history, biographical research, Lycia and Lycian.

Felicitas **Seebacher**, Mag. Dr. phil., freelance collaborator at the Institute of History at the Alpen-Adria University Klagenfurt. Research interests: history of science, history of medicine, history of academic institutions with a focus on German nationalism and academic Antisemitism.

Stefan **Sienell**, Mag. Dr. phil., MAS, archivist at the Austrian Academy of Sciences. Research interests: history of science, archive studies.

Arnold **Suppan**, Dr. phil., Professor of East European History at the University of Vienna, Vice-President of the Austrian Academy of Sciences. Research interests: nation building and communities of conflict in East Central and Southeast Europe, empires and nation states, First World War – interwar period – Second World War.

Klaus **Taschwer**, Mag. Dr. phil., writes for the newspaper "*Der Standard.*" Research interests: history of science and universities in the 20th century.

Heidemarie **Uhl**, PD Mag. Dr. phil., historian at the Institute for Culture Studies and Theatre History at the Austrian Academy of Sciences. Research interests: contemporary history, the history and theories of memory, cultural theory. Co-leader of the research project: *Continuity and Transformation. The Austrian Academy of Sciences in the 20th Century*

Marlene **Wahlmüller**, Mag. phil., research interests: history of science, archive studies.